8 Story & Art by Maki Enjoji

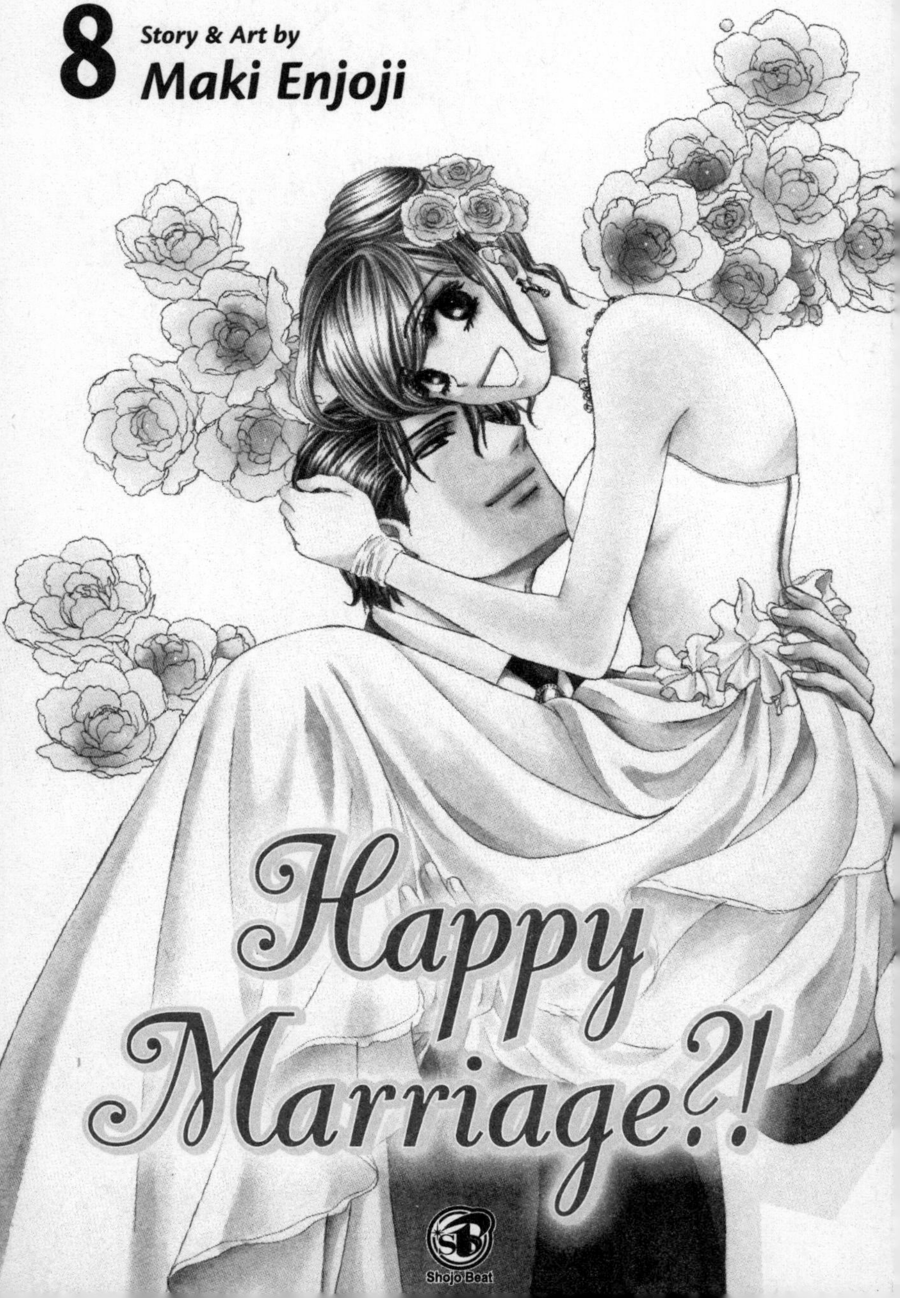
Happy Marriage?!
Shojo Beat

Happy Marriage?!

Characters

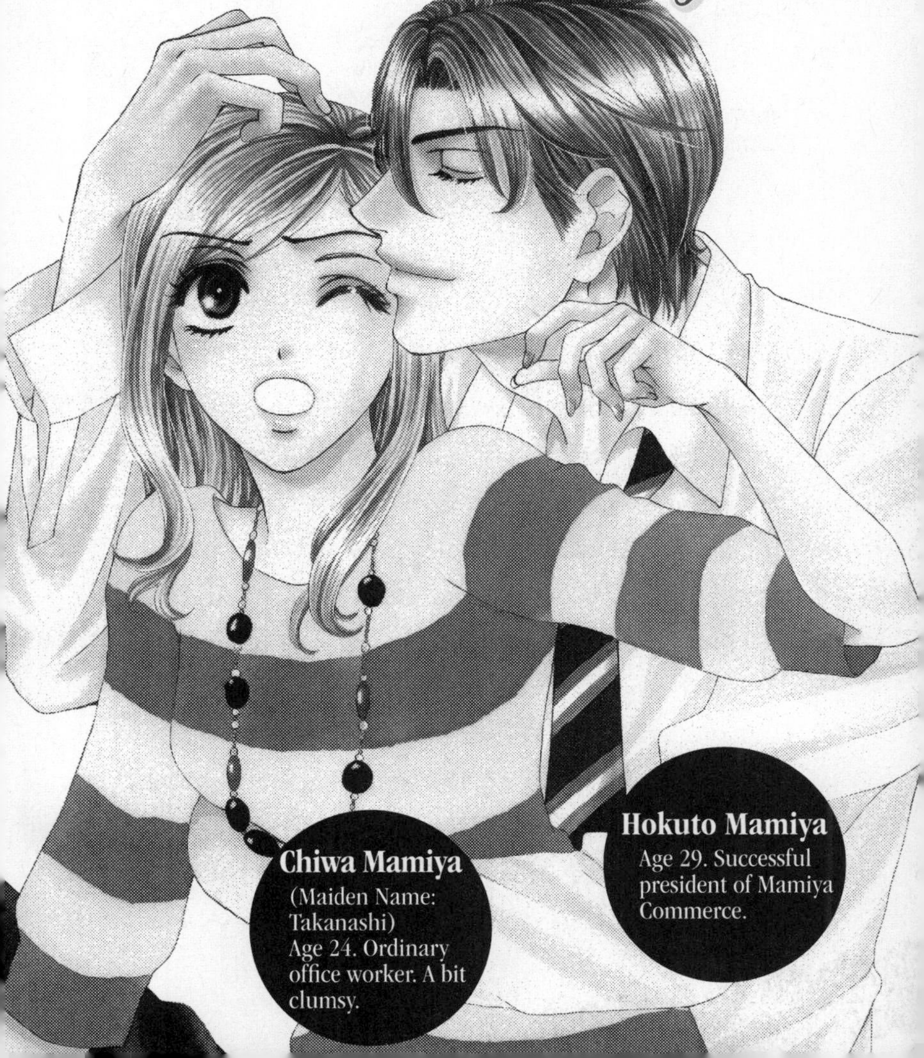
Hokuto Mamiya
Age 29. Successful president of Mamiya Commerce.
Chiwa Mamiya
(Maiden Name: Takanashi)
Age 24. Ordinary office worker. A bit clumsy.

Misaki Shitara

President of a famous brand. In the past she was in a relationship with Hokuto...?

Kaname Asahina

Two years older than Chiwa, he was an upperclassman at her university. He is now her boss at work.

Story

Chiwa Takanashi has no girlish fantasies about finding Prince Charming, and she wanted nothing but to lead a normal life until she found herself marrying company president Hokuto to pay off her father's debts. Though the marriage is in name only, Chiwa has fallen in love with her husband. The two make love for the first time, consummating their marriage. Learning about each other's past relationships brings out jealousy, but they rediscover their love through that experience. Meanwhile, Asahina has learned about the secret behind their marriage…

Happy Marriage?!

Contents

Step Twenty-Nine
What Makes You Happy? 5

Step Thirty
Shall I Tell You About My Resolution? 51

Step Thirty-One
You Won't Leave Me Alone, Will You? 97

Step Thirty-Two
What Am I Supposed to Do? 140

Bonus Story 185

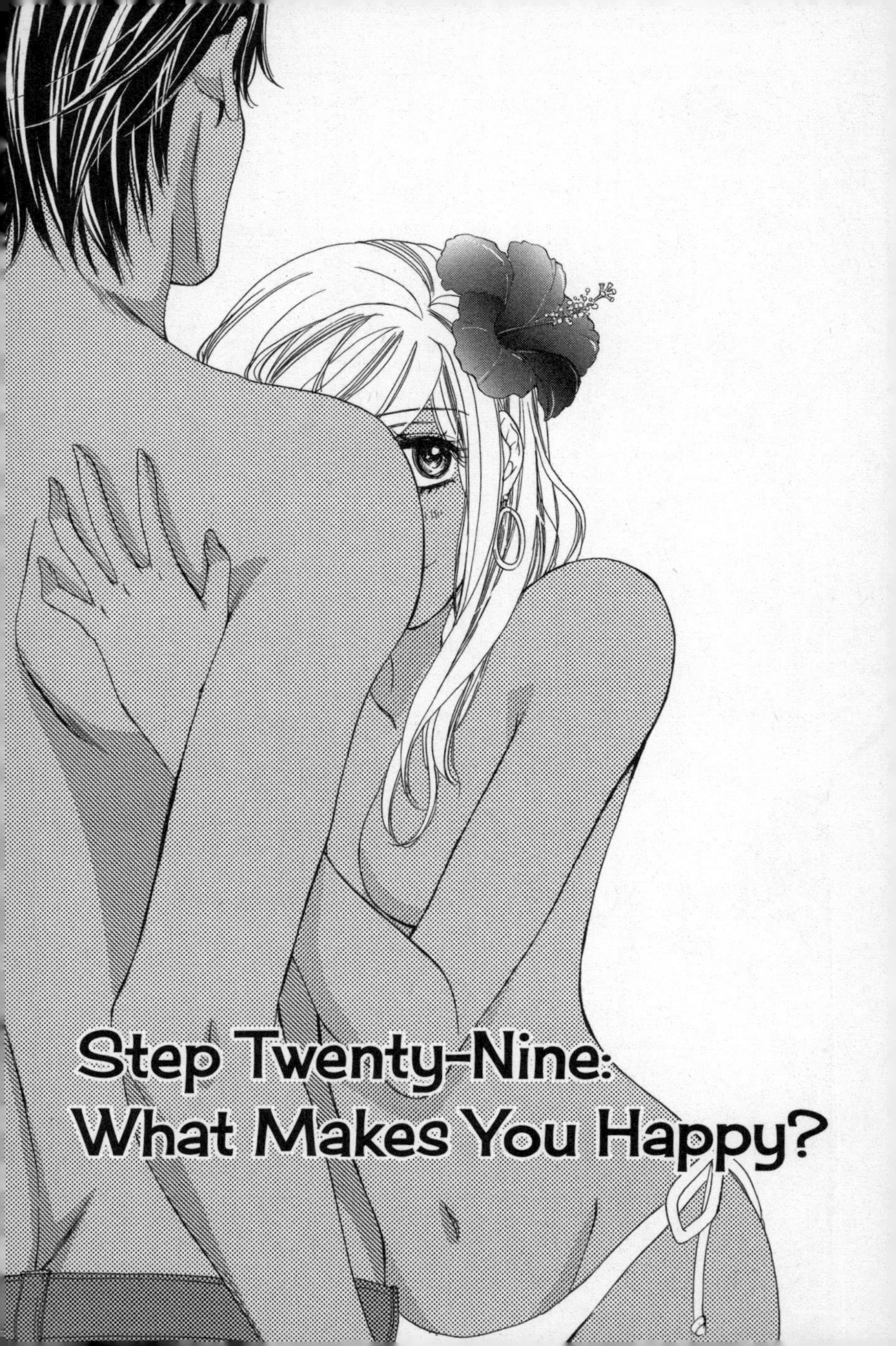
Step Twenty-Nine:
What Makes You Happy?

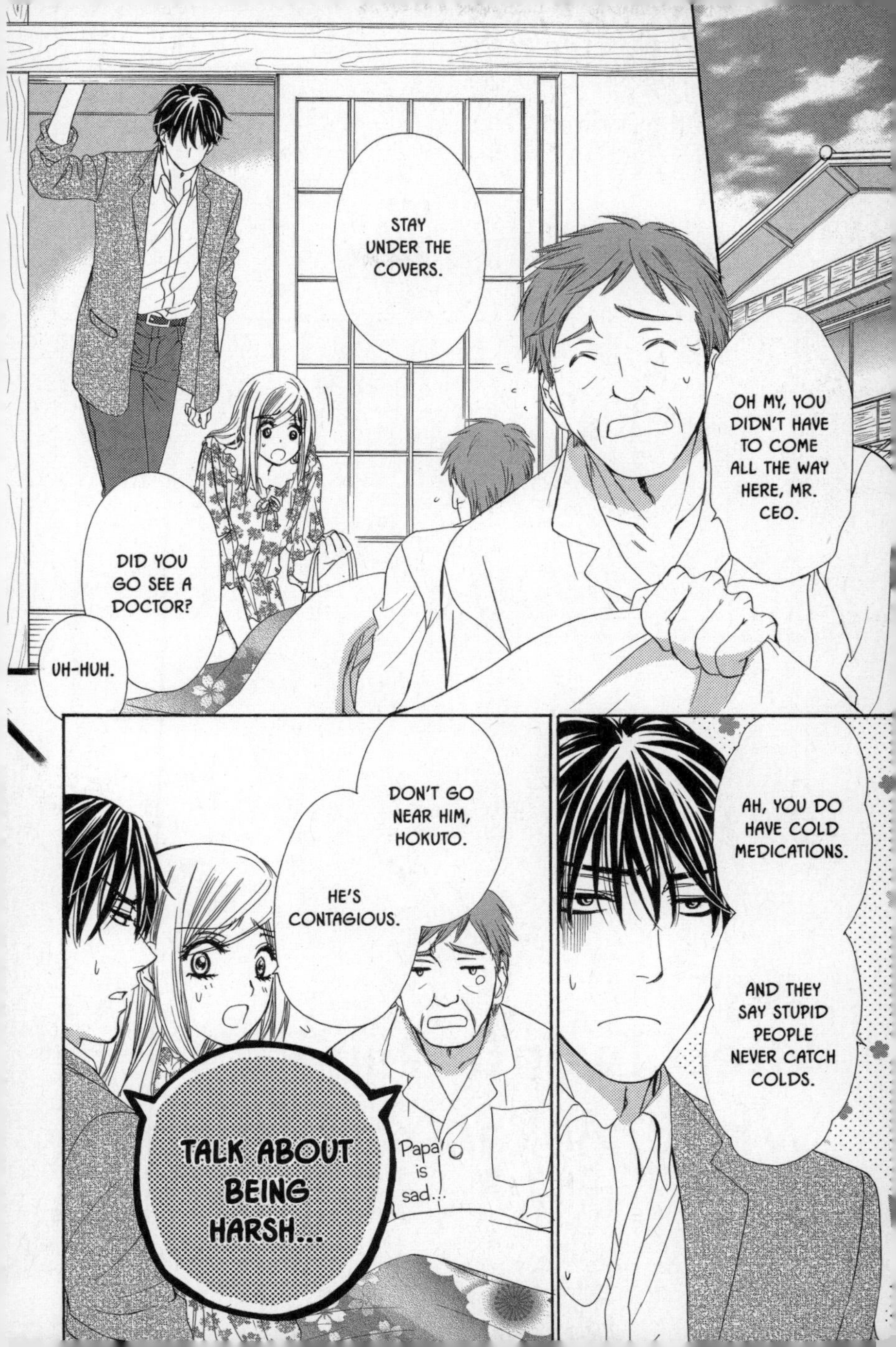
OH MY, YOU DIDN'T HAVE TO COME ALL THE WAY HERE, MR. CEO.
STAY UNDER THE COVERS.
DID YOU GO SEE A DOCTOR?
UH-HUH.
AH, YOU DO HAVE COLD MEDICATIONS.
AND THEY SAY STUPID PEOPLE NEVER CATCH COLDS.
DON'T GO NEAR HIM, HOKUTO.
HE'S CONTAGIOUS.
Papa is sad...
TALK ABOUT BEING HARSH...

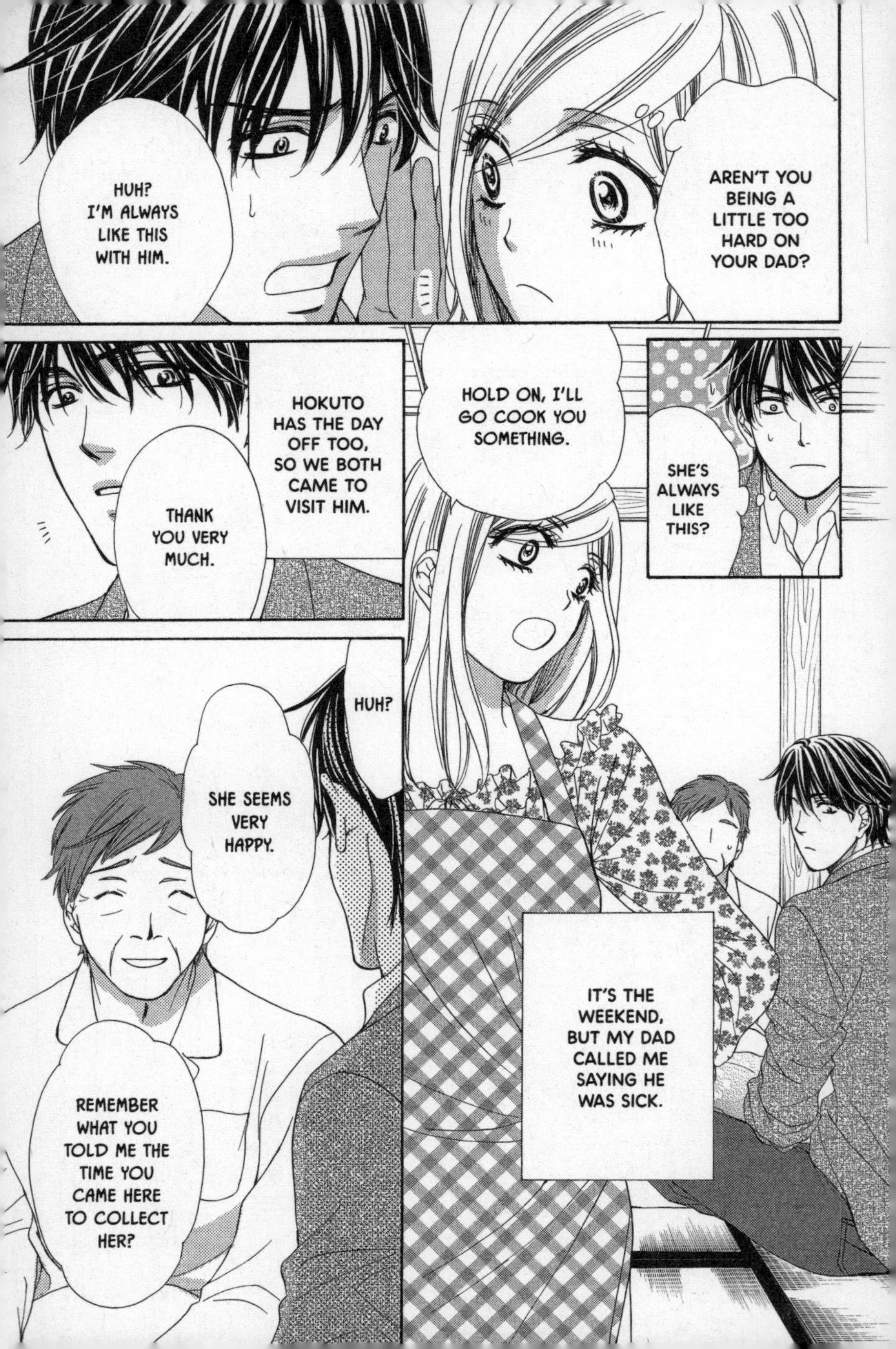
ARE'NT YOU BEING A LITTLE TOO HARD ON YOUR DAD?
HUH? I'M ALWAYS LIKE THIS WITH HIM.
SHE'S ALWAYS LIKE THIS?
IT'S THE WEEKEND, BUT MY DAD CALLED ME SAYING HE WAS SICK.
HOLD ON, I'LL GO COOK YOU SOMETHING.
HOKUTO HAS THE DAY OFF TOO, SO WE BOTH CAME TO VISIT HIM.
THANK YOU VERY MUCH.
HUH?
SHE SEEMS VERY HAPPY.
REMEMBER WHAT YOU TOLD ME THE TIME YOU CAME HERE TO COLLECT HER?

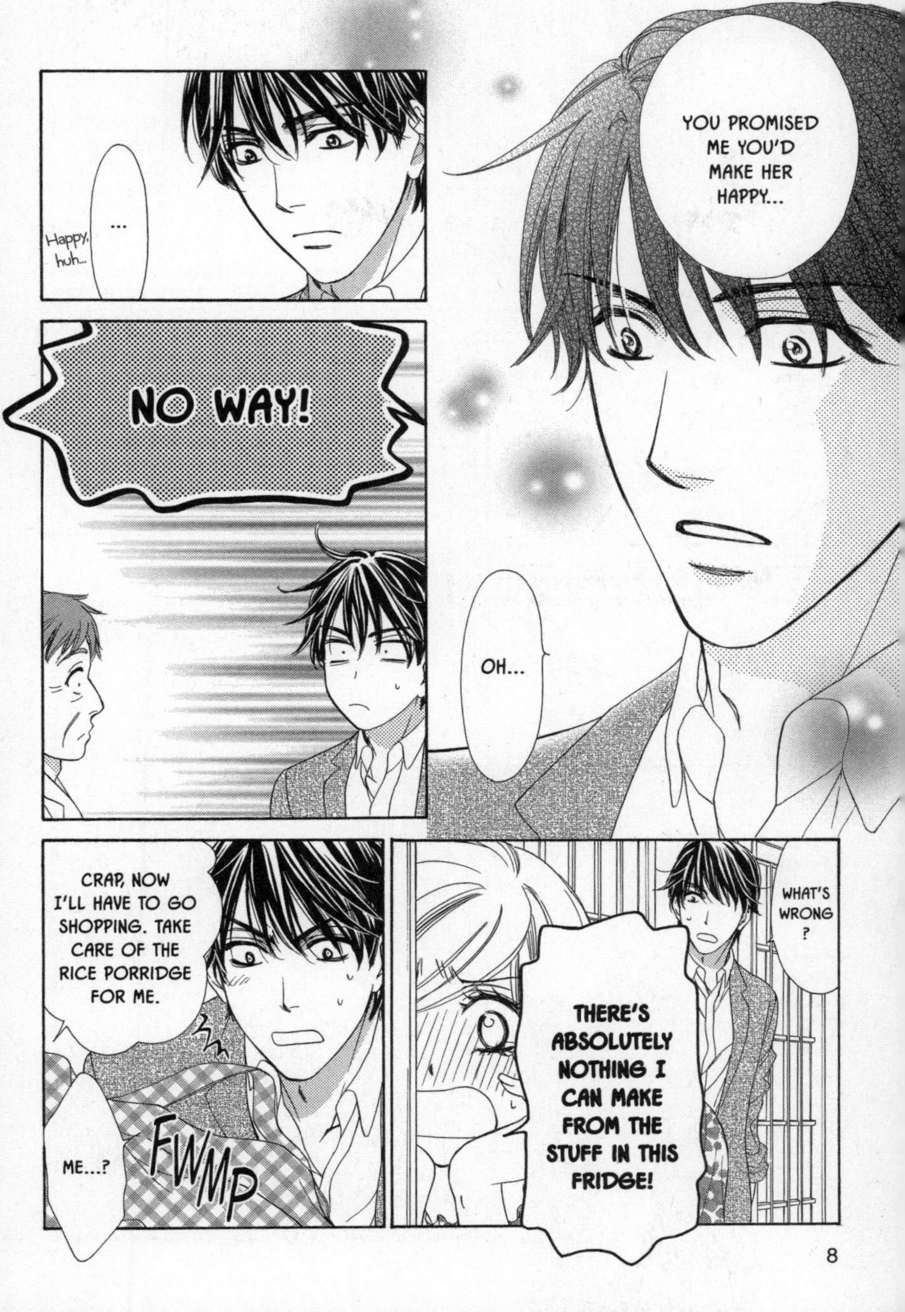
YOU PROMISED ME YOU'D MAKE HER HAPPY...
OH...
...
Happy, huh...
NO WAY!
WHAT'S WRONG?
THERE'S ABSOLUTELY NOTHING I CAN MAKE FROM THE STUFF IN THIS FRIDGE!
CRAP, NOW I'LL HAVE TO GO SHOPPING. TAKE CARE OF THE RICE PORRIDGE FOR ME.
FWMP
ME...?

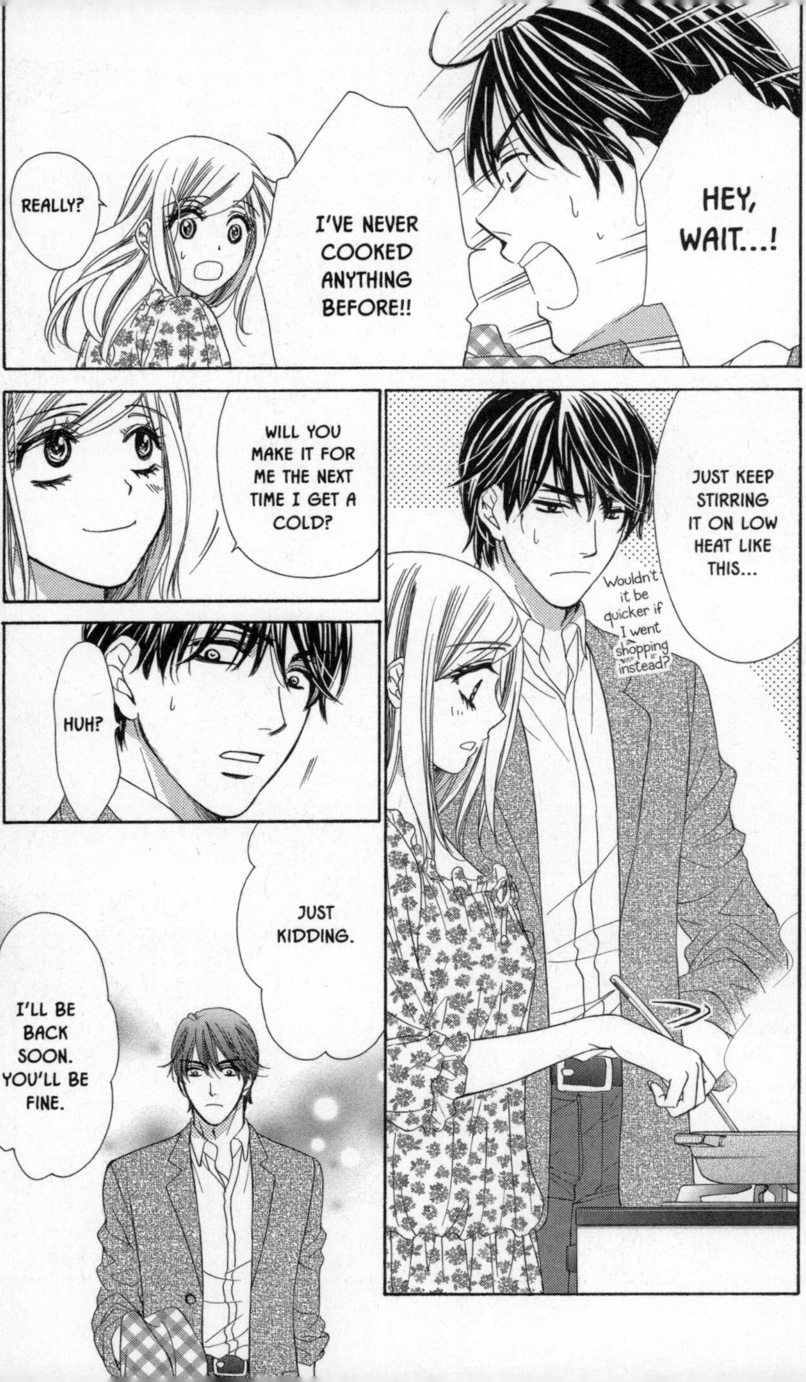
HEY, WAIT...!
I'VE NEVER COOKED ANYTHING BEFORE!!
REALLY?
JUST KEEP STIRRING IT ON LOW HEAT LIKE THIS...
Wouldn't it be quicker if I went shopping instead?
WILL YOU MAKE IT FOR ME THE NEXT TIME I GET A COLD?
HUH?
JUST KIDDING.
I'LL BE BACK SOON. YOU'LL BE FINE.

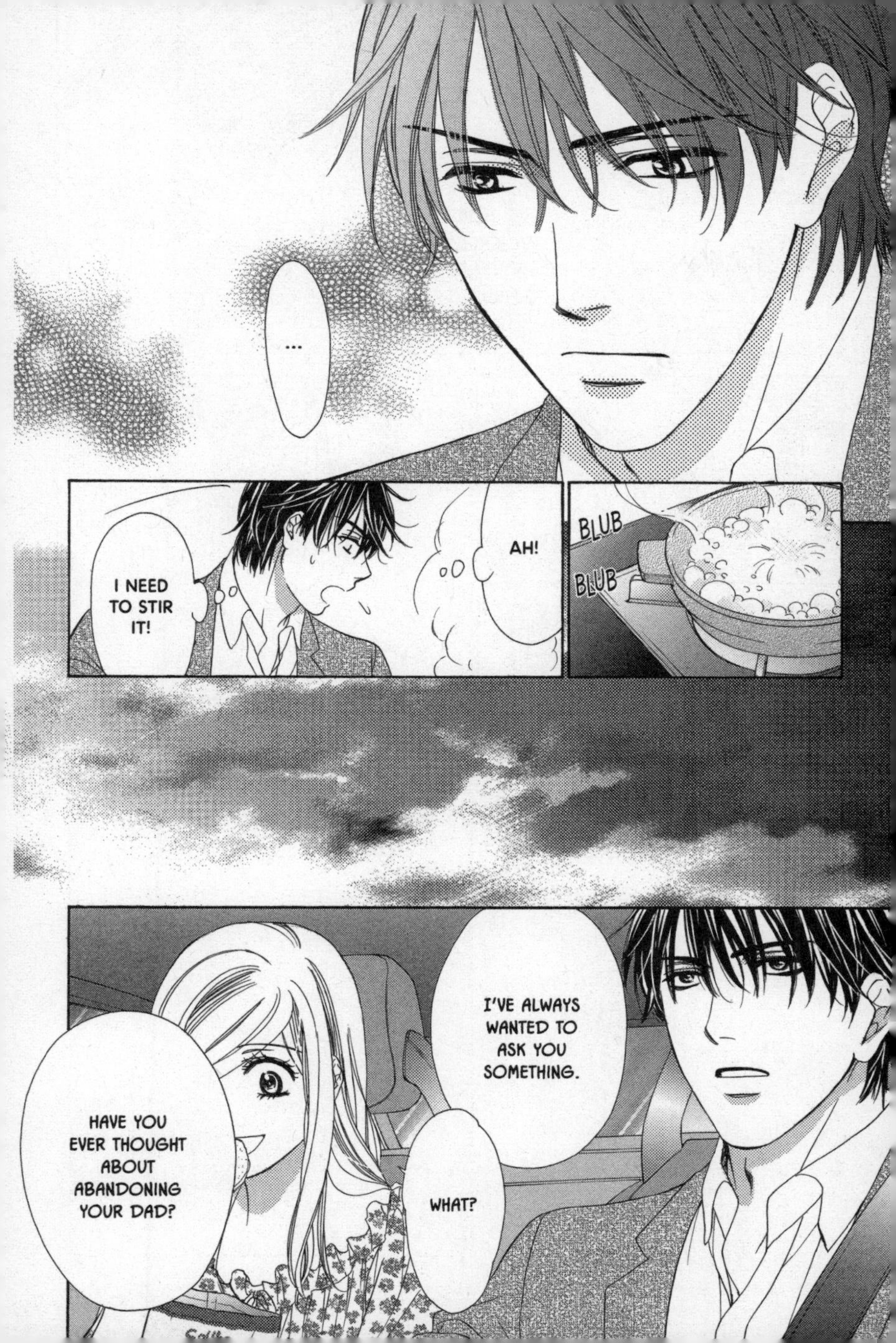
...
BLUB
BLUB
AH!
I NEED TO STIR IT!
I'VE ALWAYS WANTED TO ASK YOU SOMETHING.
WHAT?
HAVE YOU EVER THOUGHT ABOUT ABANDONING YOUR DAD?

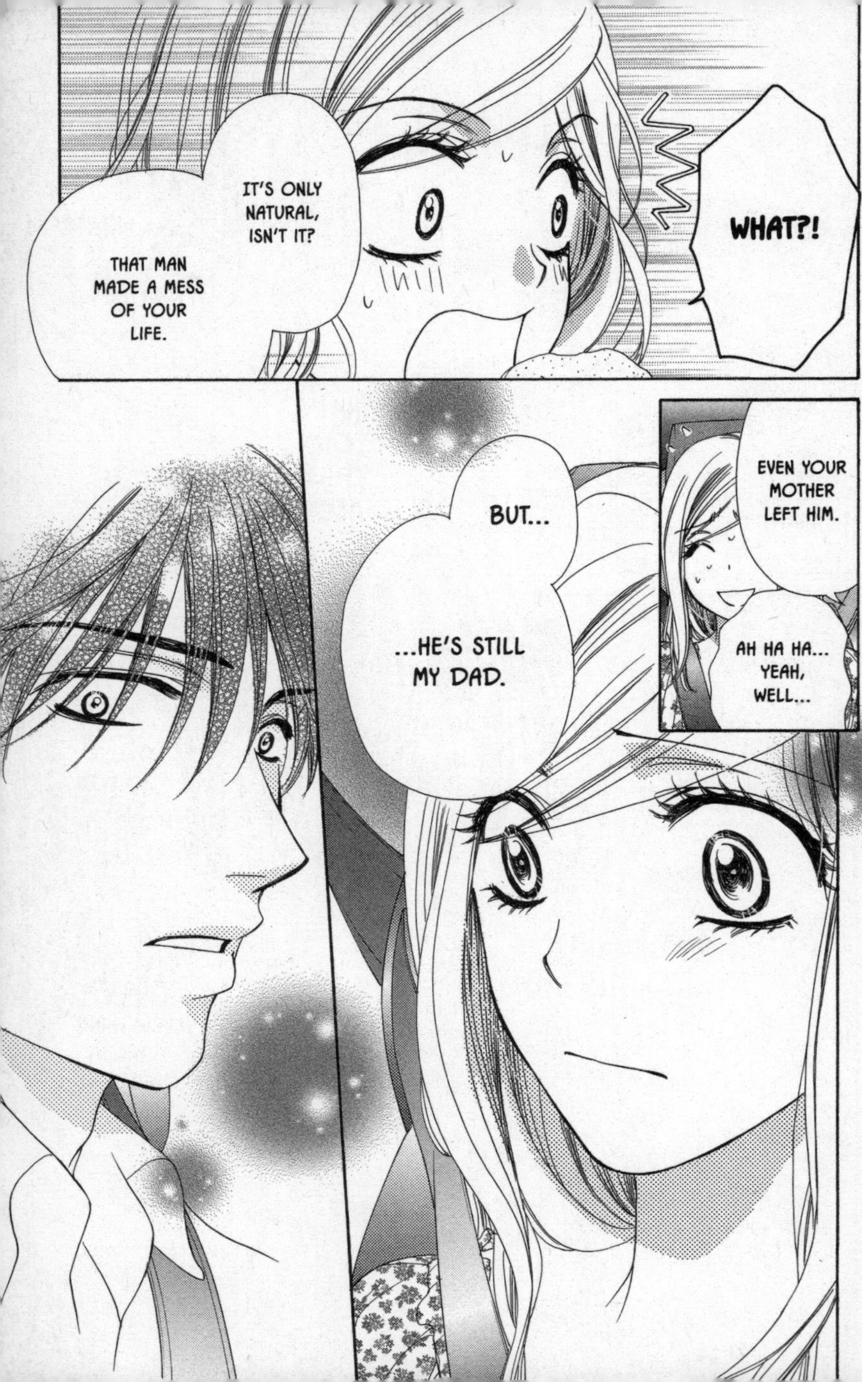
WHAT?!
IT'S ONLY NATURAL, ISN'T IT?
THAT MAN MADE A MESS OF YOUR LIFE.
EVEN YOUR MOTHER LEFT HIM.
AH HA HA... YEAH, WELL...
BUT...
...HE'S STILL MY DAD.

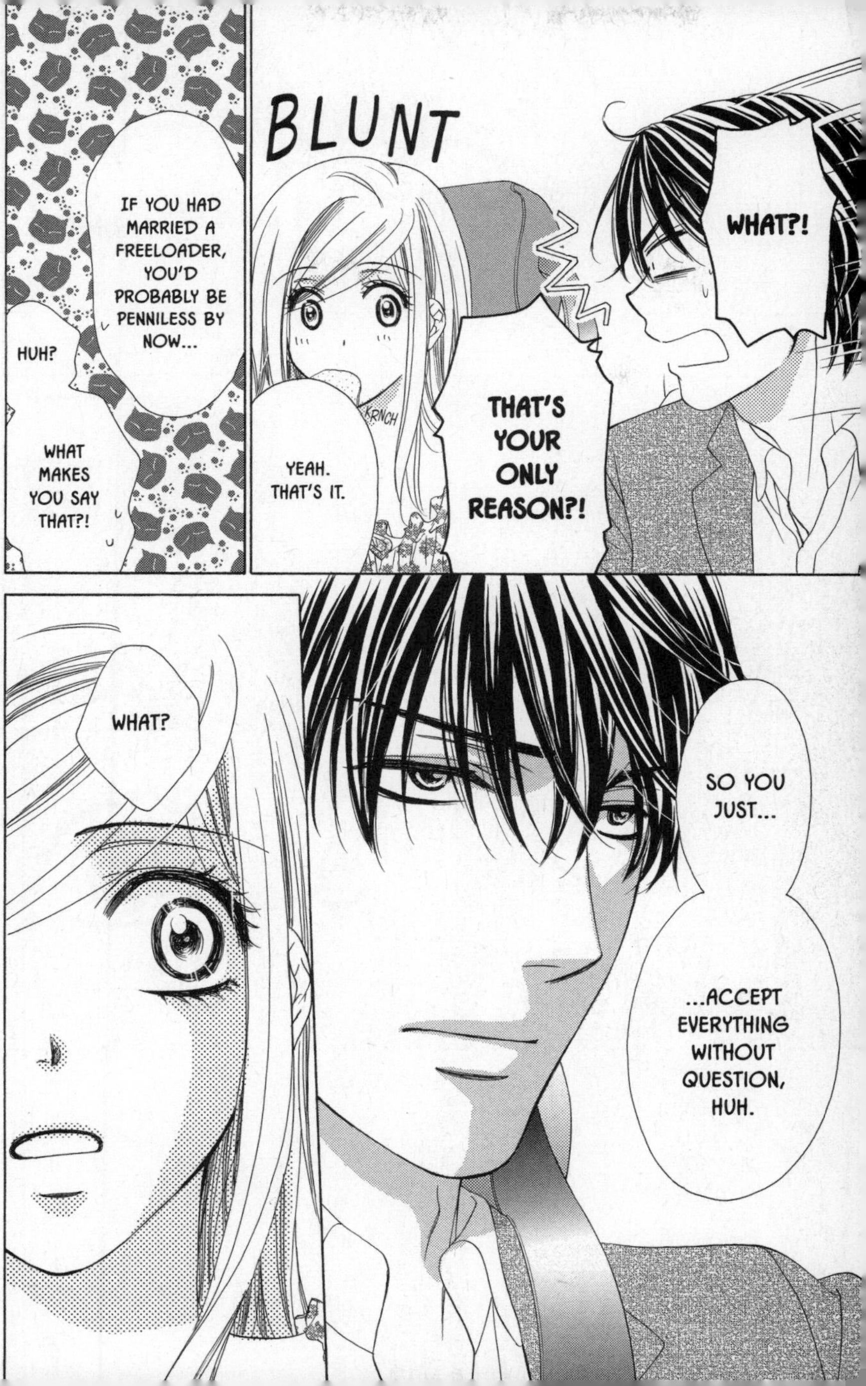
WHAT?!
BLUNT
THAT'S YOUR ONLY REASON?!
KRNCH
YEAH. THAT'S IT.
IF YOU HAD MARRIED A FREELOADER, YOU'D PROBABLY BE PENNILESS BY NOW...
HUH?
WHAT MAKES YOU SAY THAT?!
SO YOU JUST...
...ACCEPT EVERYTHING WITHOUT QUESTION, HUH.
WHAT?

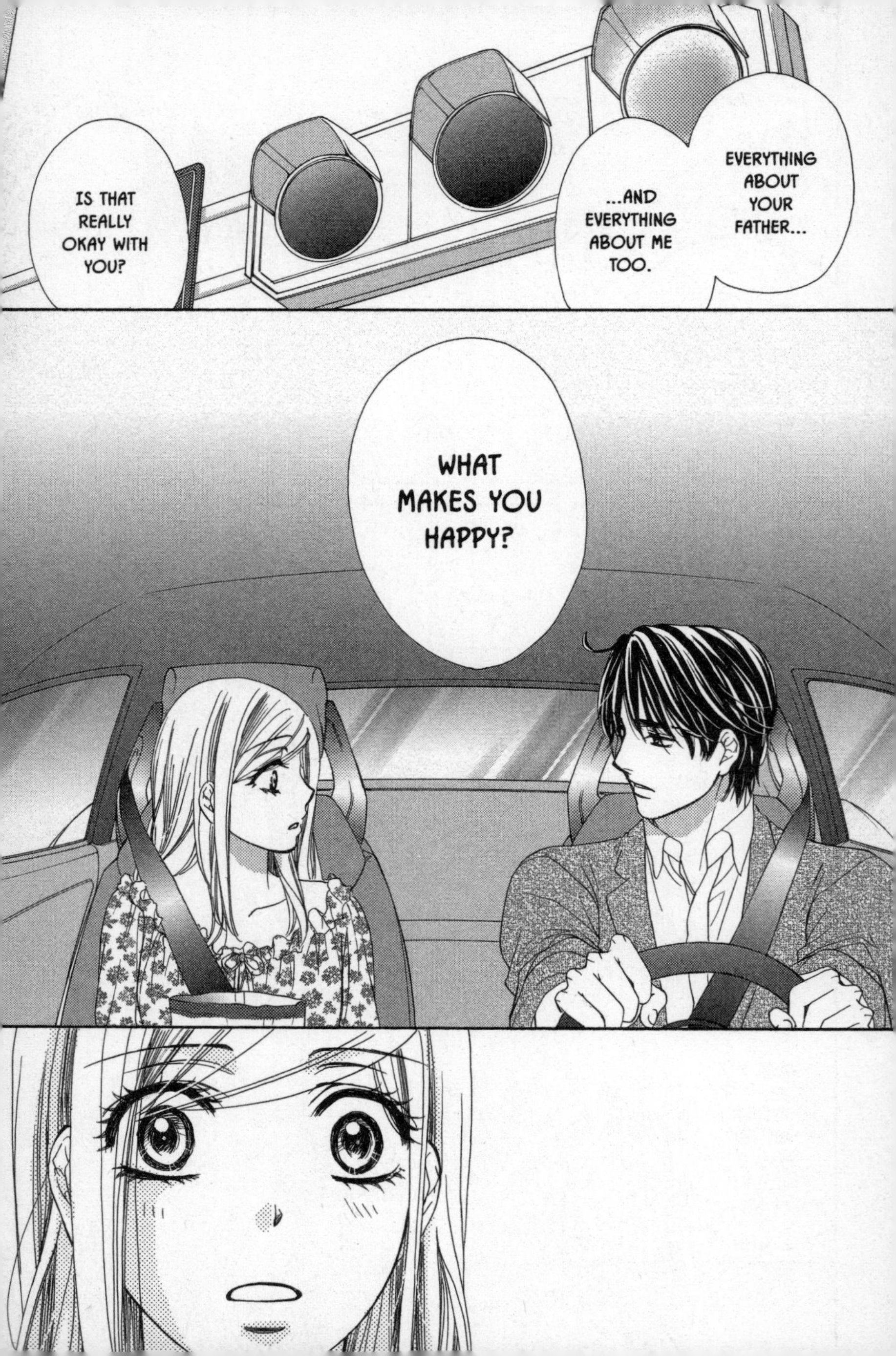
EVERYTHING ABOUT YOUR FATHER...
...AND EVERYTHING ABOUT ME TOO.
IS THAT REALLY OKAY WITH YOU?
WHAT MAKES YOU HAPPY?

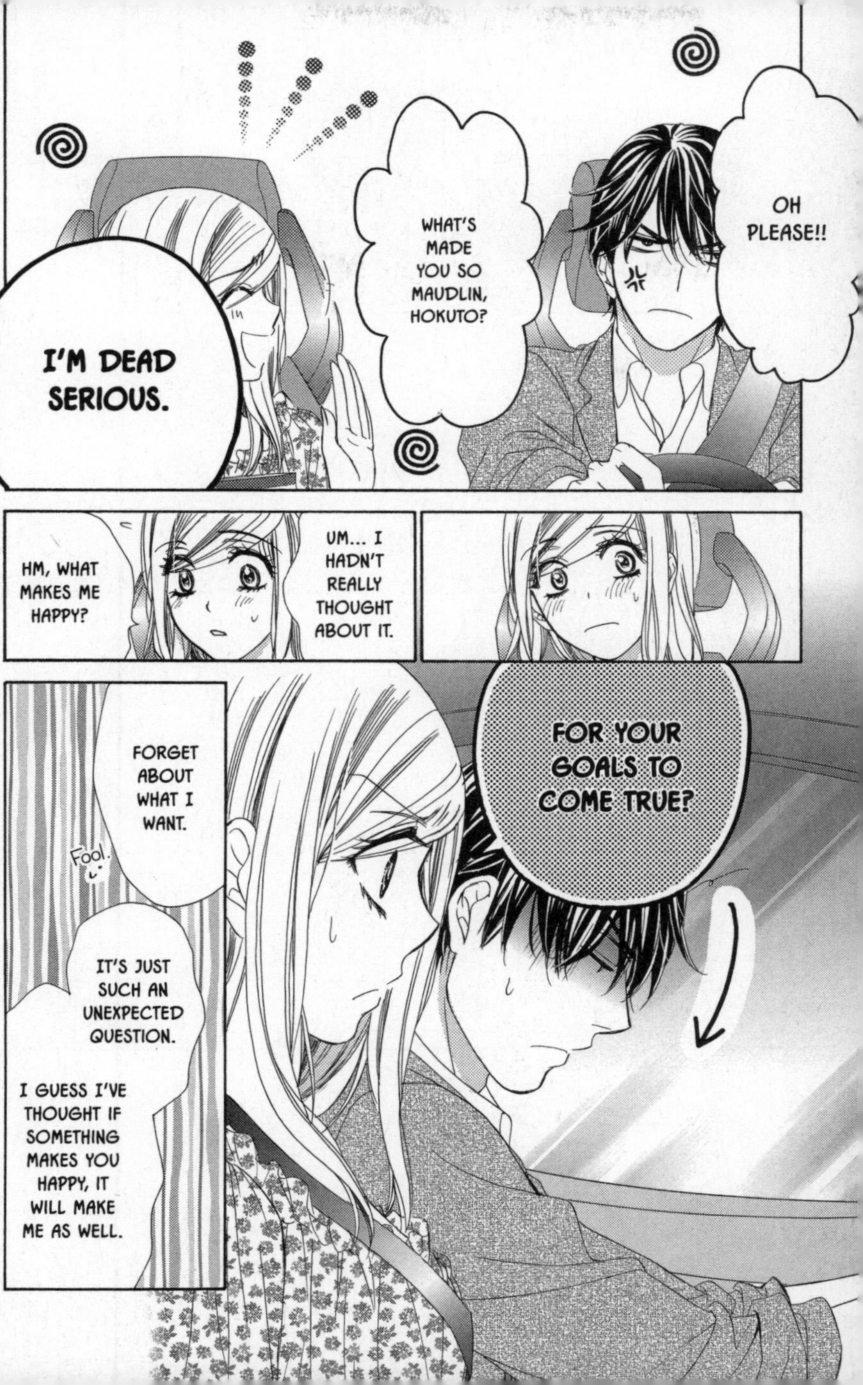
OH PLEASE!!
WHAT'S MADE YOU SO MAUDLIN, HOKUTO?
I'M DEAD SERIOUS.
UM... I HADN'T REALLY THOUGHT ABOUT IT.
HM, WHAT MAKES ME HAPPY?
FOR YOUR GOALS TO COME TRUE?
FORGET ABOUT WHAT I WANT.
Fool.
IT'S JUST SUCH AN UNEXPECTED QUESTION.
I GUESS I'VE THOUGHT IF SOMETHING MAKES YOU HAPPY, IT WILL MAKE ME AS WELL.

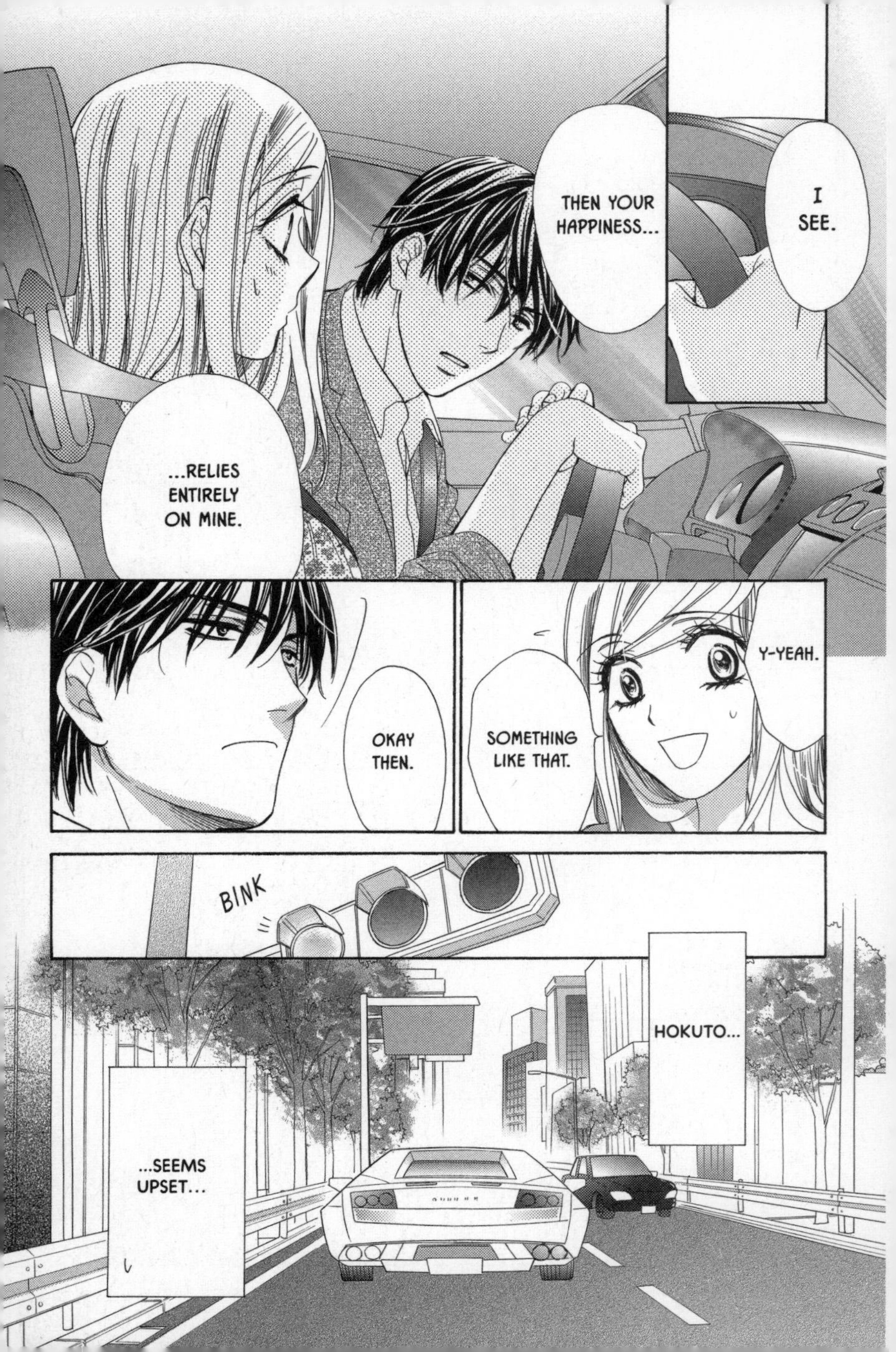
I SEE.
THEN YOUR HAPPINESS...
...RELIES ENTIRELY ON MINE.
Y-YEAH.
SOMETHING LIKE THAT.
OKAY THEN.
BINK
HOKUTO...
...SEEMS UPSET...

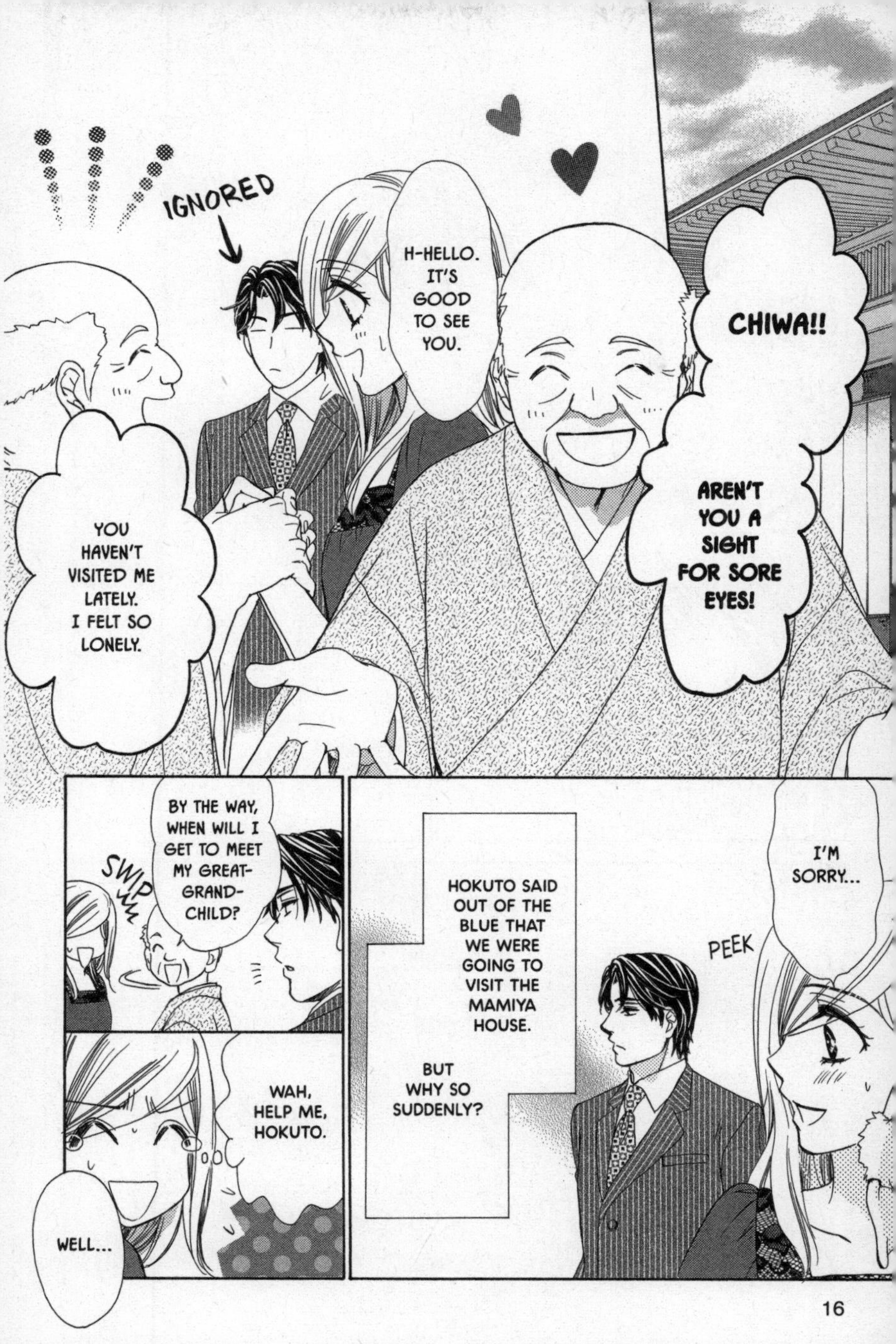
CHIWA!!
AREN'T YOU A SIGHT FOR SORE EYES!
H-HELLO. IT'S GOOD TO SEE YOU.
IGNORED
YOU HAVEN'T VISITED ME LATELY. I FELT SO LONELY.
I'M SORRY...
PEEK
HOKUTO SAID OUT OF THE BLUE THAT WE WERE GOING TO VISIT THE MAMIYA HOUSE.
BUT WHY SO SUDDENLY?
BY THE WAY, WHEN WILL I GET TO MEET MY GREAT-GRAND-CHILD?
SWIP
WAH, HELP ME, HOKUTO.
WELL...

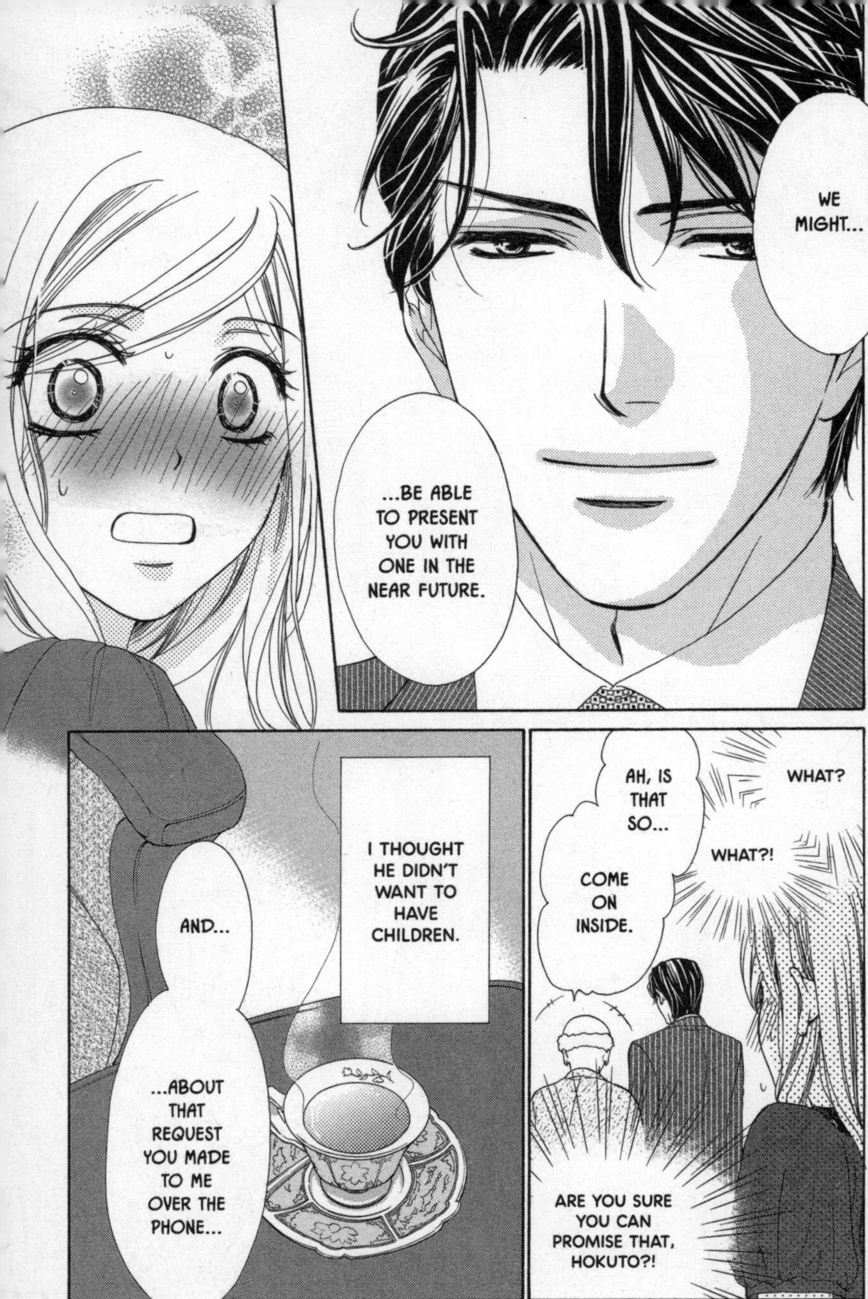
WE MIGHT...
...BE ABLE TO PRESENT YOU WITH ONE IN THE NEAR FUTURE.
WHAT?
AH, IS THAT SO...
WHAT?!
COME ON INSIDE.
ARE YOU SURE YOU CAN PROMISE THAT, HOKUTO?!
I THOUGHT HE DIDN'T WANT TO HAVE CHILDREN.
AND...
...ABOUT THAT REQUEST YOU MADE TO ME OVER THE PHONE...

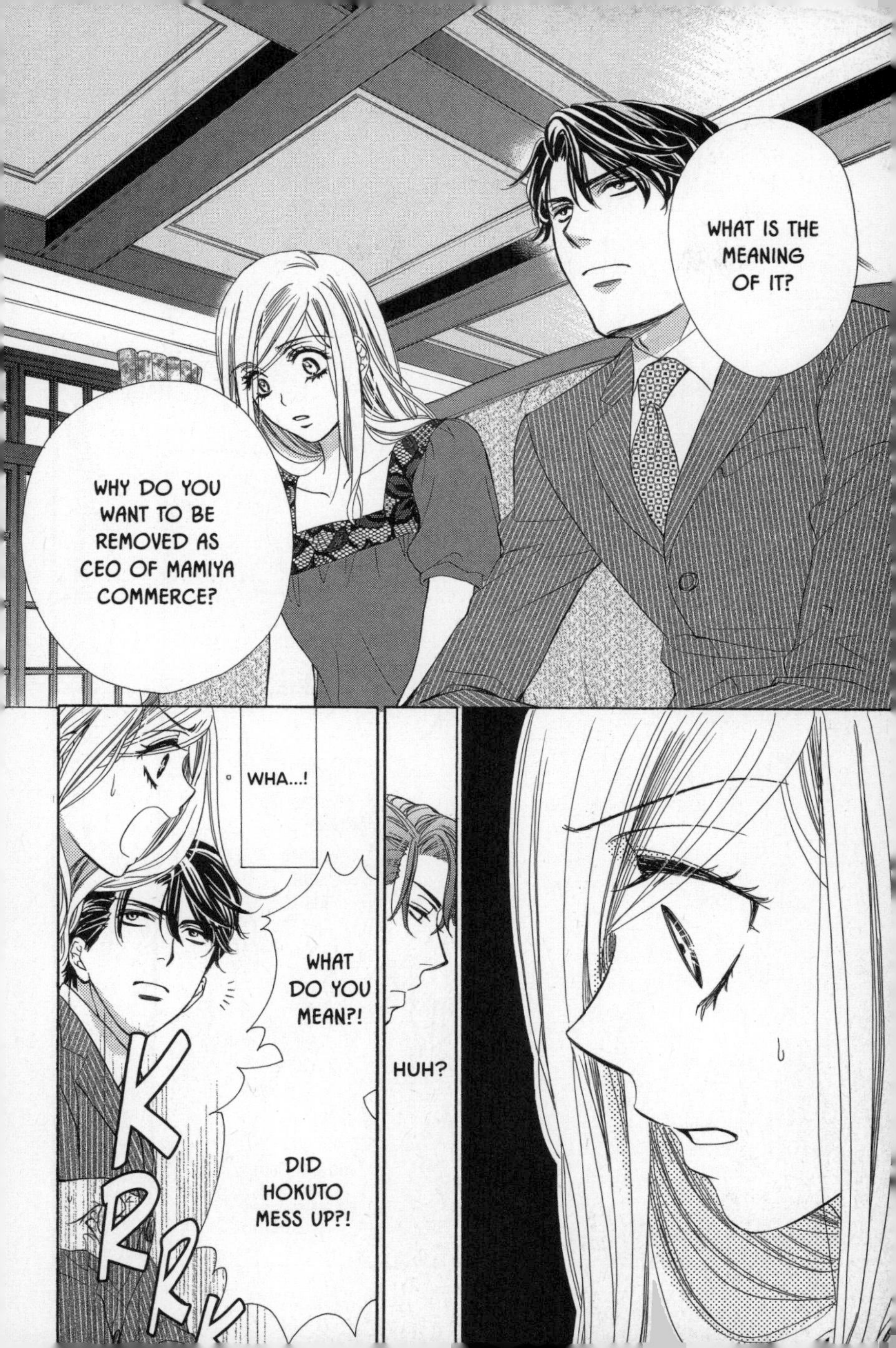
WHAT IS THE MEANING OF IT?
WHY DO YOU WANT TO BE REMOVED AS CEO OF MAMIYA COMMERCE?
HUH?
WHA...!
WHAT DO YOU MEAN?!
DID HOKUTO MESS UP?!
KRR

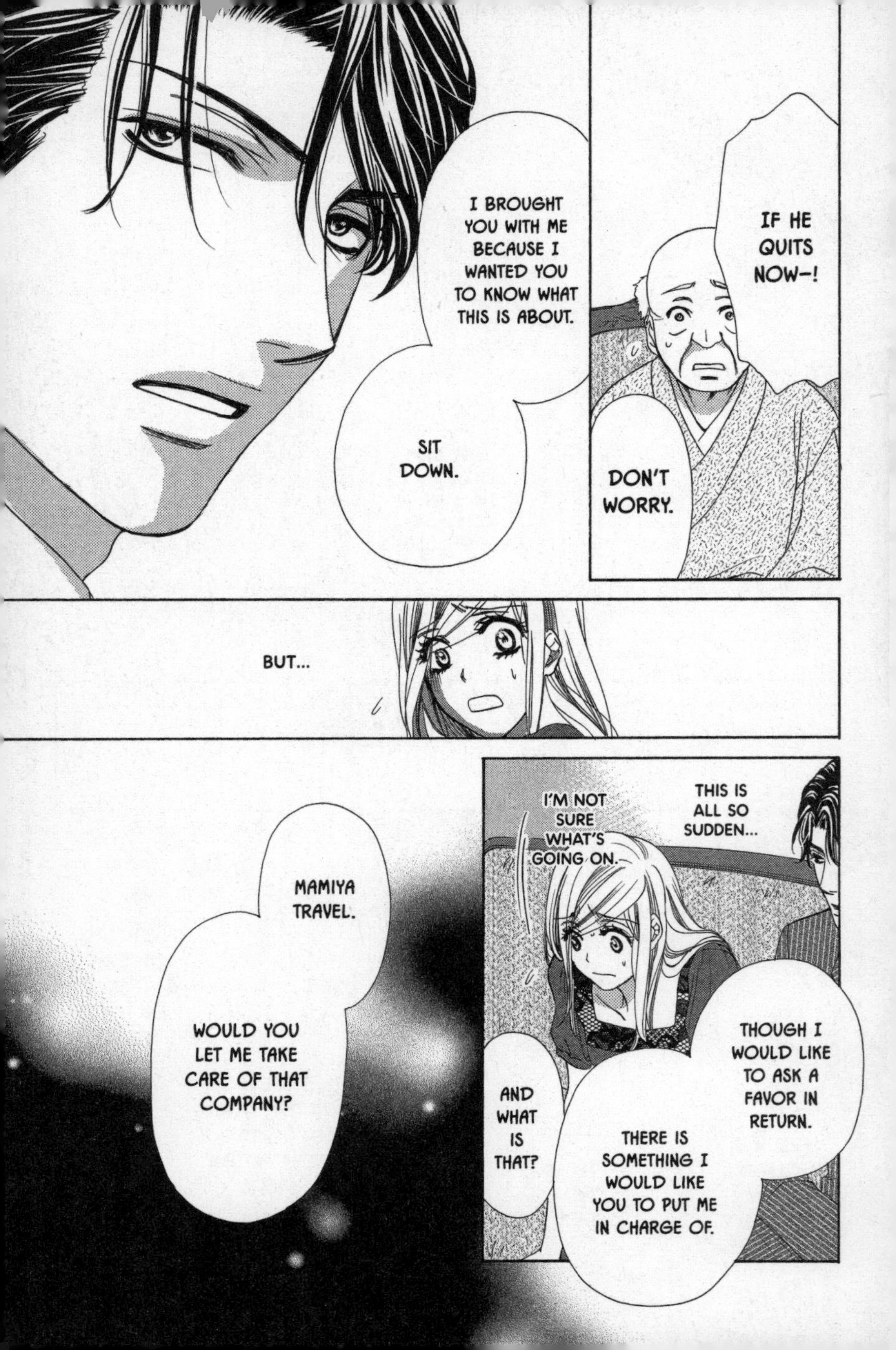

IF HE QUITS NOW–!
DON'T WORRY.
I BROUGHT YOU WITH ME BECAUSE I WANTED YOU TO KNOW WHAT THIS IS ABOUT.
SIT DOWN.
BUT...
THIS IS ALL SO SUDDEN...
I'M NOT SURE WHAT'S GOING ON.
THOUGH I WOULD LIKE TO ASK A FAVOR IN RETURN.
AND WHAT IS THAT?
THERE IS SOMETHING I WOULD LIKE YOU TO PUT ME IN CHARGE OF.
MAMIYA TRAVEL.
WOULD YOU LET ME TAKE CARE OF THAT COMPANY?

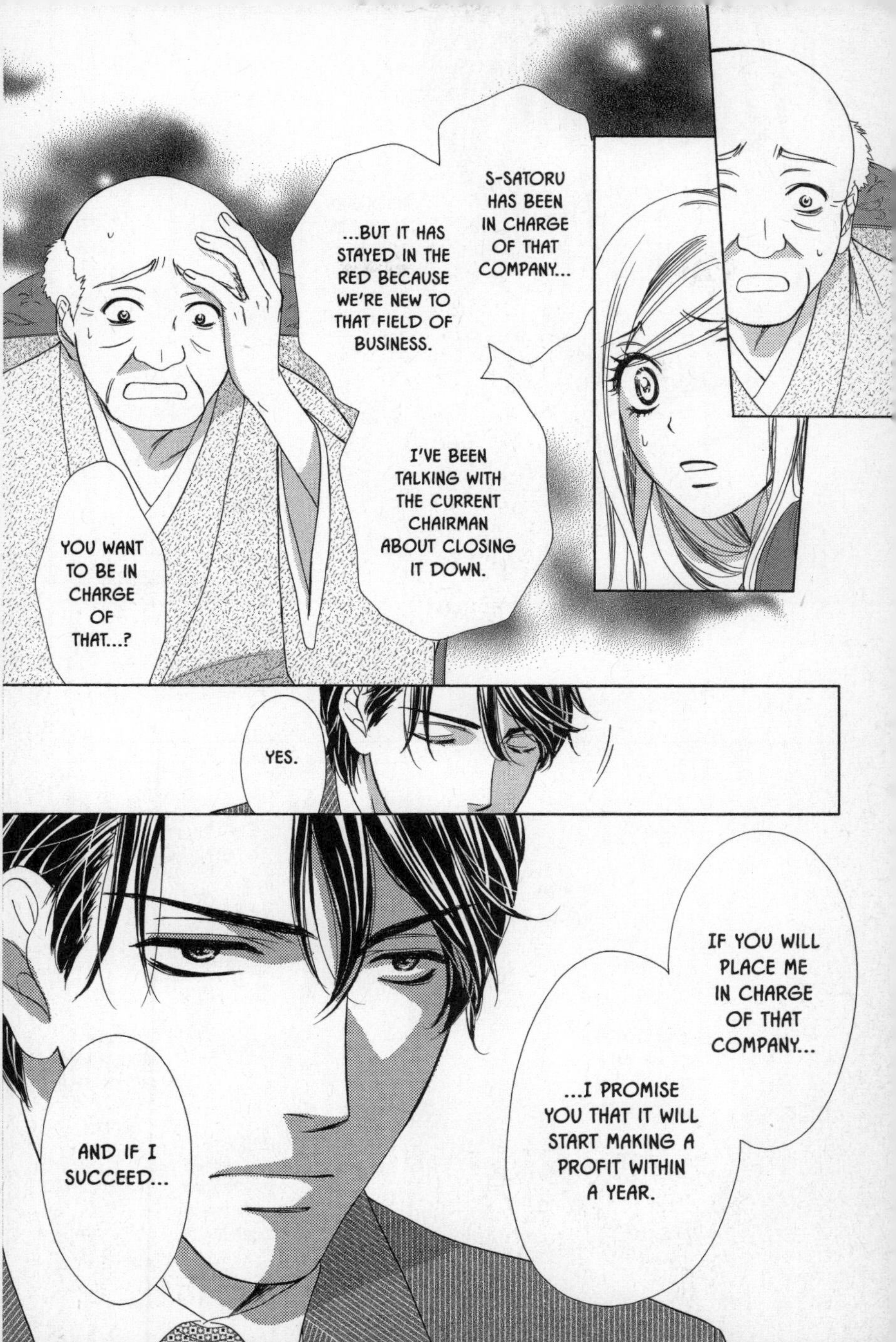
S-SATORU HAS BEEN IN CHARGE OF THAT COMPANY...
...BUT IT HAS STAYED IN THE RED BECAUSE WE'RE NEW TO THAT FIELD OF BUSINESS.
I'VE BEEN TALKING WITH THE CURRENT CHAIRMAN ABOUT CLOSING IT DOWN.
YOU WANT TO BE IN CHARGE OF THAT...?
YES.
IF YOU WILL PLACE ME IN CHARGE OF THAT COMPANY...
...I PROMISE YOU THAT IT WILL START MAKING A PROFIT WITHIN A YEAR.
AND IF I SUCCEED...

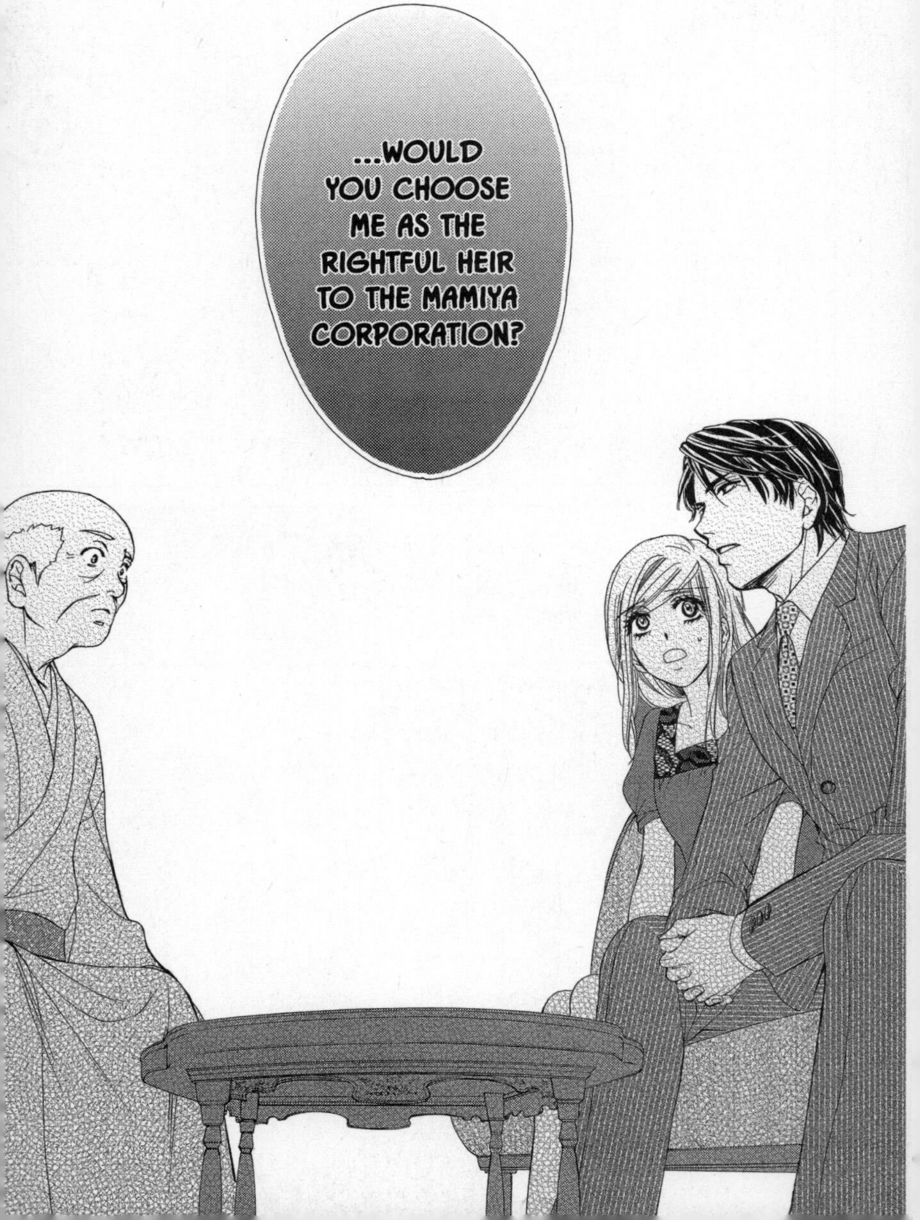
...WOULD YOU CHOOSE ME AS THE RIGHTFUL HEIR TO THE MAMIYA CORPORATION?

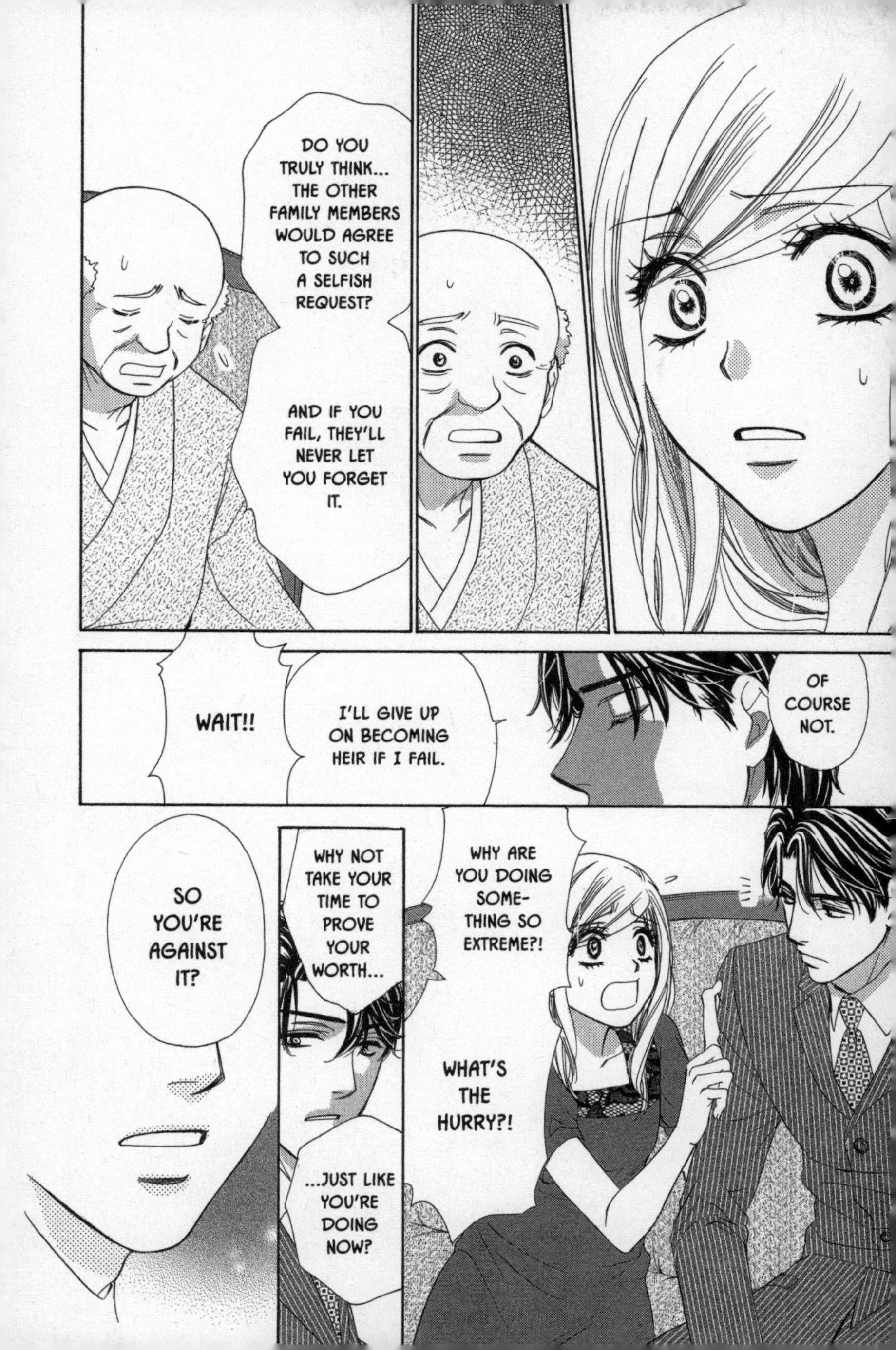
DO YOU TRULY THINK... THE OTHER FAMILY MEMBERS WOULD AGREE TO SUCH A SELFISH REQUEST?
AND IF YOU FAIL, THEY'LL NEVER LET YOU FORGET IT.
OF COURSE NOT.
I'LL GIVE UP ON BECOMING HEIR IF I FAIL.
WAIT!!
WHY ARE YOU DOING SOME-THING SO EXTREME?!
WHAT'S THE HURRY?!
WHY NOT TAKE YOUR TIME TO PROVE YOUR WORTH...
...JUST LIKE YOU'RE DOING NOW?
SO YOU'RE AGAINST IT?

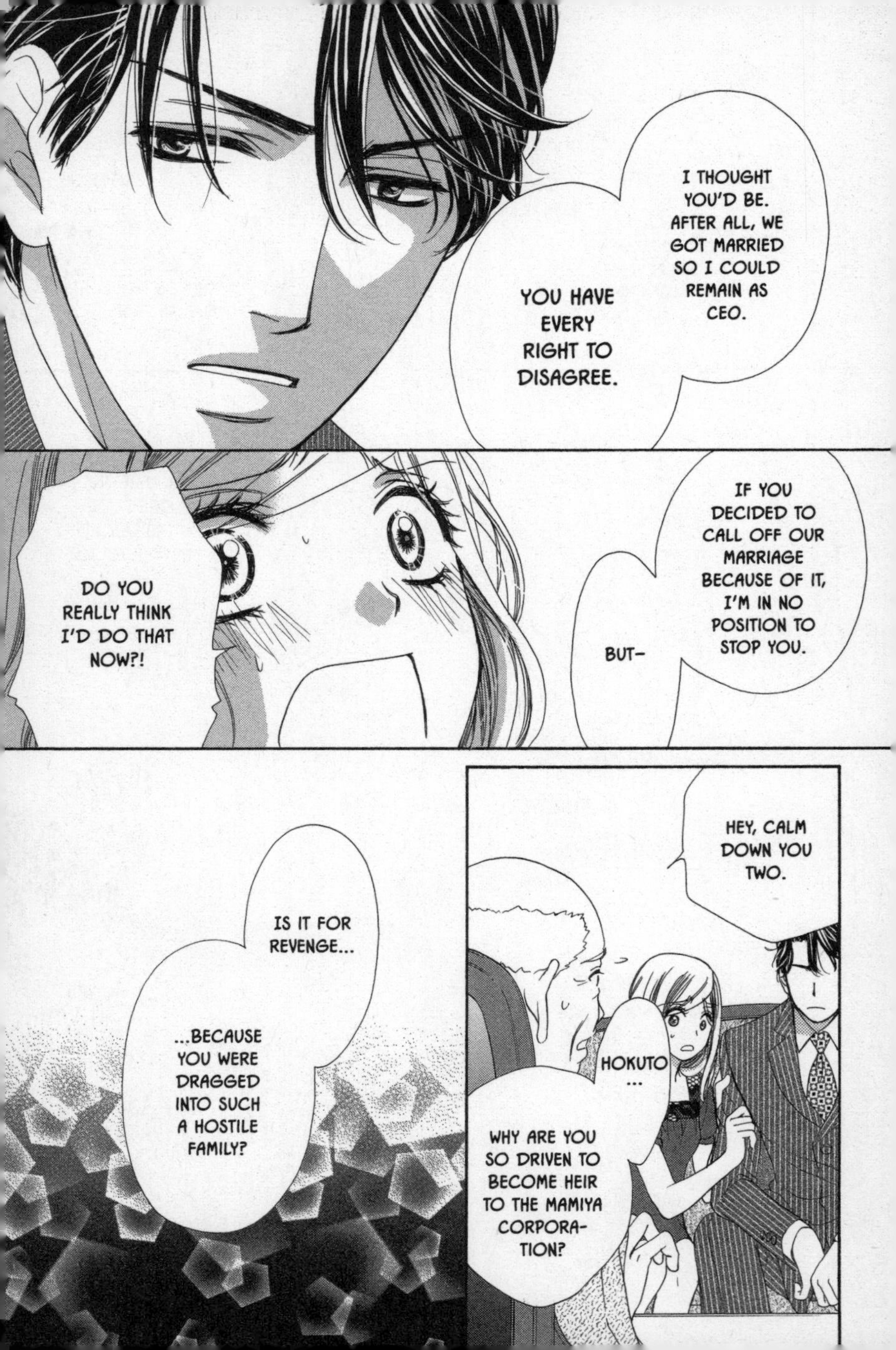
I THOUGHT YOU'D BE. AFTER ALL, WE GOT MARRIED SO I COULD REMAIN AS CEO.
YOU HAVE EVERY RIGHT TO DISAGREE.
IF YOU DECIDED TO CALL OFF OUR MARRIAGE BECAUSE OF IT, I'M IN NO POSITION TO STOP YOU.
BUT–
DO YOU REALLY THINK I'D DO THAT NOW?!
HEY, CALM DOWN YOU TWO.
HOKUTO...
WHY ARE YOU SO DRIVEN TO BECOME HEIR TO THE MAMIYA CORPORA-TION?
IS IT FOR REVENGE...
...BECAUSE YOU WERE DRAGGED INTO SUCH A HOSTILE FAMILY?

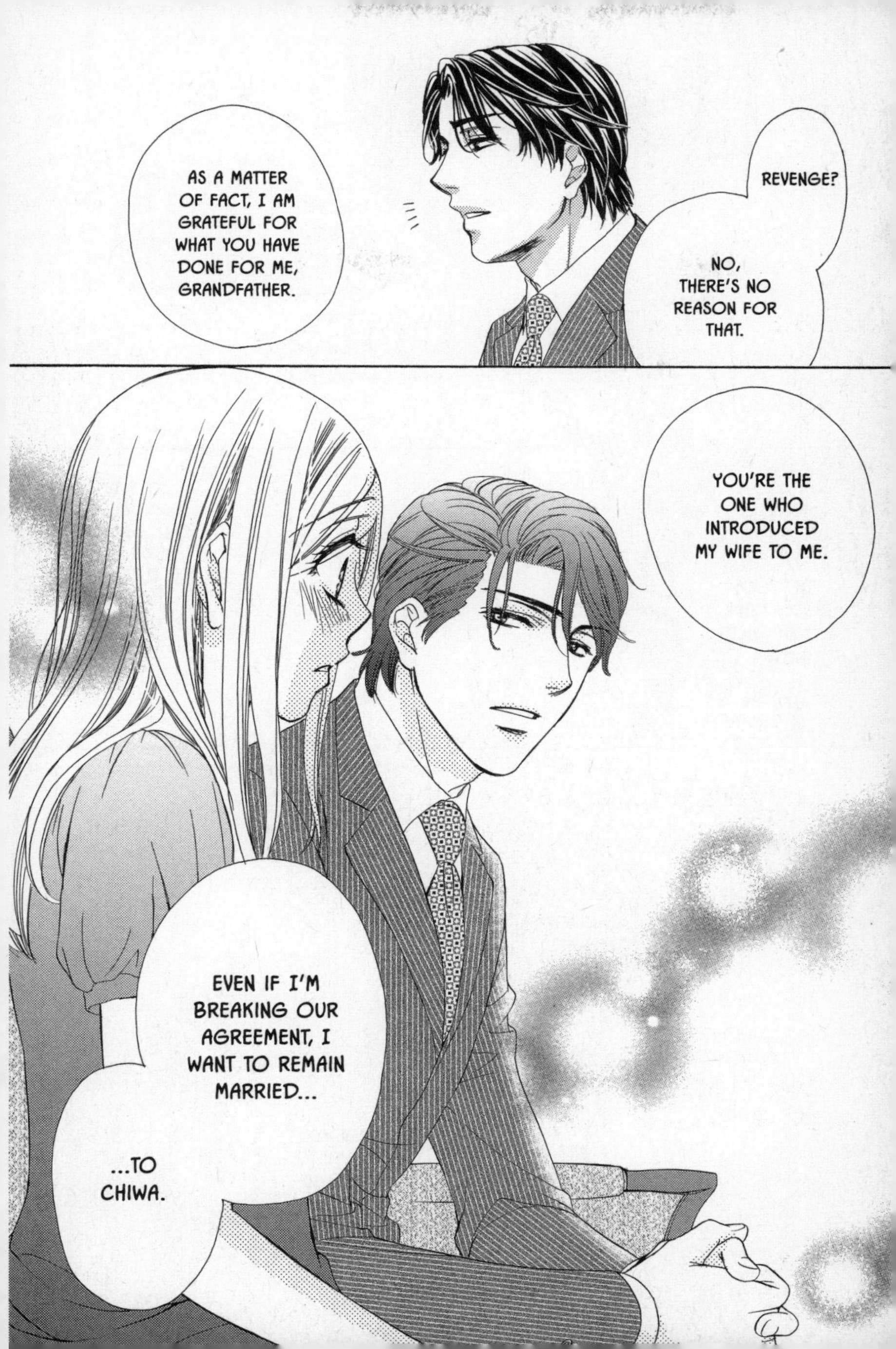
REVENGE?
NO, THERE'S NO REASON FOR THAT.
AS A MATTER OF FACT, I AM GRATEFUL FOR WHAT YOU HAVE DONE FOR ME, GRANDFATHER.
YOU'RE THE ONE WHO INTRODUCED MY WIFE TO ME.
EVEN IF I'M BREAKING OUR AGREEMENT, I WANT TO REMAIN MARRIED...
...TO CHIWA.

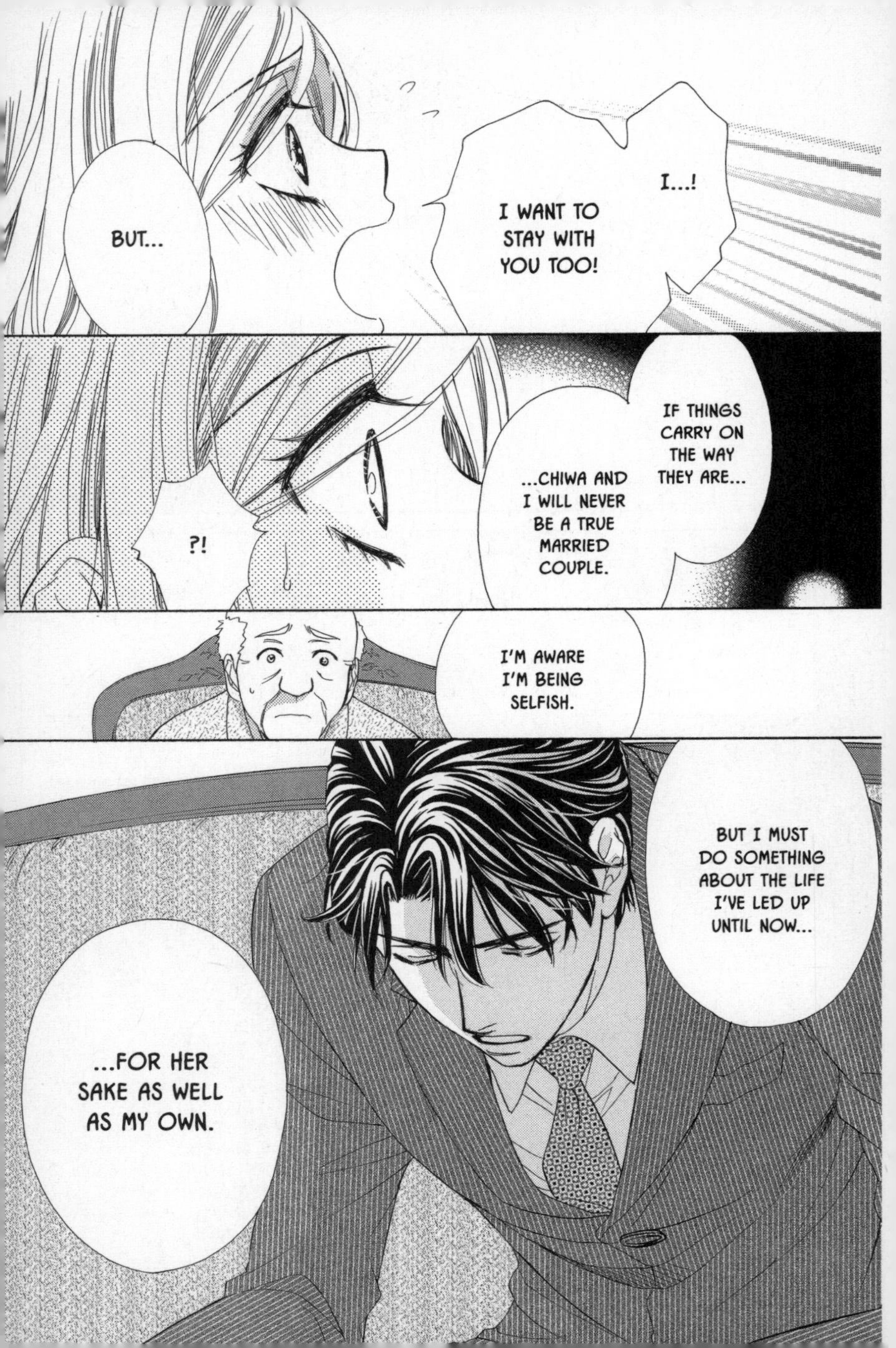
I...!
I WANT TO STAY WITH YOU TOO!
BUT...
IF THINGS CARRY ON THE WAY THEY ARE...
...CHIWA AND I WILL NEVER BE A TRUE MARRIED COUPLE.
?!
I'M AWARE I'M BEING SELFISH.
BUT I MUST DO SOMETHING ABOUT THE LIFE I'VE LED UP UNTIL NOW...
...FOR HER SAKE AS WELL AS MY OWN.

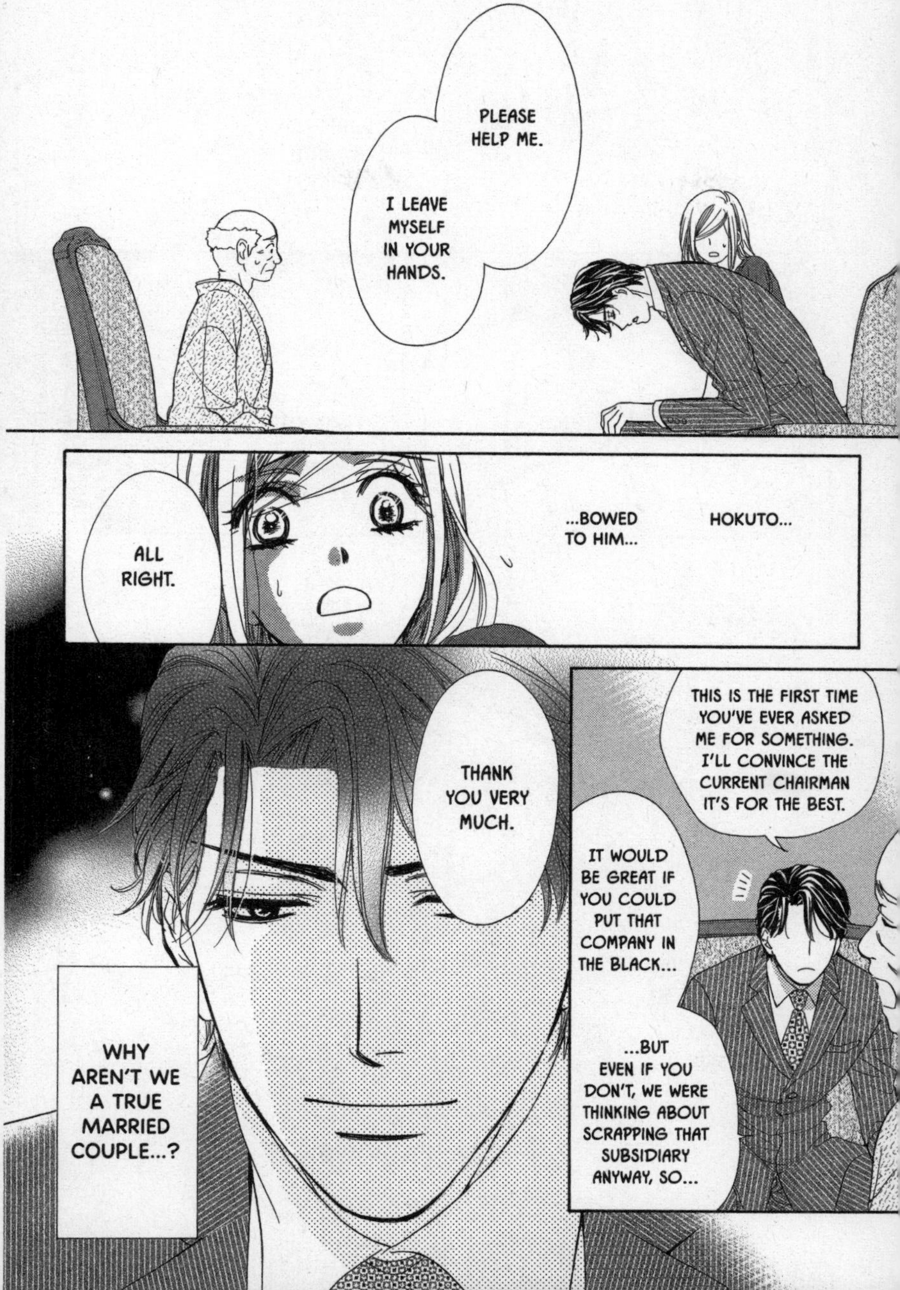
PLEASE HELP ME.
I LEAVE MYSELF IN YOUR HANDS.
HOKUTO...
...BOWED TO HIM...
ALL RIGHT.
THIS IS THE FIRST TIME YOU'VE EVER ASKED ME FOR SOMETHING. I'LL CONVINCE THE CURRENT CHAIRMAN IT'S FOR THE BEST.
IT WOULD BE GREAT IF YOU COULD PUT THAT COMPANY IN THE BLACK...
...BUT EVEN IF YOU DON'T, WE WERE THINKING ABOUT SCRAPPING THAT SUBSIDIARY ANYWAY, SO...
THANK YOU VERY MUCH.
WHY AREN'T WE A TRUE MARRIED COUPLE...?

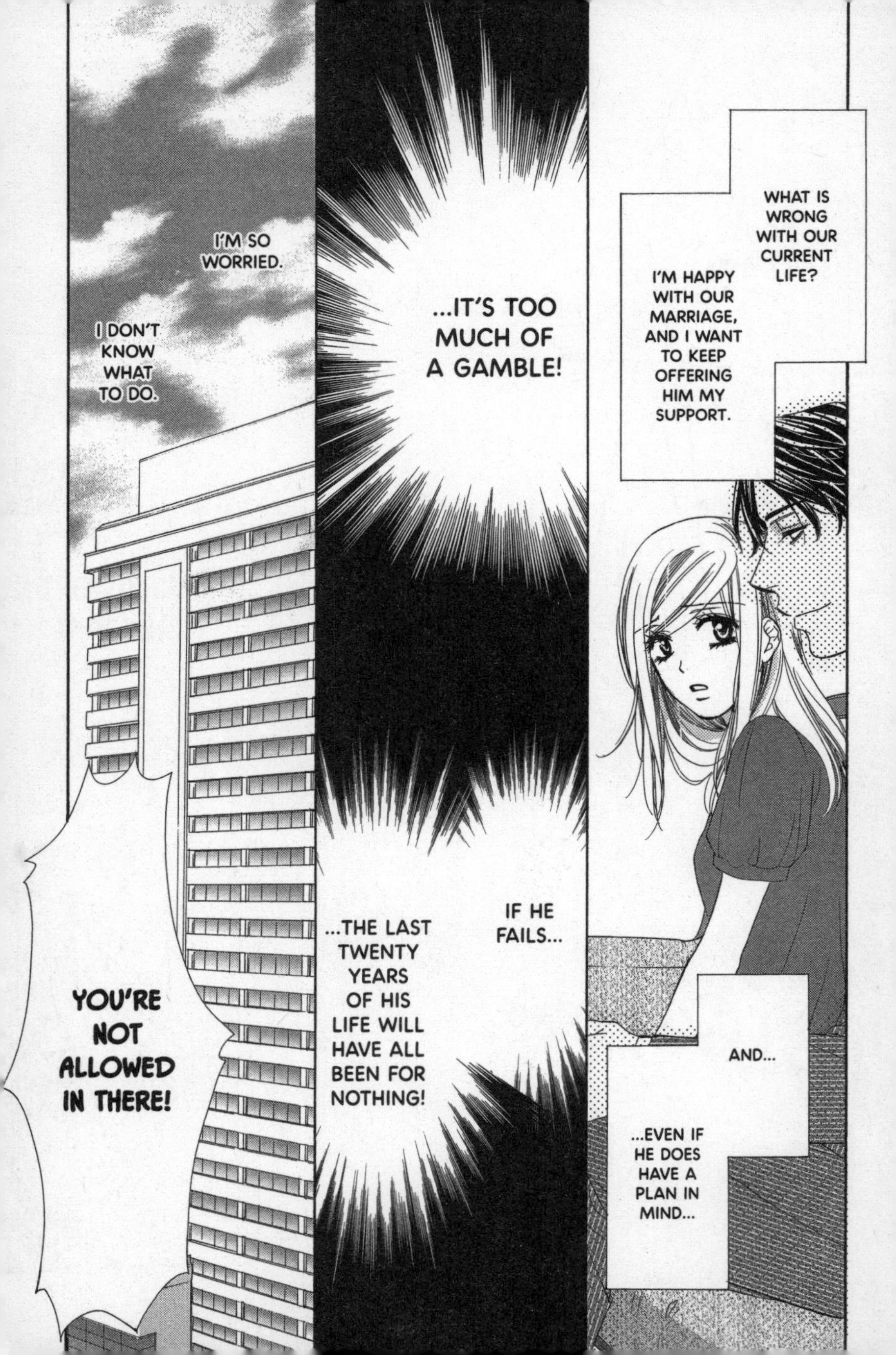
WHAT IS WRONG WITH OUR CURRENT LIFE?
I'M HAPPY WITH OUR MARRIAGE, AND I WANT TO KEEP OFFERING HIM MY SUPPORT.
AND...
...EVEN IF HE DOES HAVE A PLAN IN MIND...
...IT'S TOO MUCH OF A GAMBLE!
IF HE FAILS...
...THE LAST TWENTY YEARS OF HIS LIFE WILL HAVE ALL BEEN FOR NOTHING!
I'M SO WORRIED.
I DON'T KNOW WHAT TO DO.
YOU'RE NOT ALLOWED IN THERE!

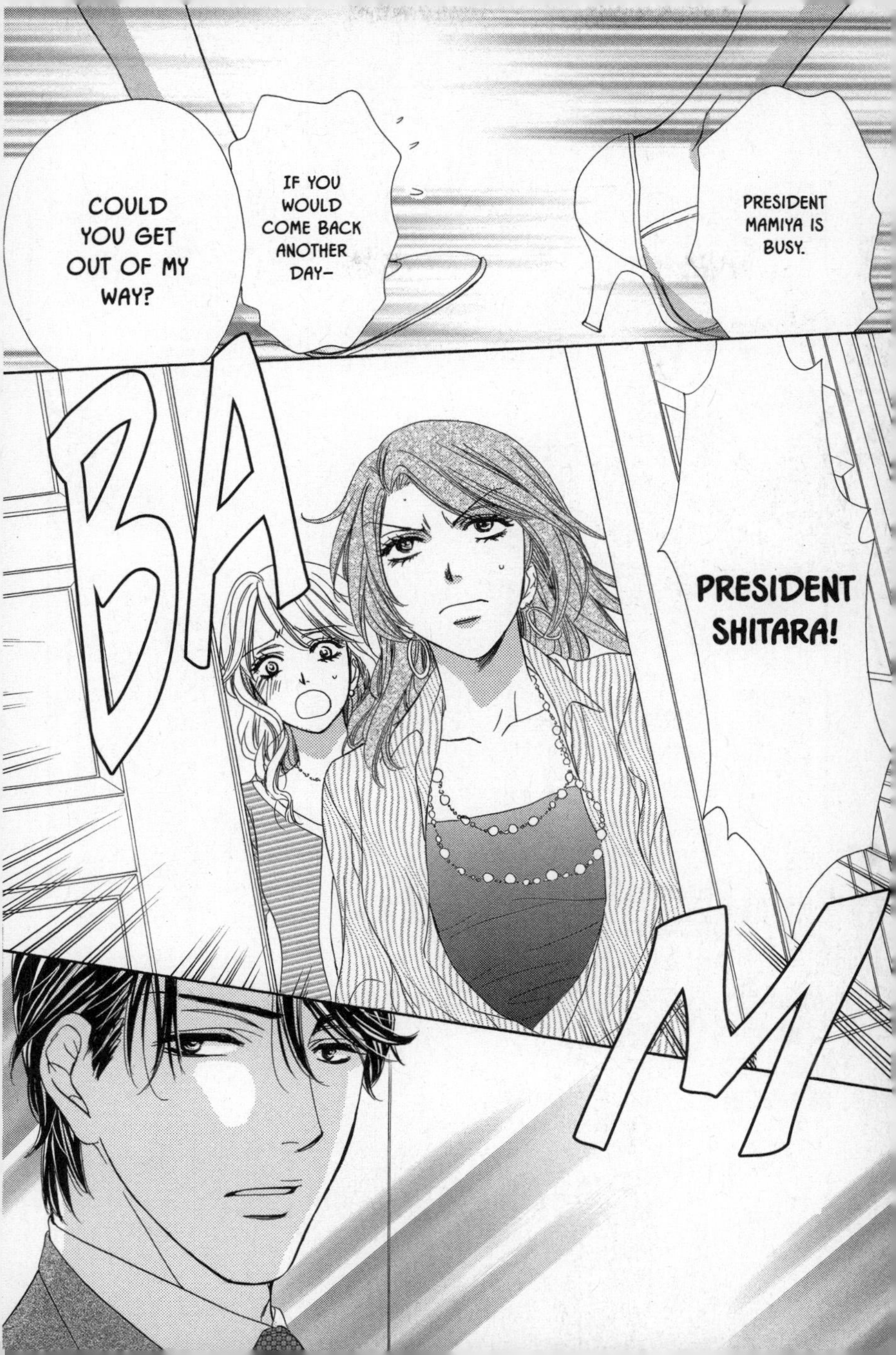
PRESIDENT MAMIYA IS BUSY.
IF YOU WOULD COME BACK ANOTHER DAY—
COULD YOU GET OUT OF MY WAY?
PRESIDENT SHITARA!
BAM

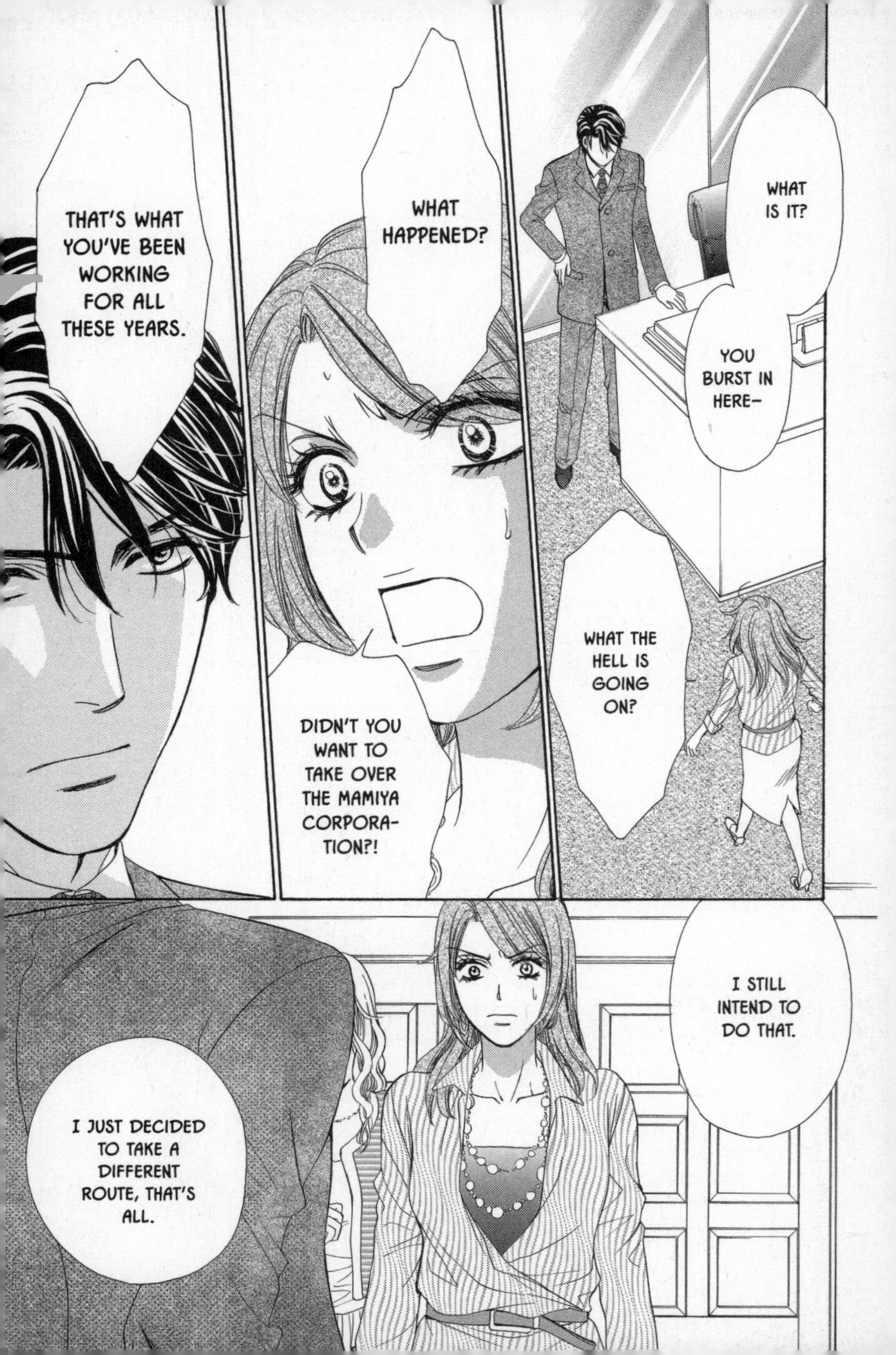
WHAT IS IT?
YOU BURST IN HERE—
WHAT THE HELL IS GOING ON?
WHAT HAPPENED?
DIDN'T YOU WANT TO TAKE OVER THE MAMIYA CORPORATION?!
THAT'S WHAT YOU'VE BEEN WORKING FOR ALL THESE YEARS.
I STILL INTEND TO DO THAT.
I JUST DECIDED TO TAKE A DIFFERENT ROUTE, THAT'S ALL.

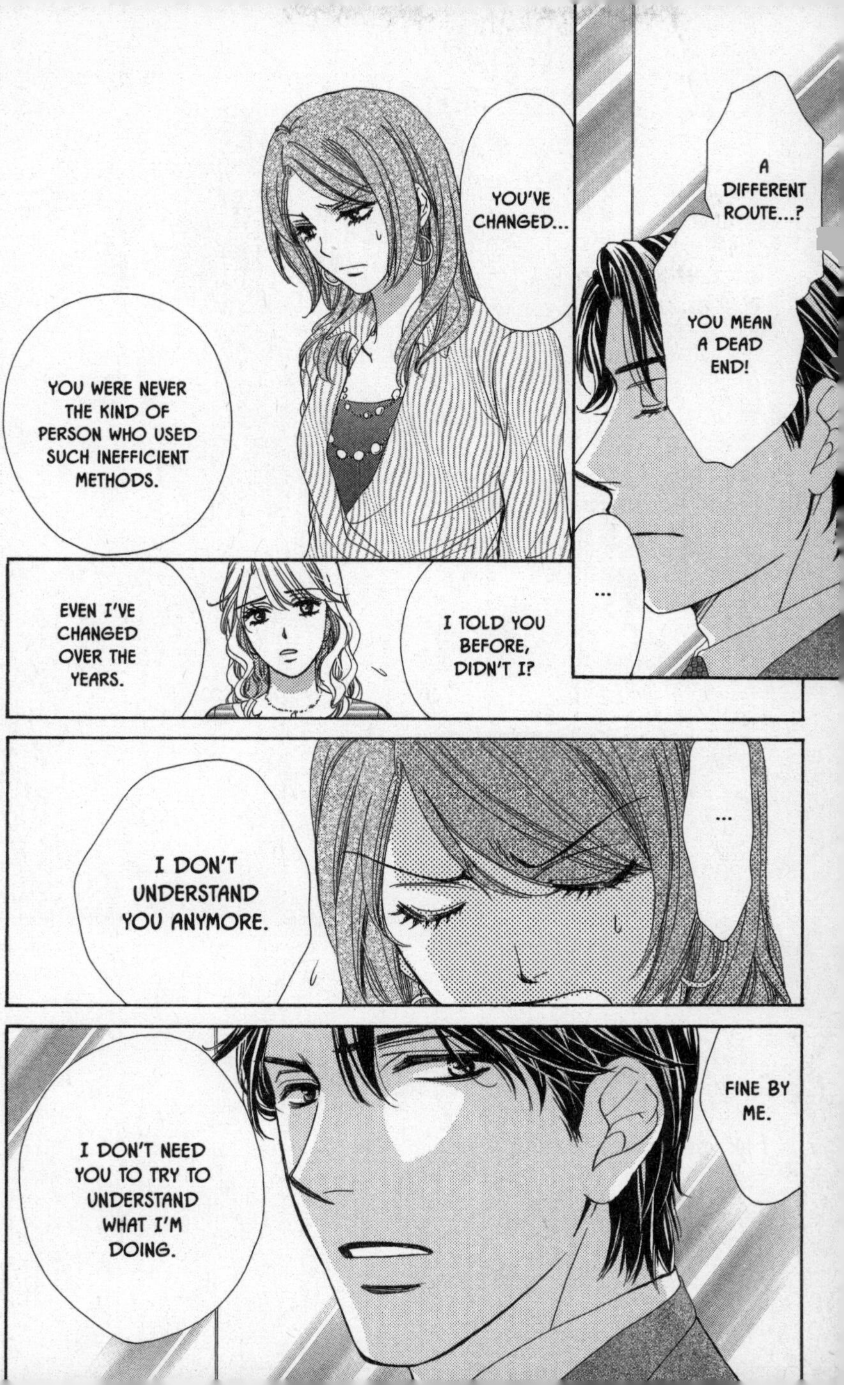
A DIFFERENT ROUTE...?
YOU MEAN A DEAD END!
...
YOU'VE CHANGED...
YOU WERE NEVER THE KIND OF PERSON WHO USED SUCH INEFFICIENT METHODS.
I TOLD YOU BEFORE, DIDN'T I?
EVEN I'VE CHANGED OVER THE YEARS.
...
I DON'T UNDERSTAND YOU ANYMORE.
FINE BY ME.
I DON'T NEED YOU TO TRY TO UNDERSTAND WHAT I'M DOING.

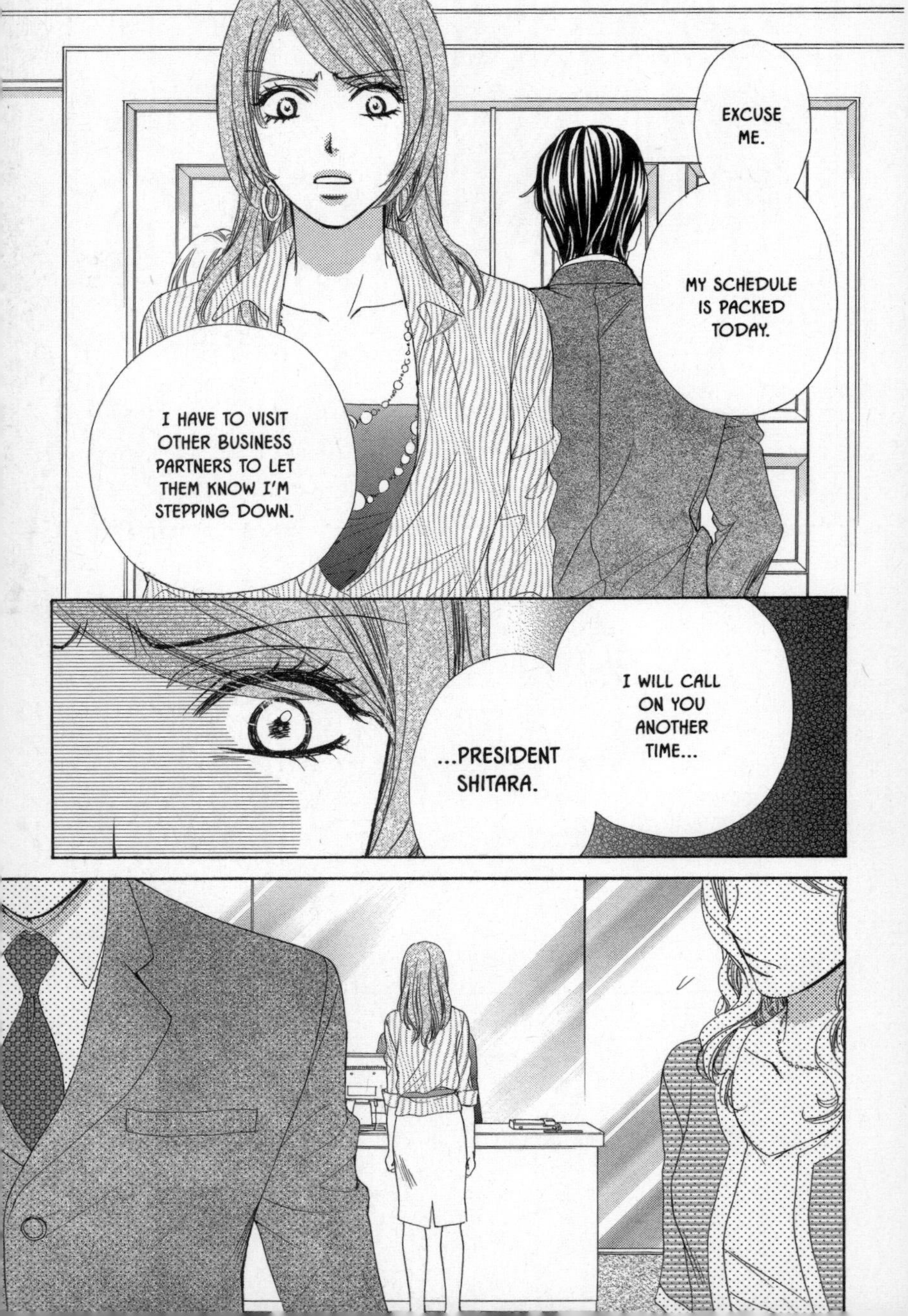
EXCUSE ME.
MY SCHEDULE IS PACKED TODAY.
I HAVE TO VISIT OTHER BUSINESS PARTNERS TO LET THEM KNOW I'M STEPPING DOWN.
I WILL CALL ON YOU ANOTHER TIME...
...PRESIDENT SHITARA.

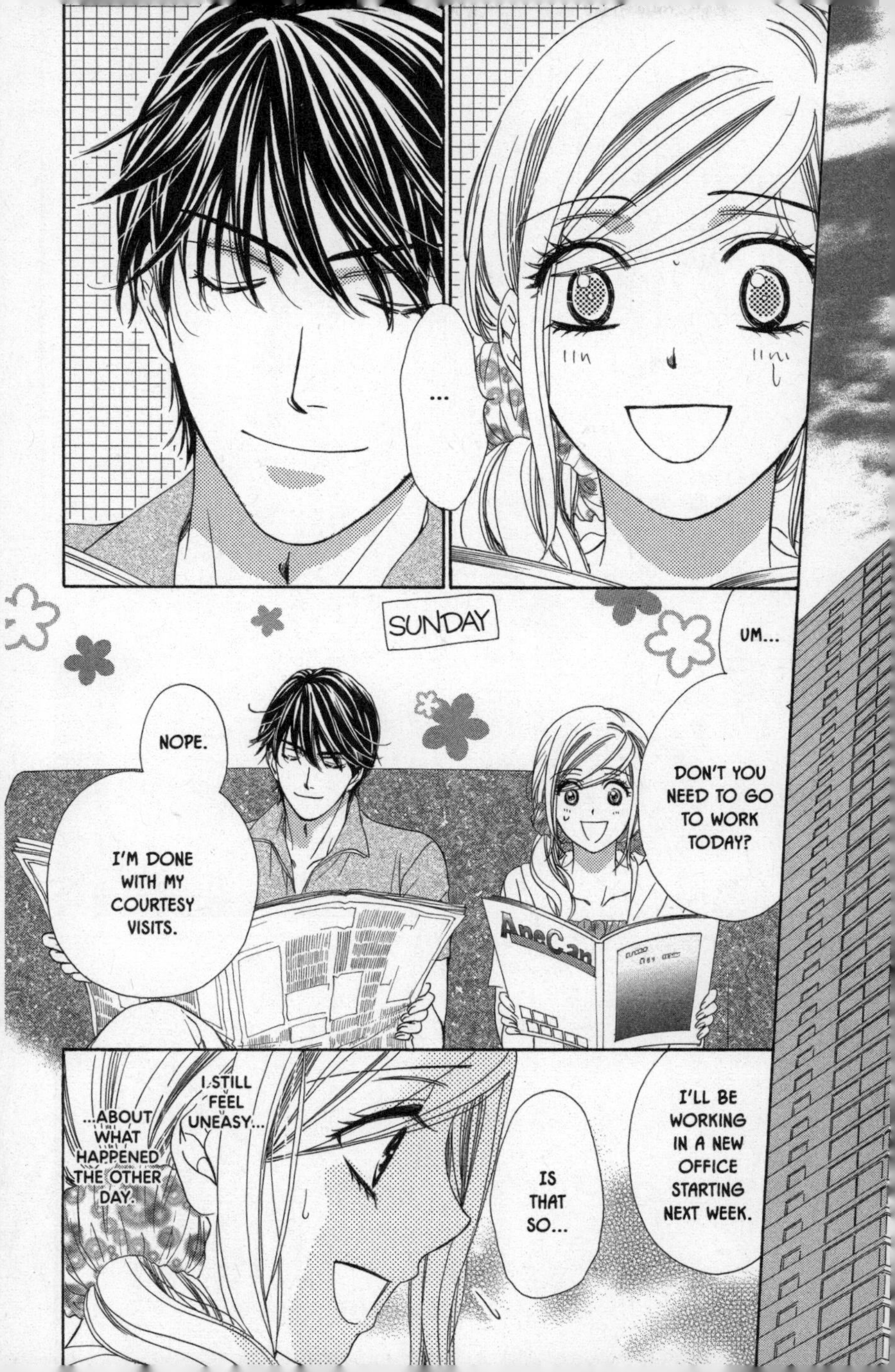
...
SUNDAY
UM...
DON'T YOU NEED TO GO TO WORK TODAY?
NOPE.
I'M DONE WITH MY COURTESY VISITS.
I'LL BE WORKING IN A NEW OFFICE STARTING NEXT WEEK.
IS THAT SO...
I STILL FEEL UNEASY...
...ABOUT WHAT HAPPENED THE OTHER DAY.

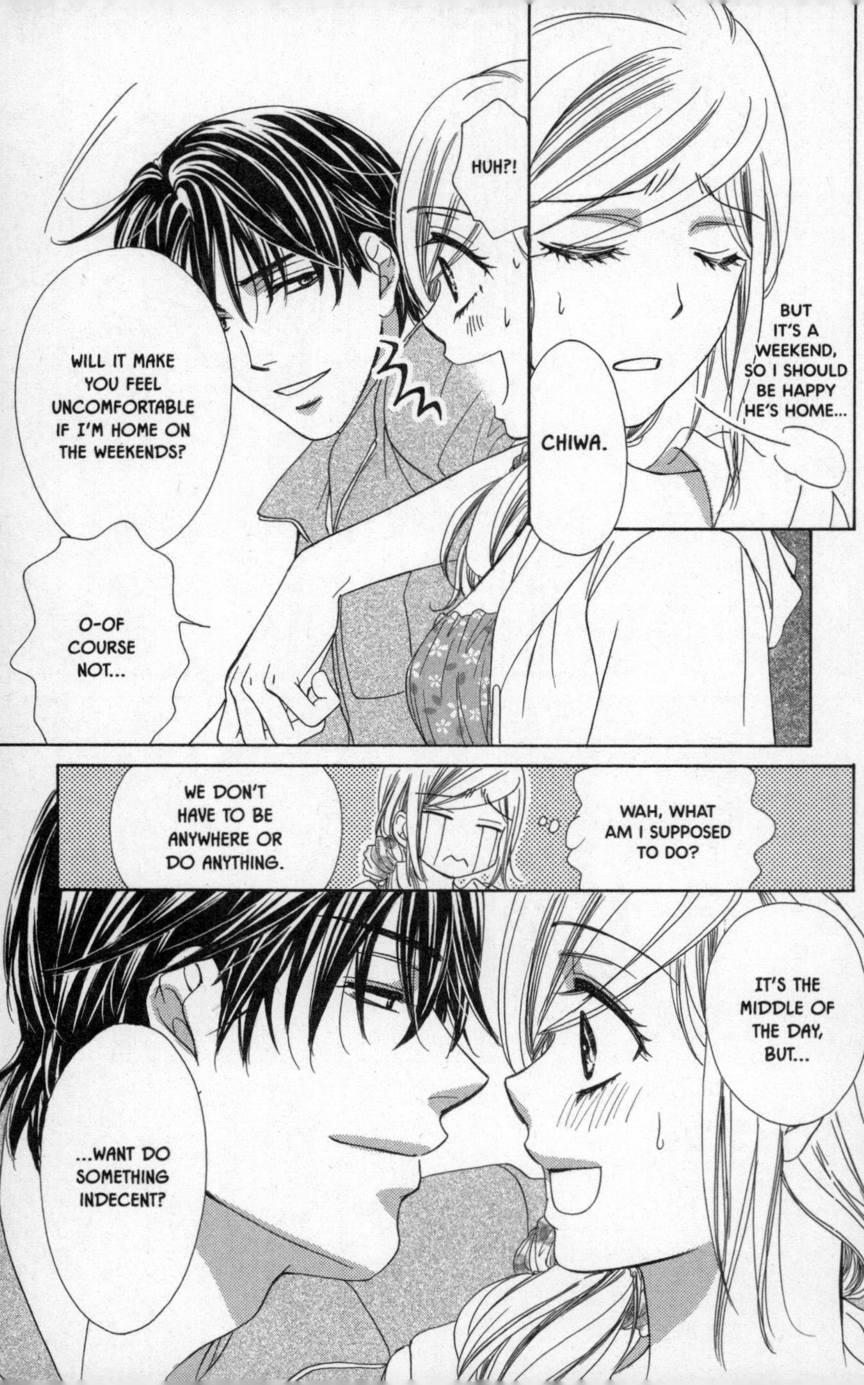
BUT IT'S A WEEKEND, SO I SHOULD BE HAPPY HE'S HOME...
CHIWA.
HUH?!
WILL IT MAKE YOU FEEL UNCOMFORTABLE IF I'M HOME ON THE WEEKENDS?
O-OF COURSE NOT...
WAH, WHAT AM I SUPPOSED TO DO?
WE DON'T HAVE TO BE ANYWHERE OR DO ANYTHING.
IT'S THE MIDDLE OF THE DAY, BUT...
...WANT DO SOMETHING INDECENT?

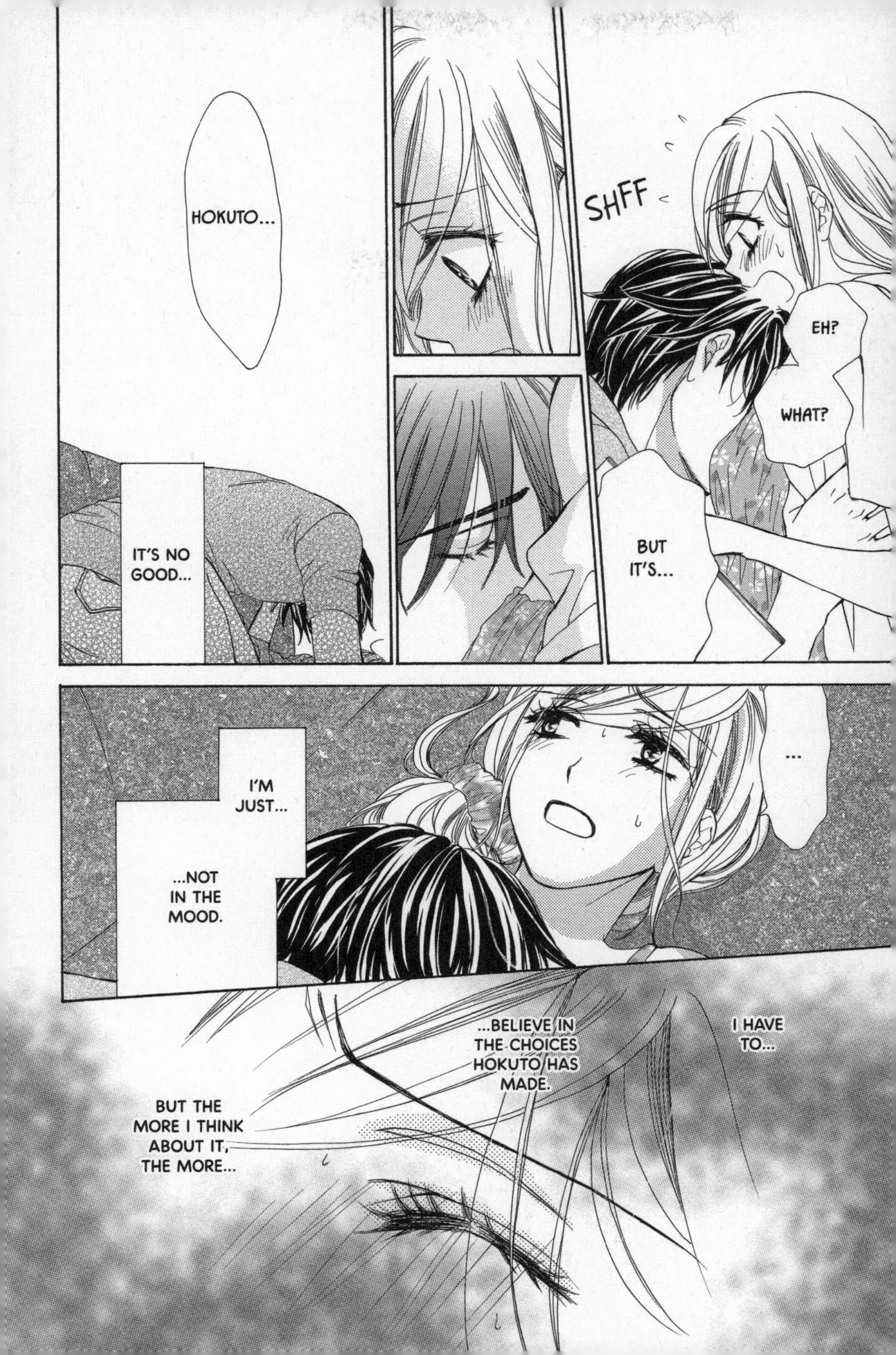
SHFF
EH?
WHAT?
BUT IT'S...
HOKUTO...
IT'S NO GOOD...
...
I'M JUST...
...NOT IN THE MOOD.
I HAVE TO...
...BELIEVE IN THE CHOICES HOKUTO HAS MADE.
BUT THE MORE I THINK ABOUT IT, THE MORE...

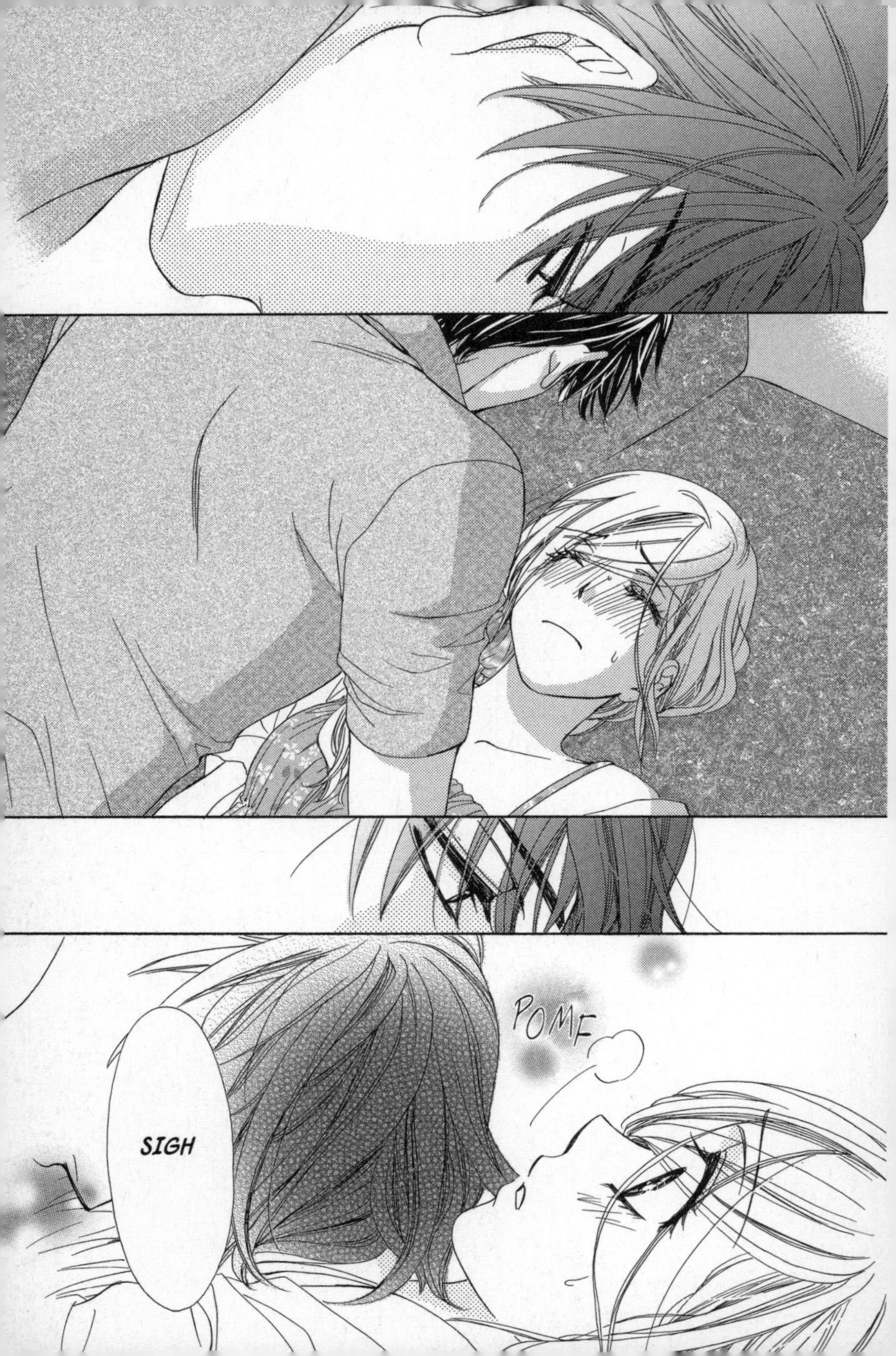
POMF
SIGH

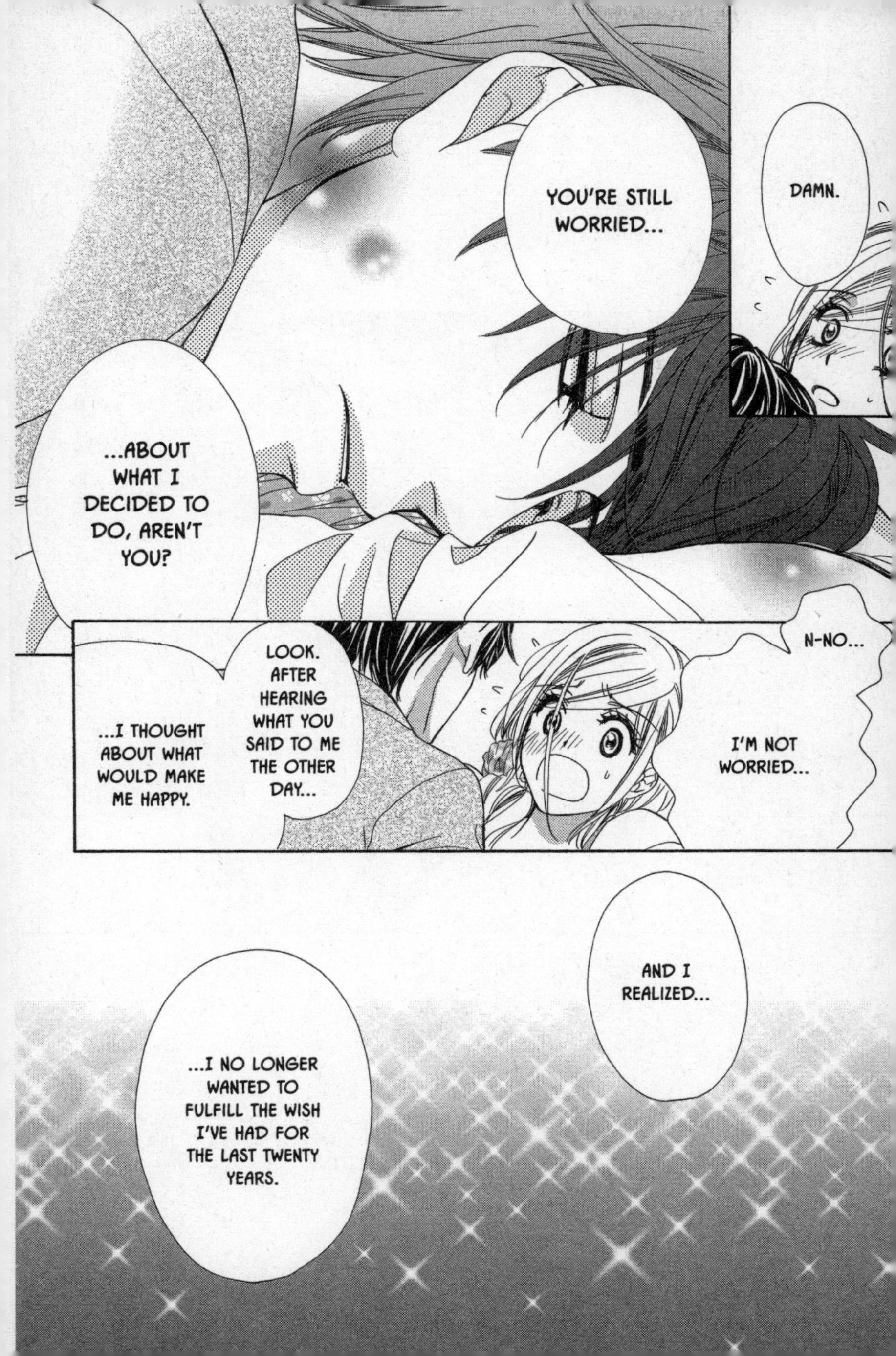
DAMN.
YOU'RE STILL WORRIED...
...ABOUT WHAT I DECIDED TO DO, AREN'T YOU?
N-NO...
I'M NOT WORRIED...
LOOK. AFTER HEARING WHAT YOU SAID TO ME THE OTHER DAY...
...I THOUGHT ABOUT WHAT WOULD MAKE ME HAPPY.
AND I REALIZED...
...I NO LONGER WANTED TO FULFILL THE WISH I'VE HAD FOR THE LAST TWENTY YEARS.

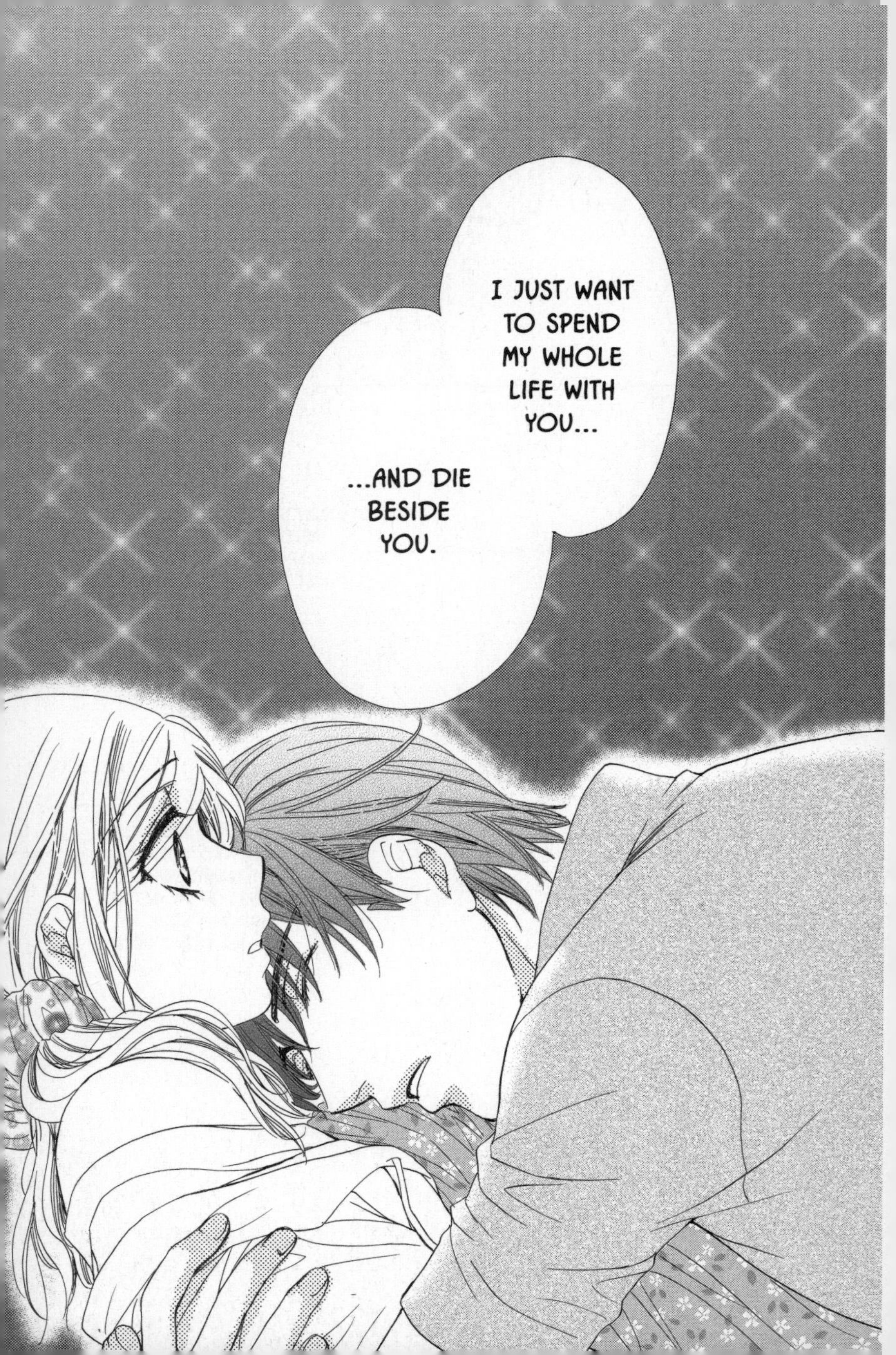
I JUST WANT TO SPEND MY WHOLE LIFE WITH YOU...
...AND DIE BESIDE YOU.

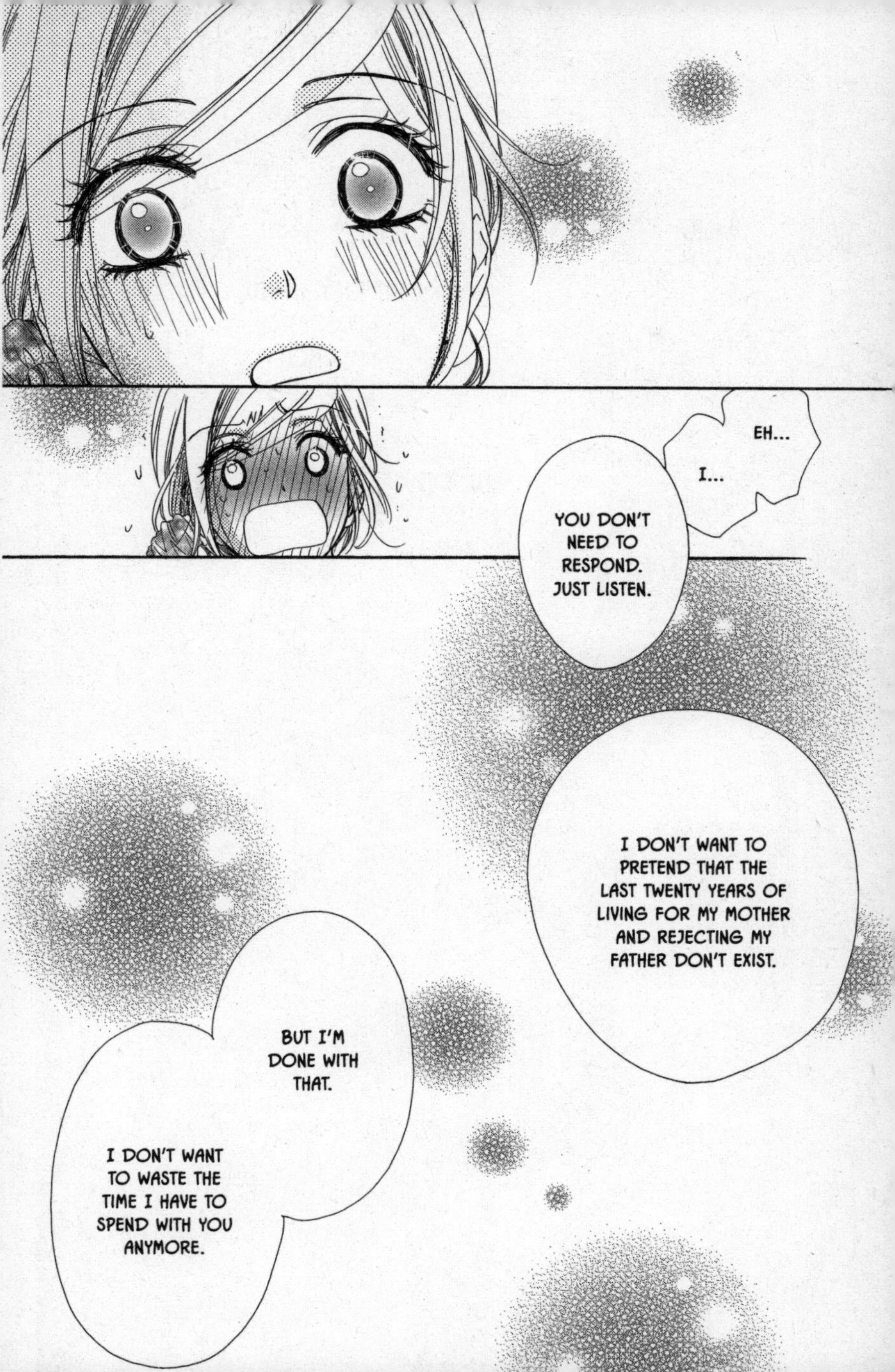
EH... I...
YOU DON'T NEED TO RESPOND. JUST LISTEN.
I DON'T WANT TO PRETEND THAT THE LAST TWENTY YEARS OF LIVING FOR MY MOTHER AND REJECTING MY FATHER DON'T EXIST.
BUT I'M DONE WITH THAT.
I DON'T WANT TO WASTE THE TIME I HAVE TO SPEND WITH YOU ANYMORE.

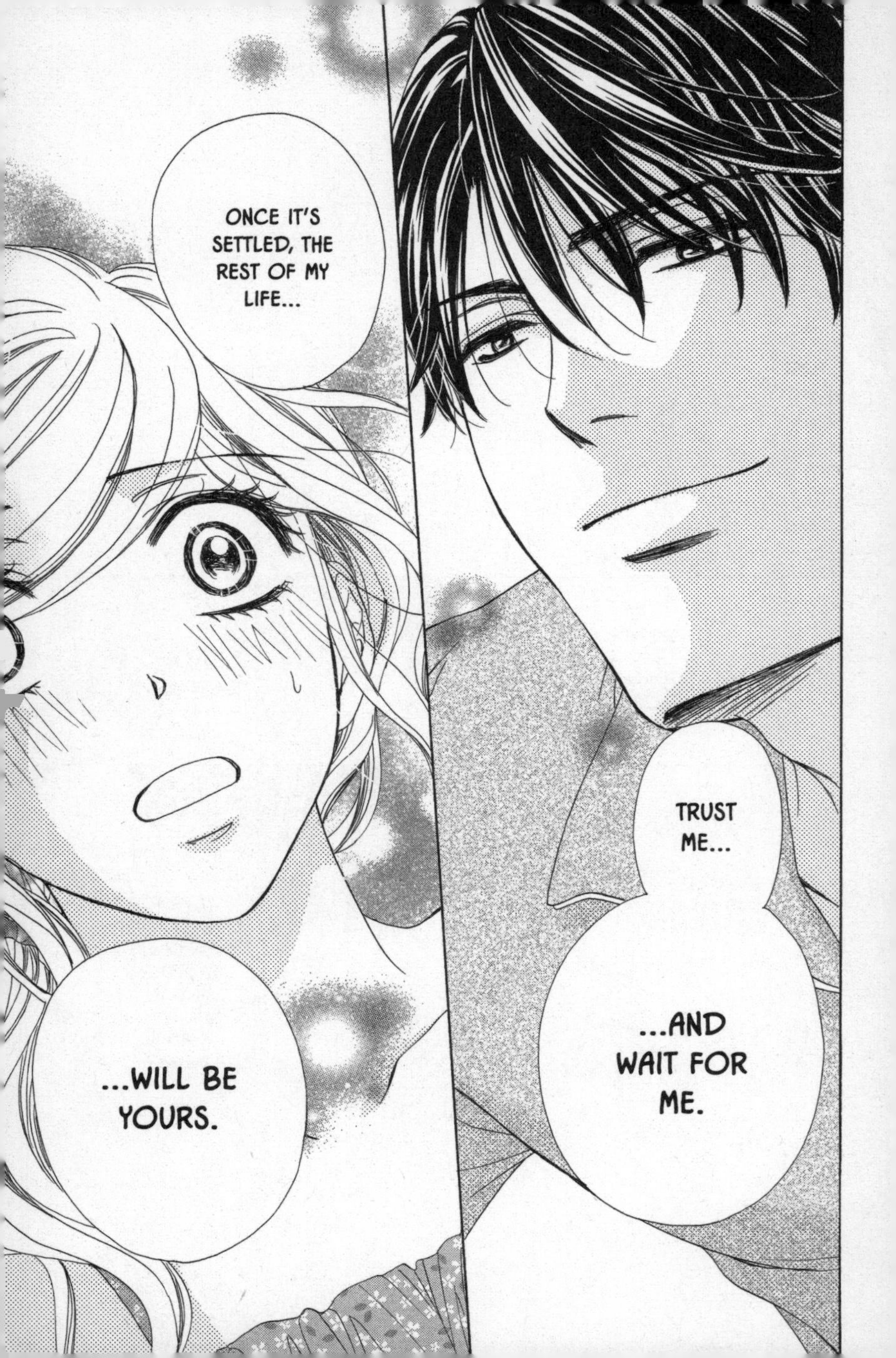
TRUST ME...
...AND WAIT FOR ME.
ONCE IT'S SETTLED, THE REST OF MY LIFE...
...WILL BE YOURS.

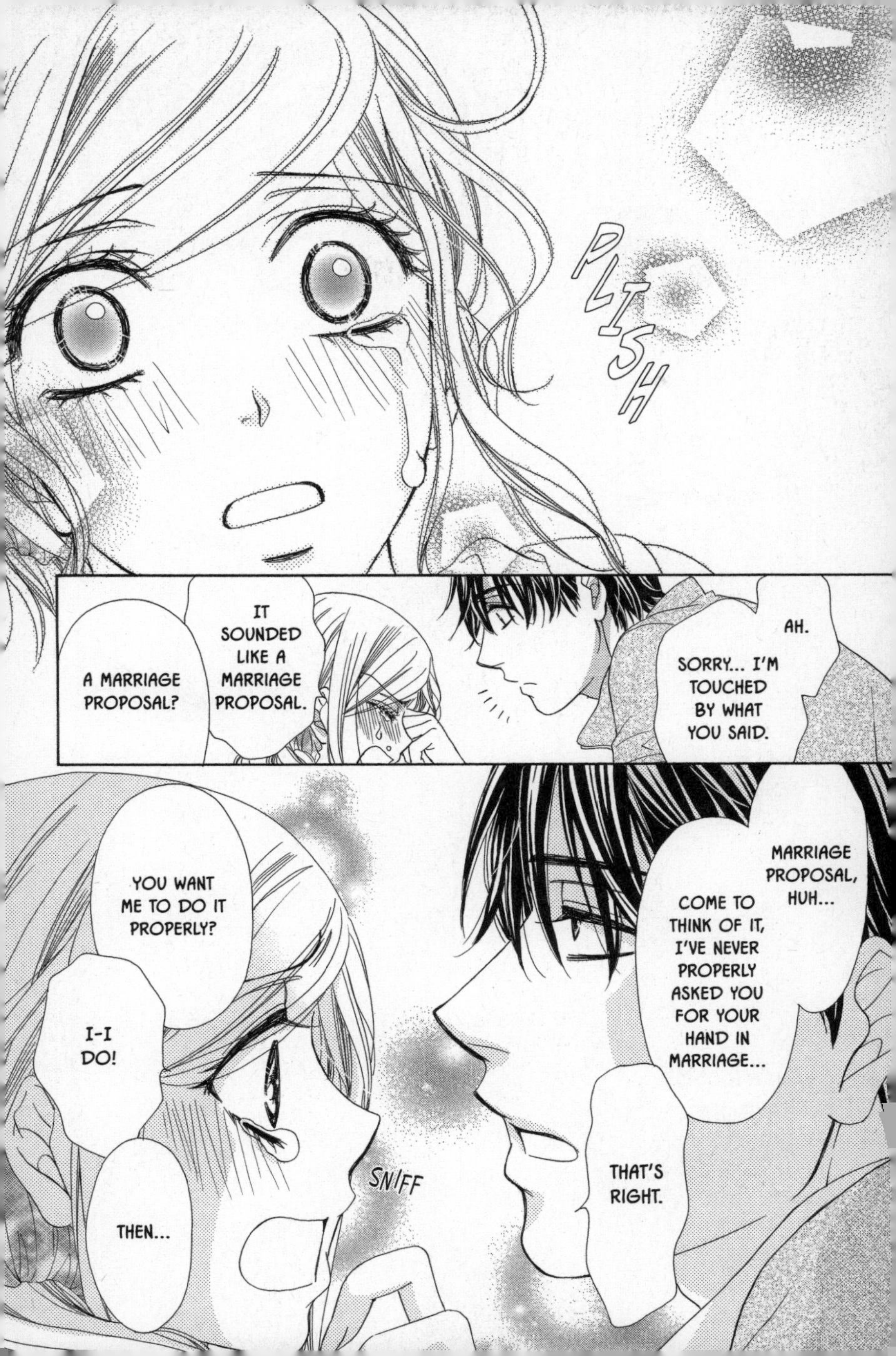
PLISH
AH.
SORRY... I'M TOUCHED BY WHAT YOU SAID.
IT SOUNDED LIKE A MARRIAGE PROPOSAL.
A MARRIAGE PROPOSAL?
MARRIAGE PROPOSAL, HUH...
COME TO THINK OF IT, I'VE NEVER PROPERLY ASKED YOU FOR YOUR HAND IN MARRIAGE...
YOU WANT ME TO DO IT PROPERLY?
I-I DO!
THAT'S RIGHT.
SNIFF
THEN...

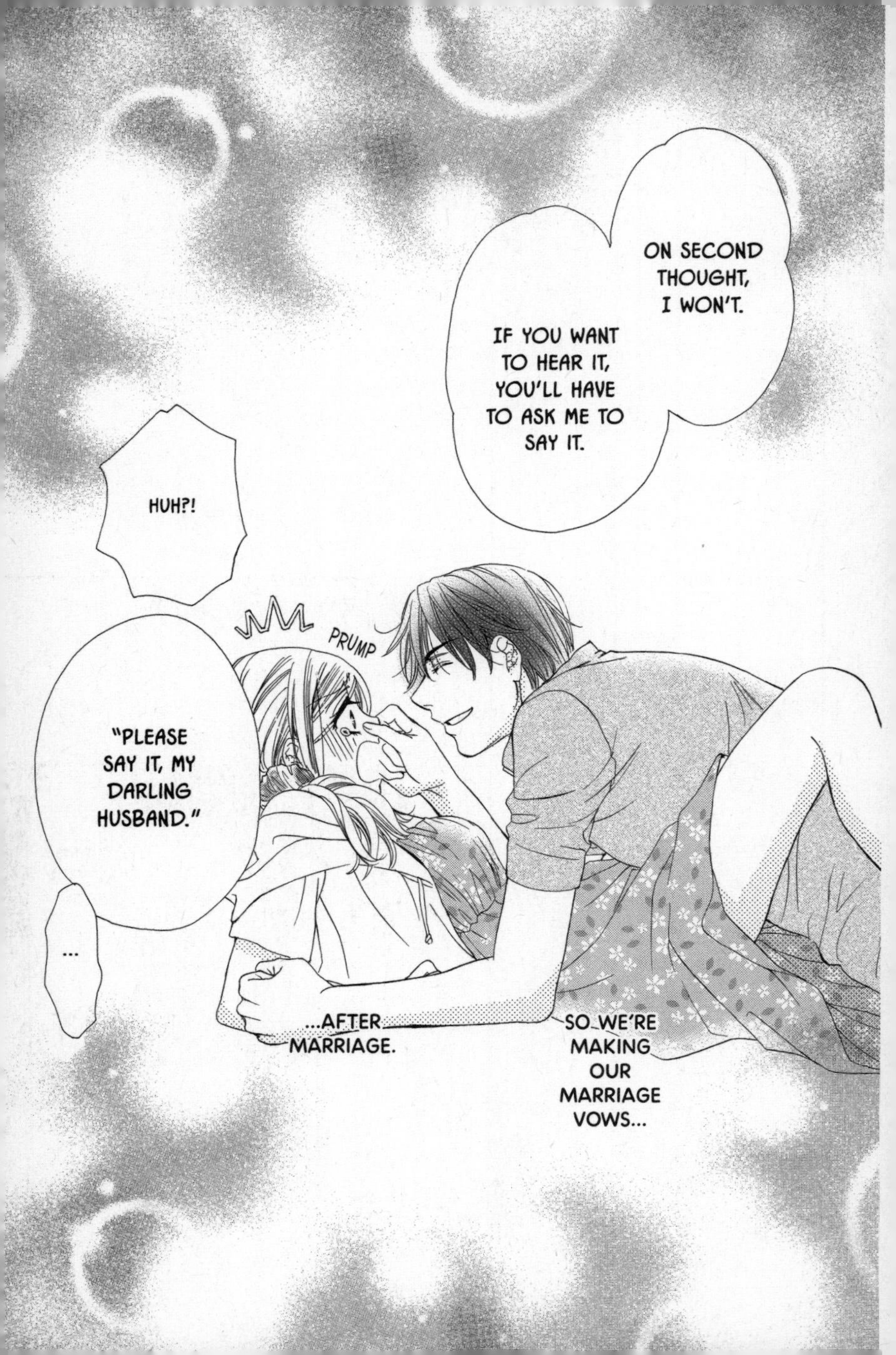
ON SECOND THOUGHT, I WON'T.
IF YOU WANT TO HEAR IT, YOU'LL HAVE TO ASK ME TO SAY IT.
HUH?!
PRUMP
"PLEASE SAY IT, MY DARLING HUSBAND."
...
SO WE'RE MAKING OUR MARRIAGE VOWS...
...AFTER MARRIAGE.

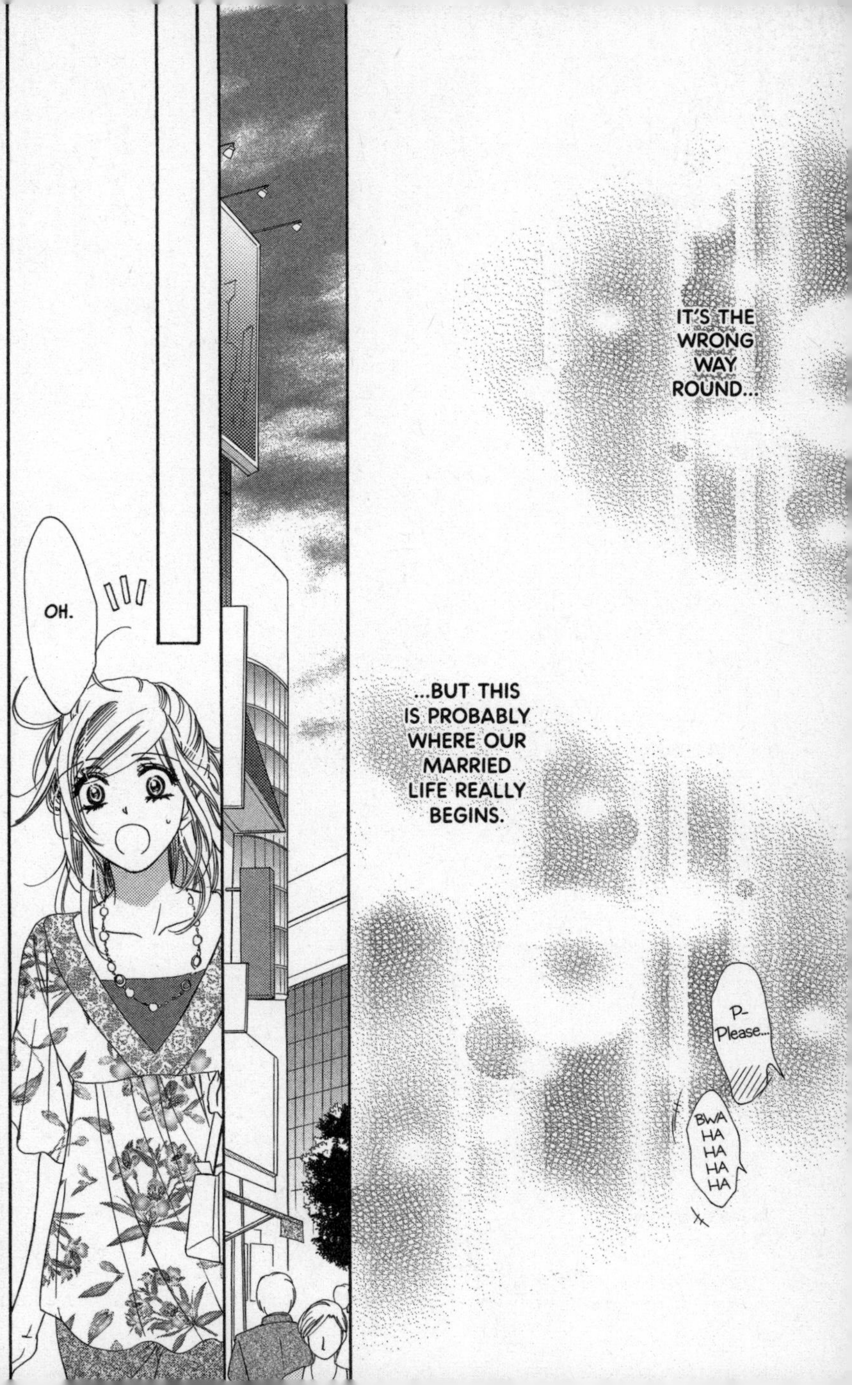
IT'S THE WRONG WAY ROUND...
...BUT THIS IS PROBABLY WHERE OUR MARRIED LIFE REALLY BEGINS.
P-Please...
BWA HA HA HA HA
OH.

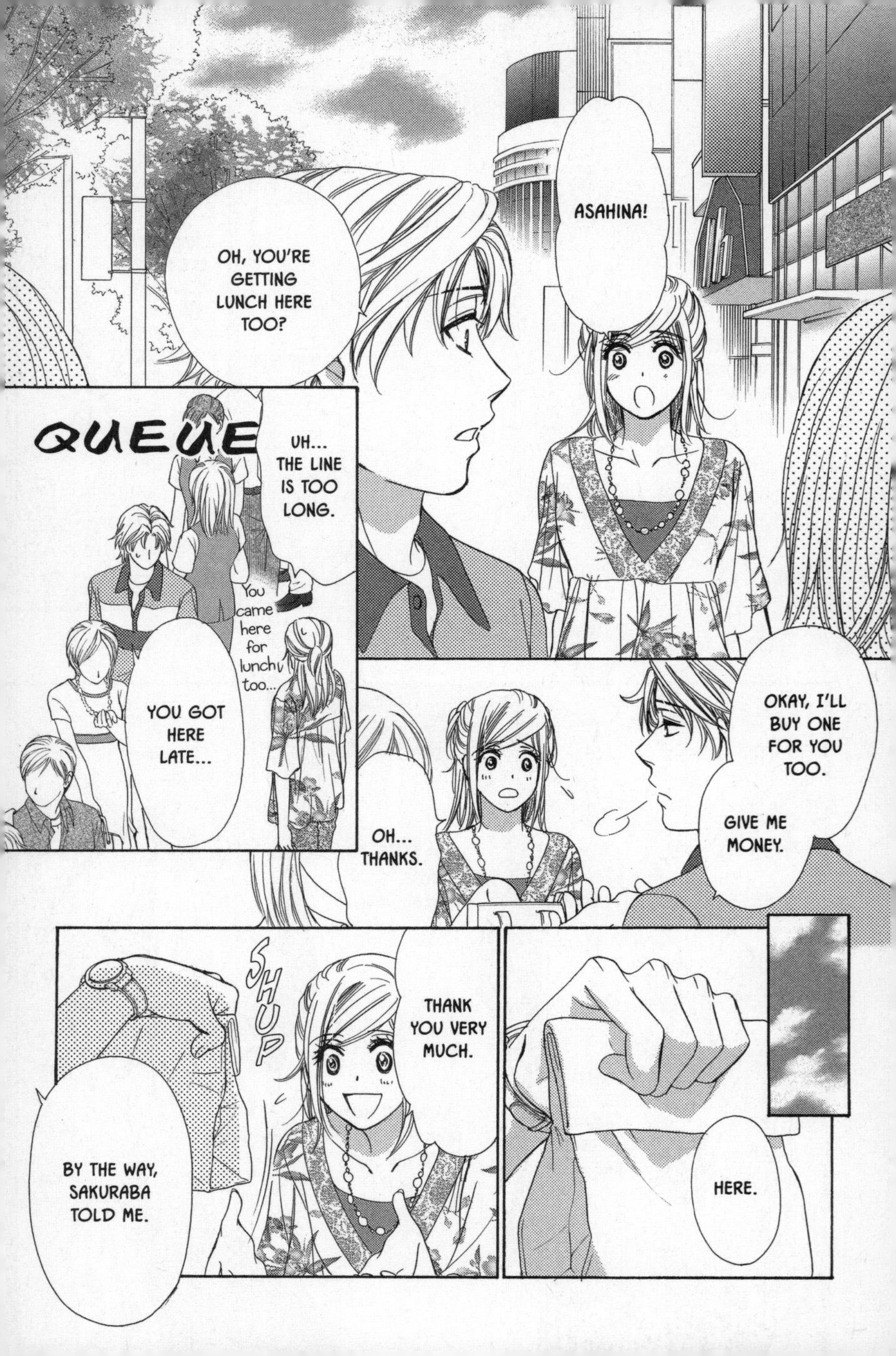
ASAHINA!
OH, YOU'RE GETTING LUNCH HERE TOO?
QUEUE
UH... THE LINE IS TOO LONG.
You came here for lunch too...
YOU GOT HERE LATE...
OKAY, I'LL BUY ONE FOR YOU TOO.
GIVE ME MONEY.
OH... THANKS.
HERE.
SHUP
THANK YOU VERY MUCH.
BY THE WAY, SAKURABA TOLD ME.

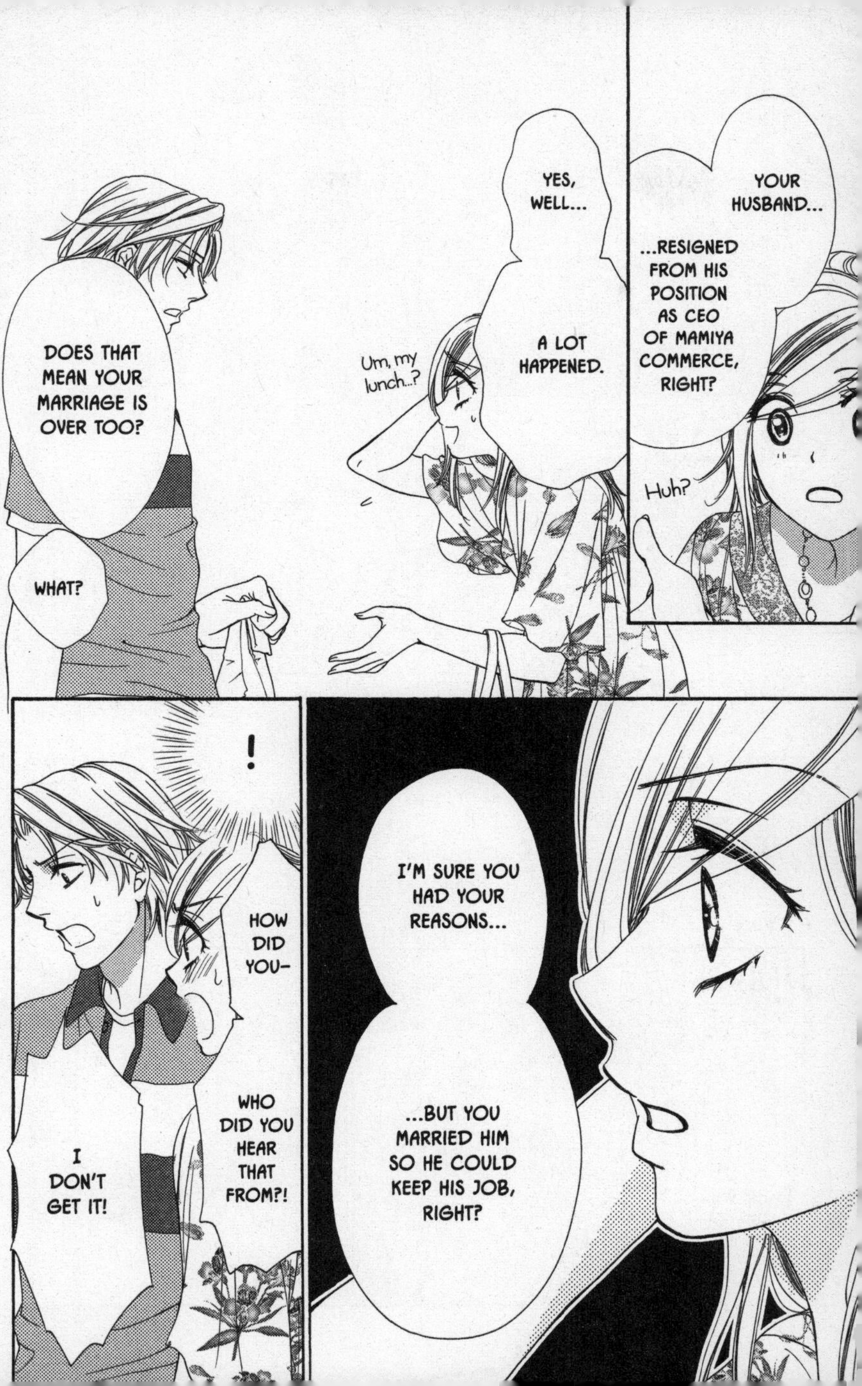
YOUR HUSBAND...
...RESIGNED FROM HIS POSITION AS CEO OF MAMIYA COMMERCE, RIGHT?
Huh?
YES, WELL...
A LOT HAPPENED.
Um, my lunch...?
DOES THAT MEAN YOUR MARRIAGE IS OVER TOO?
WHAT?
I'M SURE YOU HAD YOUR REASONS...
...BUT YOU MARRIED HIM SO HE COULD KEEP HIS JOB, RIGHT?
!
HOW DID YOU-
WHO DID YOU HEAR THAT FROM?!
I DON'T GET IT!

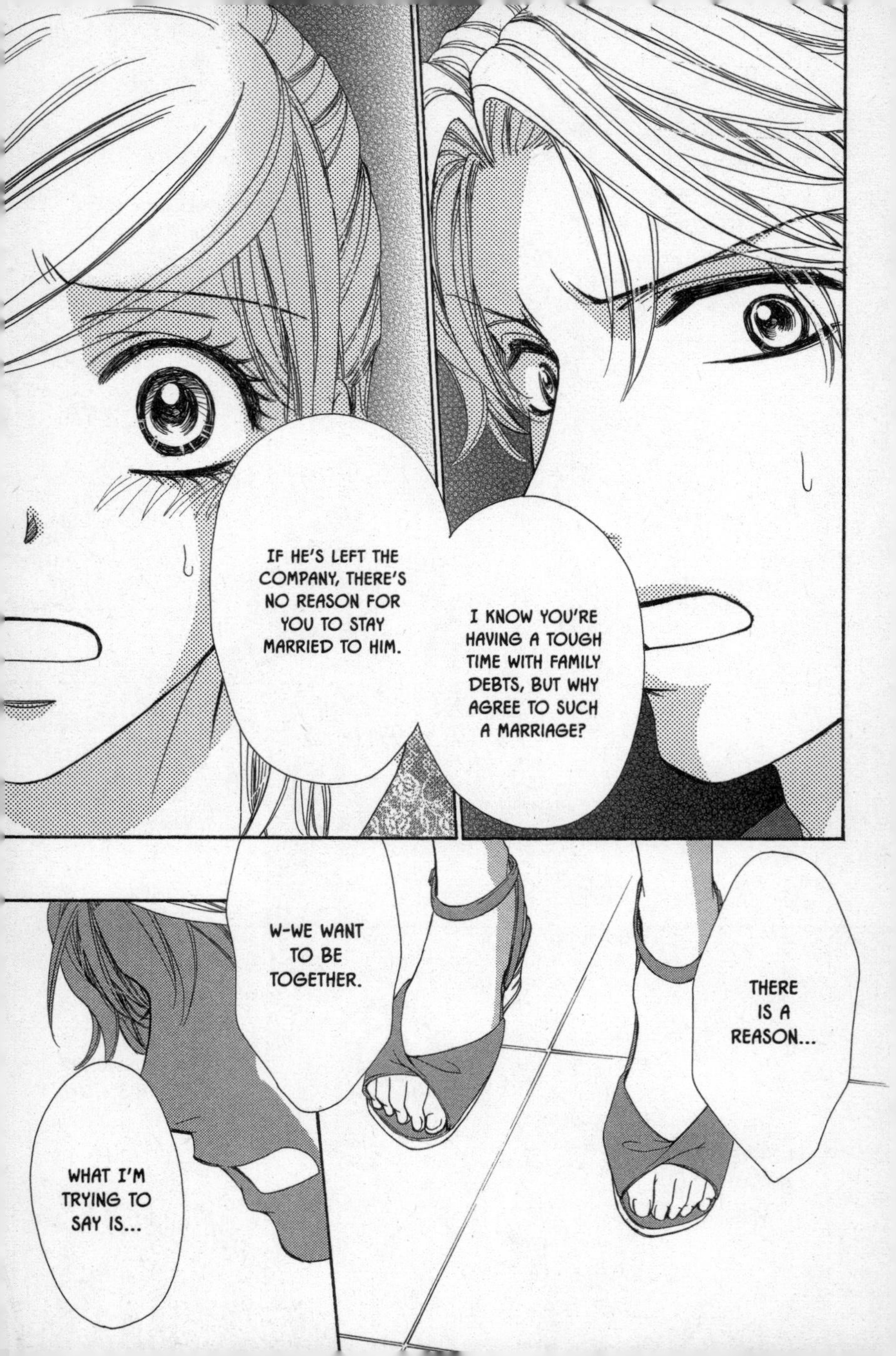
I KNOW YOU'RE HAVING A TOUGH TIME WITH FAMILY DEBTS, BUT WHY AGREE TO SUCH A MARRIAGE?
IF HE'S LEFT THE COMPANY, THERE'S NO REASON FOR YOU TO STAY MARRIED TO HIM.
THERE IS A REASON...
W-WE WANT TO BE TOGETHER.
WHAT I'M TRYING TO SAY IS...

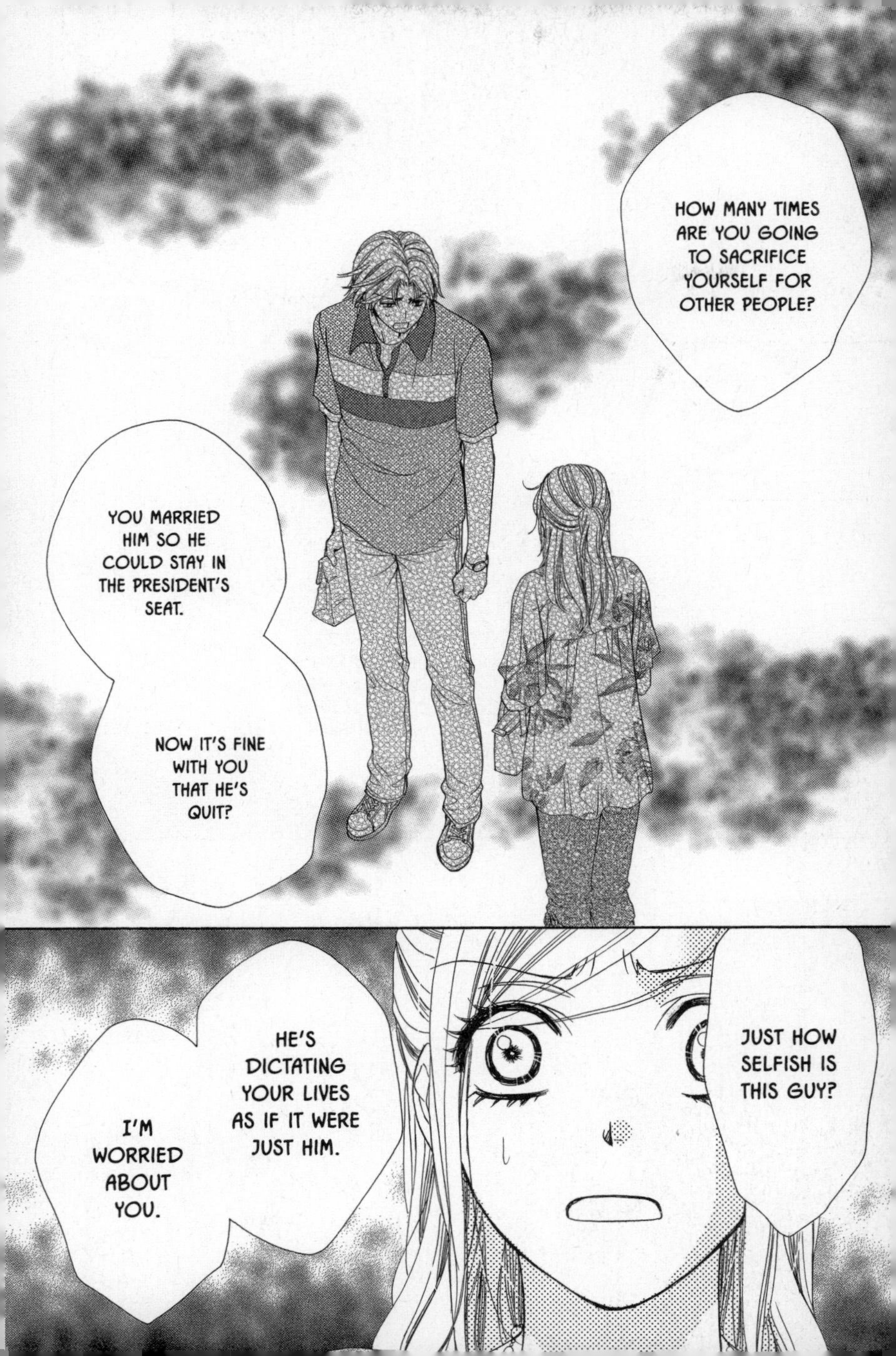
HOW MANY TIMES ARE YOU GOING TO SACRIFICE YOURSELF FOR OTHER PEOPLE?
YOU MARRIED HIM SO HE COULD STAY IN THE PRESIDENT'S SEAT.
NOW IT'S FINE WITH YOU THAT HE'S QUIT?
JUST HOW SELFISH IS THIS GUY?
HE'S DICTATING YOUR LIVES AS IF IT WERE JUST HIM.
I'M WORRIED ABOUT YOU.

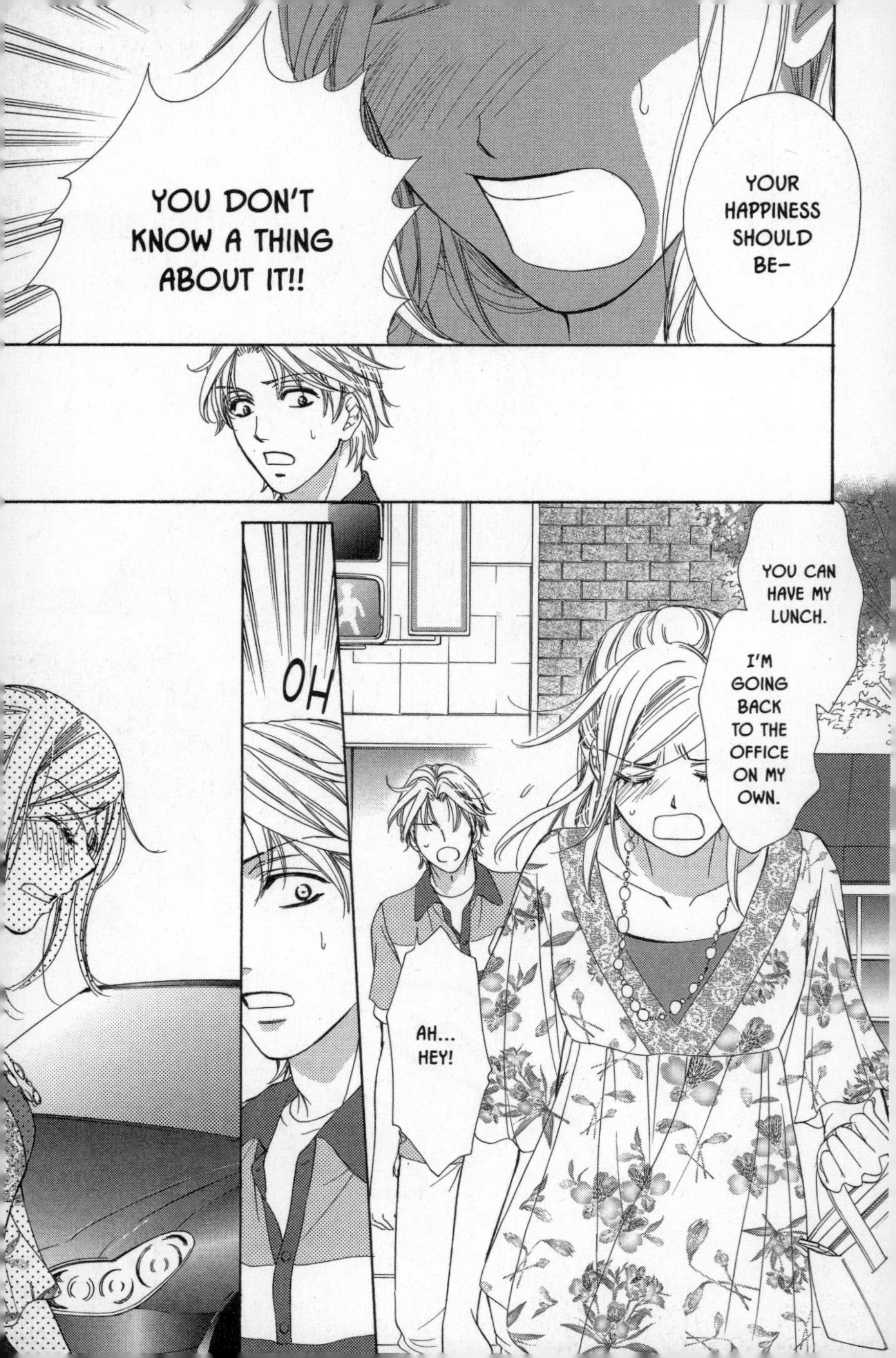
YOUR HAPPINESS SHOULD BE-
YOU DON'T KNOW A THING ABOUT IT!!
YOU CAN HAVE MY LUNCH.
I'M GOING BACK TO THE OFFICE ON MY OWN.
AH... HEY!
OH

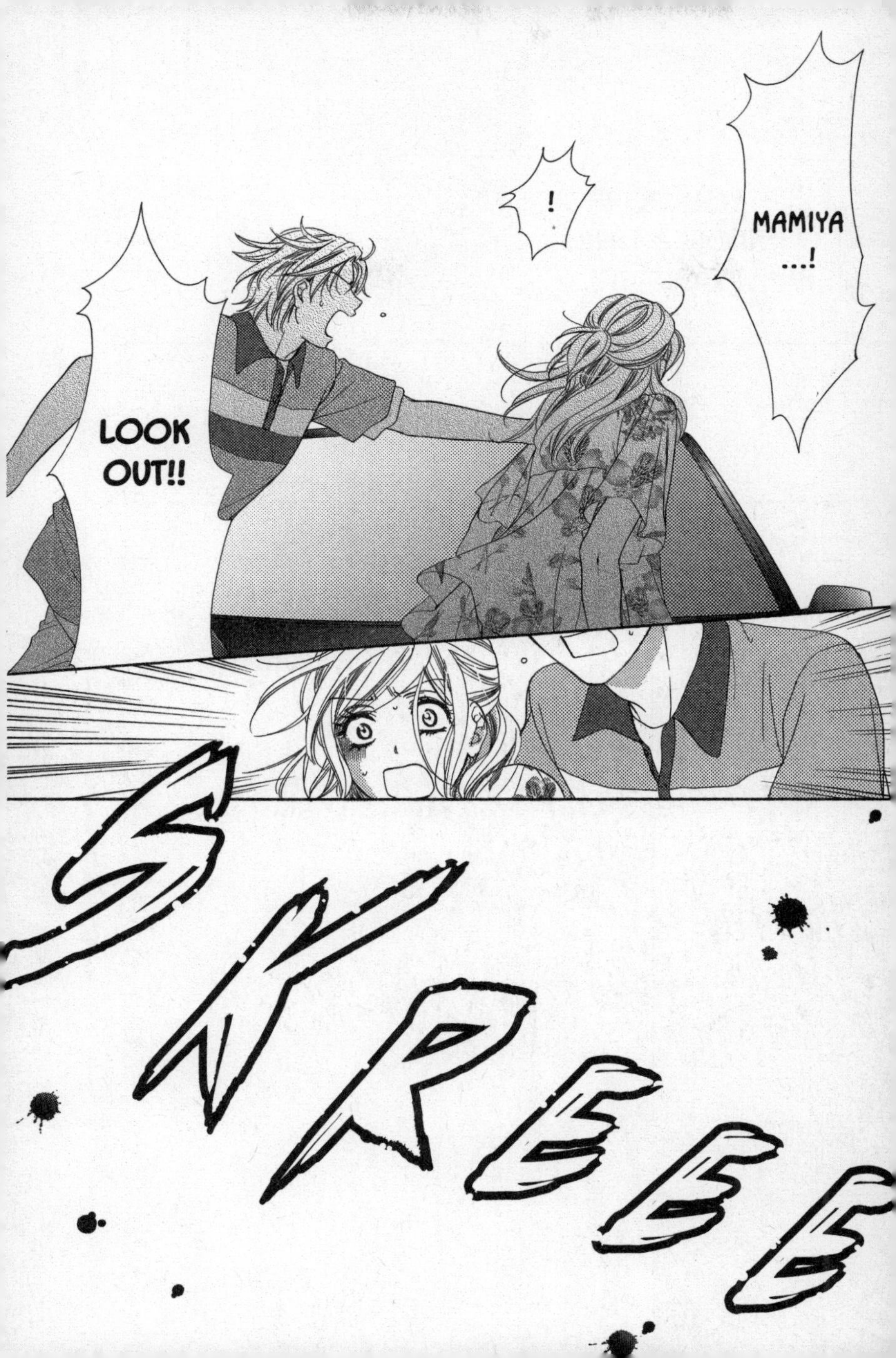
MAMIYA ...!
!
LOOK OUT!!
SKREEE

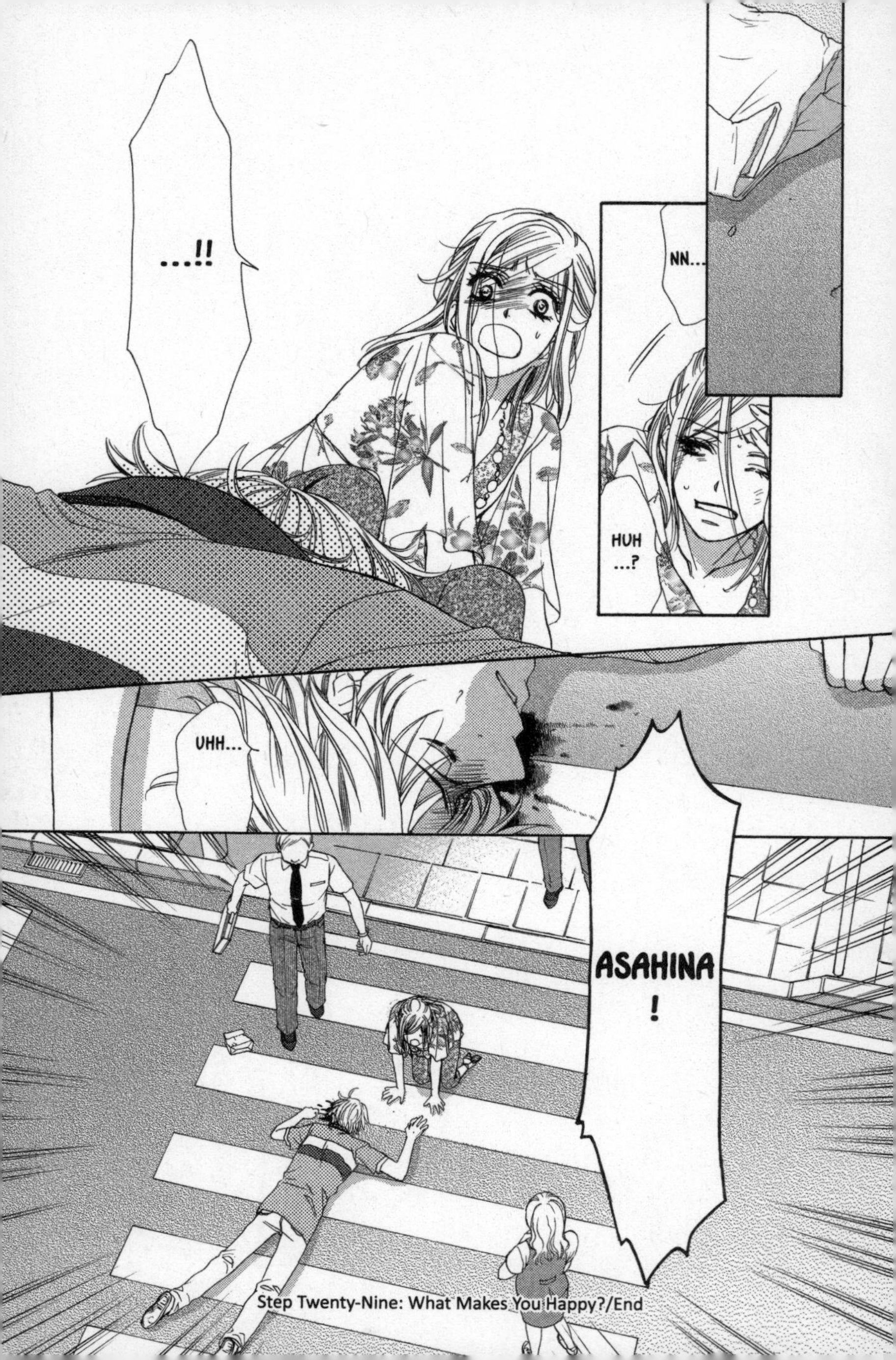
NN...
HUH ...?
...!!
UHH...
ASAHINA !

Step Twenty-Nine: What Makes You Happy?/End

KIYOHIKO IN SOUTH AMERICA

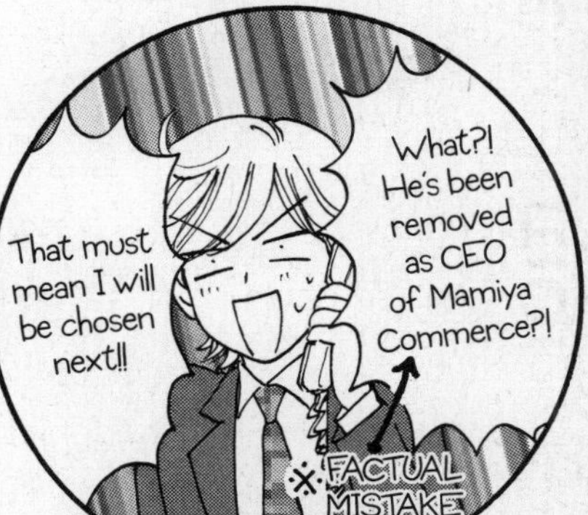
What?! He's been removed as CEO of Mamiya Commerce?!
That must mean I will be chosen next!!
※: FACTUAL MISTAKE

IT NEVER CAME TO PASS.

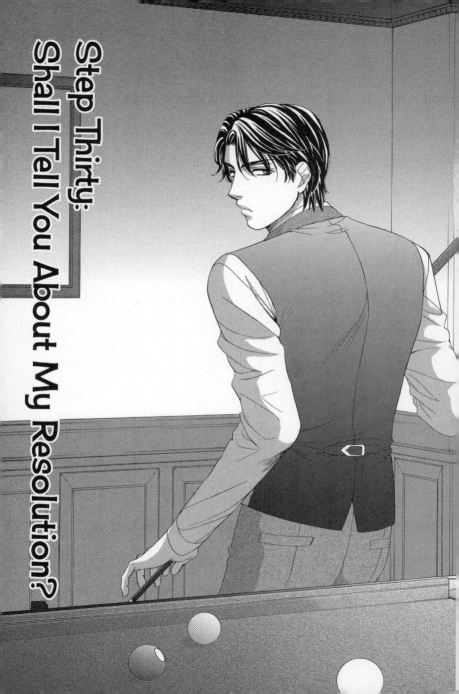

Step Thirty: Shall I Tell You About My Resolution?

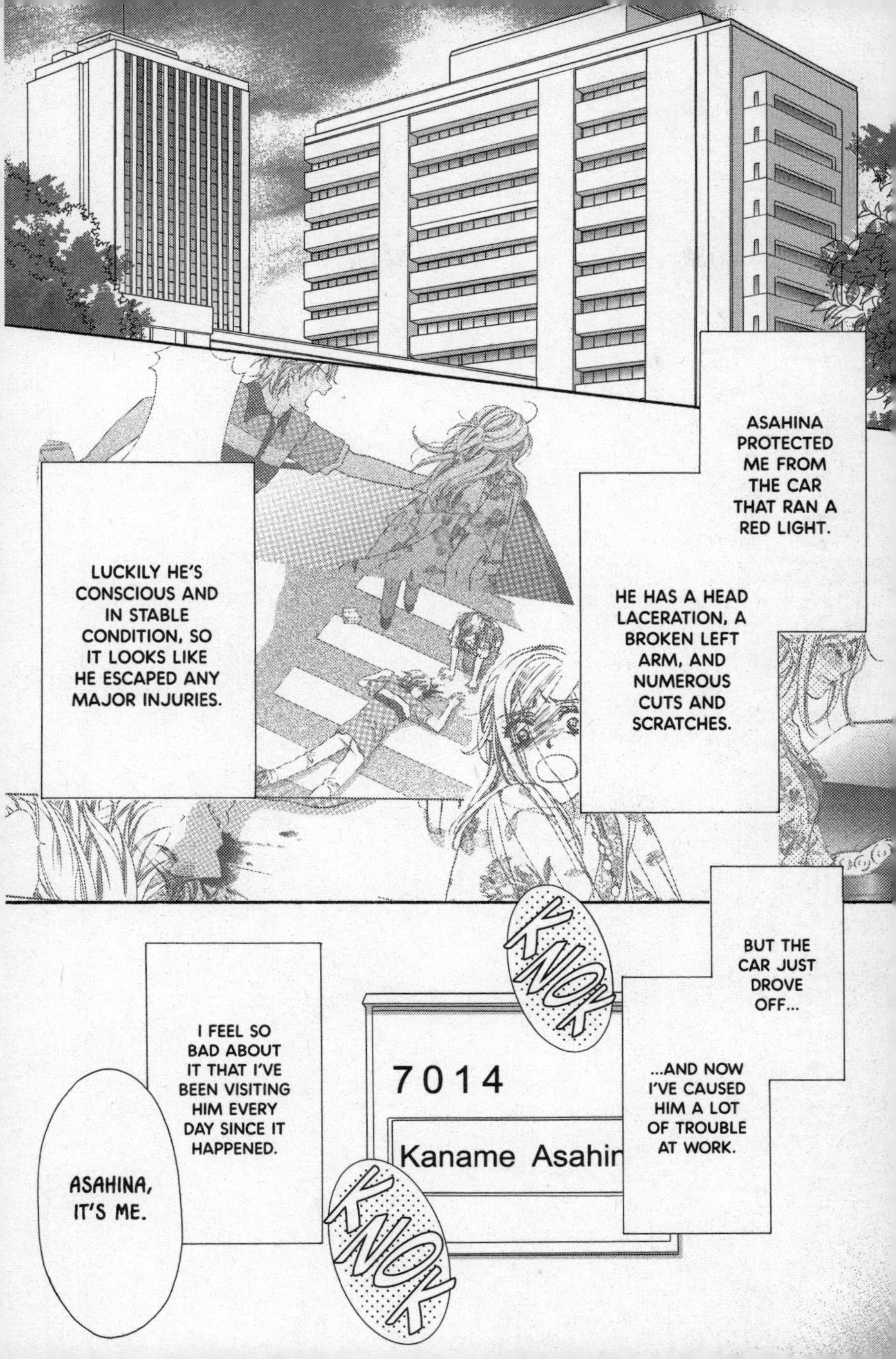

ASAHINA PROTECTED ME FROM THE CAR THAT RAN A RED LIGHT.
HE HAS A HEAD LACERATION, A BROKEN LEFT ARM, AND NUMEROUS CUTS AND SCRATCHES.
LUCKILY HE'S CONSCIOUS AND IN STABLE CONDITION, SO IT LOOKS LIKE HE ESCAPED ANY MAJOR INJURIES.
BUT THE CAR JUST DROVE OFF...
...AND NOW I'VE CAUSED HIM A LOT OF TROUBLE AT WORK.
KNOK
7014
Kaname Asahin
KNOK
I FEEL SO BAD ABOUT IT THAT I'VE BEEN VISITING HIM EVERY DAY SINCE IT HAPPENED.
ASAHINA, IT'S ME.

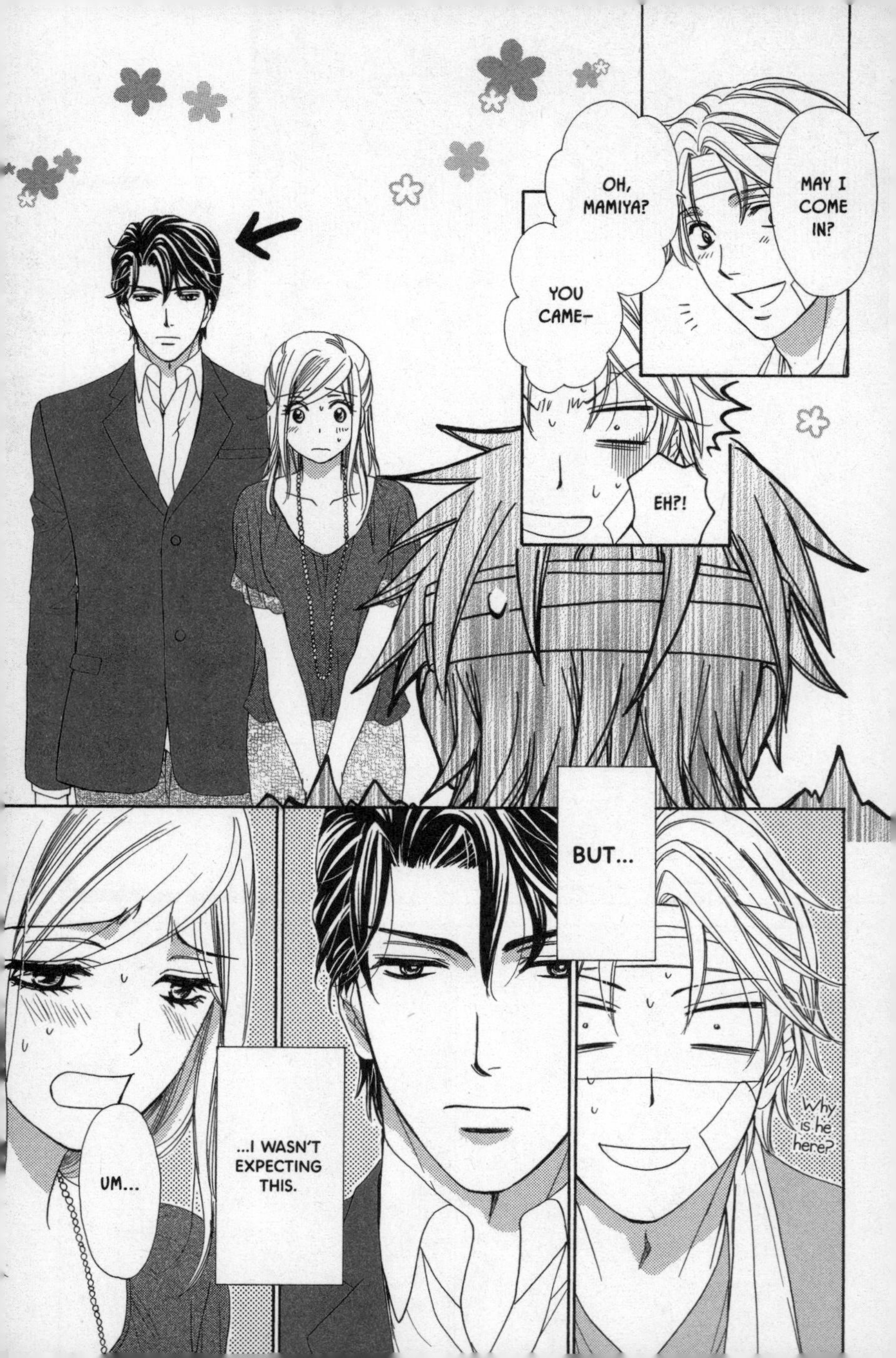
MAY I COME IN?
OH, MAMIYA?
YOU CAME—
EH?!
BUT...
Why is he here?
...I WASN'T EXPECTING THIS.
UM...

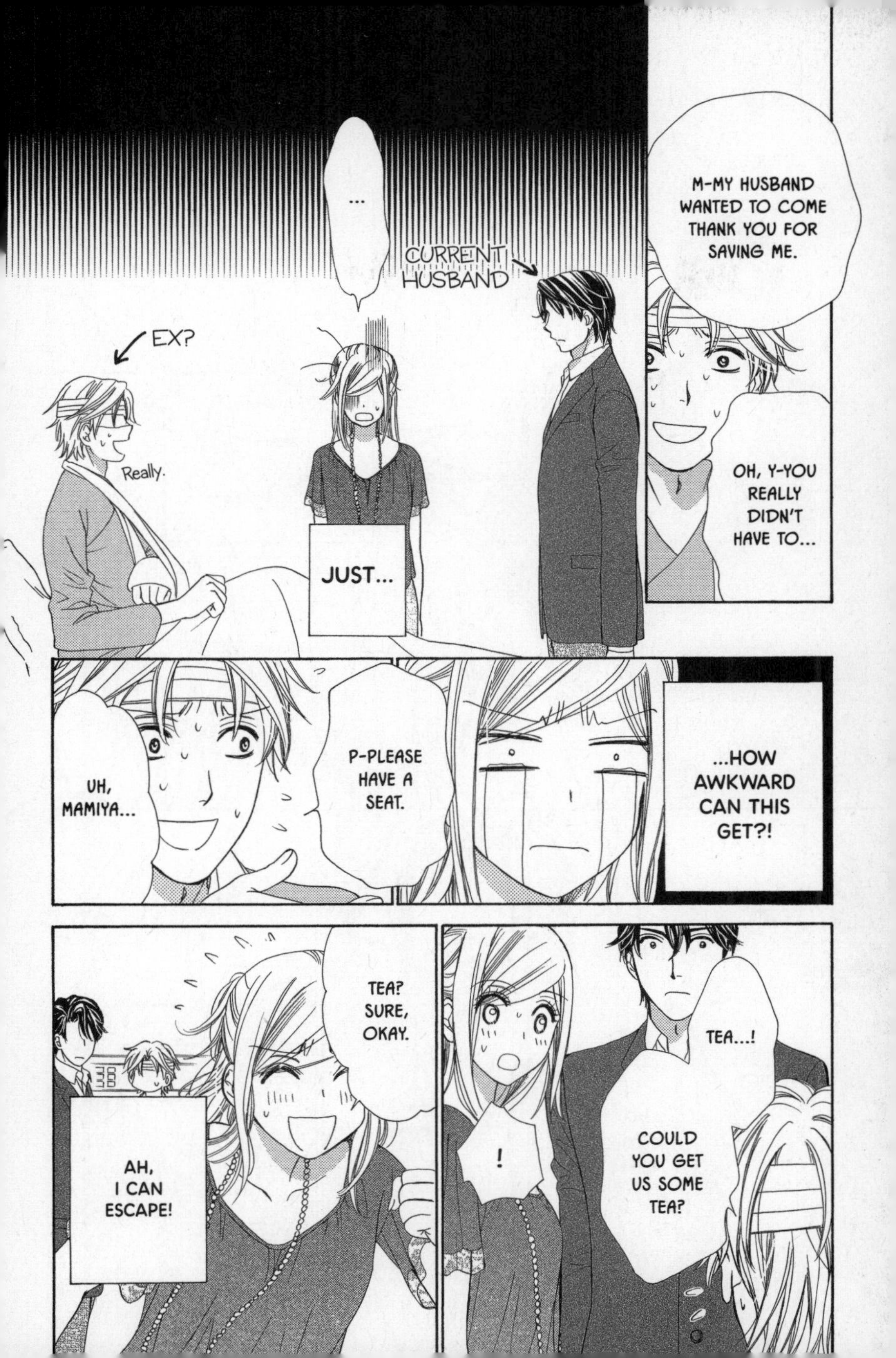

M-MY HUSBAND WANTED TO COME THANK YOU FOR SAVING ME.
OH, Y-YOU REALLY DIDN'T HAVE TO...
...
CURRENT HUSBAND
EX?
Really.
JUST...
...HOW AWKWARD CAN THIS GET?!
P-PLEASE HAVE A SEAT.
UH, MAMIYA...
TEA...!
COULD YOU GET US SOME TEA?
!
TEA? SURE, OKAY.
AH, I CAN ESCAPE!

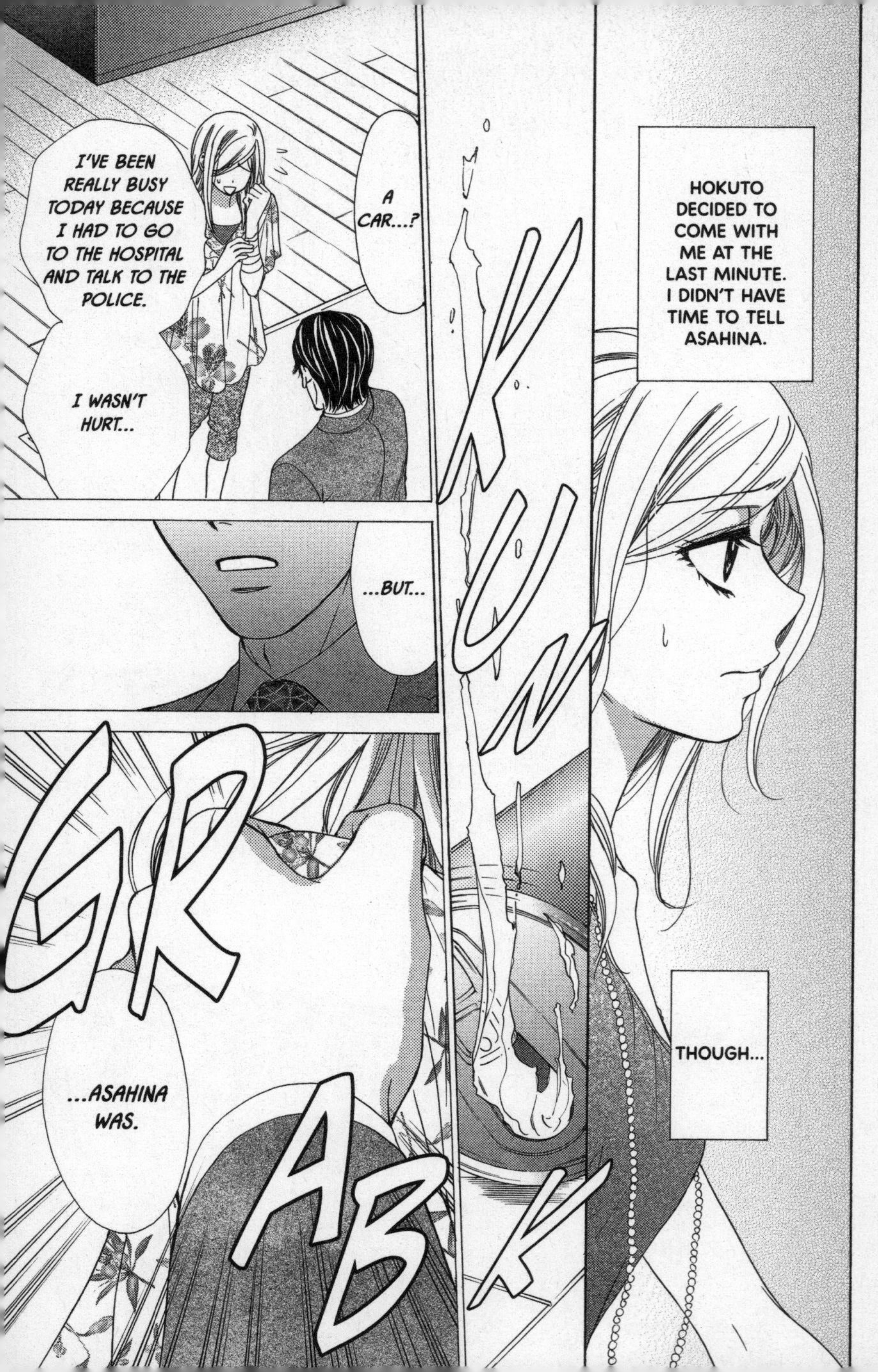
HOKUTO DECIDED TO COME WITH ME AT THE LAST MINUTE. I DIDN'T HAVE TIME TO TELL ASAHINA.
THOUGH...
KLUNK
A CAR...?
I'VE BEEN REALLY BUSY TODAY BECAUSE I HAD TO GO TO THE HOSPITAL AND TALK TO THE POLICE.
I WASN'T HURT...
...BUT...
GRAB
...ASAHINA WAS.

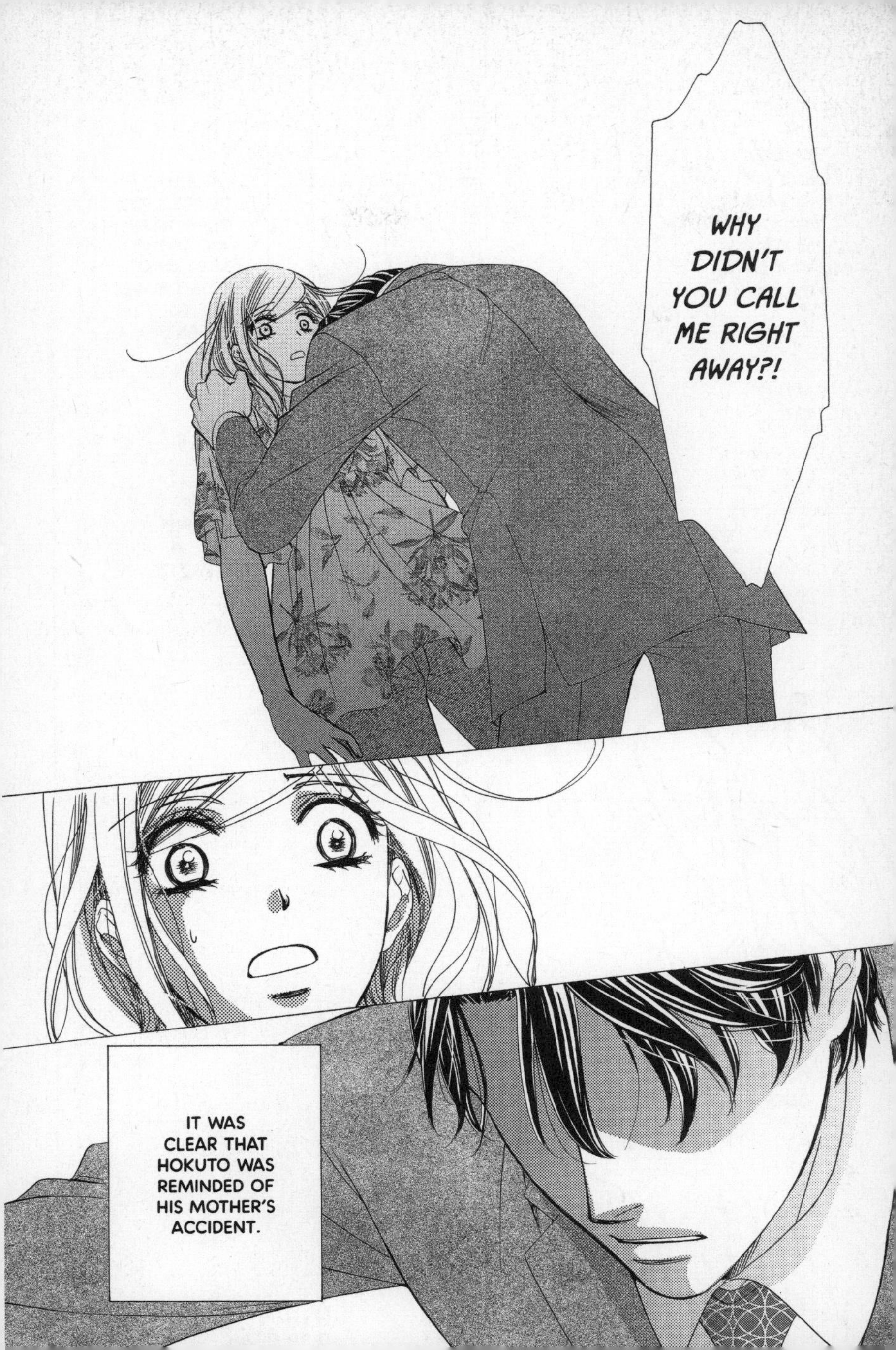
WHY DIDN'T YOU CALL ME RIGHT AWAY?!
IT WAS CLEAR THAT HOKUTO WAS REMINDED OF HIS MOTHER'S ACCIDENT.

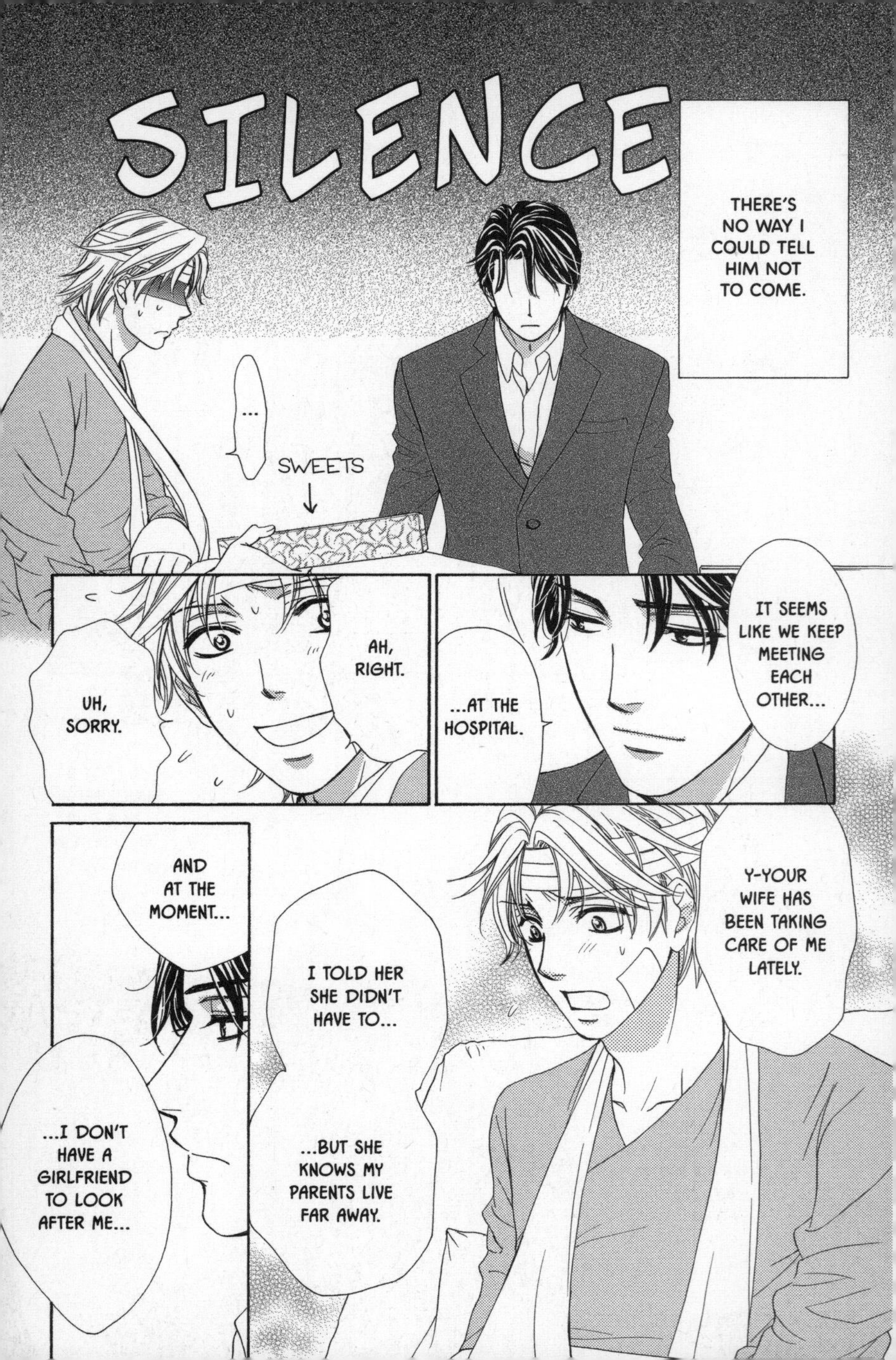
THERE'S NO WAY I COULD TELL HIM NOT TO COME.
SILENCE
...
SWEETS
IT SEEMS LIKE WE KEEP MEETING EACH OTHER...
...AT THE HOSPITAL.
AH, RIGHT.
UH, SORRY.
Y-YOUR WIFE HAS BEEN TAKING CARE OF ME LATELY.
I TOLD HER SHE DIDN'T HAVE TO...
...BUT SHE KNOWS MY PARENTS LIVE FAR AWAY.
AND AT THE MOMENT...
...I DON'T HAVE A GIRLFRIEND TO LOOK AFTER ME...

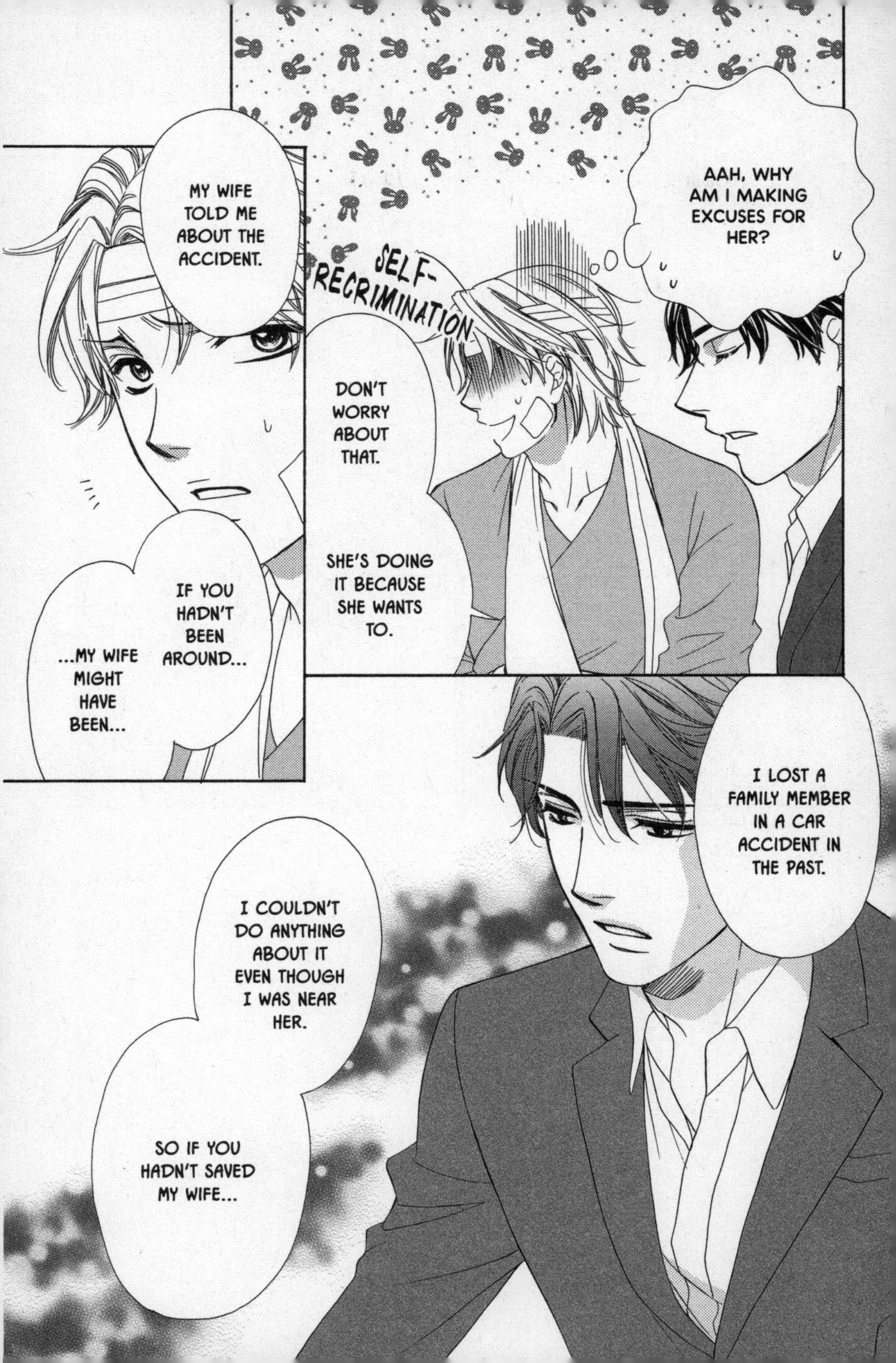
AAH, WHY AM I MAKING EXCUSES FOR HER?
SELF-RECRIMINATION
DON'T WORRY ABOUT THAT.
SHE'S DOING IT BECAUSE SHE WANTS TO.
MY WIFE TOLD ME ABOUT THE ACCIDENT.
IF YOU HADN'T BEEN AROUND...
...MY WIFE MIGHT HAVE BEEN...
I LOST A FAMILY MEMBER IN A CAR ACCIDENT IN THE PAST.
I COULDN'T DO ANYTHING ABOUT IT EVEN THOUGH I WAS NEAR HER.
SO IF YOU HADN'T SAVED MY WIFE...

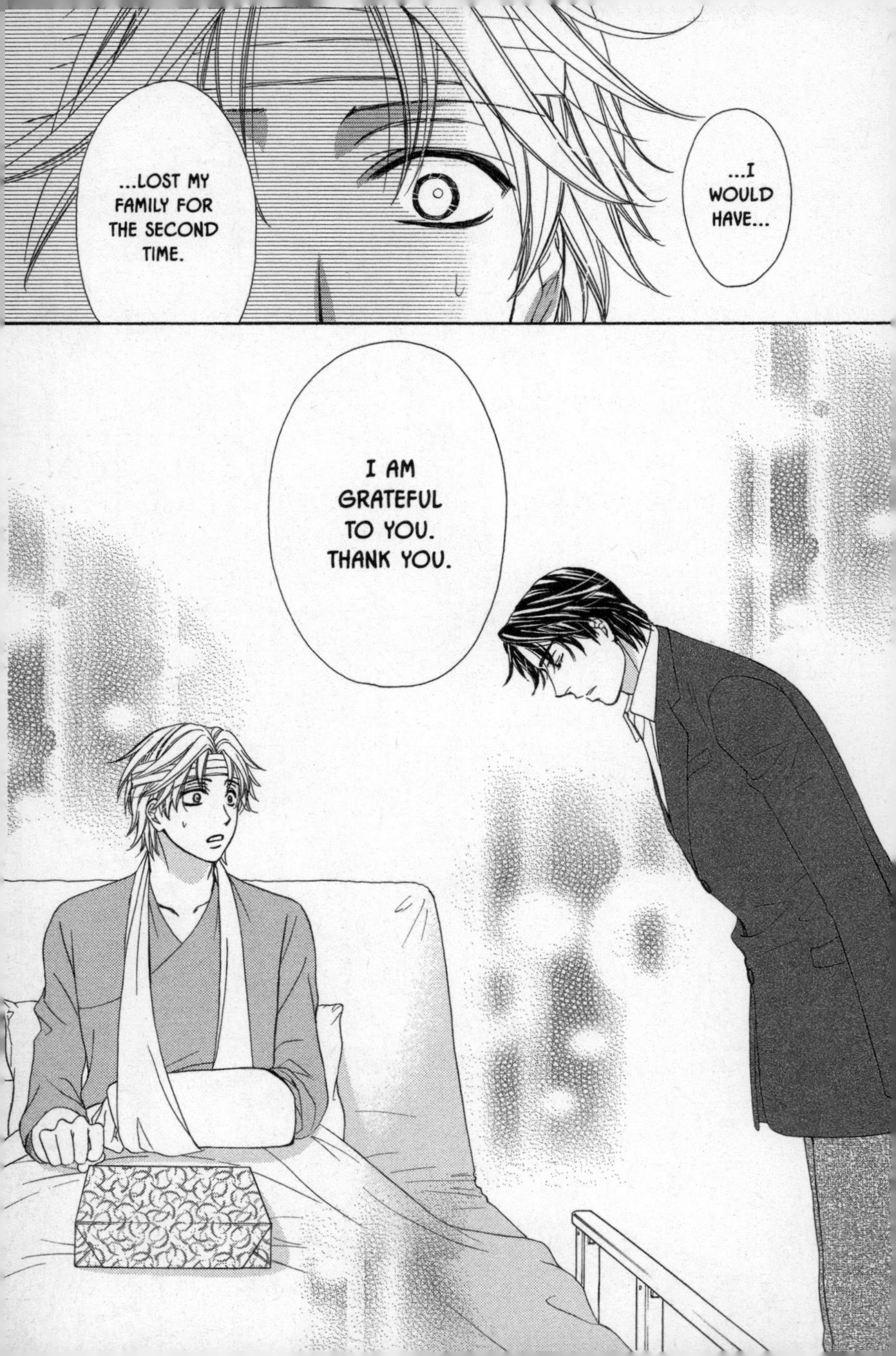
...I WOULD HAVE...
...LOST MY FAMILY FOR THE SECOND TIME.
I AM GRATEFUL TO YOU. THANK YOU.

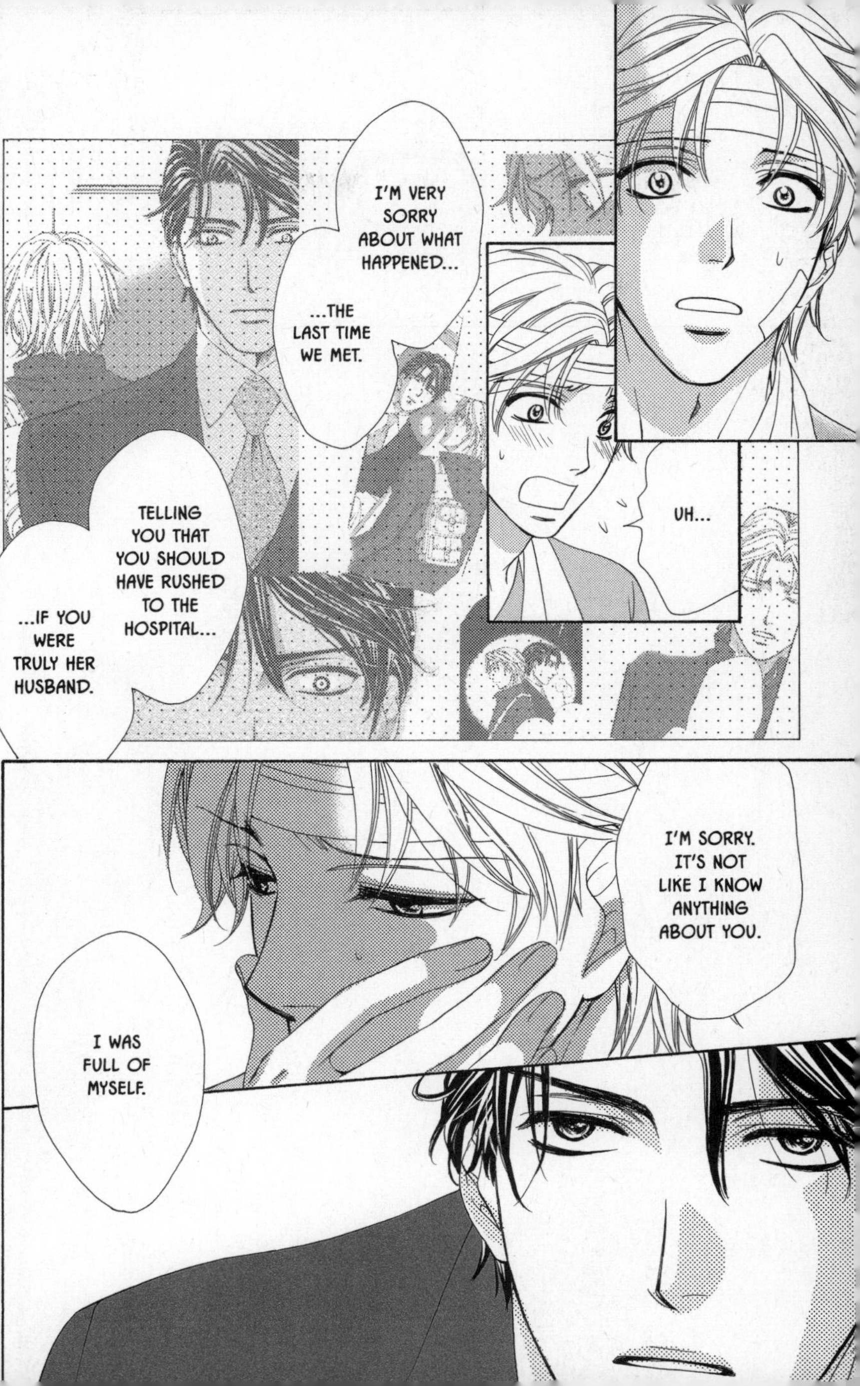
I'M VERY SORRY ABOUT WHAT HAPPENED...
...THE LAST TIME WE MET.
UH...
TELLING YOU THAT YOU SHOULD HAVE RUSHED TO THE HOSPITAL...
...IF YOU WERE TRULY HER HUSBAND.
I'M SORRY. IT'S NOT LIKE I KNOW ANYTHING ABOUT YOU.
I WAS FULL OF MYSELF.

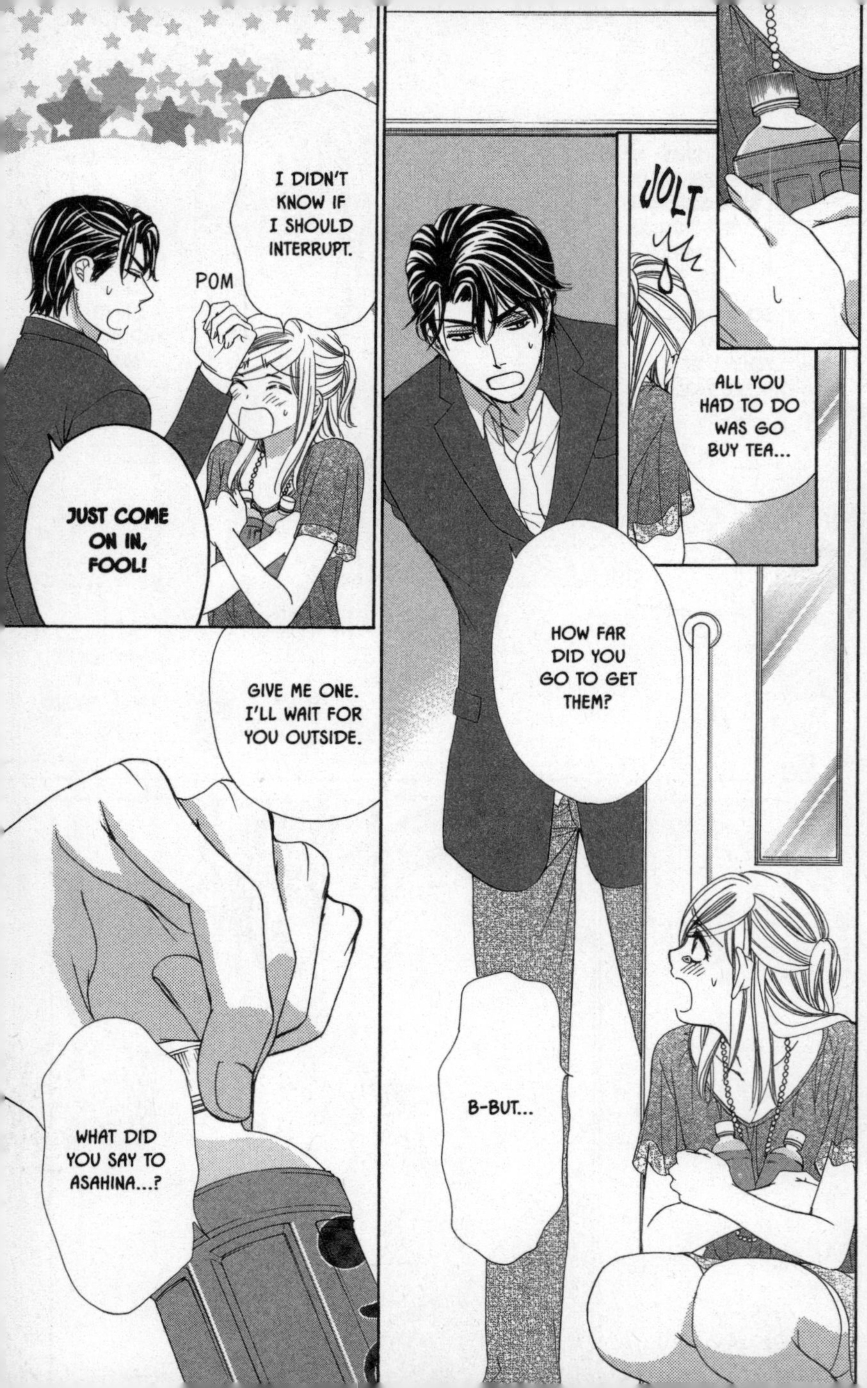
JOLT
ALL YOU HAD TO DO WAS GO BUY TEA...
HOW FAR DID YOU GO TO GET THEM?
B-BUT...
I DIDN'T KNOW IF I SHOULD INTERRUPT.
POM
JUST COME ON IN, FOOL!
GIVE ME ONE. I'LL WAIT FOR YOU OUTSIDE.
WHAT DID YOU SAY TO ASAHINA...?

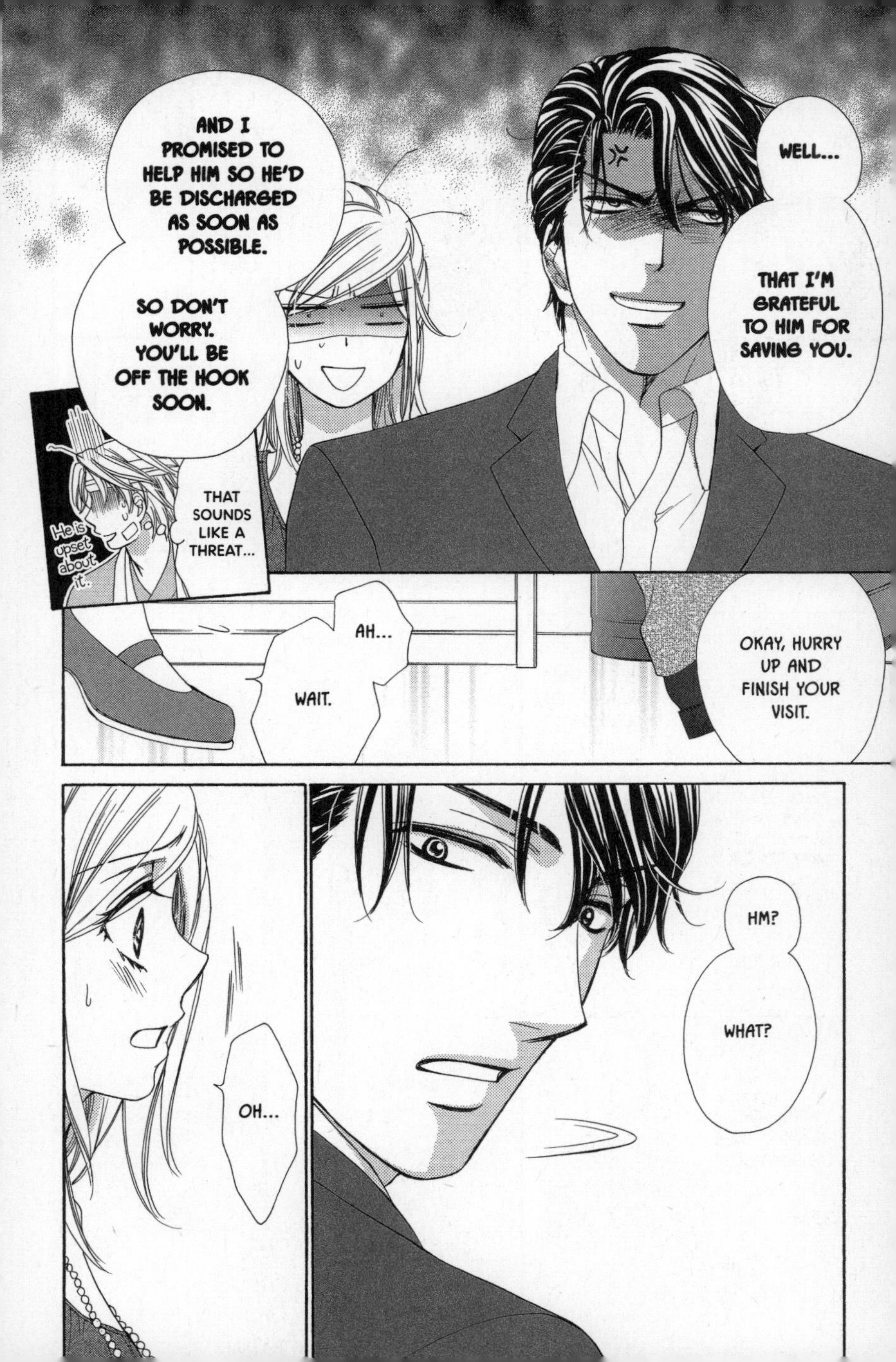
WELL...
THAT I'M GRATEFUL TO HIM FOR SAVING YOU.
AND I PROMISED TO HELP HIM SO HE'D BE DISCHARGED AS SOON AS POSSIBLE.
SO DON'T WORRY. YOU'LL BE OFF THE HOOK SOON.
THAT SOUNDS LIKE A THREAT...
He is upset about it.
OKAY, HURRY UP AND FINISH YOUR VISIT.
AH...
WAIT.
HM?
WHAT?
OH...

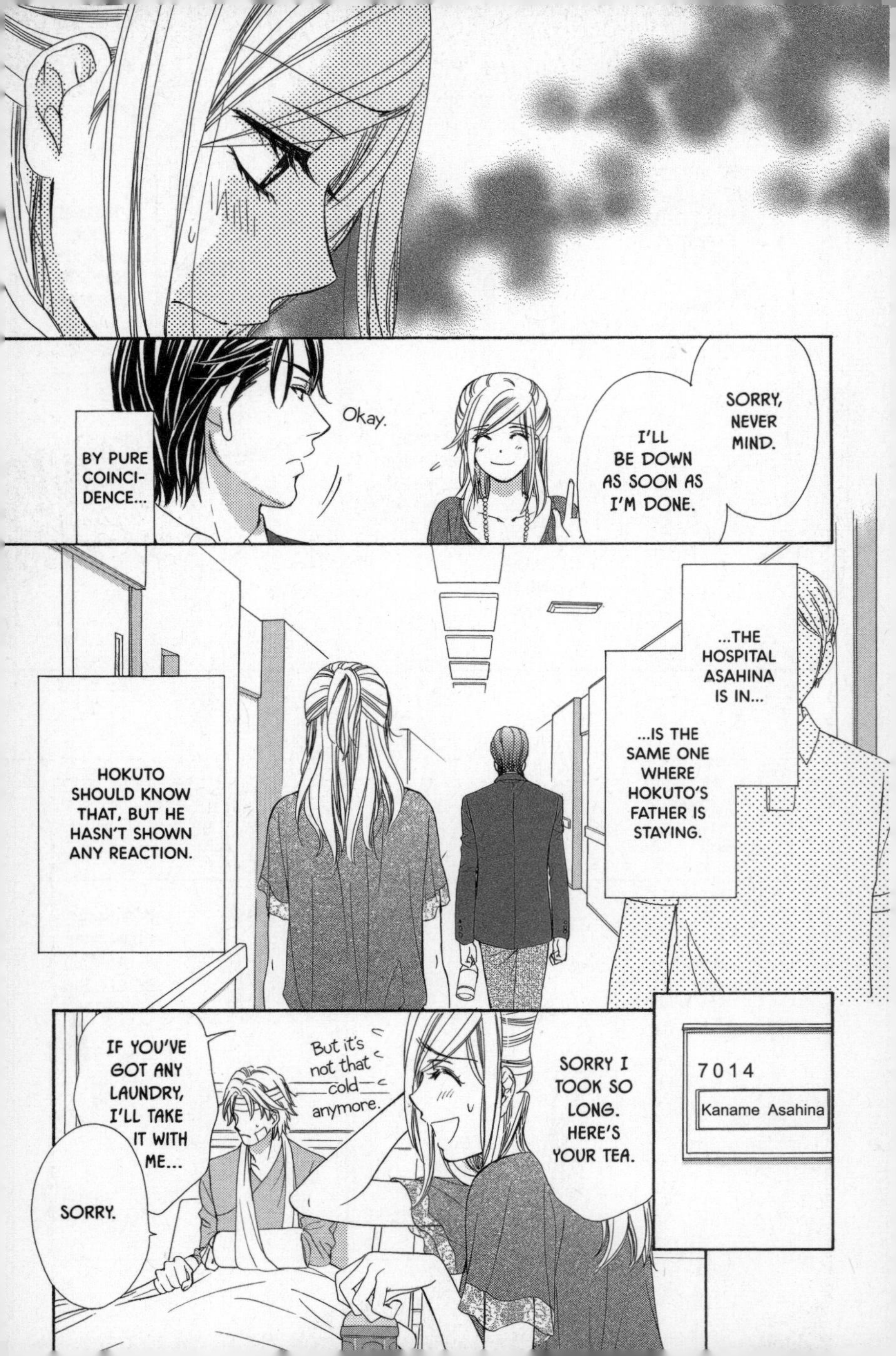
SORRY, NEVER MIND.
I'LL BE DOWN AS SOON AS I'M DONE.
Okay.
BY PURE COINCIDENCE...
...THE HOSPITAL ASAHINA IS IN...
...IS THE SAME ONE WHERE HOKUTO'S FATHER IS STAYING.
HOKUTO SHOULD KNOW THAT, BUT HE HASN'T SHOWN ANY REACTION.
7014
Kaname Asahina
SORRY I TOOK SO LONG. HERE'S YOUR TEA.
But it's not that cold anymore.
IF YOU'VE GOT ANY LAUNDRY, I'LL TAKE IT WITH ME...
SORRY.

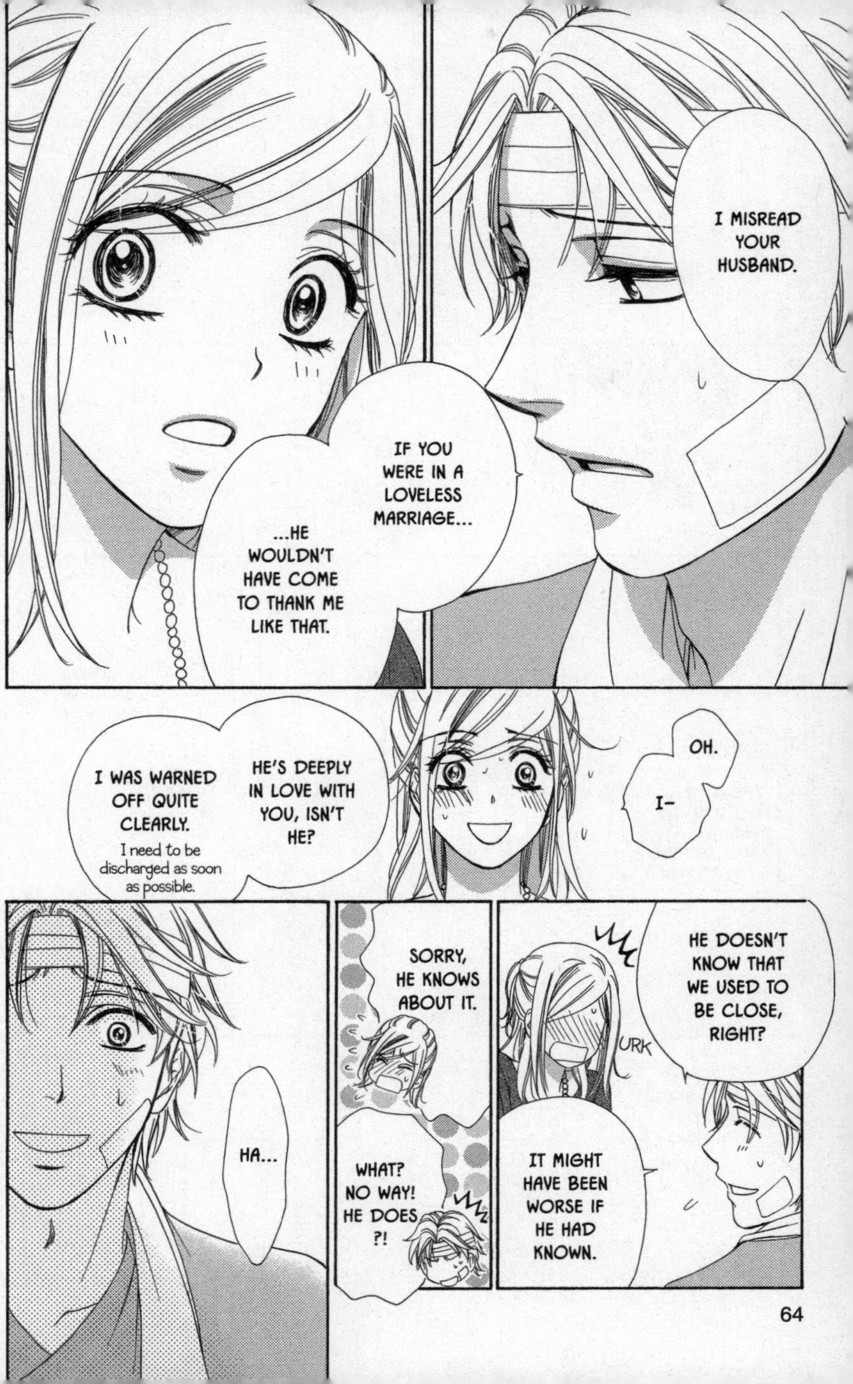
I MISREAD YOUR HUSBAND.
IF YOU WERE IN A LOVELESS MARRIAGE...
...HE WOULDN'T HAVE COME TO THANK ME LIKE THAT.
OH.
I–
HE'S DEEPLY IN LOVE WITH YOU, ISN'T HE?
I WAS WARNED OFF QUITE CLEARLY.
I need to be discharged as soon as possible.
HE DOESN'T KNOW THAT WE USED TO BE CLOSE, RIGHT?
URK
IT MIGHT HAVE BEEN WORSE IF HE HAD KNOWN.
SORRY, HE KNOWS ABOUT IT.
WHAT? NO WAY! HE DOES ?!
HA...

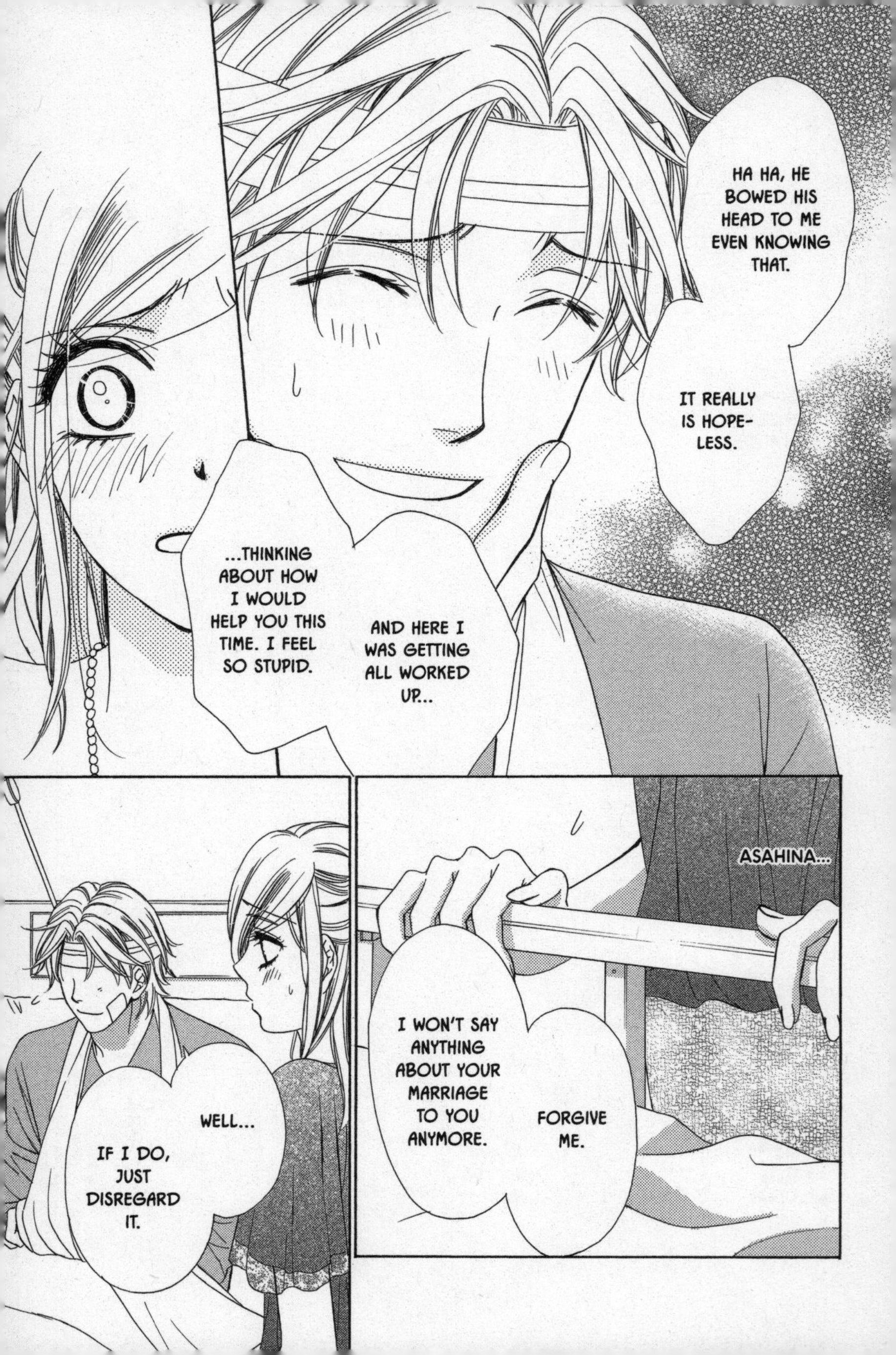
HA HA, HE BOWED HIS HEAD TO ME EVEN KNOWING THAT.
IT REALLY IS HOPE-LESS.
AND HERE I WAS GETTING ALL WORKED UP...
...THINKING ABOUT HOW I WOULD HELP YOU THIS TIME. I FEEL SO STUPID.
ASAHINA...
FORGIVE ME.
I WON'T SAY ANYTHING ABOUT YOUR MARRIAGE TO YOU ANYMORE.
WELL...
IF I DO, JUST DISREGARD IT.

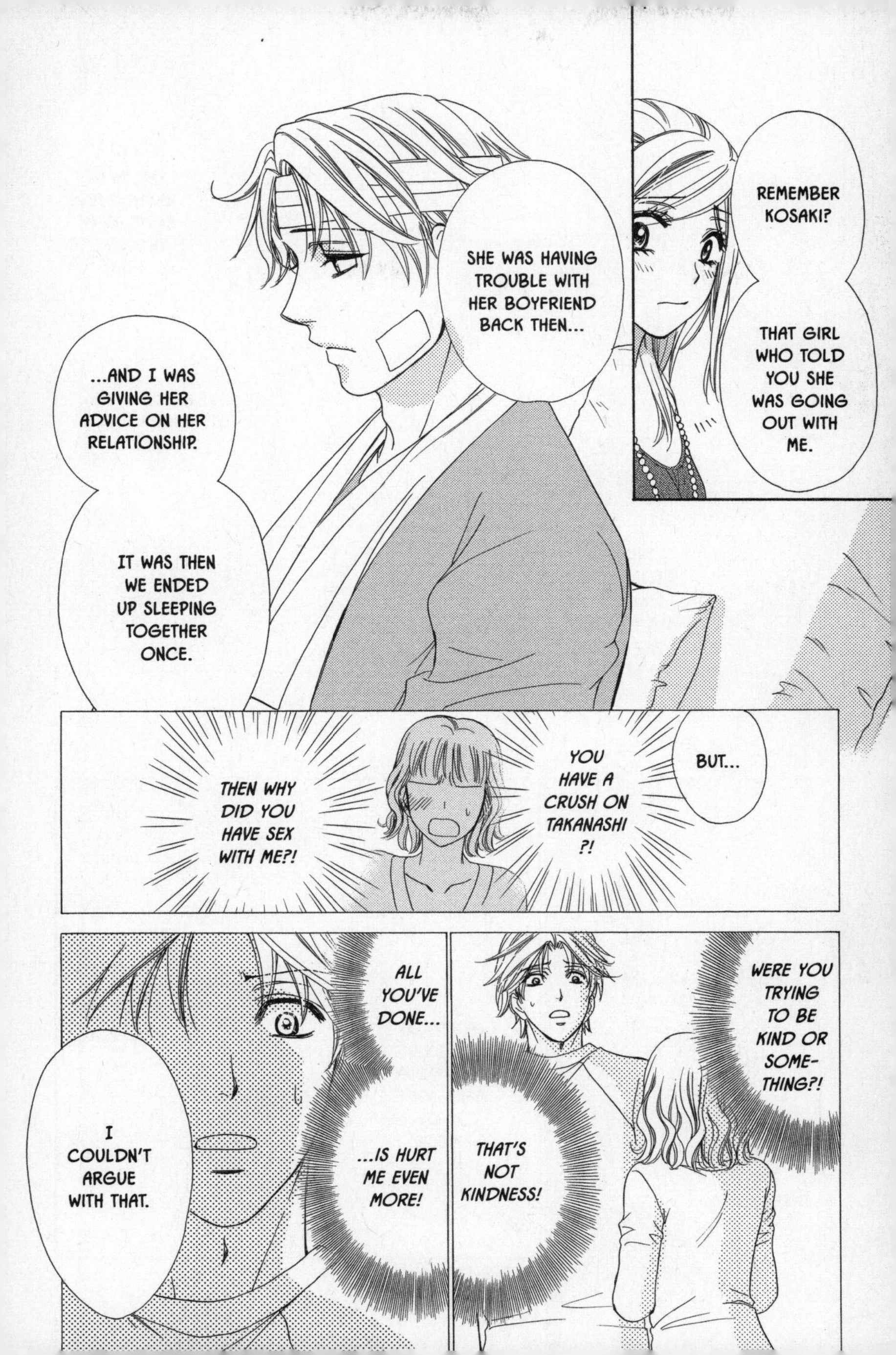

REMEMBER KOSAKI?
THAT GIRL WHO TOLD YOU SHE WAS GOING OUT WITH ME.
SHE WAS HAVING TROUBLE WITH HER BOYFRIEND BACK THEN...
...AND I WAS GIVING HER ADVICE ON HER RELATIONSHIP.
IT WAS THEN WE ENDED UP SLEEPING TOGETHER ONCE.
BUT...
YOU HAVE A CRUSH ON TAKANASHI?!
THEN WHY DID YOU HAVE SEX WITH ME?!
WERE YOU TRYING TO BE KIND OR SOME-THING?!
THAT'S NOT KINDNESS!
ALL YOU'VE DONE...
...IS HURT ME EVEN MORE!
I COULDN'T ARGUE WITH THAT.

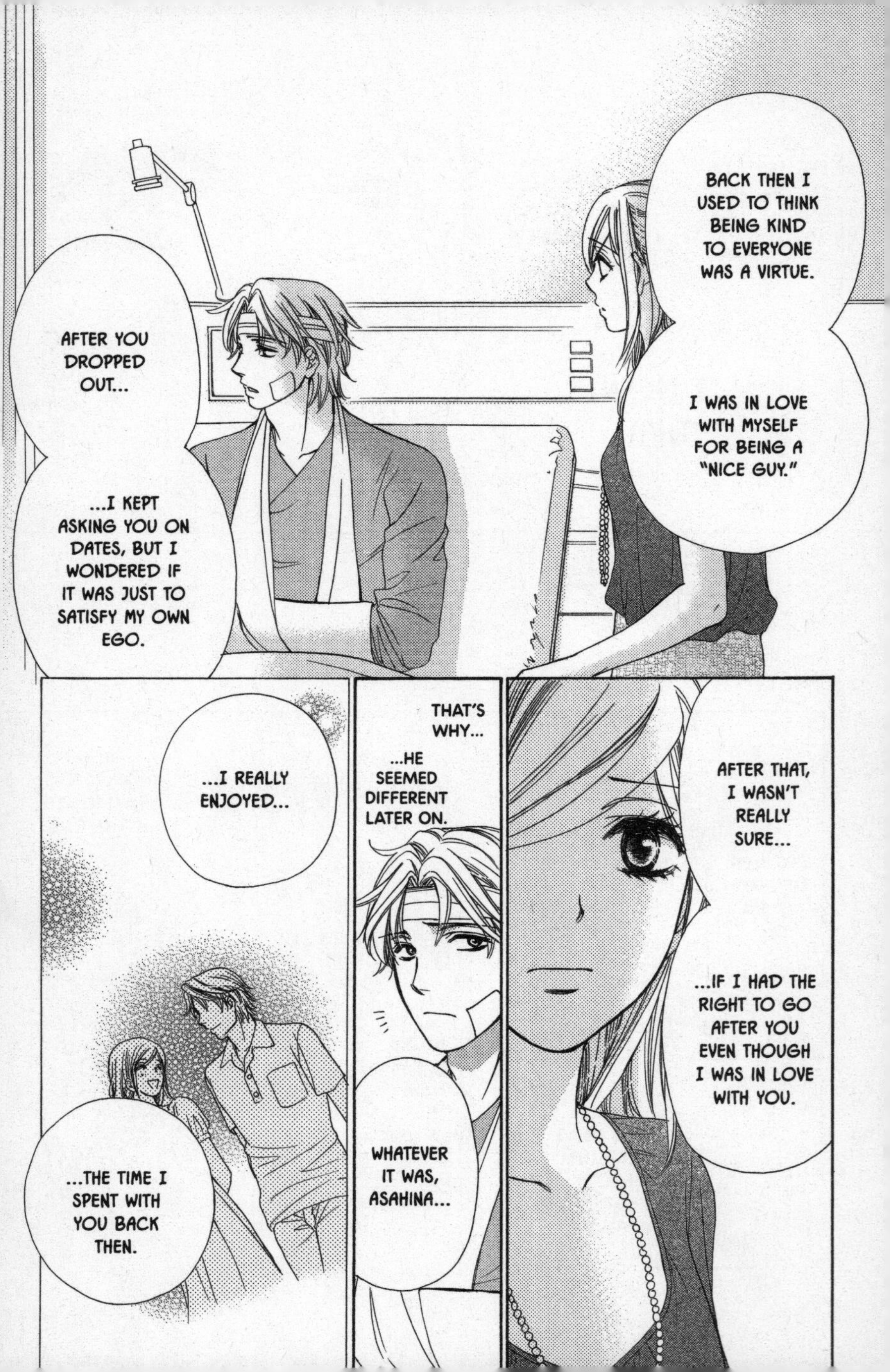
BACK THEN I USED TO THINK BEING KIND TO EVERYONE WAS A VIRTUE.
I WAS IN LOVE WITH MYSELF FOR BEING A "NICE GUY."
AFTER YOU DROPPED OUT...
...I KEPT ASKING YOU ON DATES, BUT I WONDERED IF IT WAS JUST TO SATISFY MY OWN EGO.
AFTER THAT, I WASN'T REALLY SURE...
...IF I HAD THE RIGHT TO GO AFTER YOU EVEN THOUGH I WAS IN LOVE WITH YOU.
THAT'S WHY...
...HE SEEMED DIFFERENT LATER ON.
WHATEVER IT WAS, ASAHINA...
...I REALLY ENJOYED...
...THE TIME I SPENT WITH YOU BACK THEN.

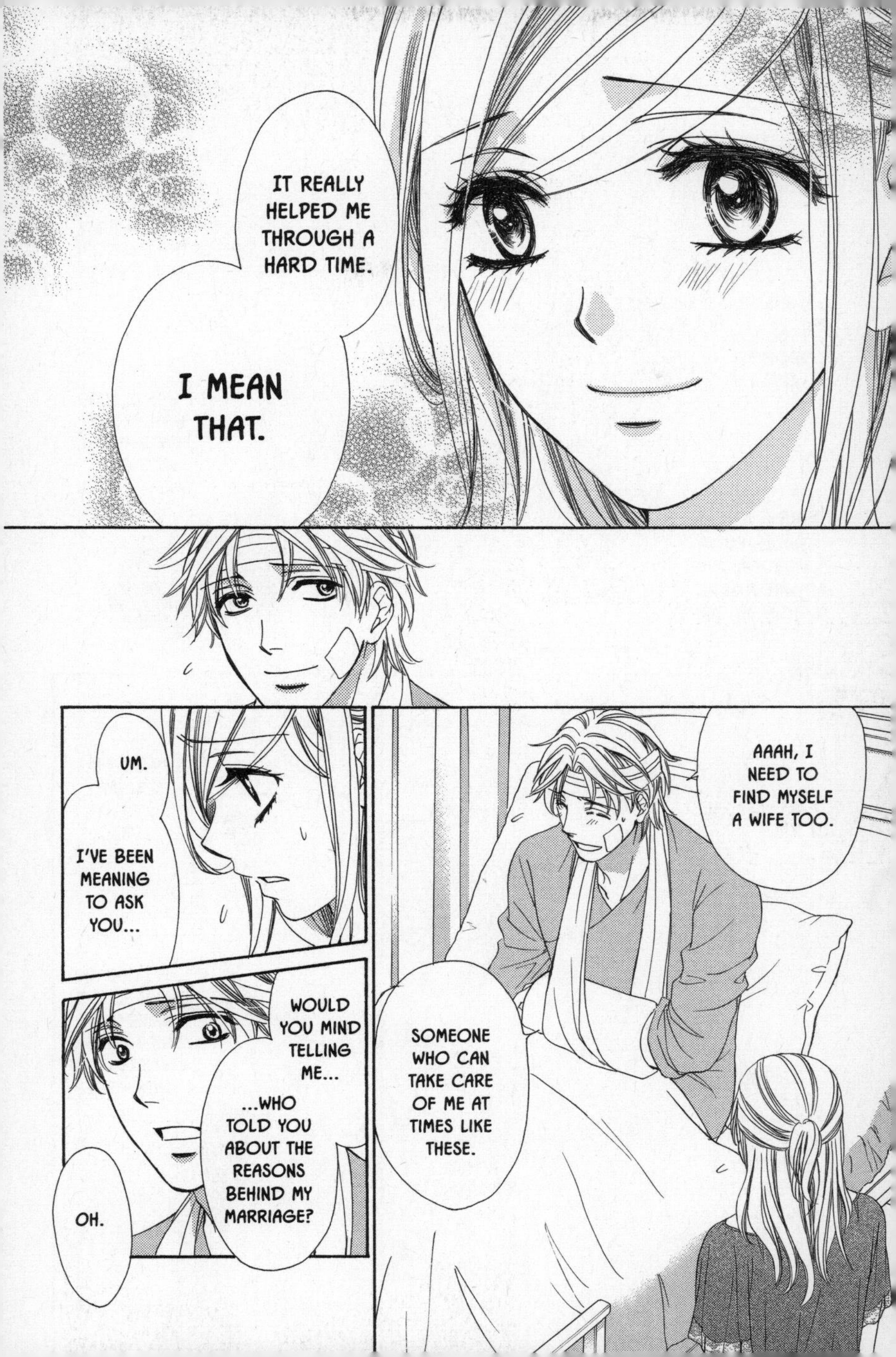
IT REALLY HELPED ME THROUGH A HARD TIME.
I MEAN THAT.
AAAH, I NEED TO FIND MYSELF A WIFE TOO.
SOMEONE WHO CAN TAKE CARE OF ME AT TIMES LIKE THESE.
UM.
I'VE BEEN MEANING TO ASK YOU...
WOULD YOU MIND TELLING ME...
...WHO TOLD YOU ABOUT THE REASONS BEHIND MY MARRIAGE?
OH.

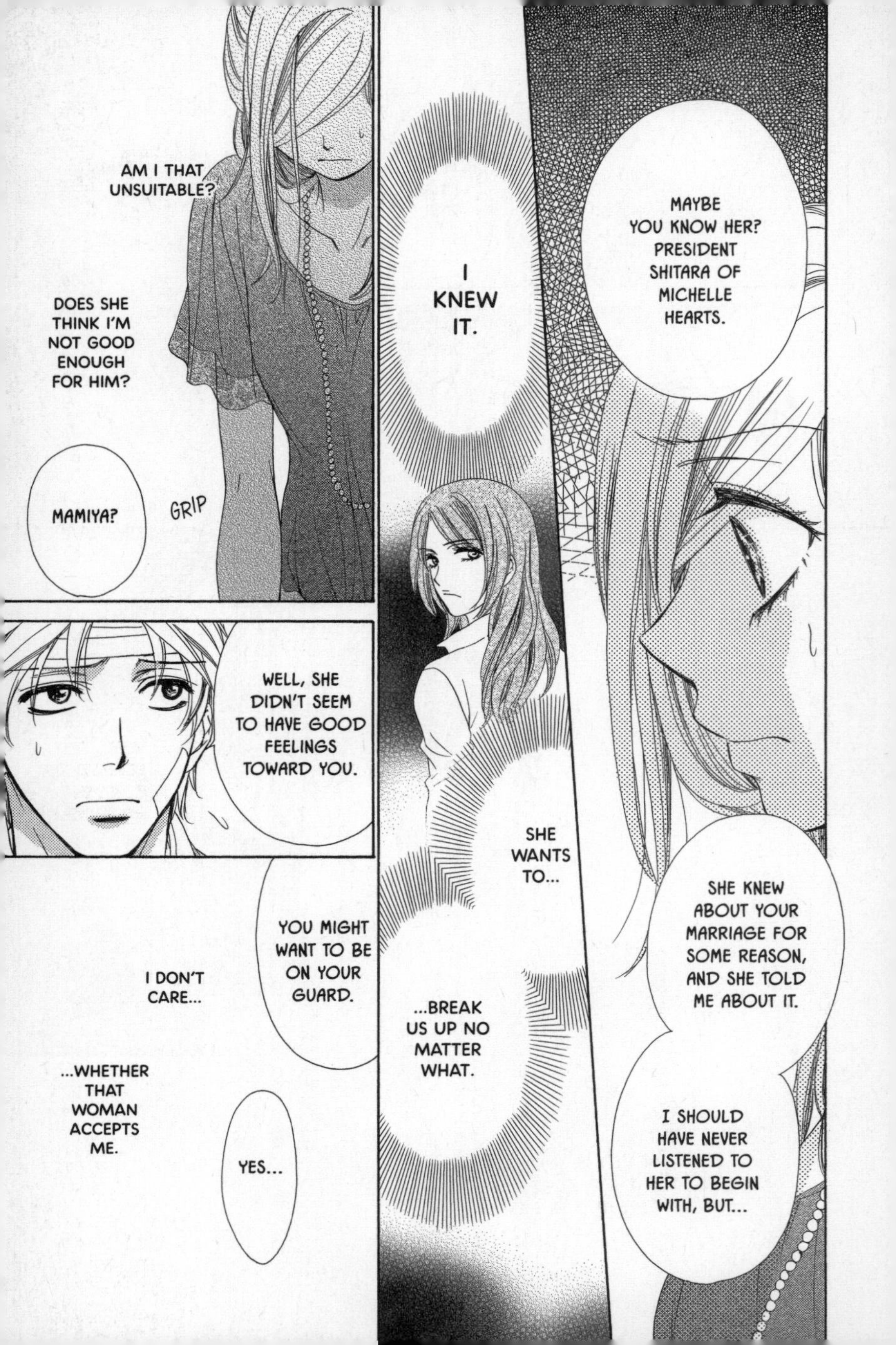
MAYBE YOU KNOW HER? PRESIDENT SHITARA OF MICHELLE HEARTS.
SHE KNEW ABOUT YOUR MARRIAGE FOR SOME REASON, AND SHE TOLD ME ABOUT IT.
I SHOULD HAVE NEVER LISTENED TO HER TO BEGIN WITH, BUT...
I KNEW IT.
SHE WANTS TO...
...BREAK US UP NO MATTER WHAT.
AM I THAT UNSUITABLE?
DOES SHE THINK I'M NOT GOOD ENOUGH FOR HIM?
GRIP
MAMIYA?
WELL, SHE DIDN'T SEEM TO HAVE GOOD FEELINGS TOWARD YOU.
YOU MIGHT WANT TO BE ON YOUR GUARD.
YES...
I DON'T CARE...
...WHETHER THAT WOMAN ACCEPTS ME.

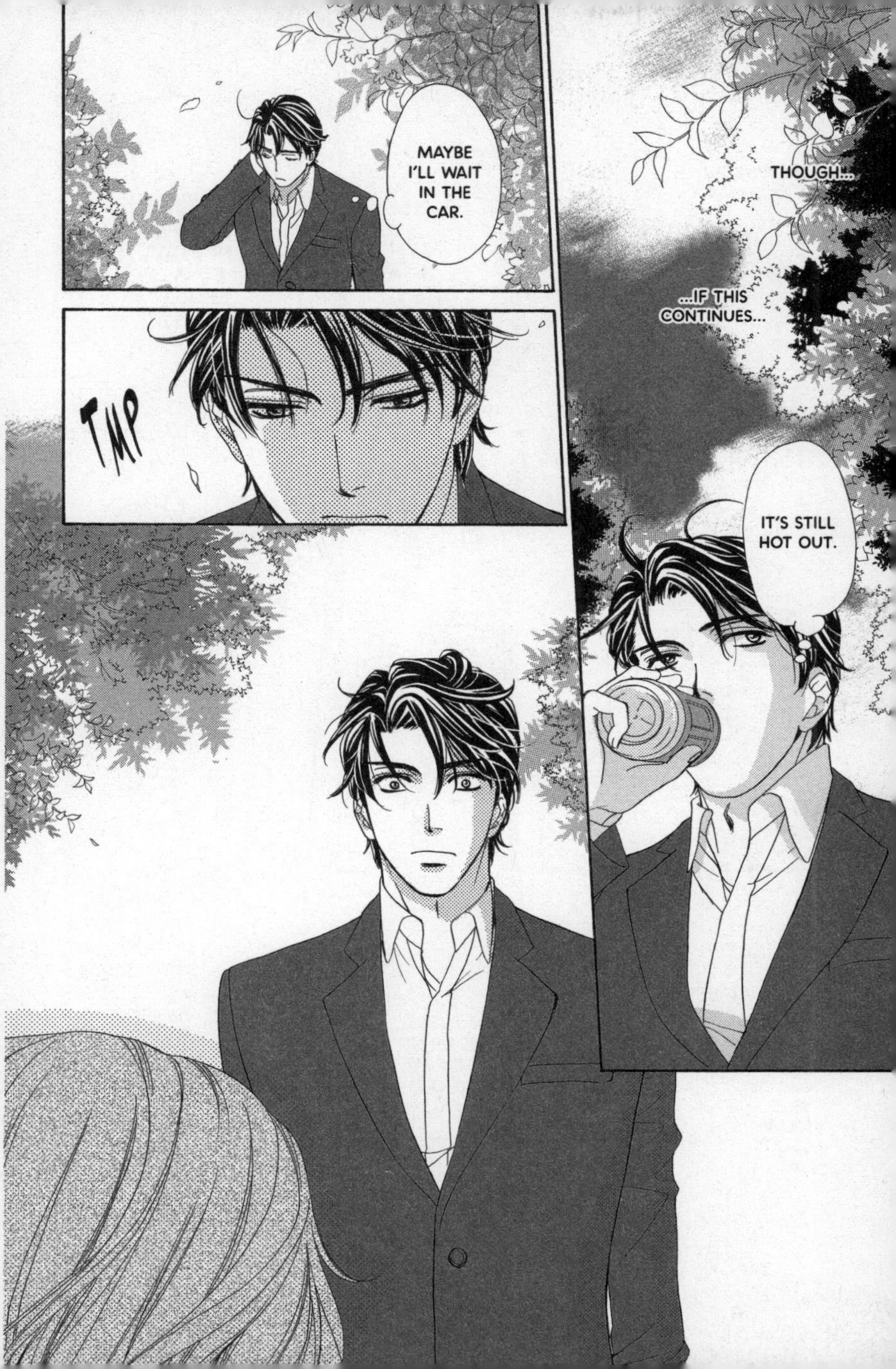
THOUGH...
...IF THIS CONTINUES...
IT'S STILL HOT OUT.
MAYBE I'LL WAIT IN THE CAR.
TMP

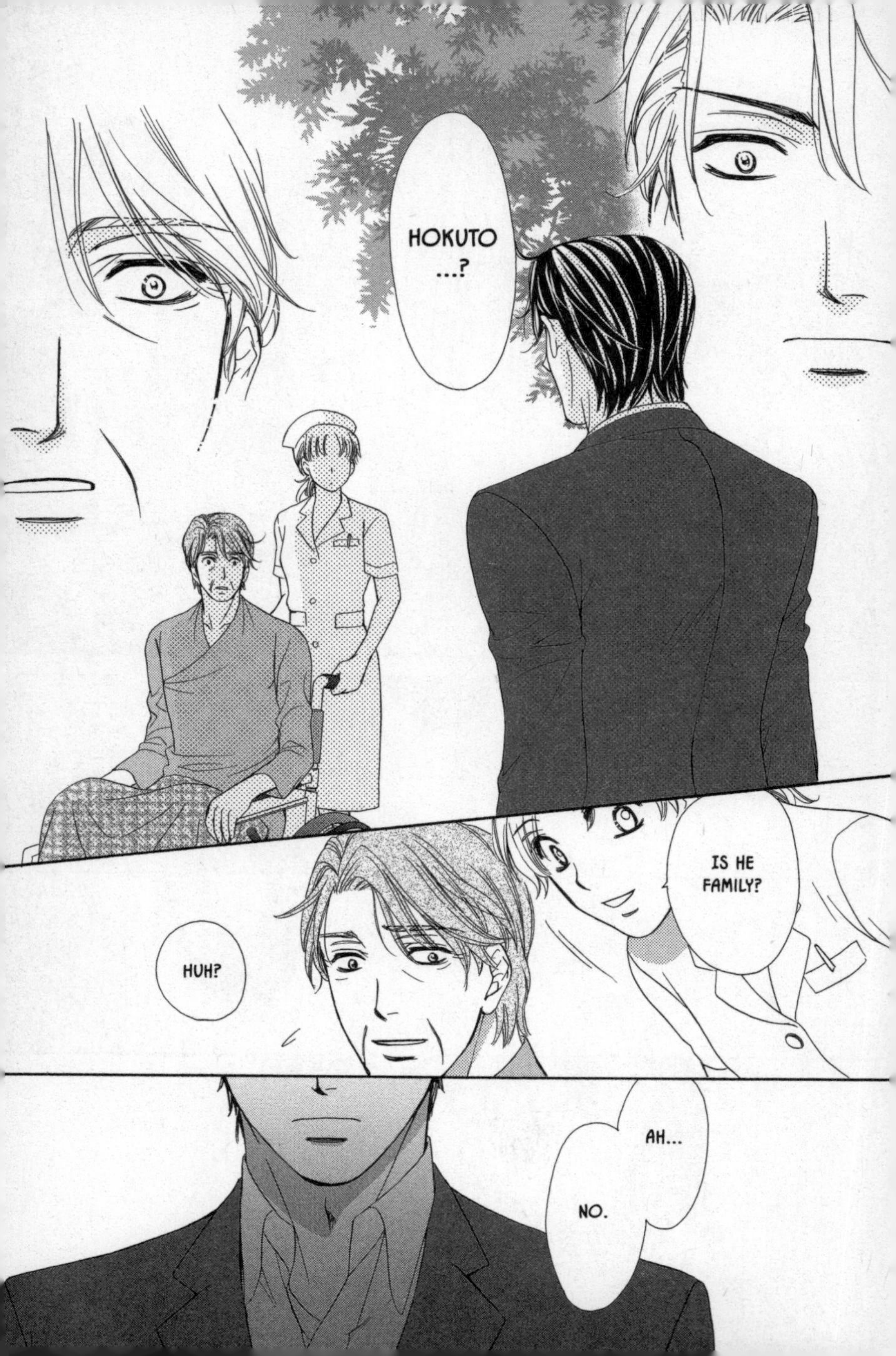
HOKUTO ...?
IS HE FAMILY?
HUH?
AH...
NO.

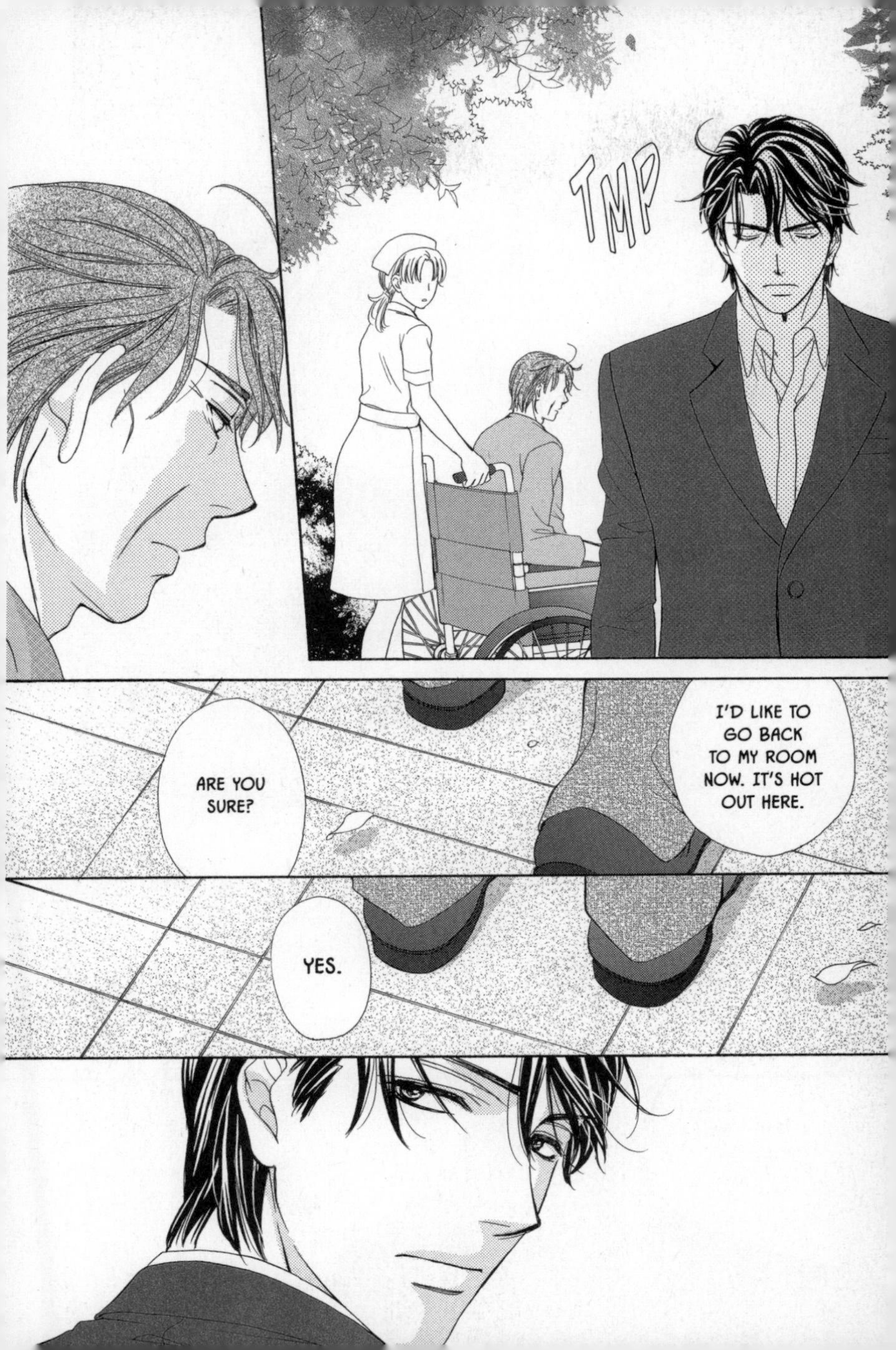
TMP
I'D LIKE TO GO BACK TO MY ROOM NOW. IT'S HOT OUT HERE.
ARE YOU SURE?
YES.

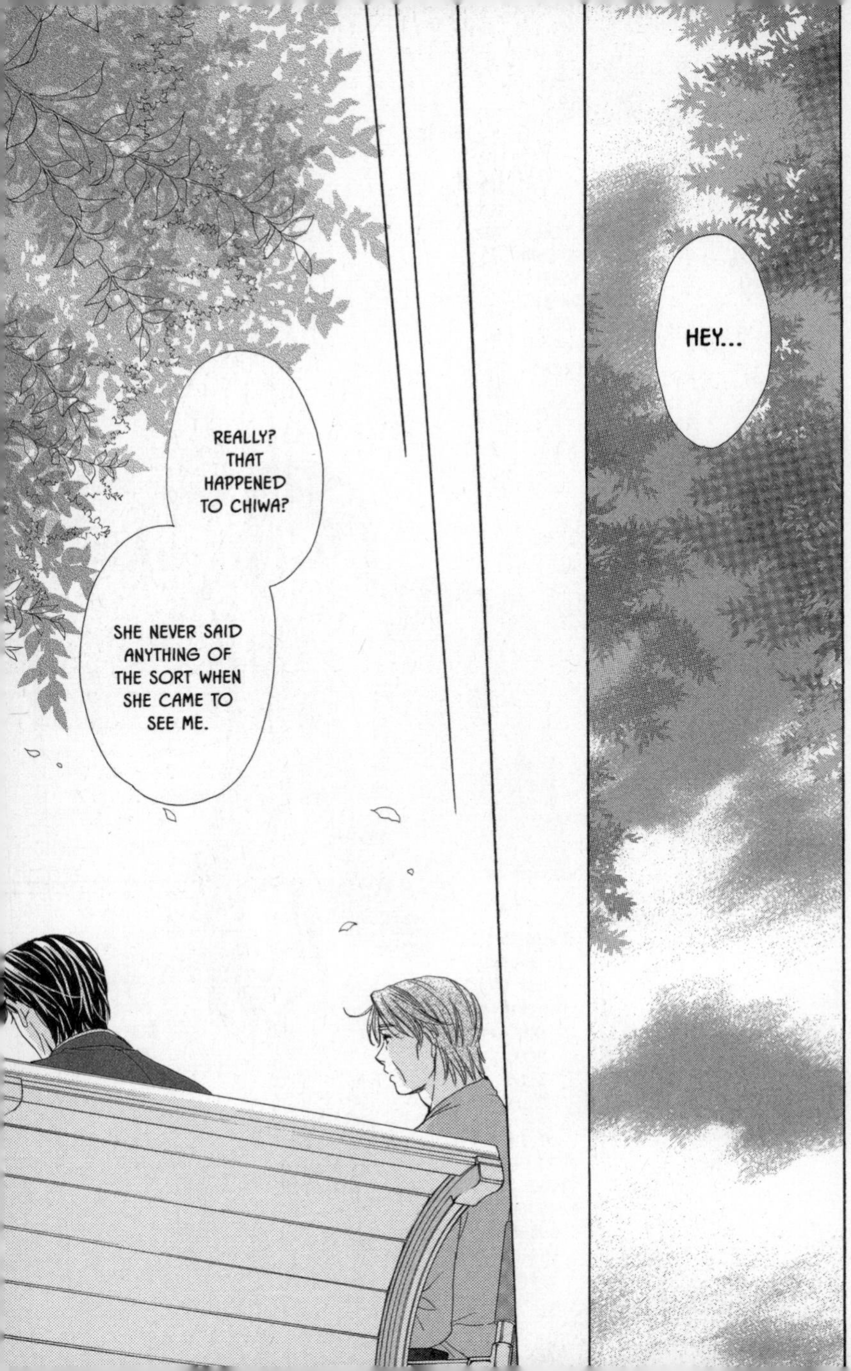
HEY...
REALLY? THAT HAPPENED TO CHIWA?
SHE NEVER SAID ANYTHING OF THE SORT WHEN SHE CAME TO SEE ME.

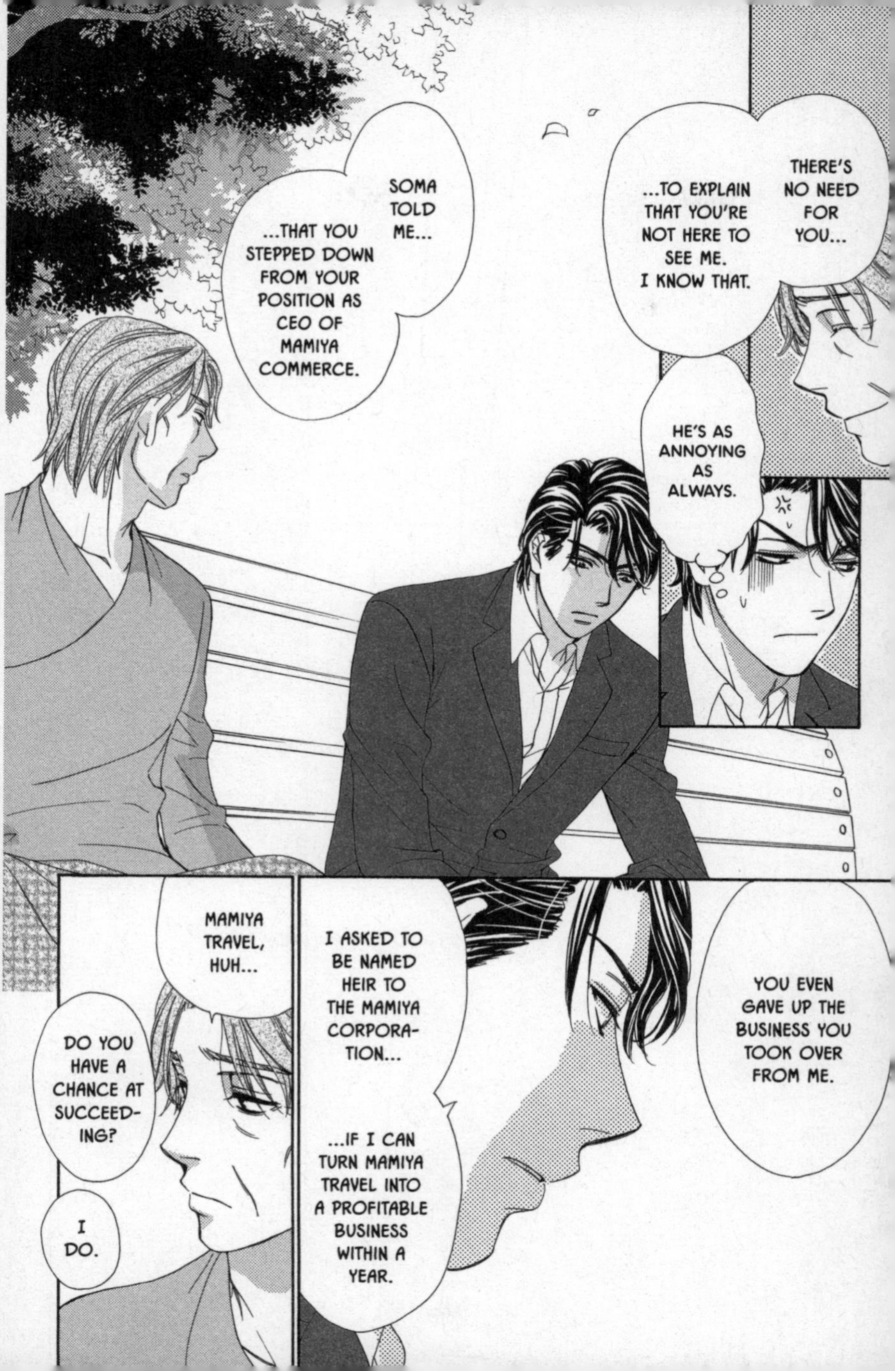
THERE'S NO NEED FOR YOU...
...TO EXPLAIN THAT YOU'RE NOT HERE TO SEE ME. I KNOW THAT.
HE'S AS ANNOYING AS ALWAYS.
SOMA TOLD ME...
...THAT YOU STEPPED DOWN FROM YOUR POSITION AS CEO OF MAMIYA COMMERCE.
YOU EVEN GAVE UP THE BUSINESS YOU TOOK OVER FROM ME.
I ASKED TO BE NAMED HEIR TO THE MAMIYA CORPORA-TION...
...IF I CAN TURN MAMIYA TRAVEL INTO A PROFITABLE BUSINESS WITHIN A YEAR.
MAMIYA TRAVEL, HUH...
DO YOU HAVE A CHANCE AT SUCCEED-ING?
I DO.

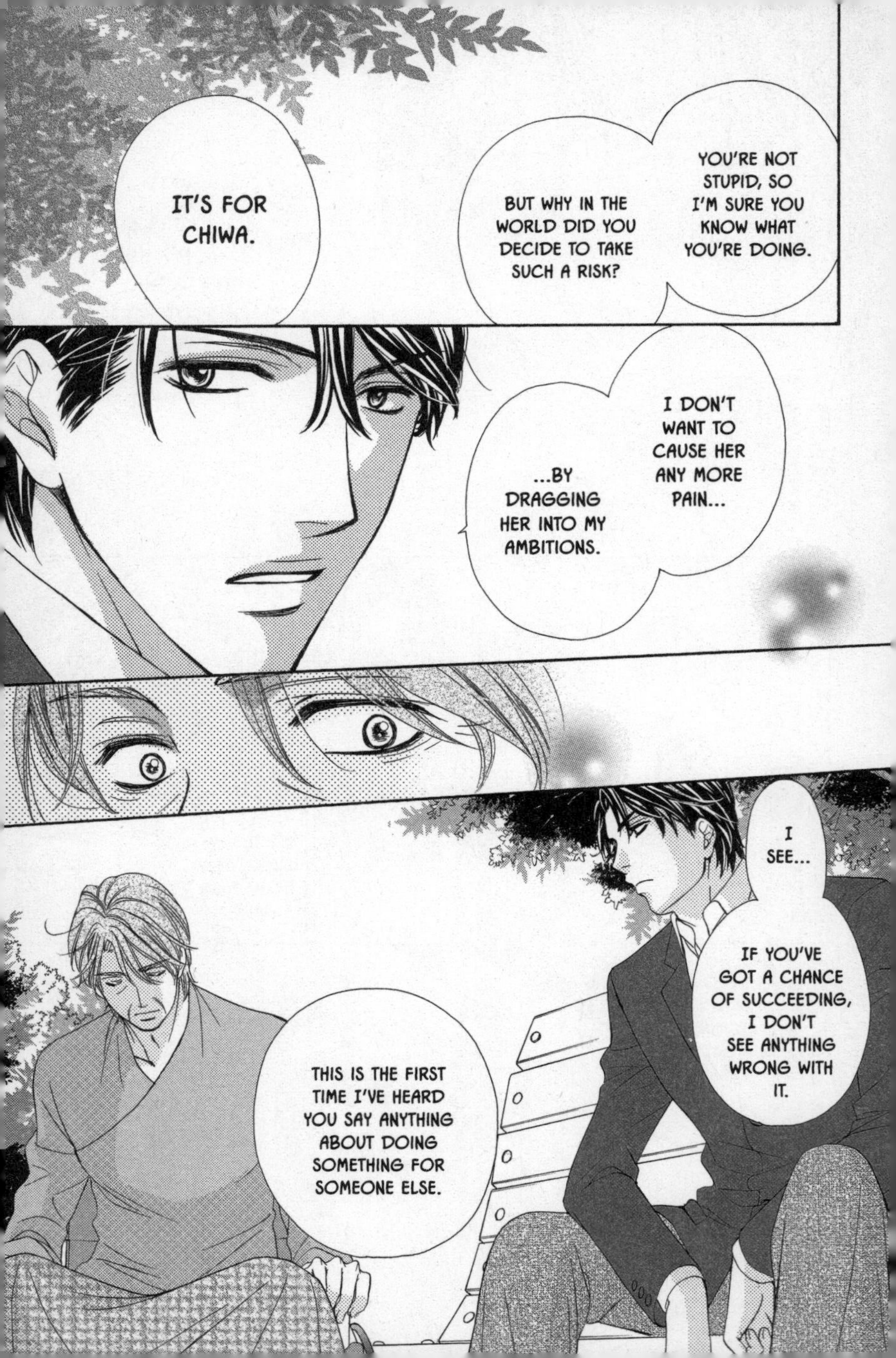
YOU'RE NOT STUPID, SO I'M SURE YOU KNOW WHAT YOU'RE DOING.
BUT WHY IN THE WORLD DID YOU DECIDE TO TAKE SUCH A RISK?
IT'S FOR CHIWA.
I DON'T WANT TO CAUSE HER ANY MORE PAIN...
...BY DRAGGING HER INTO MY AMBITIONS.
I SEE...
IF YOU'VE GOT A CHANCE OF SUCCEEDING, I DON'T SEE ANYTHING WRONG WITH IT.
THIS IS THE FIRST TIME I'VE HEARD YOU SAY ANYTHING ABOUT DOING SOMETHING FOR SOMEONE ELSE.

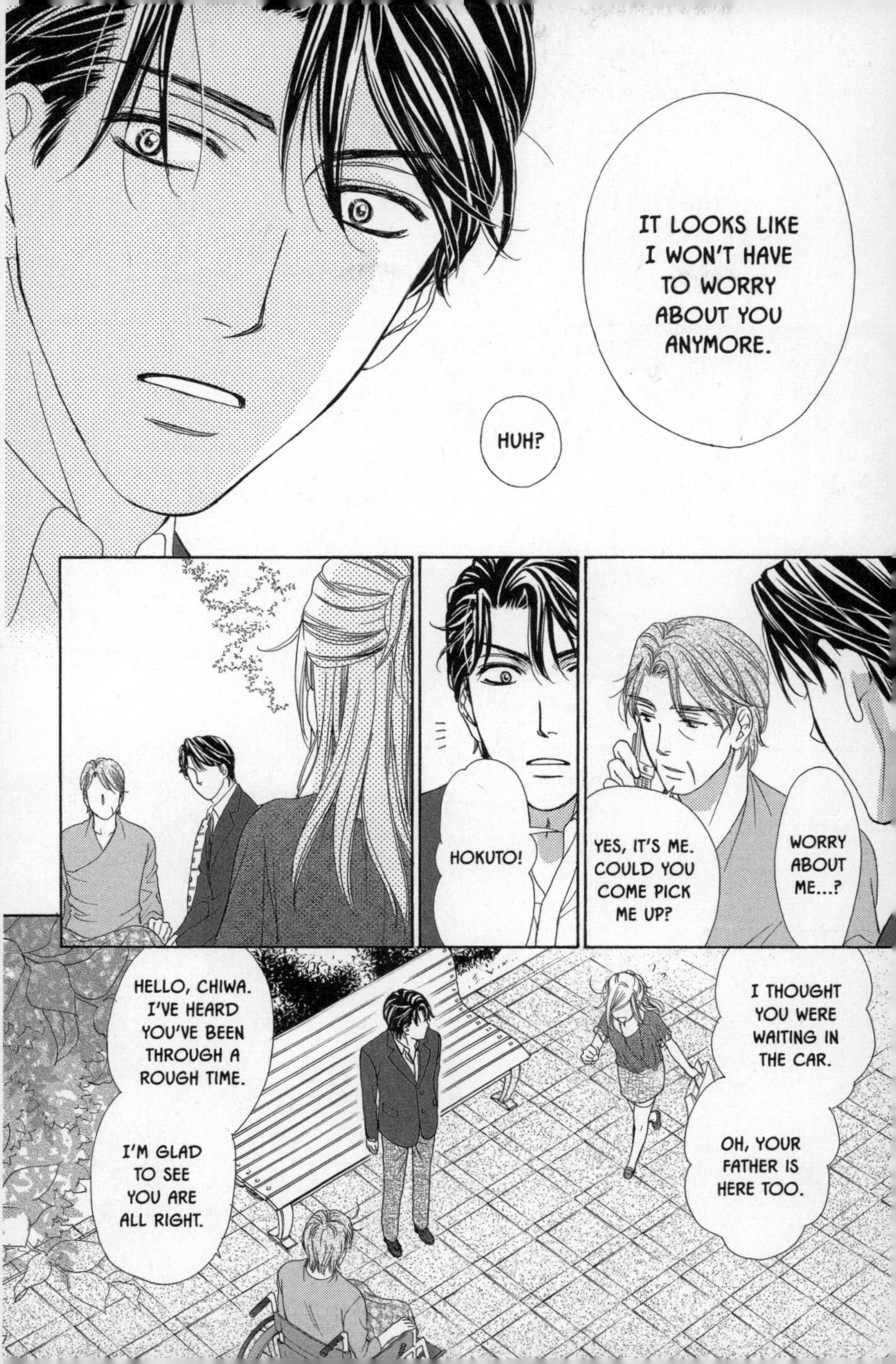
IT LOOKS LIKE I WON'T HAVE TO WORRY ABOUT YOU ANYMORE.
HUH?
WORRY ABOUT ME...?
YES, IT'S ME. COULD YOU COME PICK ME UP?
HOKUTO!
I THOUGHT YOU WERE WAITING IN THE CAR.
OH, YOUR FATHER IS HERE TOO.
HELLO, CHIWA. I'VE HEARD YOU'VE BEEN THROUGH A ROUGH TIME.
I'M GLAD TO SEE YOU ARE ALL RIGHT.

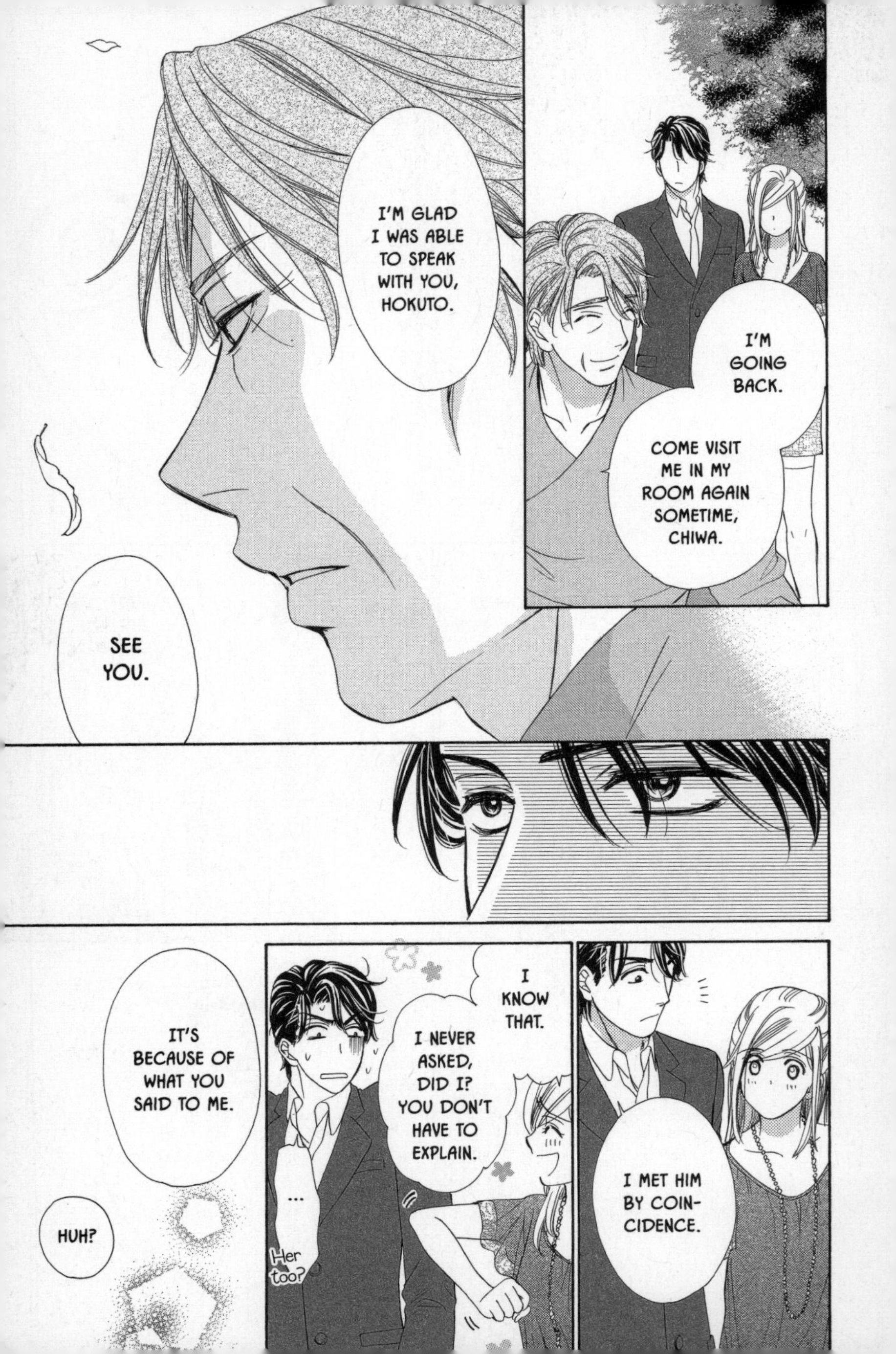
I'M GOING BACK.
COME VISIT ME IN MY ROOM AGAIN SOMETIME, CHIWA.
I'M GLAD I WAS ABLE TO SPEAK WITH YOU, HOKUTO.
SEE YOU.
I MET HIM BY COINCIDENCE.
I KNOW THAT.
I NEVER ASKED, DID I? YOU DON'T HAVE TO EXPLAIN.
...
Her too?
IT'S BECAUSE OF WHAT YOU SAID TO ME.
HUH?

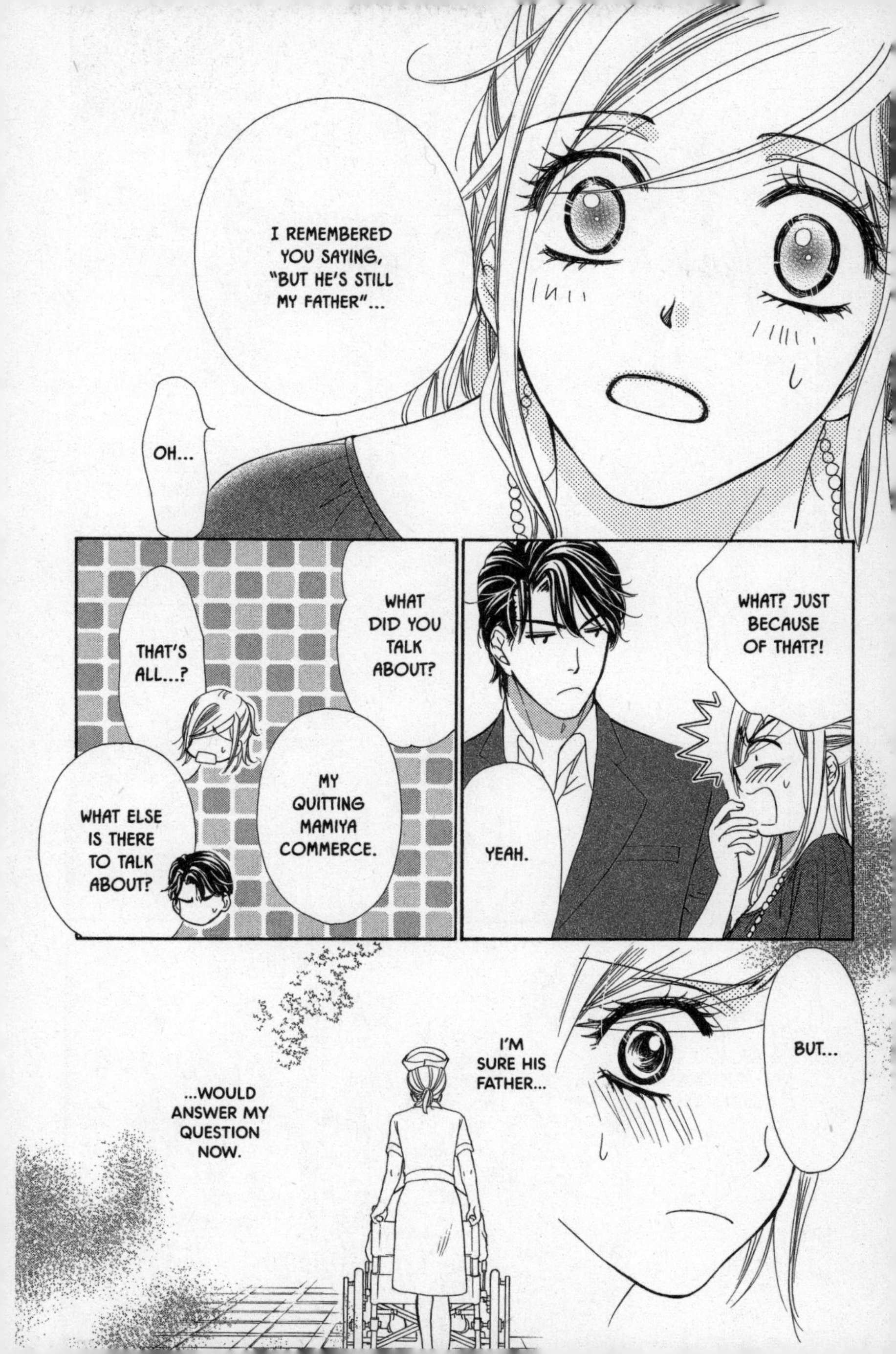
I REMEMBERED YOU SAYING, "BUT HE'S STILL MY FATHER"...
OH...
WHAT? JUST BECAUSE OF THAT?!
YEAH.
WHAT DID YOU TALK ABOUT?
THAT'S ALL...?
MY QUITTING MAMIYA COMMERCE.
WHAT ELSE IS THERE TO TALK ABOUT?
BUT...
I'M SURE HIS FATHER...
...WOULD ANSWER MY QUESTION NOW.

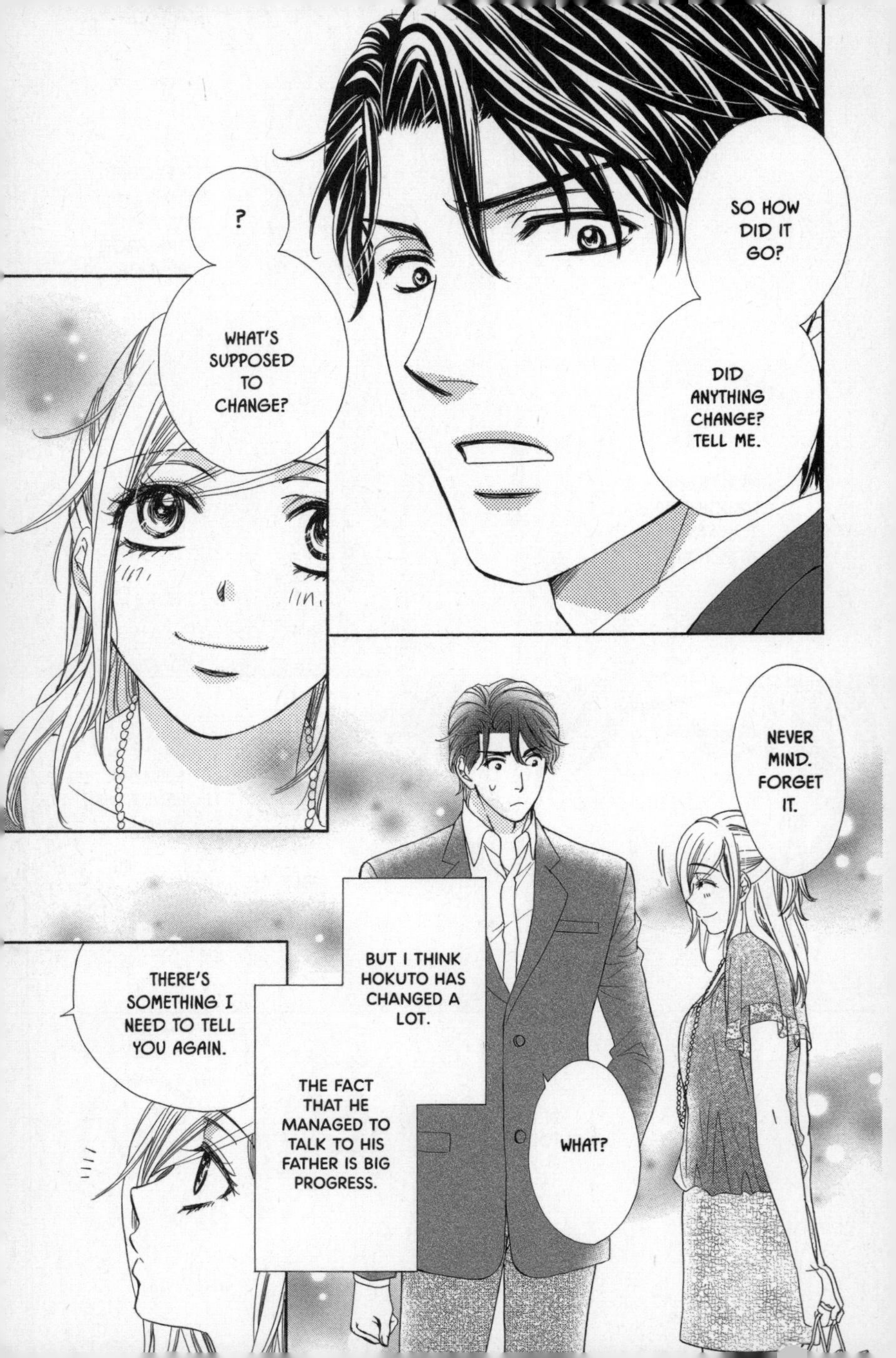
SO HOW DID IT GO?
DID ANYTHING CHANGE? TELL ME.
?
WHAT'S SUPPOSED TO CHANGE?
NEVER MIND. FORGET IT.
BUT I THINK HOKUTO HAS CHANGED A LOT.
THE FACT THAT HE MANAGED TO TALK TO HIS FATHER IS BIG PROGRESS.
WHAT?
THERE'S SOMETHING I NEED TO TELL YOU AGAIN.

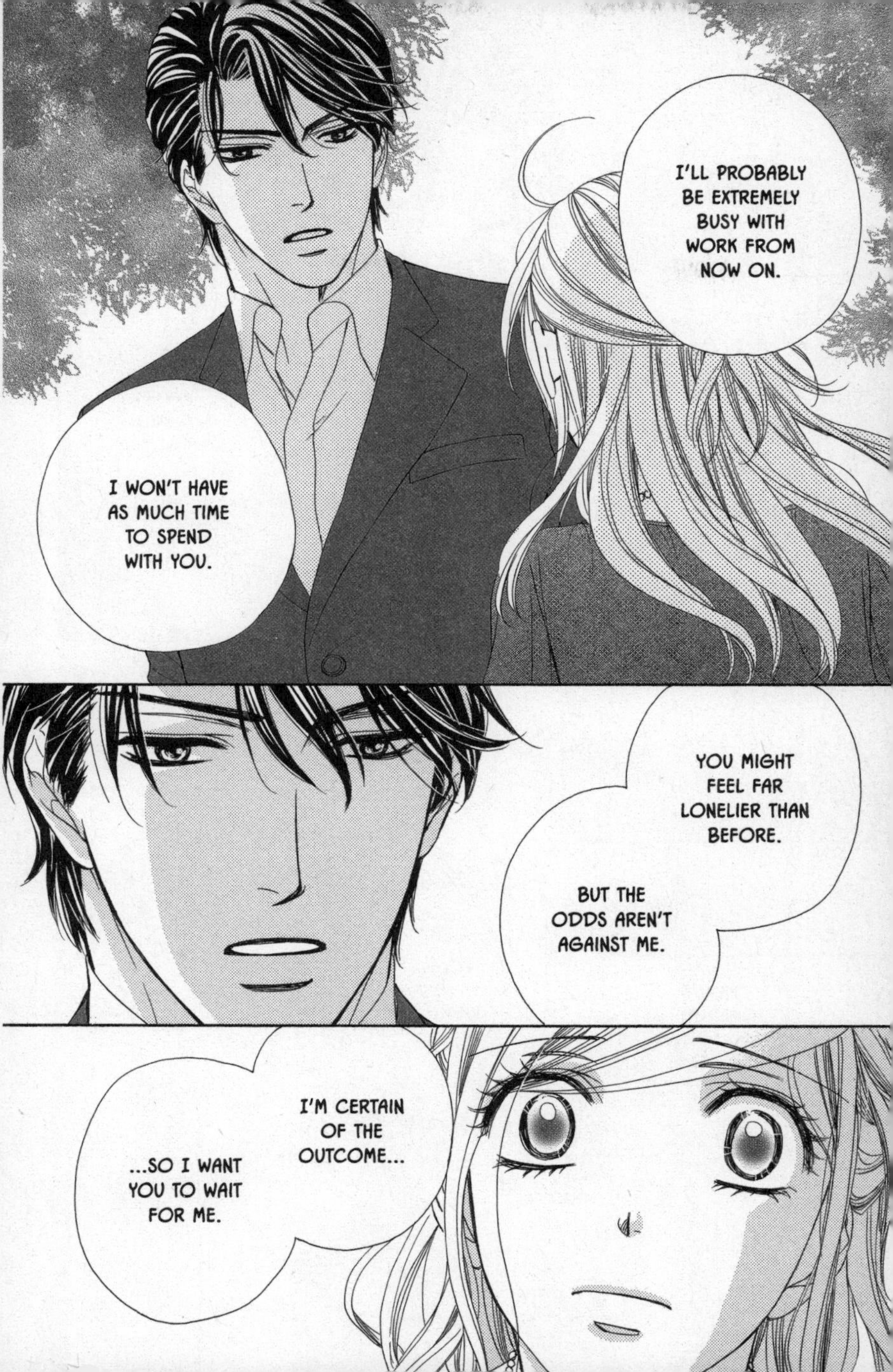
I'LL PROBABLY BE EXTREMELY BUSY WITH WORK FROM NOW ON.
I WON'T HAVE AS MUCH TIME TO SPEND WITH YOU.
YOU MIGHT FEEL FAR LONELIER THAN BEFORE.
BUT THE ODDS AREN'T AGAINST ME.
I'M CERTAIN OF THE OUTCOME...
...SO I WANT YOU TO WAIT FOR ME.

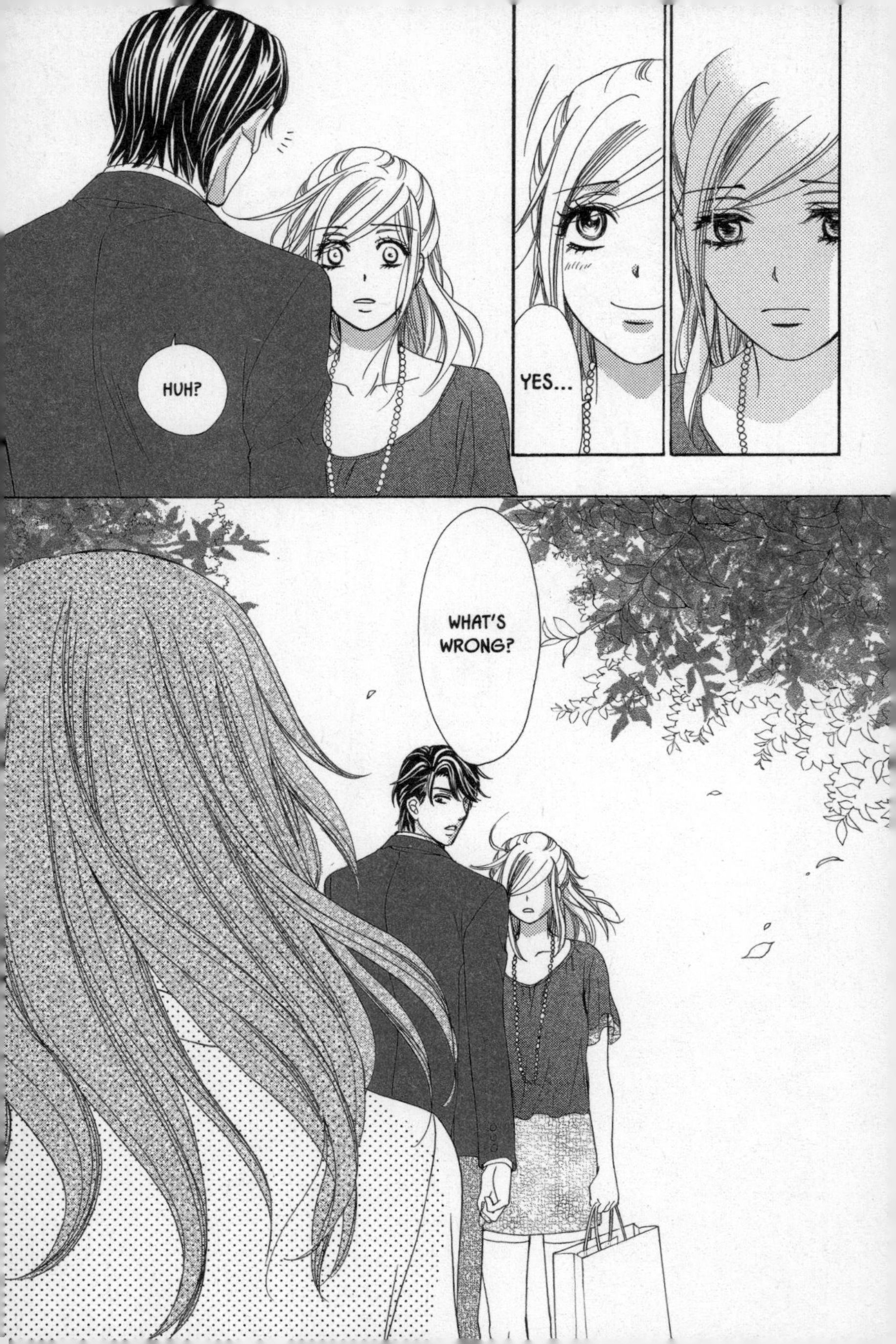
YES...
HUH?
WHAT'S WRONG?

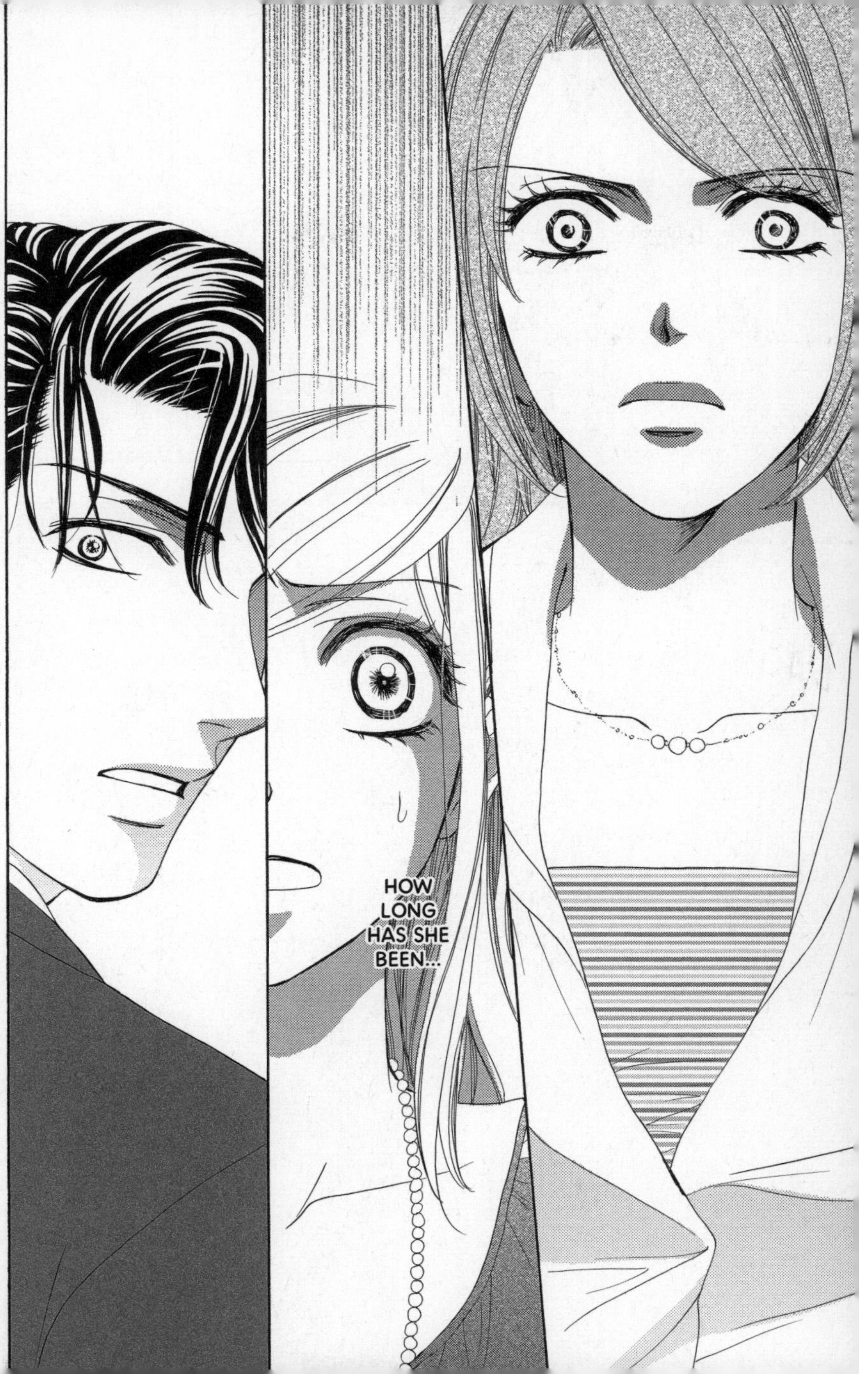
HOW LONG HAS SHE BEEN...

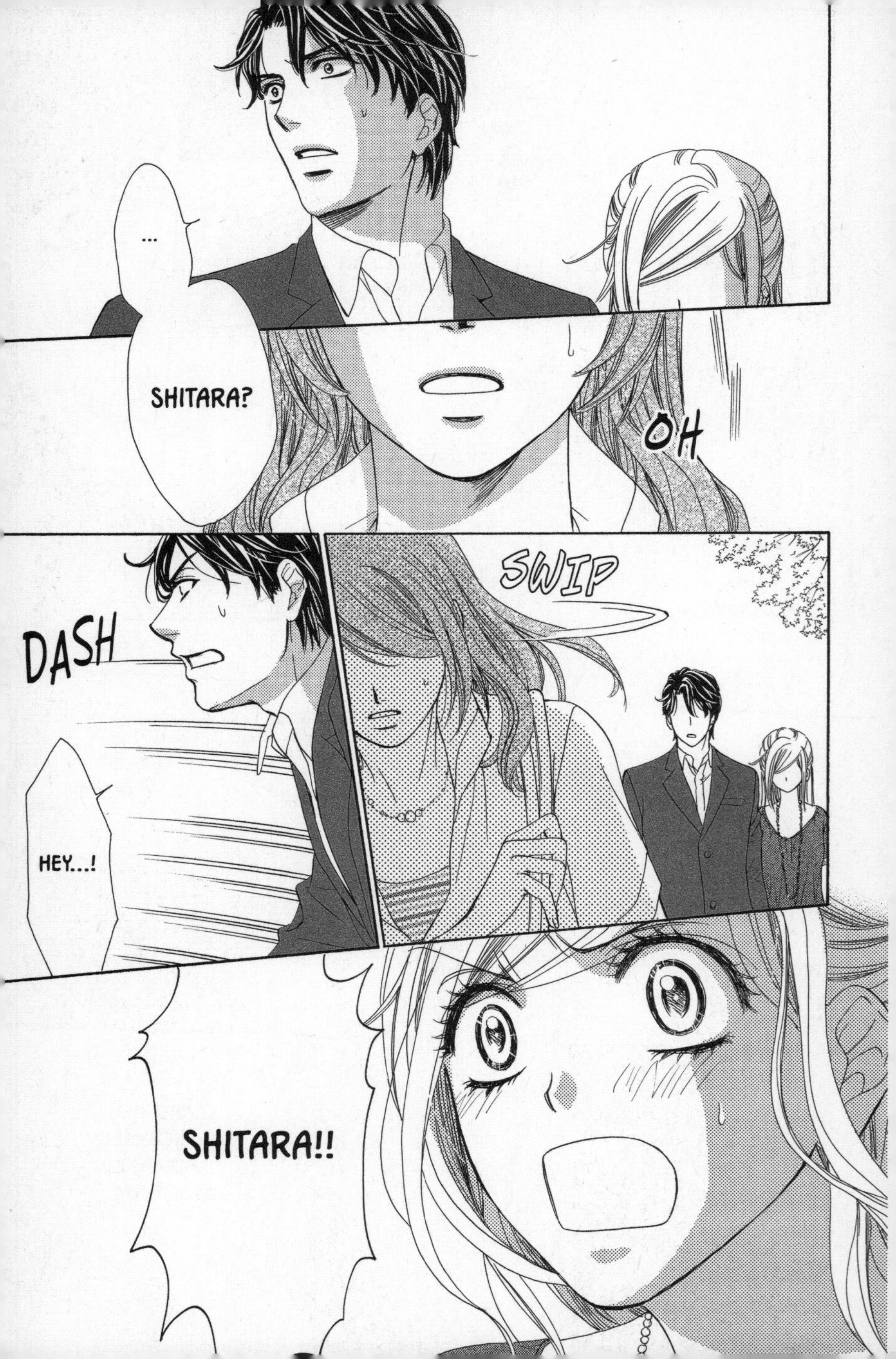
...
SHITARA?
OH
SWIP
DASH
HEY...!
SHITARA!!

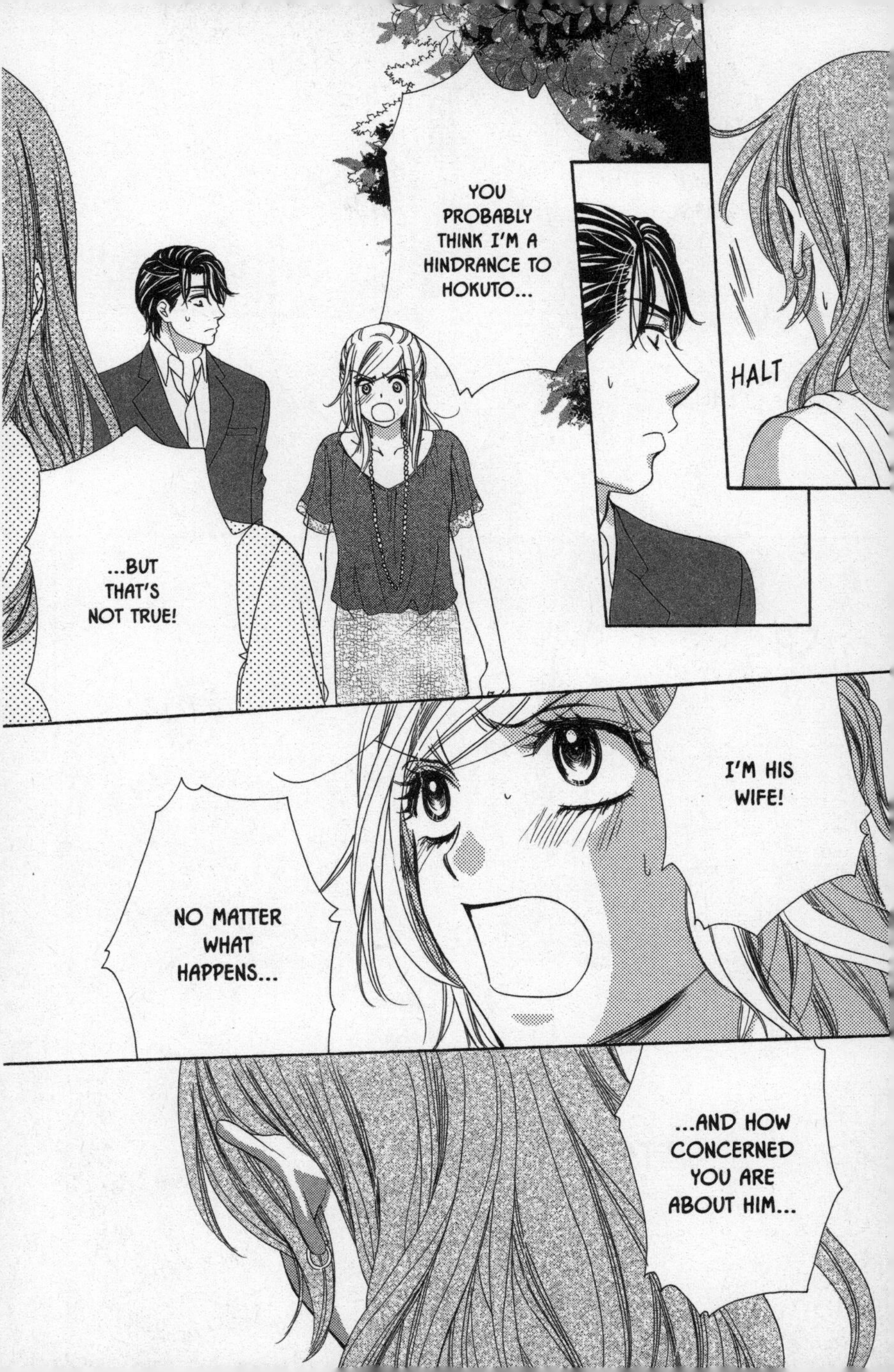
HALT
YOU PROBABLY THINK I'M A HINDRANCE TO HOKUTO...
...BUT THAT'S NOT TRUE!
I'M HIS WIFE!
NO MATTER WHAT HAPPENS...
...AND HOW CONCERNED YOU ARE ABOUT HIM...

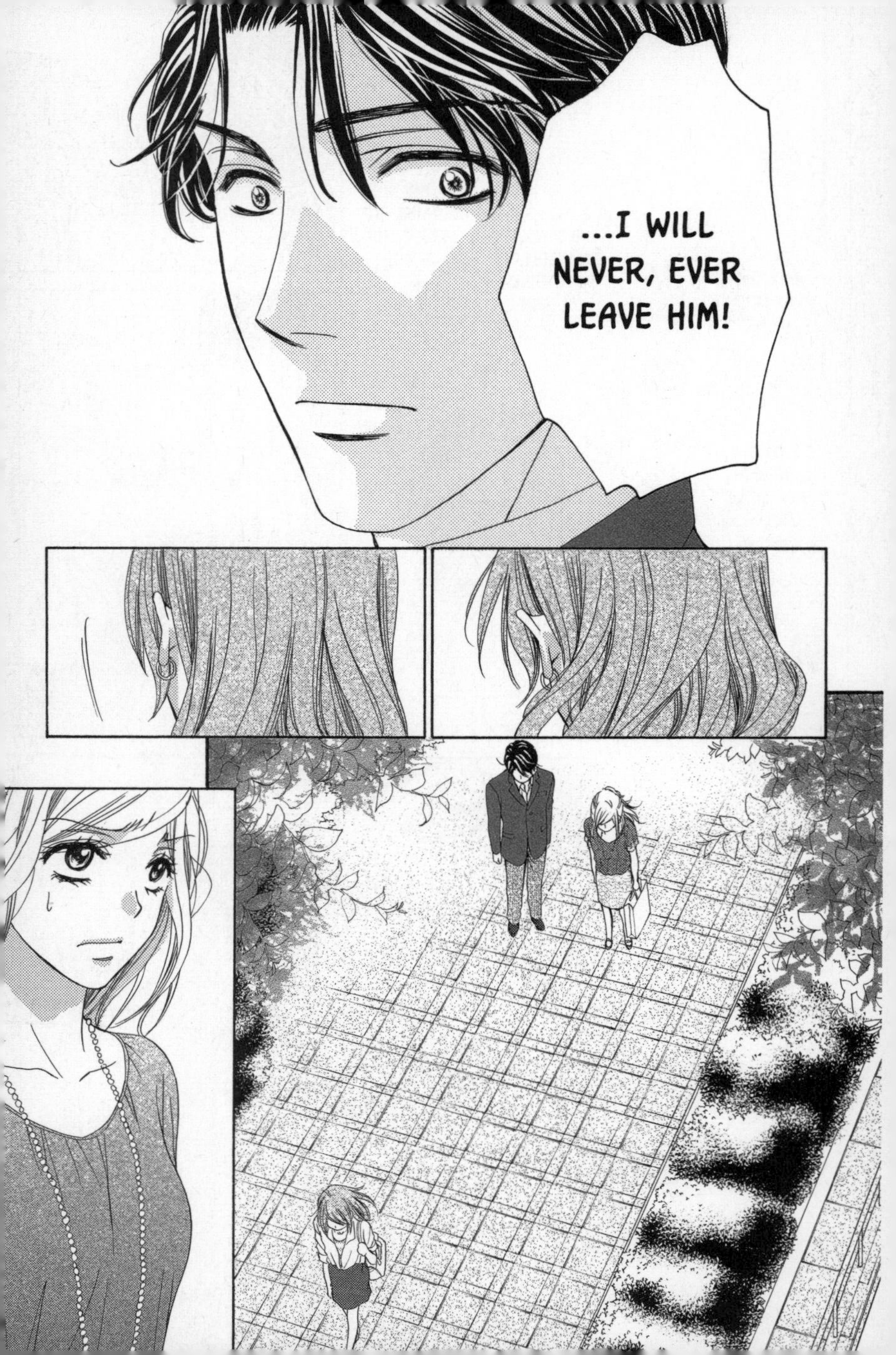
...I WILL NEVER, EVER LEAVE HIM!

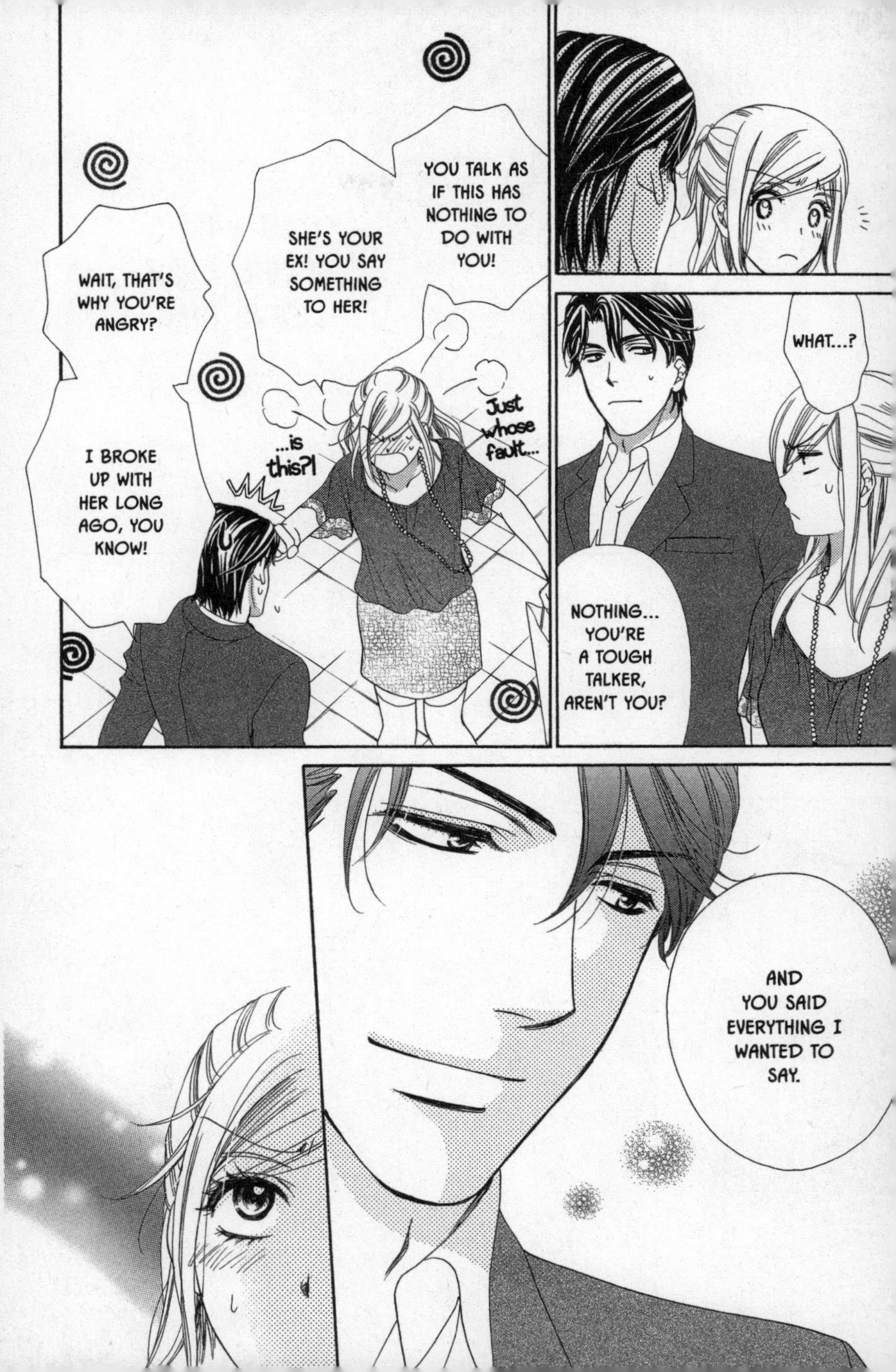
WAIT, THAT'S WHY YOU'RE ANGRY?
SHE'S YOUR EX! YOU SAY SOMETHING TO HER!
YOU TALK AS IF THIS HAS NOTHING TO DO WITH YOU!
I BROKE UP WITH HER LONG AGO, YOU KNOW!
Just whose fault...
...is this?!
WHAT...?
NOTHING... YOU'RE A TOUGH TALKER, AREN'T YOU?
AND YOU SAID EVERYTHING I WANTED TO SAY.

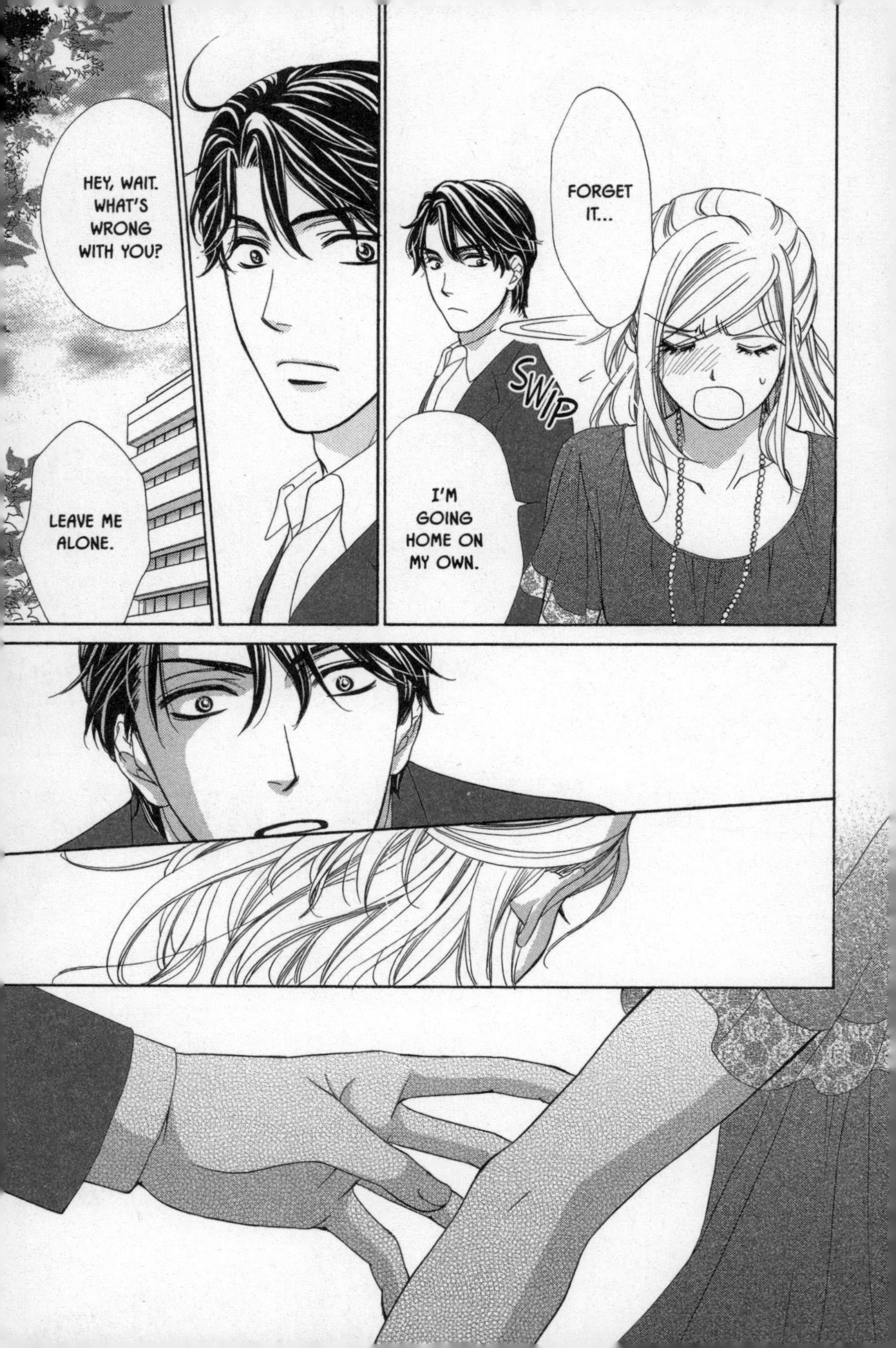
FORGET IT...
SWIP
I'M GOING HOME ON MY OWN.
HEY, WAIT. WHAT'S WRONG WITH YOU?
LEAVE ME ALONE.

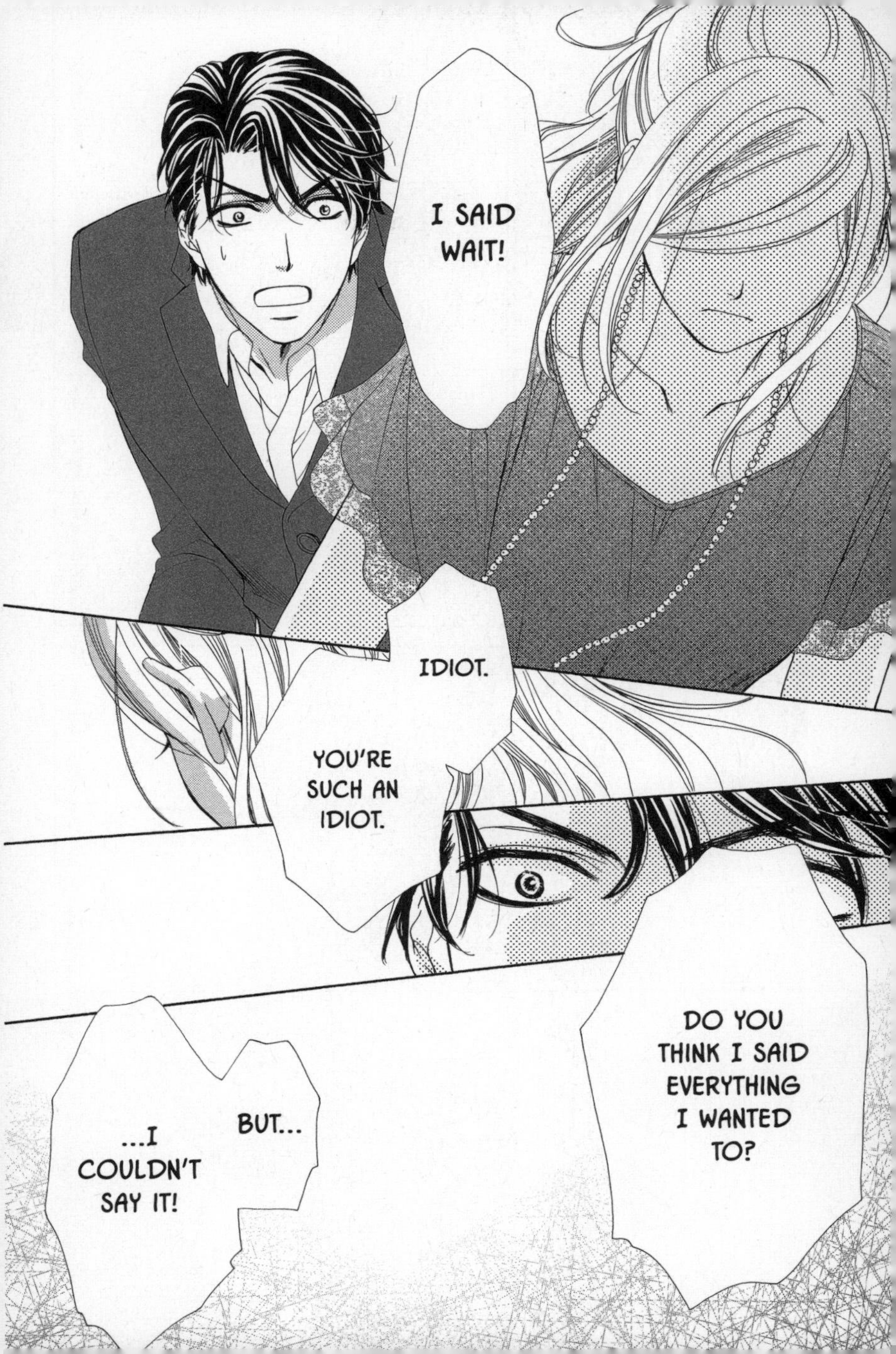
I SAID WAIT!
IDIOT.
YOU'RE SUCH AN IDIOT.
DO YOU THINK I SAID EVERYTHING I WANTED TO?
BUT...
...I COULDN'T SAY IT!

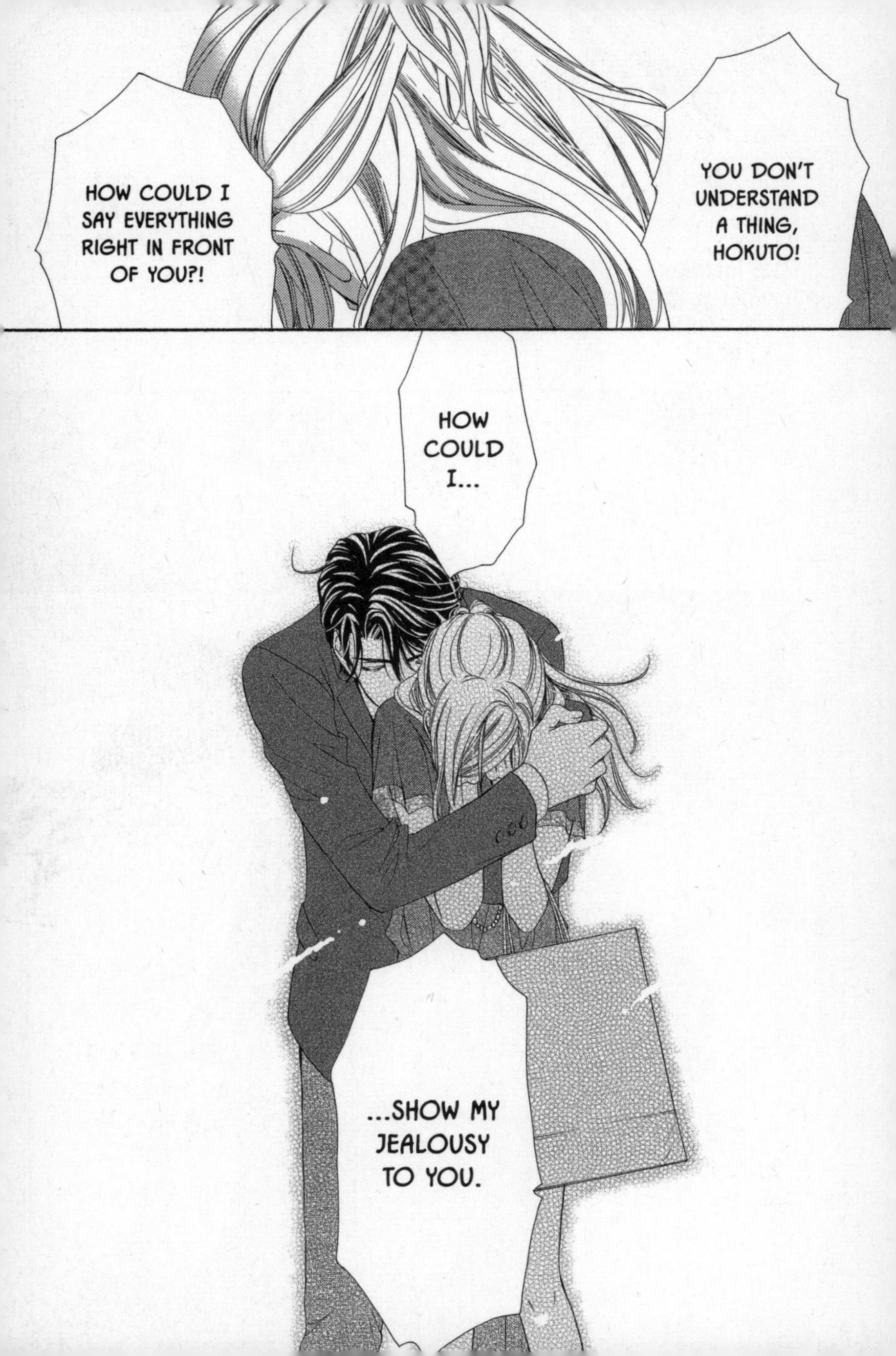
YOU DON'T UNDERSTAND A THING, HOKUTO!
HOW COULD I SAY EVERYTHING RIGHT IN FRONT OF YOU?!
HOW COULD I...
...SHOW MY JEALOUSY TO YOU.

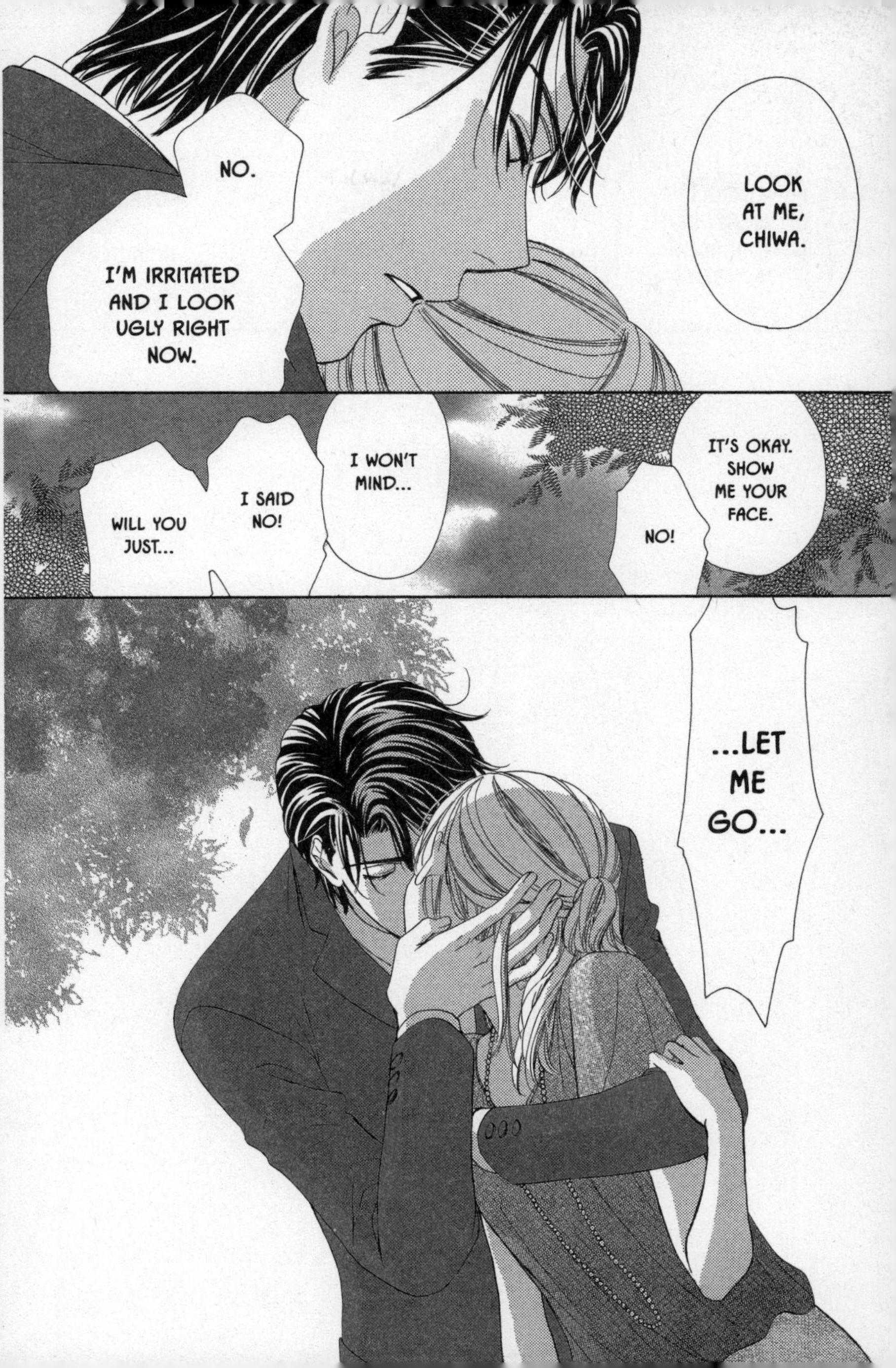
LOOK AT ME, CHIWA.
NO.
I'M IRRITATED AND I LOOK UGLY RIGHT NOW.
IT'S OKAY. SHOW ME YOUR FACE.
NO!
I WON'T MIND...
I SAID NO!
WILL YOU JUST...
...LET ME GO...

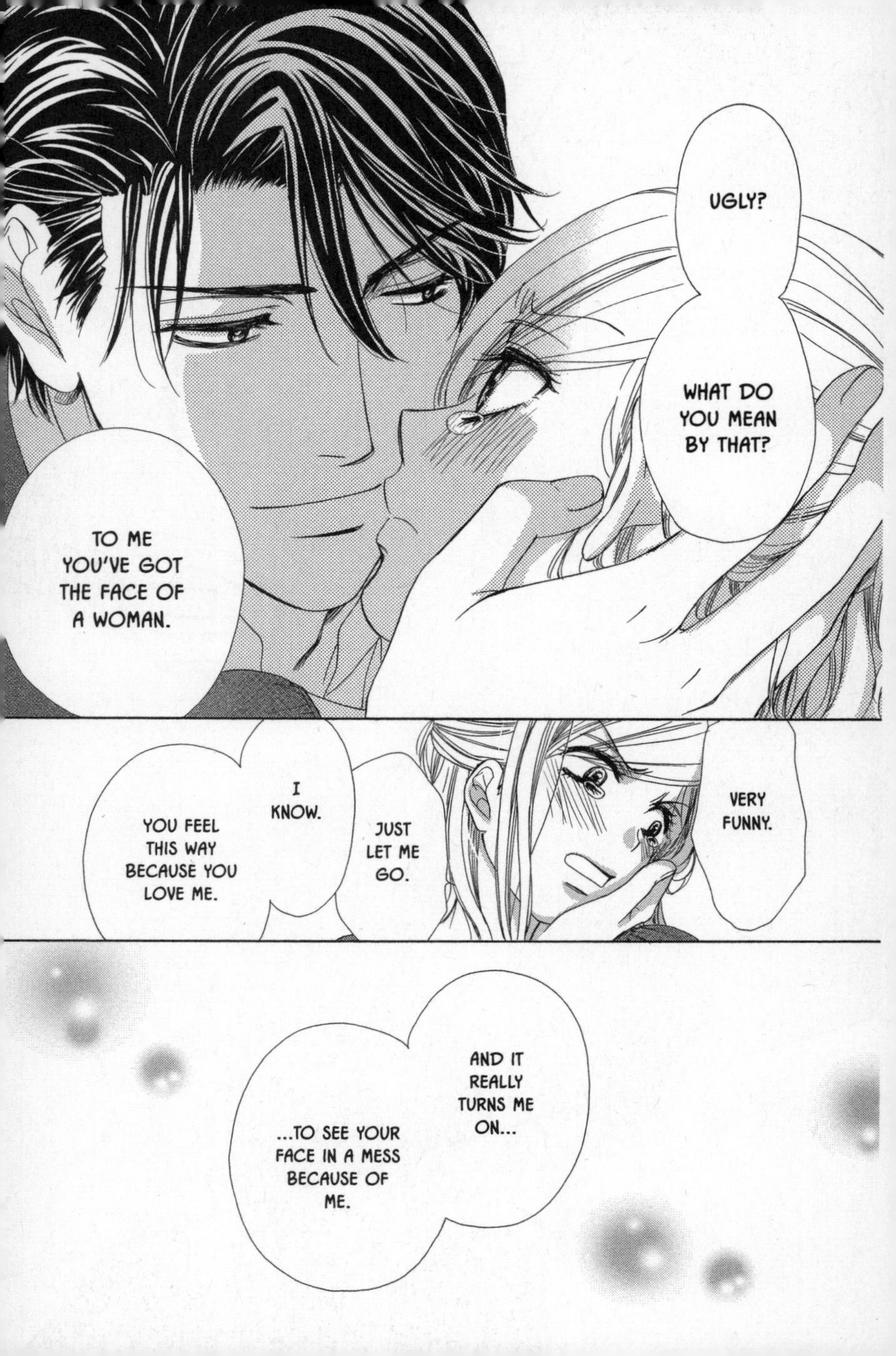
UGLY?
WHAT DO YOU MEAN BY THAT?
TO ME YOU'VE GOT THE FACE OF A WOMAN.
VERY FUNNY.
JUST LET ME GO.
I KNOW.
YOU FEEL THIS WAY BECAUSE YOU LOVE ME.
AND IT REALLY TURNS ME ON...
...TO SEE YOUR FACE IN A MESS BECAUSE OF ME.

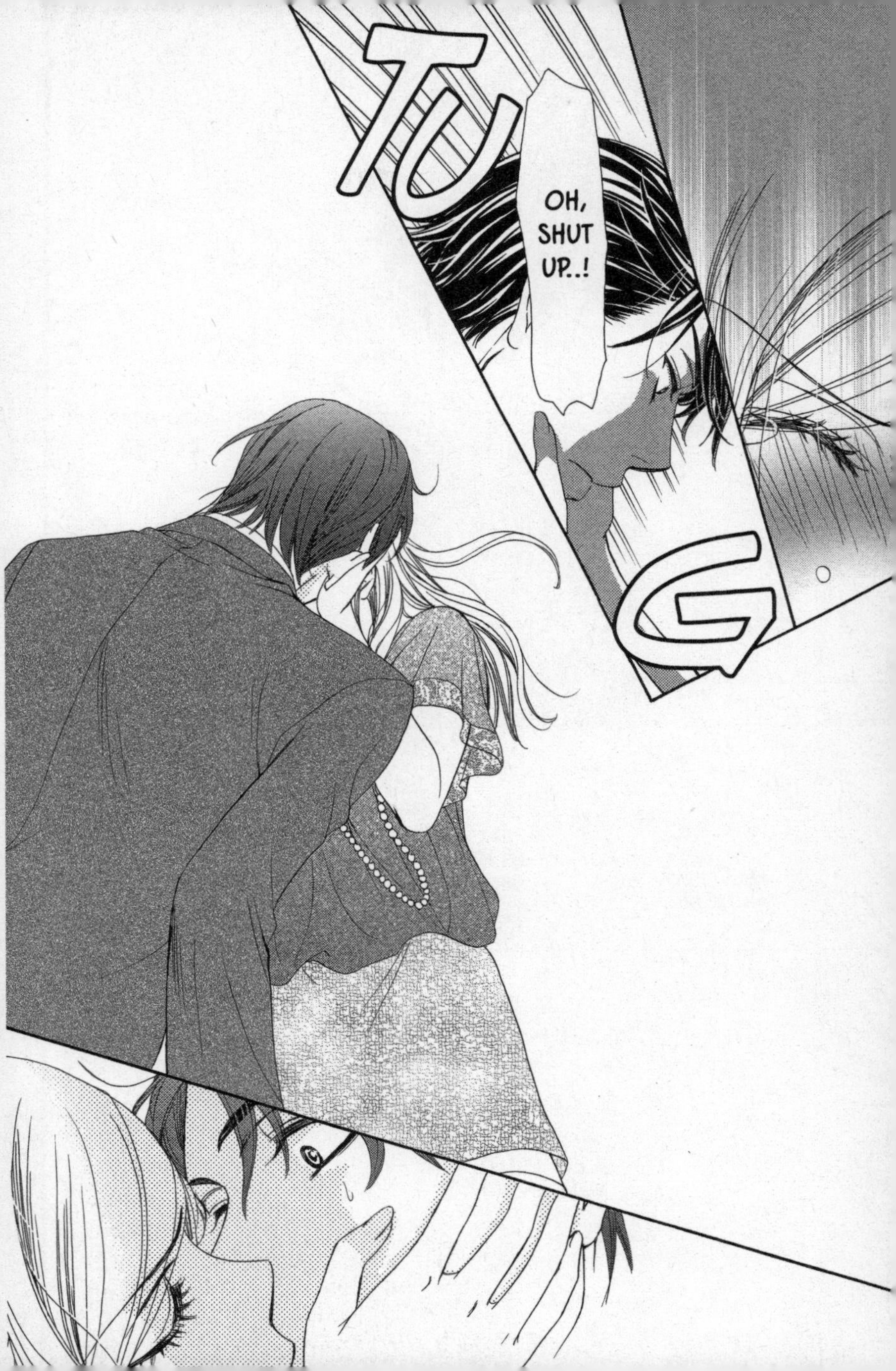
OH, SHUT UP..!
TUG

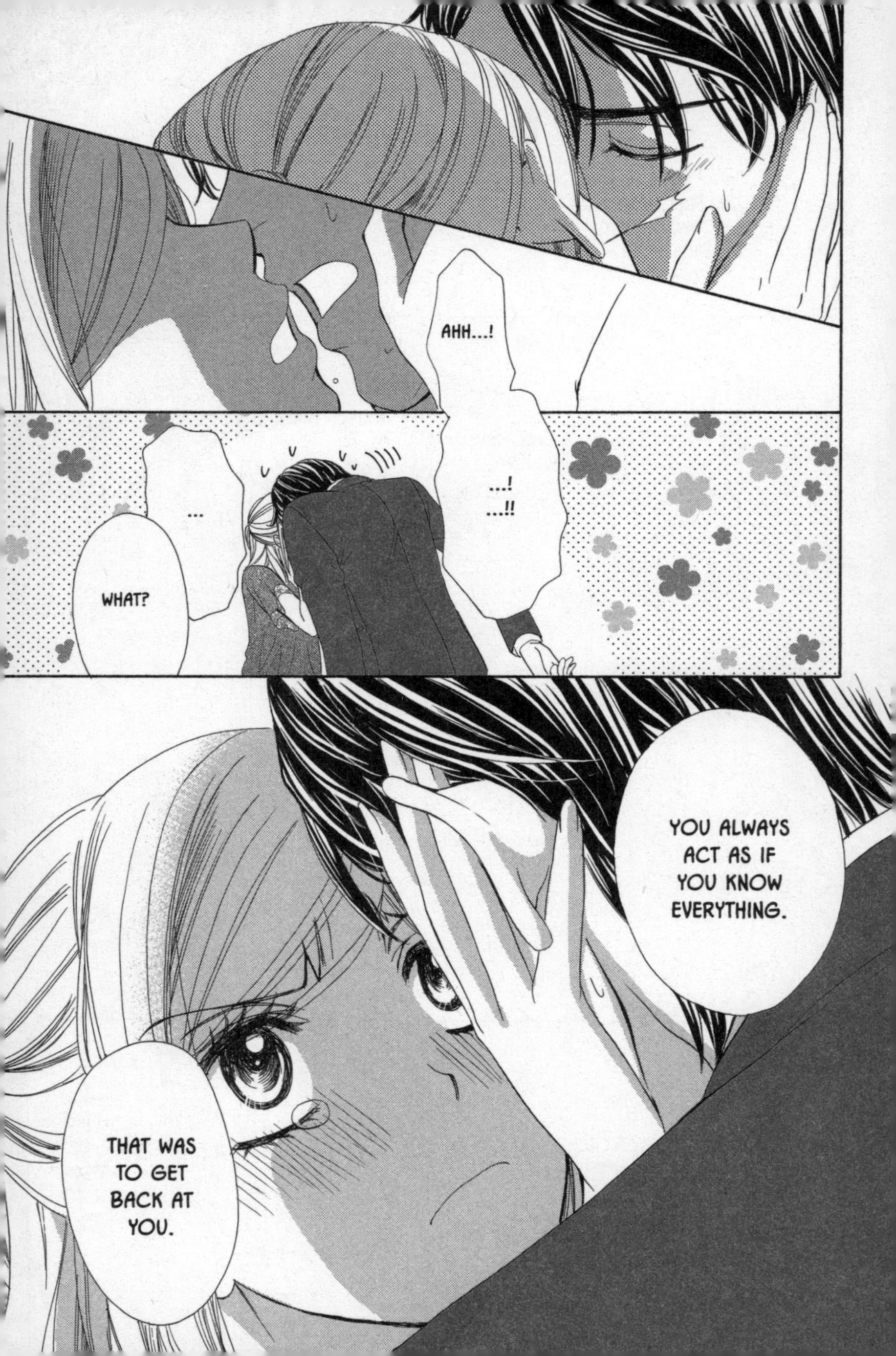

AHH...!
...!
...!!
...
WHAT?
YOU ALWAYS ACT AS IF YOU KNOW EVERYTHING.
THAT WAS TO GET BACK AT YOU.

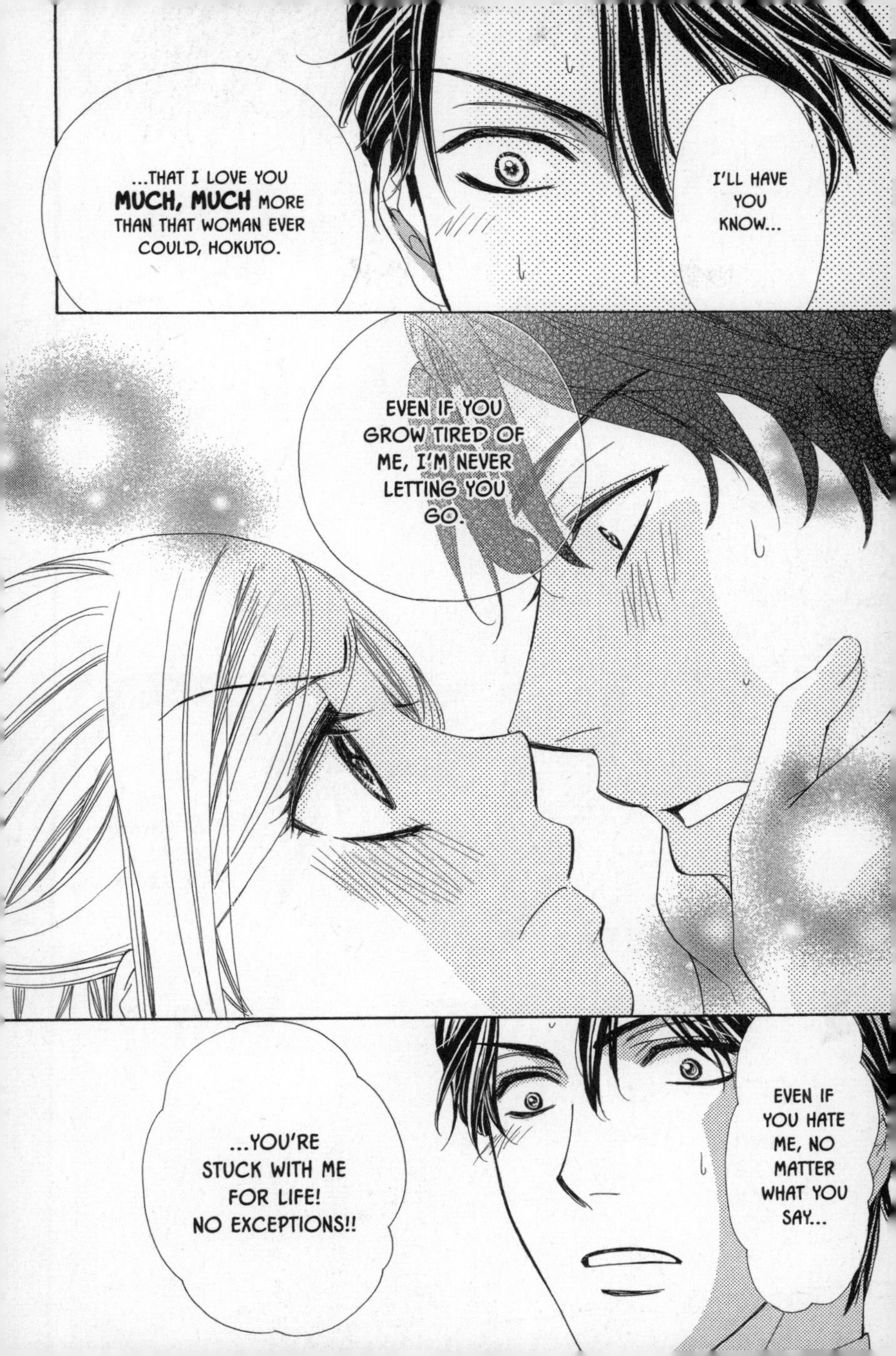
I'LL HAVE YOU KNOW...
...THAT I LOVE YOU **MUCH, MUCH** MORE THAN THAT WOMAN EVER COULD, HOKUTO.
EVEN IF YOU GROW TIRED OF ME, I'M NEVER LETTING YOU GO.
EVEN IF YOU HATE ME, NO MATTER WHAT YOU SAY...
...YOU'RE STUCK WITH ME FOR LIFE! NO EXCEPTIONS!!

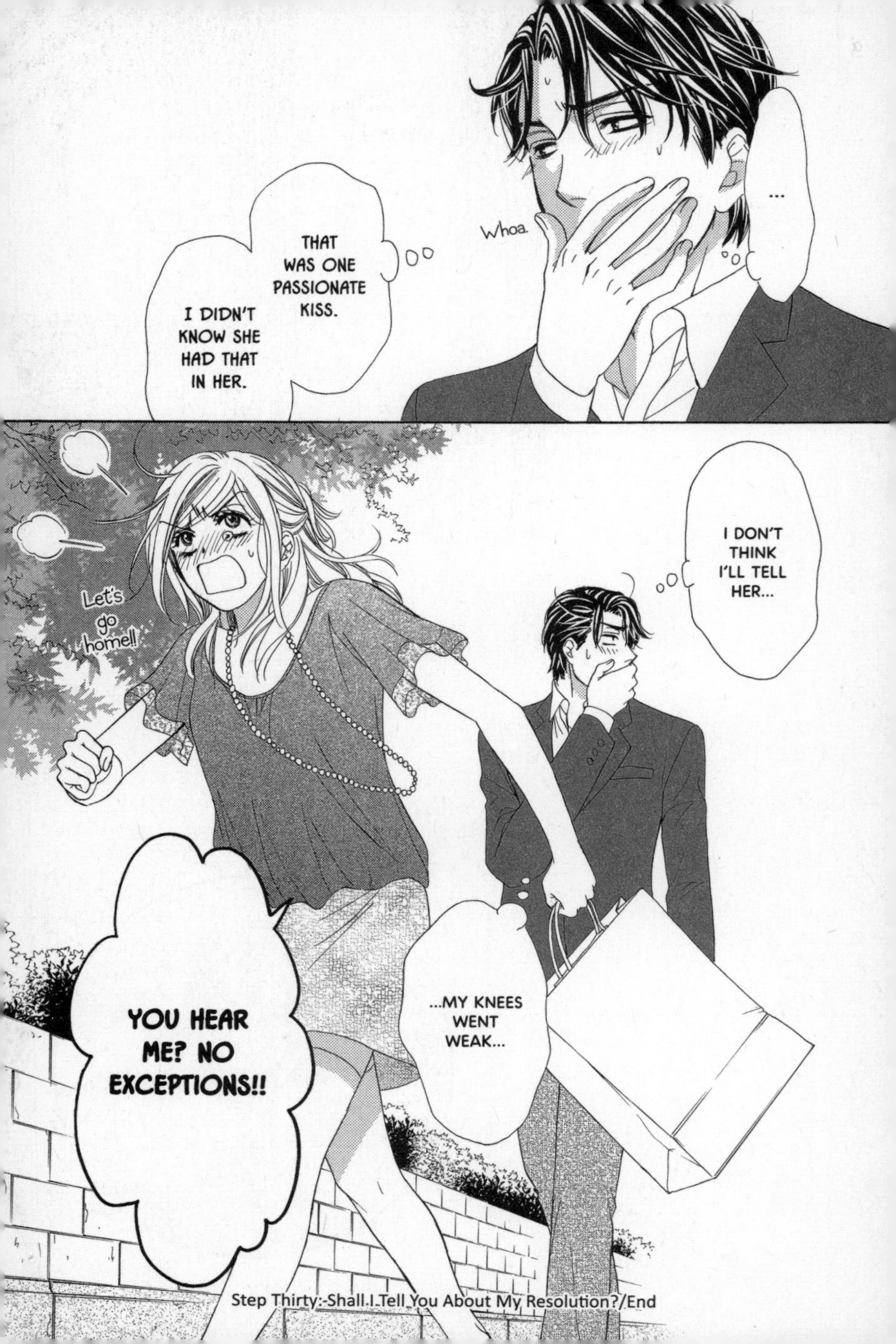
...
Whoa.
THAT WAS ONE PASSIONATE KISS.
I DIDN'T KNOW SHE HAD THAT IN HER.
I DON'T THINK I'LL TELL HER...
...MY KNEES WENT WEAK...
Let's go home!!
YOU HEAR ME? NO EXCEPTIONS!!
Step Thirty: Shall I Tell You About My Resolution?/End

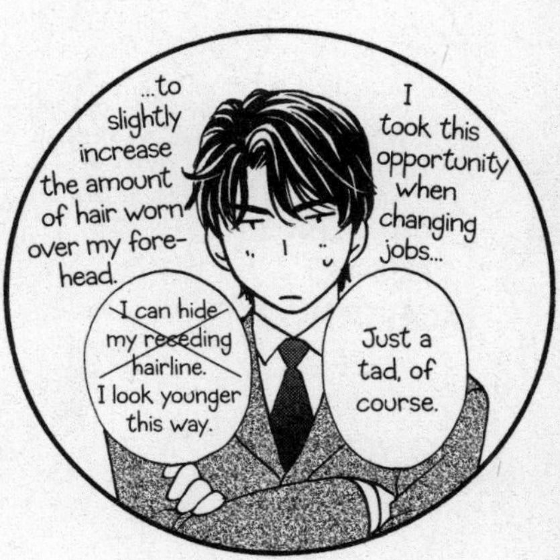
I took this opportunity when changing jobs...
...to slightly increase the amount of hair worn over my fore-head.
Just a tad, of course.
~~I can hide my receding hairline.~~ I look younger this way.

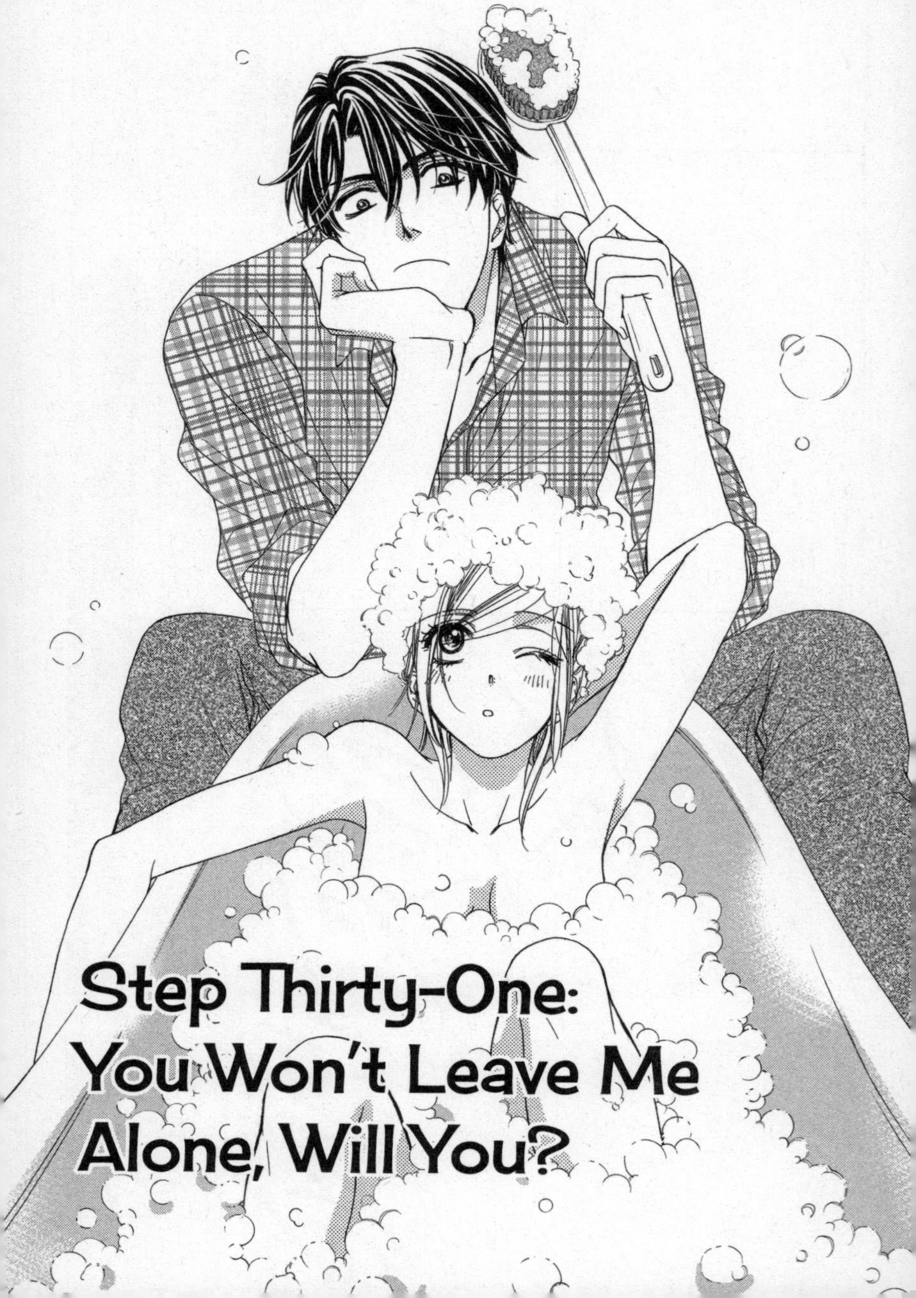

Step Thirty-One: You Won't Leave Me Alone, Will You?

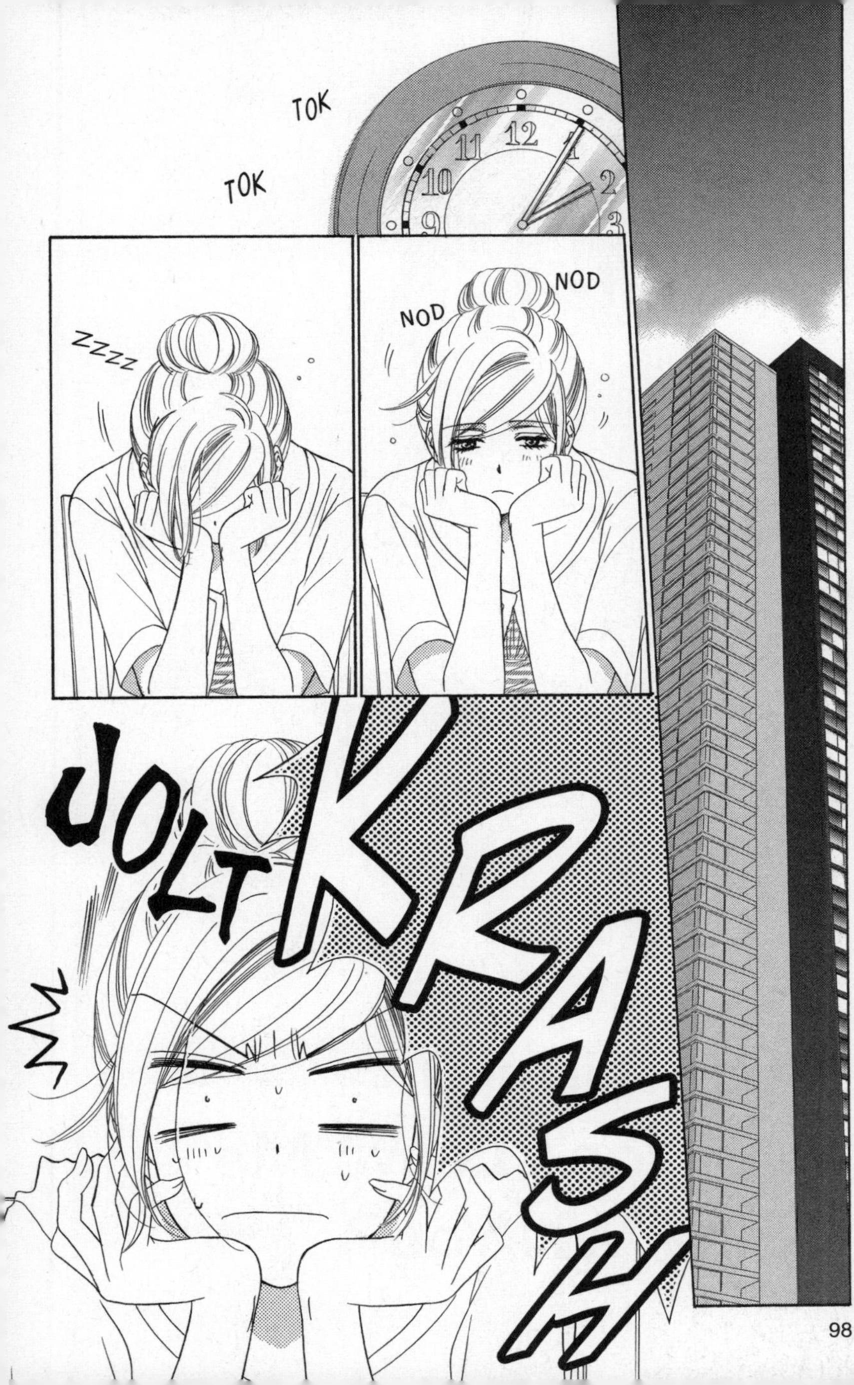
TOK
TOK
NOD
NOD
ZZZZ
KRASH
JOLT

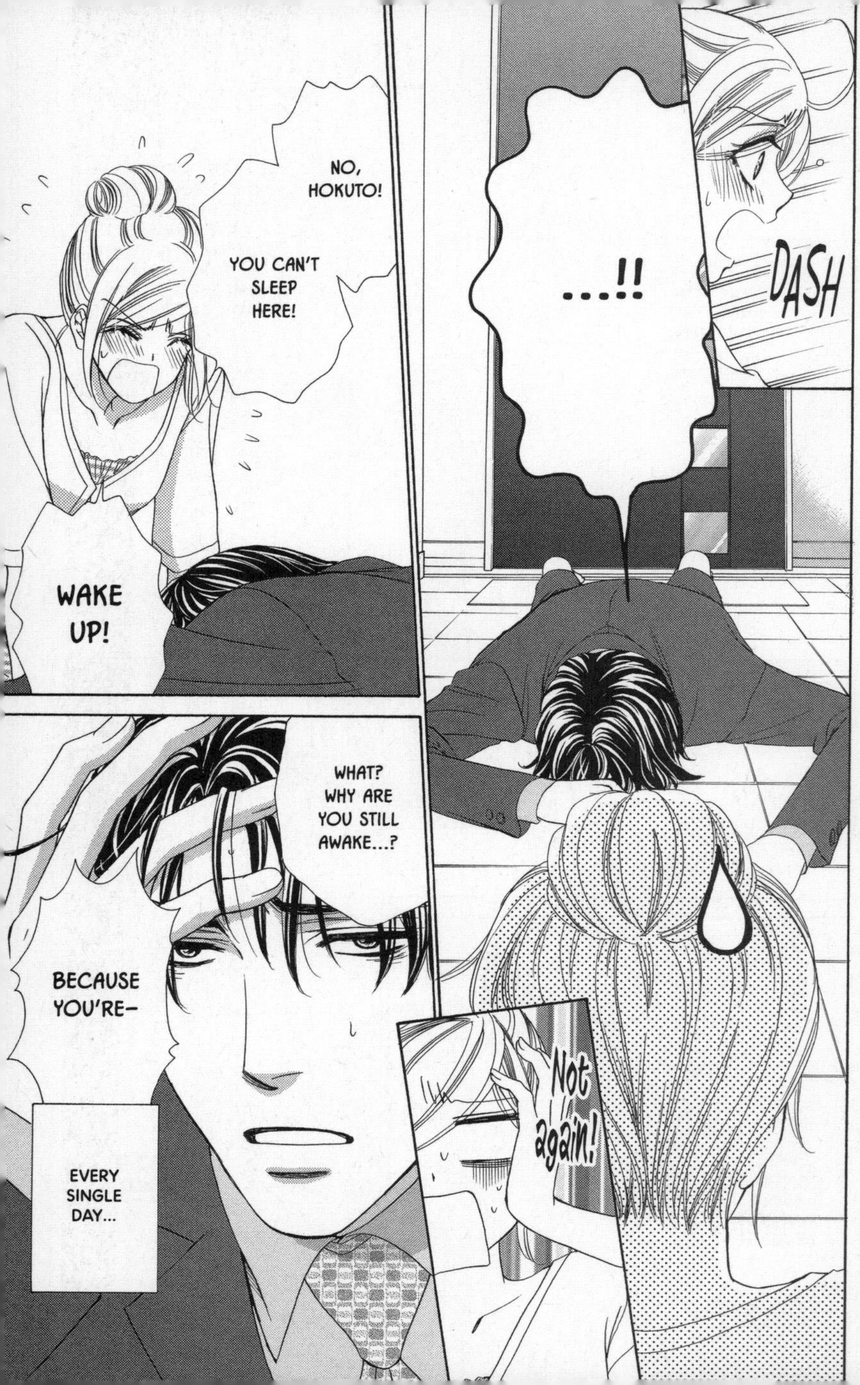

DASH
...!!
Not again!
NO, HOKUTO!
YOU CAN'T SLEEP HERE!
WAKE UP!
WHAT? WHY ARE YOU STILL AWAKE...?
BECAUSE YOU'RE—
EVERY SINGLE DAY...

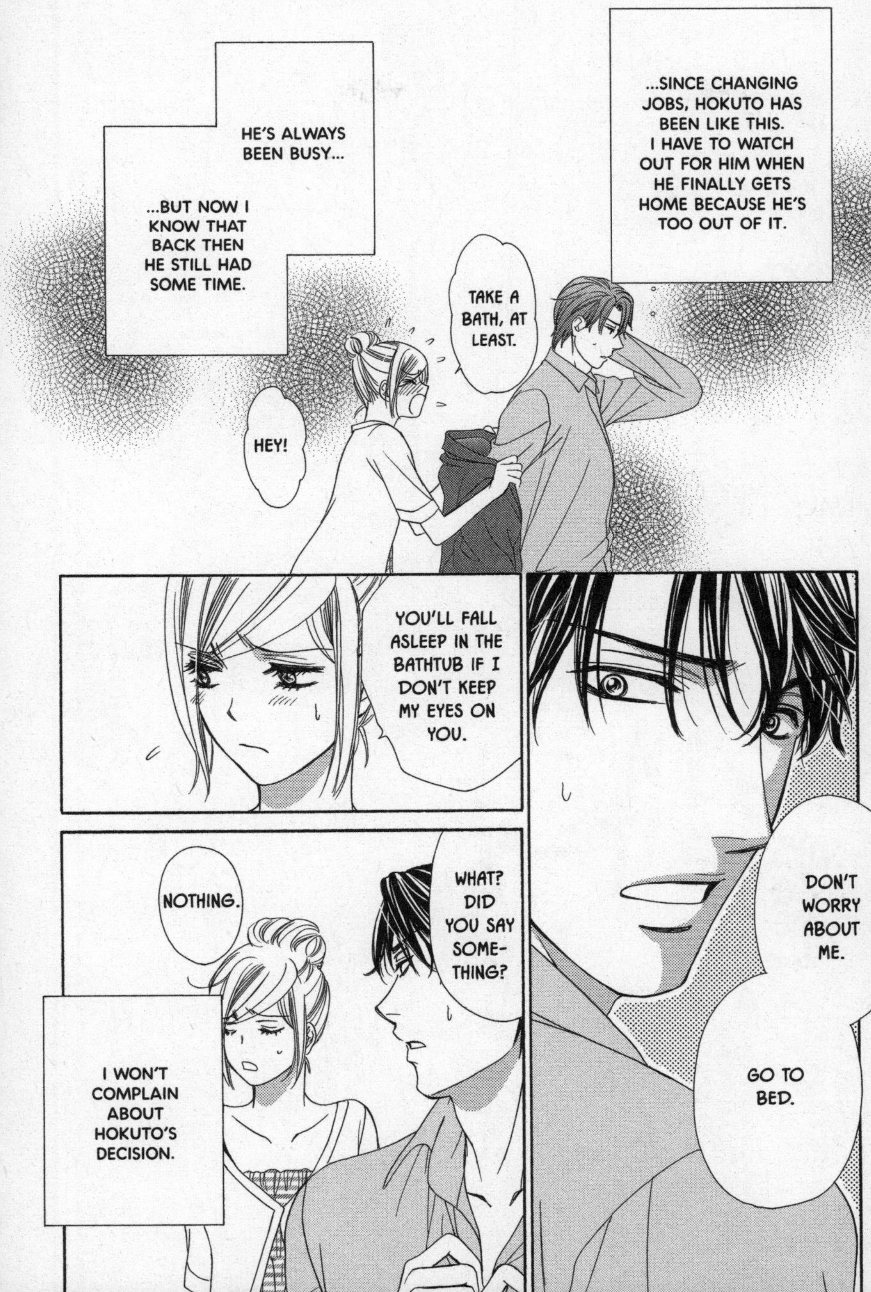
...SINCE CHANGING JOBS, HOKUTO HAS BEEN LIKE THIS. I HAVE TO WATCH OUT FOR HIM WHEN HE FINALLY GETS HOME BECAUSE HE'S TOO OUT OF IT.
HE'S ALWAYS BEEN BUSY...
...BUT NOW I KNOW THAT BACK THEN HE STILL HAD SOME TIME.
TAKE A BATH, AT LEAST.
HEY!
DON'T WORRY ABOUT ME.
GO TO BED.
YOU'LL FALL ASLEEP IN THE BATHTUB IF I DON'T KEEP MY EYES ON YOU.
WHAT? DID YOU SAY SOME-THING?
NOTHING.
I WON'T COMPLAIN ABOUT HOKUTO'S DECISION.

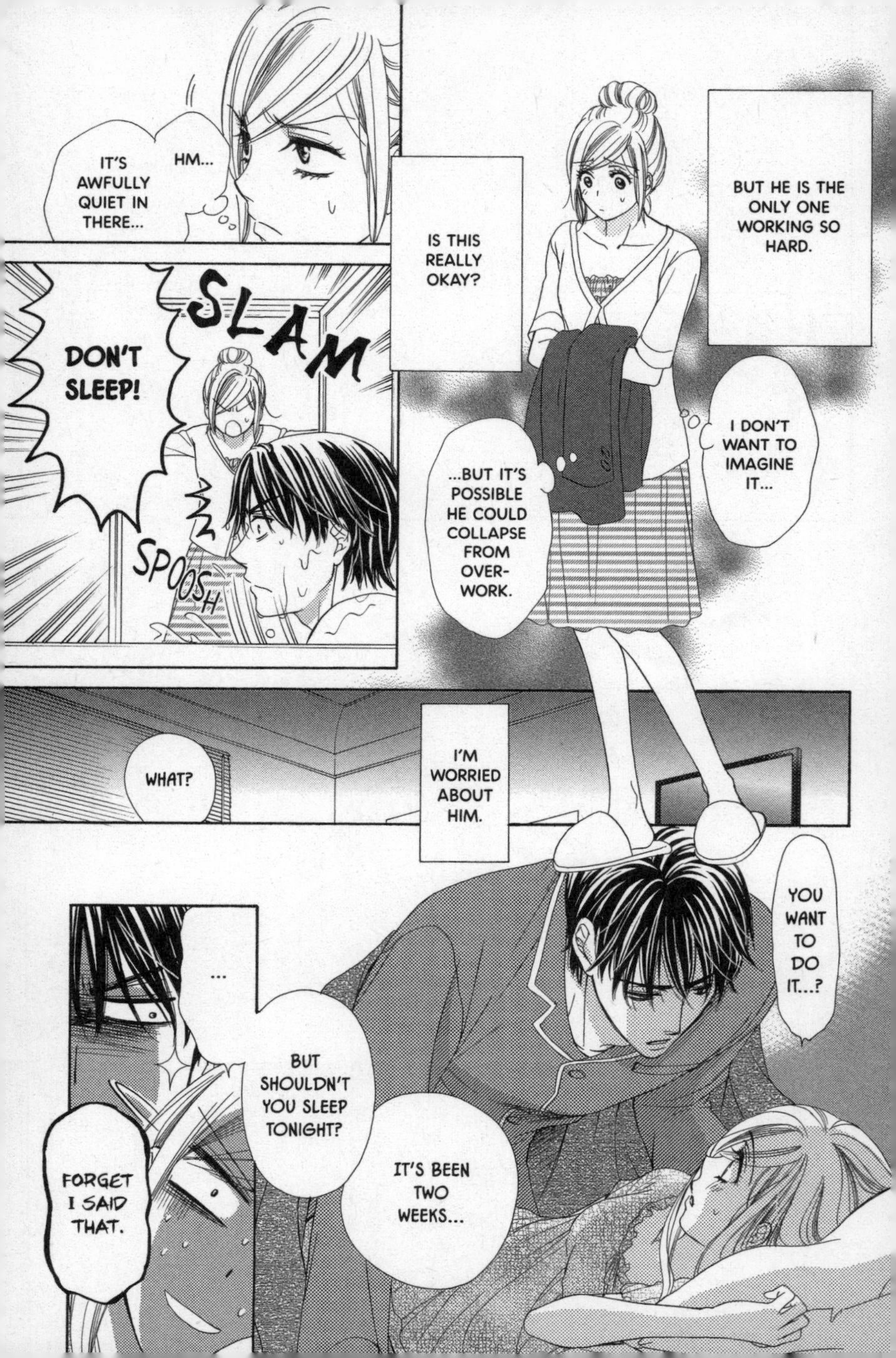
BUT HE IS THE ONLY ONE WORKING SO HARD.
IS THIS REALLY OKAY?
I DON'T WANT TO IMAGINE IT...
...BUT IT'S POSSIBLE HE COULD COLLAPSE FROM OVER-WORK.
HM...
IT'S AWFULLY QUIET IN THERE...
SLAM
DON'T SLEEP!
SPOOSH
I'M WORRIED ABOUT HIM.
WHAT?
YOU WANT TO DO IT...?
BUT SHOULDN'T YOU SLEEP TONIGHT?
IT'S BEEN TWO WEEKS...
...
FORGET I SAID THAT.

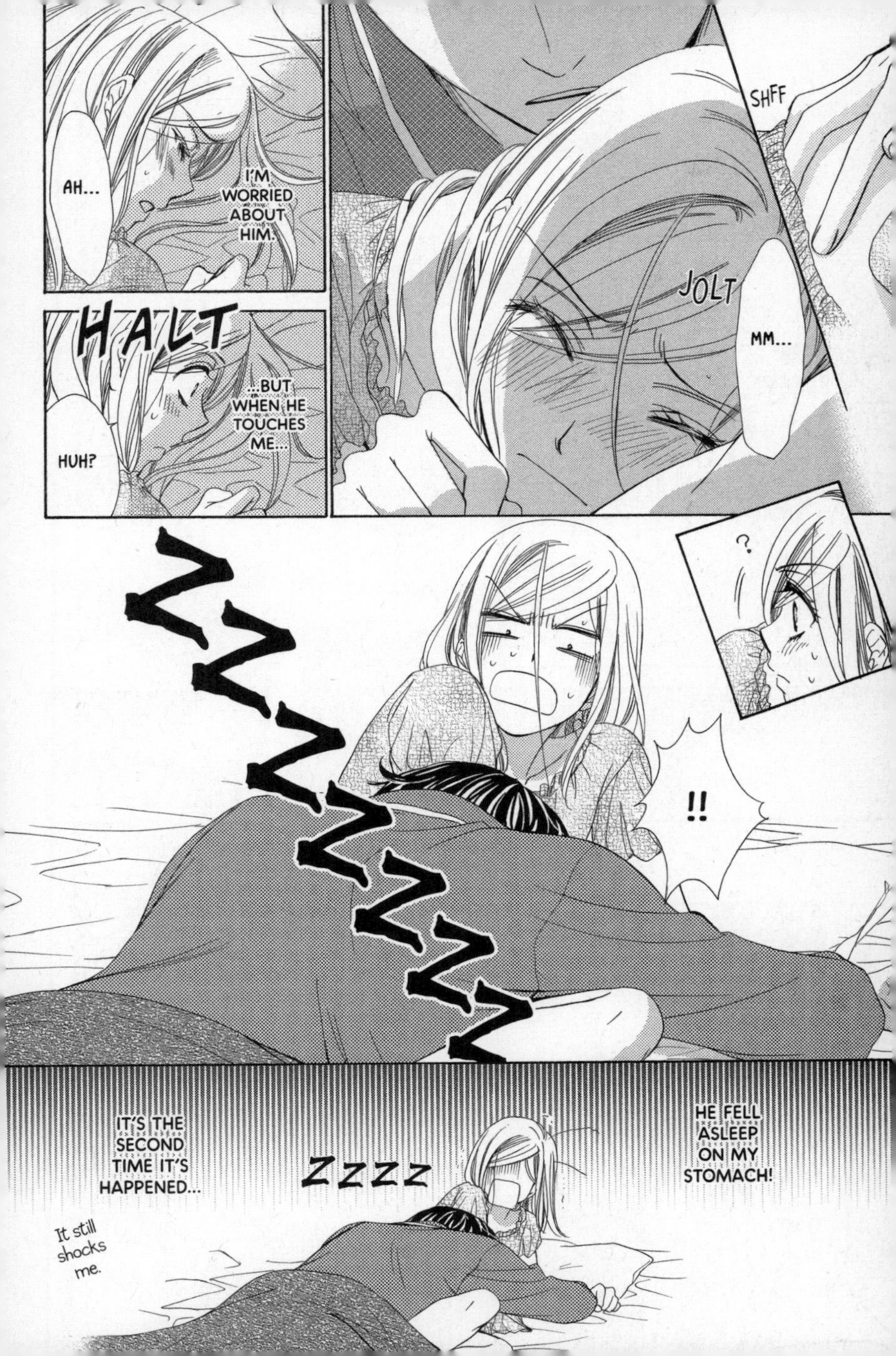
SHFF
JOLT
MM...
I'M WORRIED ABOUT HIM.
AH...
HALT
...BUT WHEN HE TOUCHES ME...
HUH?
?
!!
ZZZZZZZZ
HE FELL ASLEEP ON MY STOMACH!
ZZZZ
IT'S THE SECOND TIME IT'S HAPPENED...
It still shocks me.

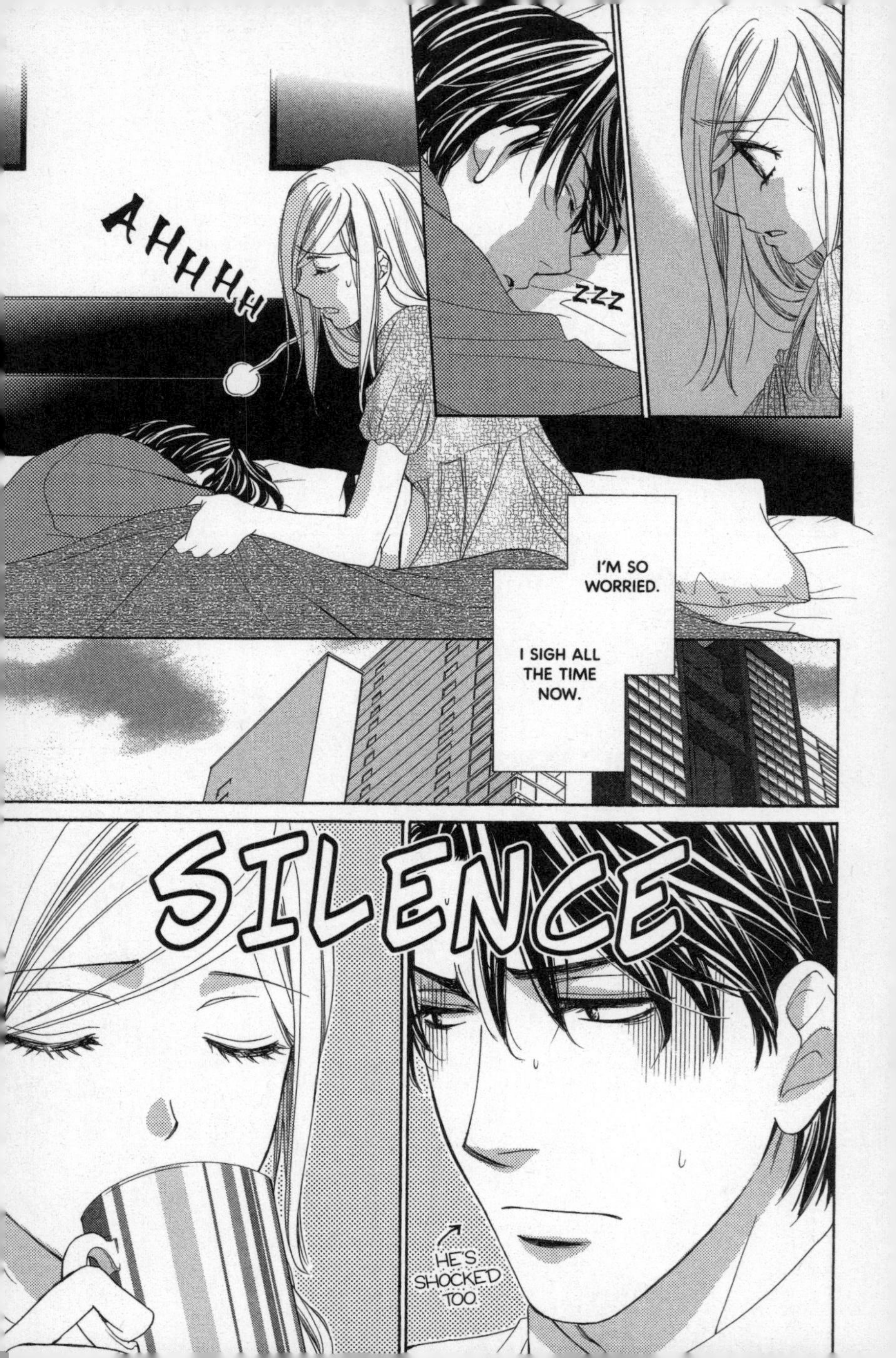
ZZZ
AHHHHH
I'M SO WORRIED.
I SIGH ALL THE TIME NOW.
SILENCE
HE'S SHOCKED TOO.

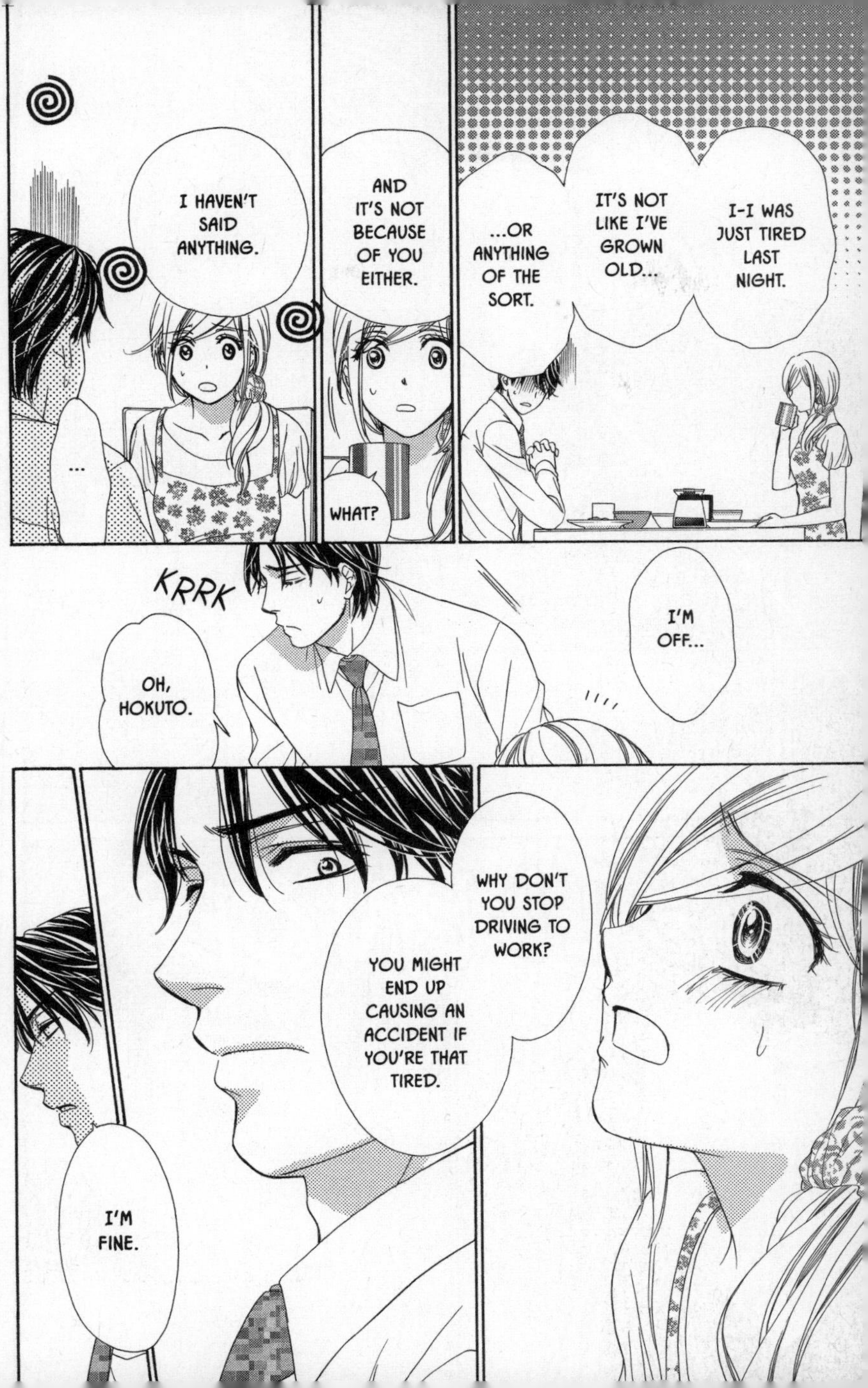
I-I WAS JUST TIRED LAST NIGHT.
IT'S NOT LIKE I'VE GROWN OLD...
...OR ANYTHING OF THE SORT.
AND IT'S NOT BECAUSE OF YOU EITHER.
WHAT?
I HAVEN'T SAID ANYTHING.
...
I'M OFF...
KRRK
OH, HOKUTO.
WHY DON'T YOU STOP DRIVING TO WORK?
YOU MIGHT END UP CAUSING AN ACCIDENT IF YOU'RE THAT TIRED.
I'M FINE.

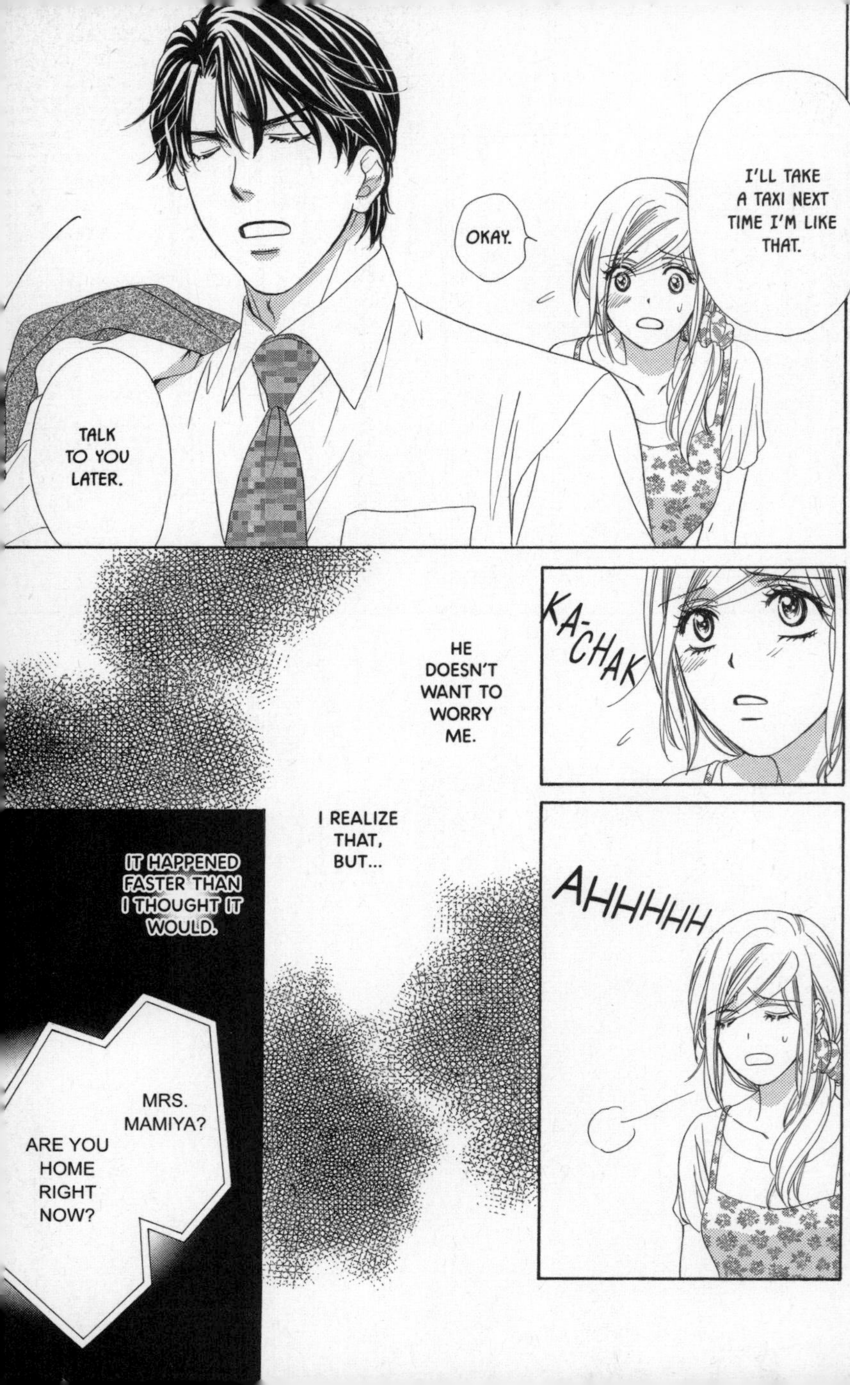
I'LL TAKE A TAXI NEXT TIME I'M LIKE THAT.
OKAY.
TALK TO YOU LATER.
KA-CHAK
HE DOESN'T WANT TO WORRY ME.
AHHHHH
I REALIZE THAT, BUT...
IT HAPPENED FASTER THAN I THOUGHT IT WOULD.
MRS. MAMIYA? ARE YOU HOME RIGHT NOW?

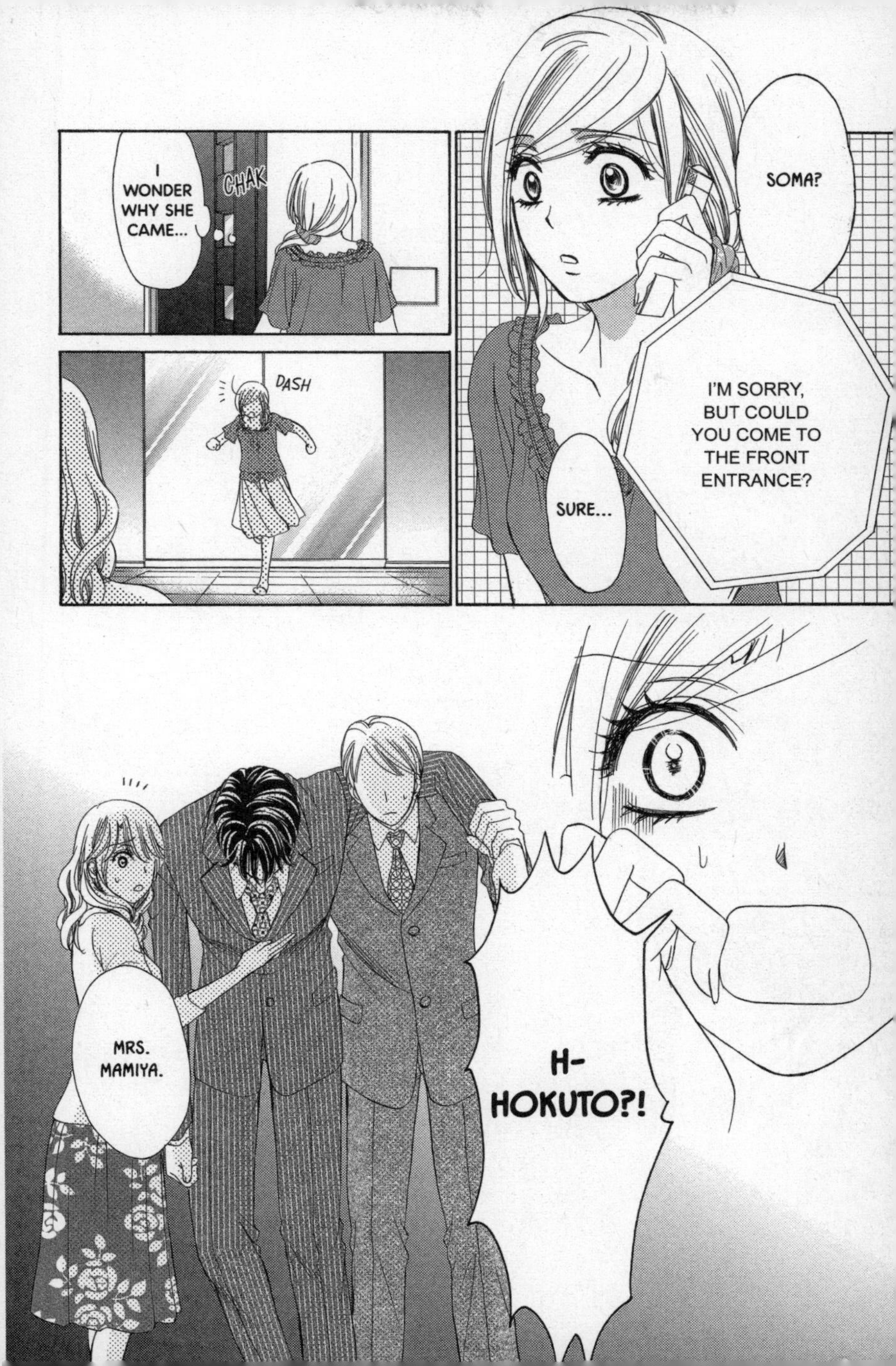
SOMA?
I'M SORRY, BUT COULD YOU COME TO THE FRONT ENTRANCE?
SURE...
I WONDER WHY SHE CAME...
CHAK
DASH
H- HOKUTO?!
MRS. MAMIYA.

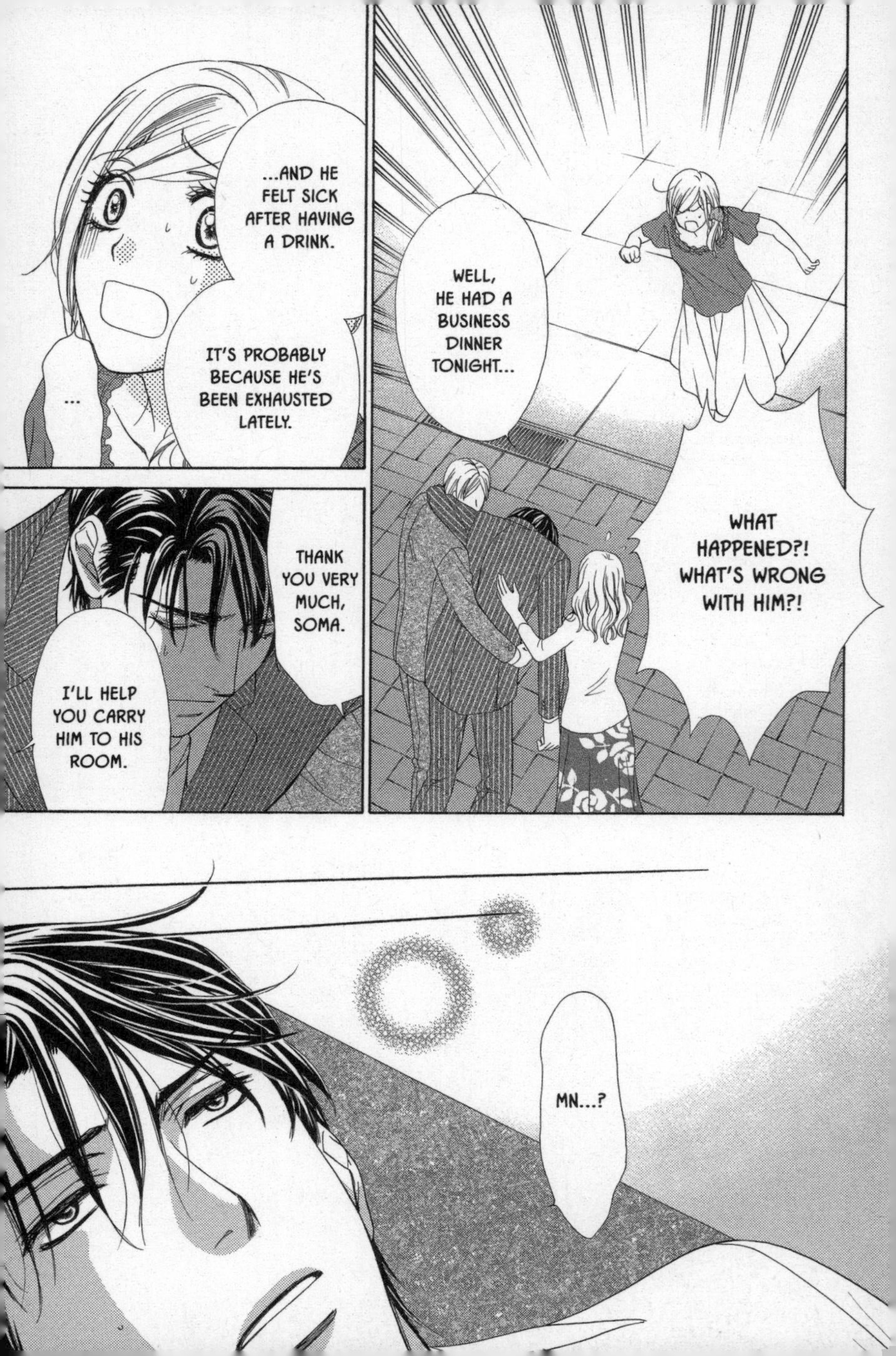
WHAT HAPPENED?! WHAT'S WRONG WITH HIM?!
WELL, HE HAD A BUSINESS DINNER TONIGHT...
...AND HE FELT SICK AFTER HAVING A DRINK.
IT'S PROBABLY BECAUSE HE'S BEEN EXHAUSTED LATELY.
...
THANK YOU VERY MUCH, SOMA.
I'LL HELP YOU CARRY HIM TO HIS ROOM.
MN...?

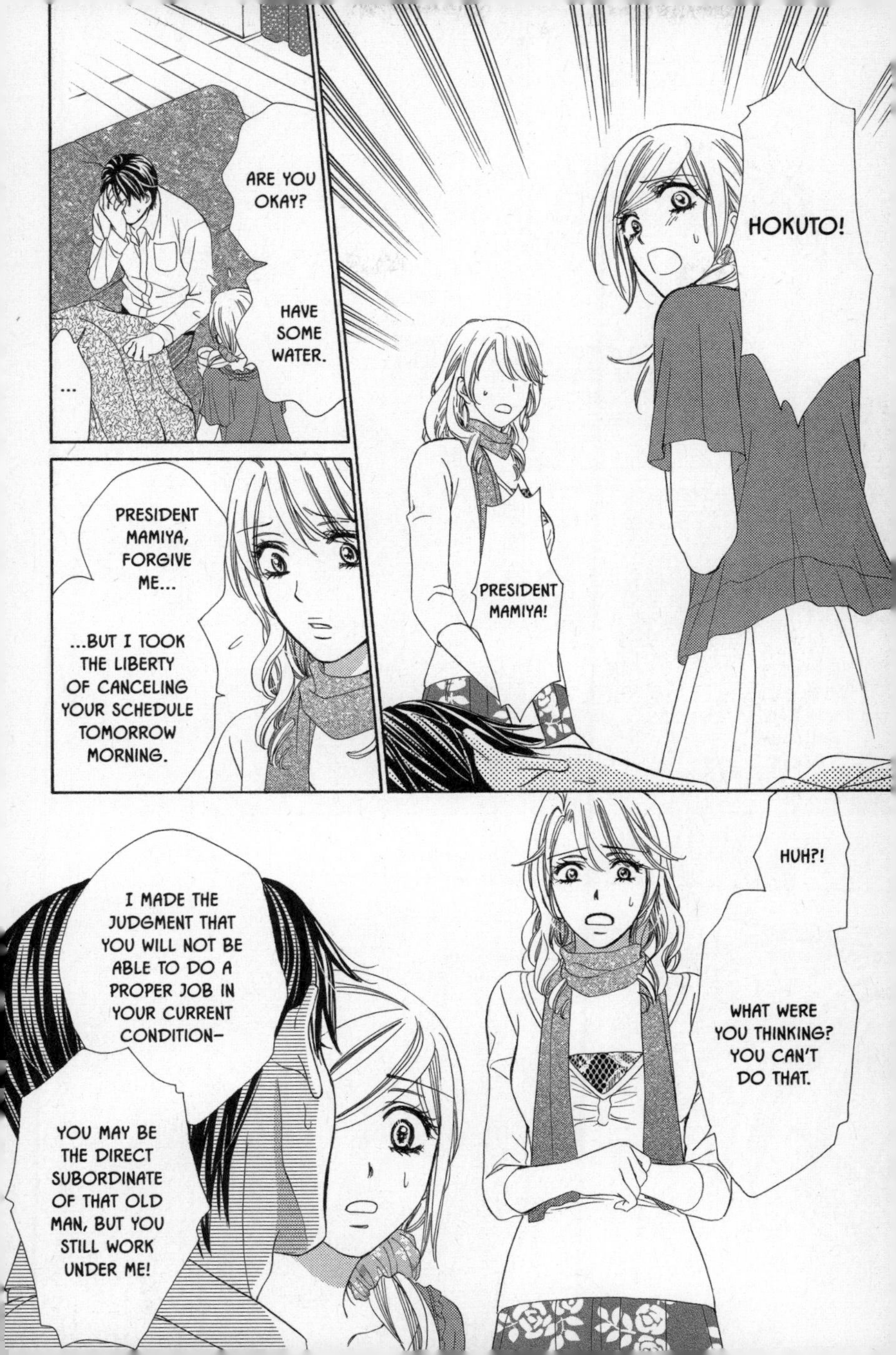
HOKUTO!
PRESIDENT MAMIYA!
ARE YOU OKAY?
HAVE SOME WATER.
...
PRESIDENT MAMIYA, FORGIVE ME...
...BUT I TOOK THE LIBERTY OF CANCELING YOUR SCHEDULE TOMORROW MORNING.
HUH?!
WHAT WERE YOU THINKING? YOU CAN'T DO THAT.
I MADE THE JUDGMENT THAT YOU WILL NOT BE ABLE TO DO A PROPER JOB IN YOUR CURRENT CONDITION–
YOU MAY BE THE DIRECT SUBORDINATE OF THAT OLD MAN, BUT YOU STILL WORK UNDER ME!

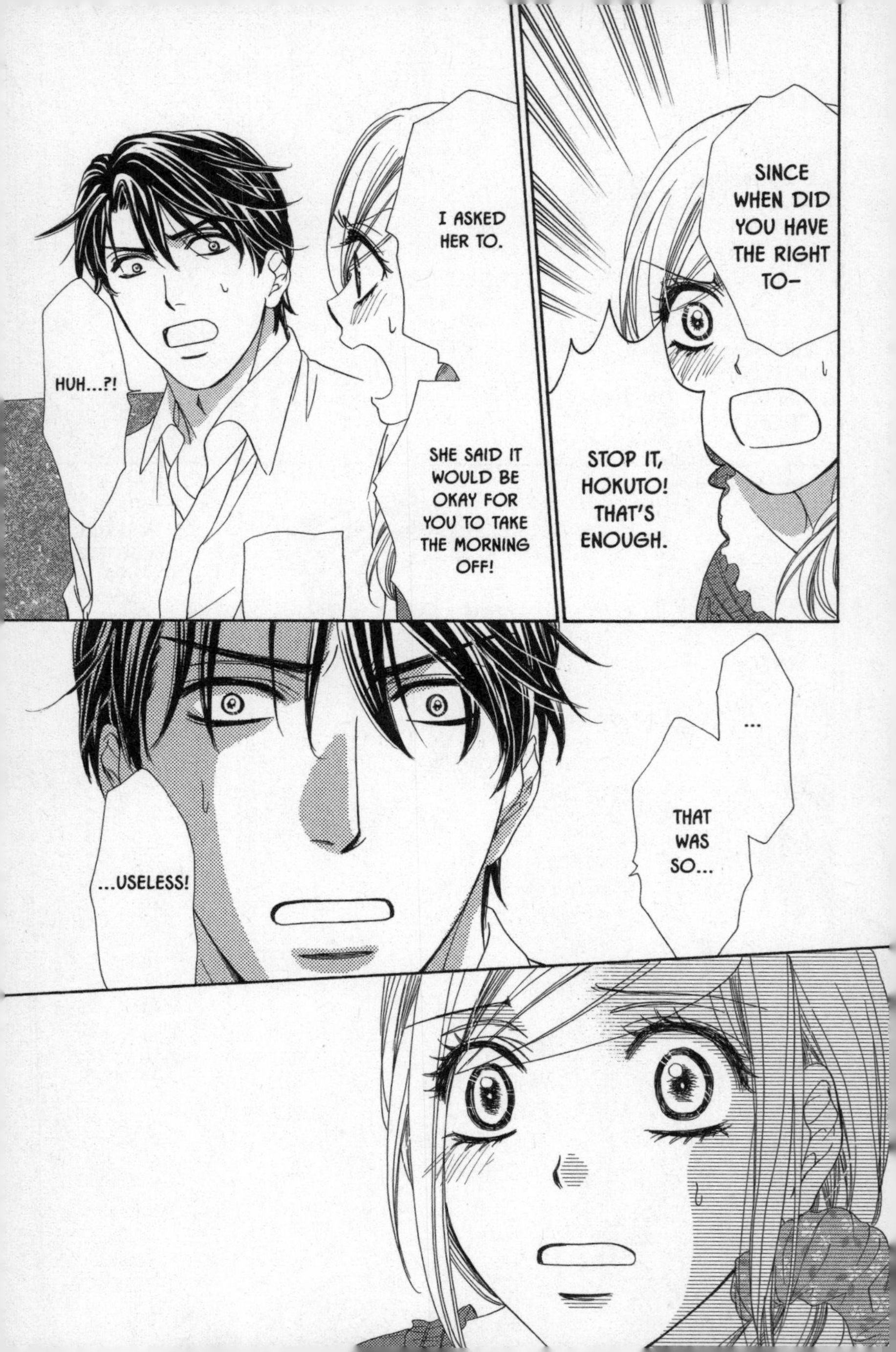
SINCE WHEN DID YOU HAVE THE RIGHT TO–
STOP IT, HOKUTO! THAT'S ENOUGH.
I ASKED HER TO.
SHE SAID IT WOULD BE OKAY FOR YOU TO TAKE THE MORNING OFF!
HUH...?!
...
THAT WAS SO...
...USELESS!

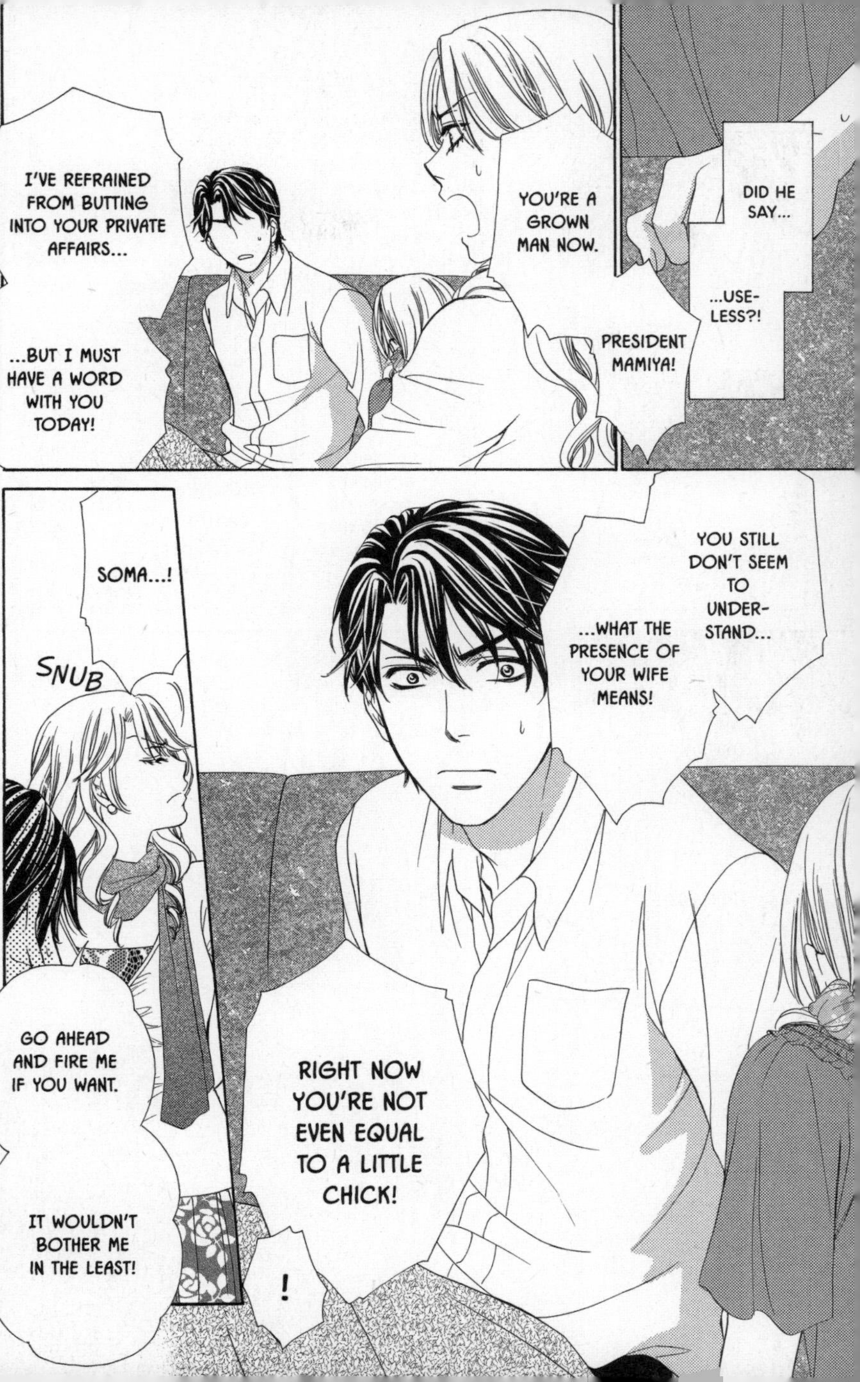
DID HE SAY...
...USE-LESS?!
PRESIDENT MAMIYA!
YOU'RE A GROWN MAN NOW.
I'VE REFRAINED FROM BUTTING INTO YOUR PRIVATE AFFAIRS...
...BUT I MUST HAVE A WORD WITH YOU TODAY!
YOU STILL DON'T SEEM TO UNDER-STAND...
...WHAT THE PRESENCE OF YOUR WIFE MEANS!
RIGHT NOW YOU'RE NOT EVEN EQUAL TO A LITTLE CHICK!
!
SOMA...!
SNUB
GO AHEAD AND FIRE ME IF YOU WANT.
IT WOULDN'T BOTHER ME IN THE LEAST!

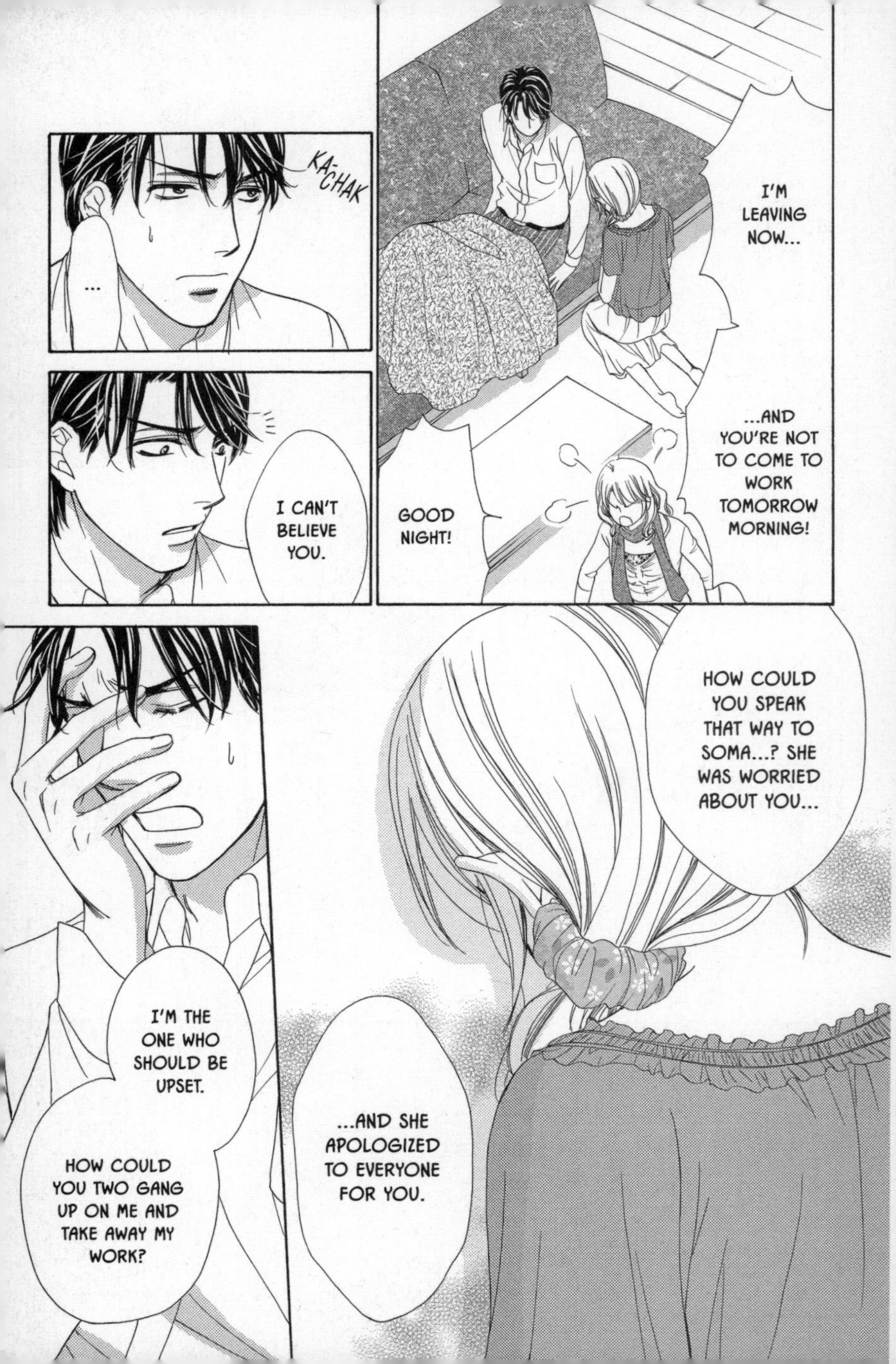

I'M LEAVING NOW...
...AND YOU'RE NOT TO COME TO WORK TOMORROW MORNING!
GOOD NIGHT!
KA-CHAK
...
I CAN'T BELIEVE YOU.
HOW COULD YOU SPEAK THAT WAY TO SOMA...? SHE WAS WORRIED ABOUT YOU...
...AND SHE APOLOGIZED TO EVERYONE FOR YOU.
I'M THE ONE WHO SHOULD BE UPSET.
HOW COULD YOU TWO GANG UP ON ME AND TAKE AWAY MY WORK?

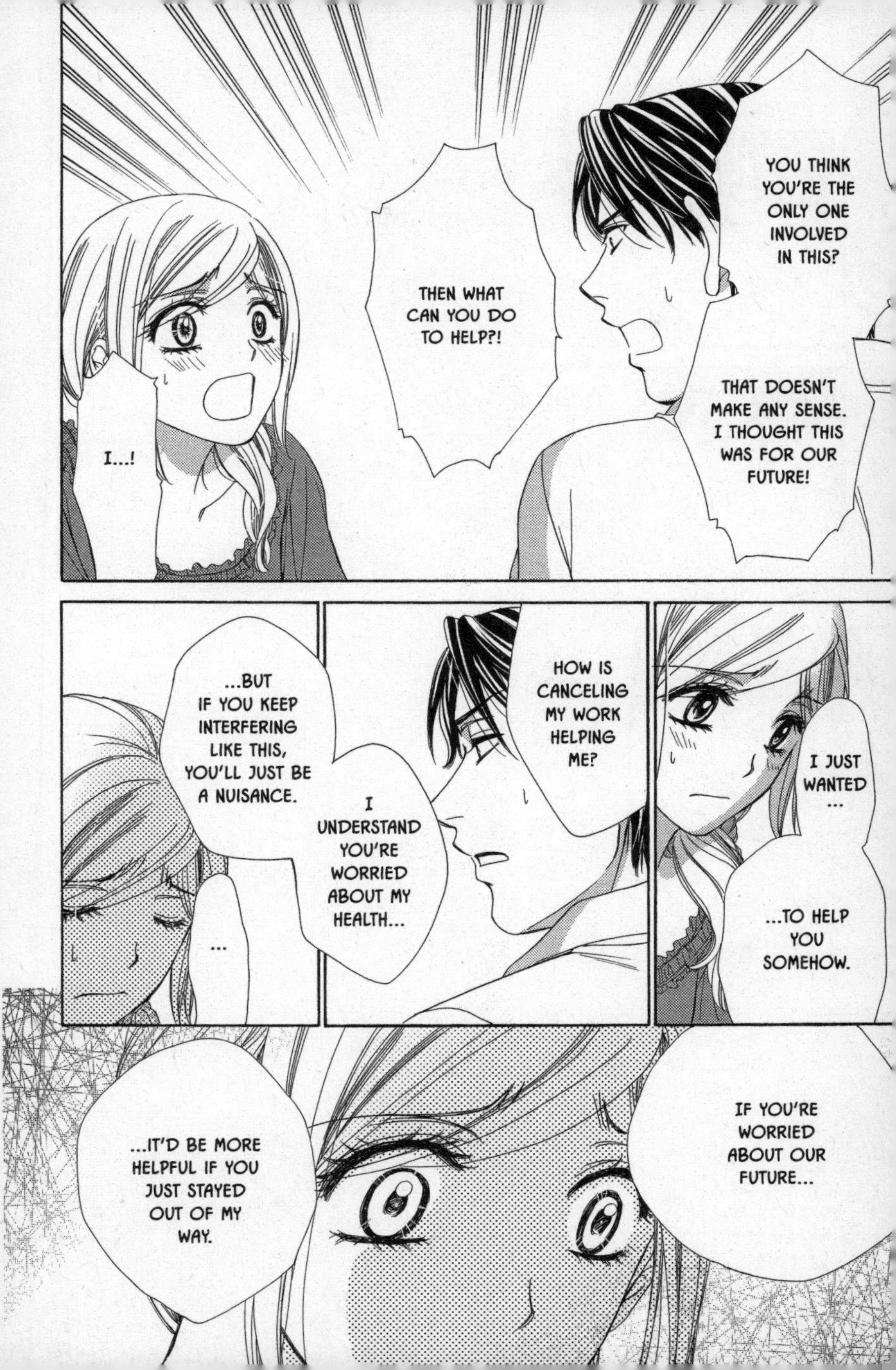
YOU THINK YOU'RE THE ONLY ONE INVOLVED IN THIS?
THAT DOESN'T MAKE ANY SENSE. I THOUGHT THIS WAS FOR OUR FUTURE!
THEN WHAT CAN YOU DO TO HELP?!
I...!
I JUST WANTED ...
...TO HELP YOU SOMEHOW.
HOW IS CANCELING MY WORK HELPING ME?
I UNDERSTAND YOU'RE WORRIED ABOUT MY HEALTH...
...BUT IF YOU KEEP INTERFERING LIKE THIS, YOU'LL JUST BE A NUISANCE.
...
IF YOU'RE WORRIED ABOUT OUR FUTURE...
...IT'D BE MORE HELPFUL IF YOU JUST STAYED OUT OF MY WAY.

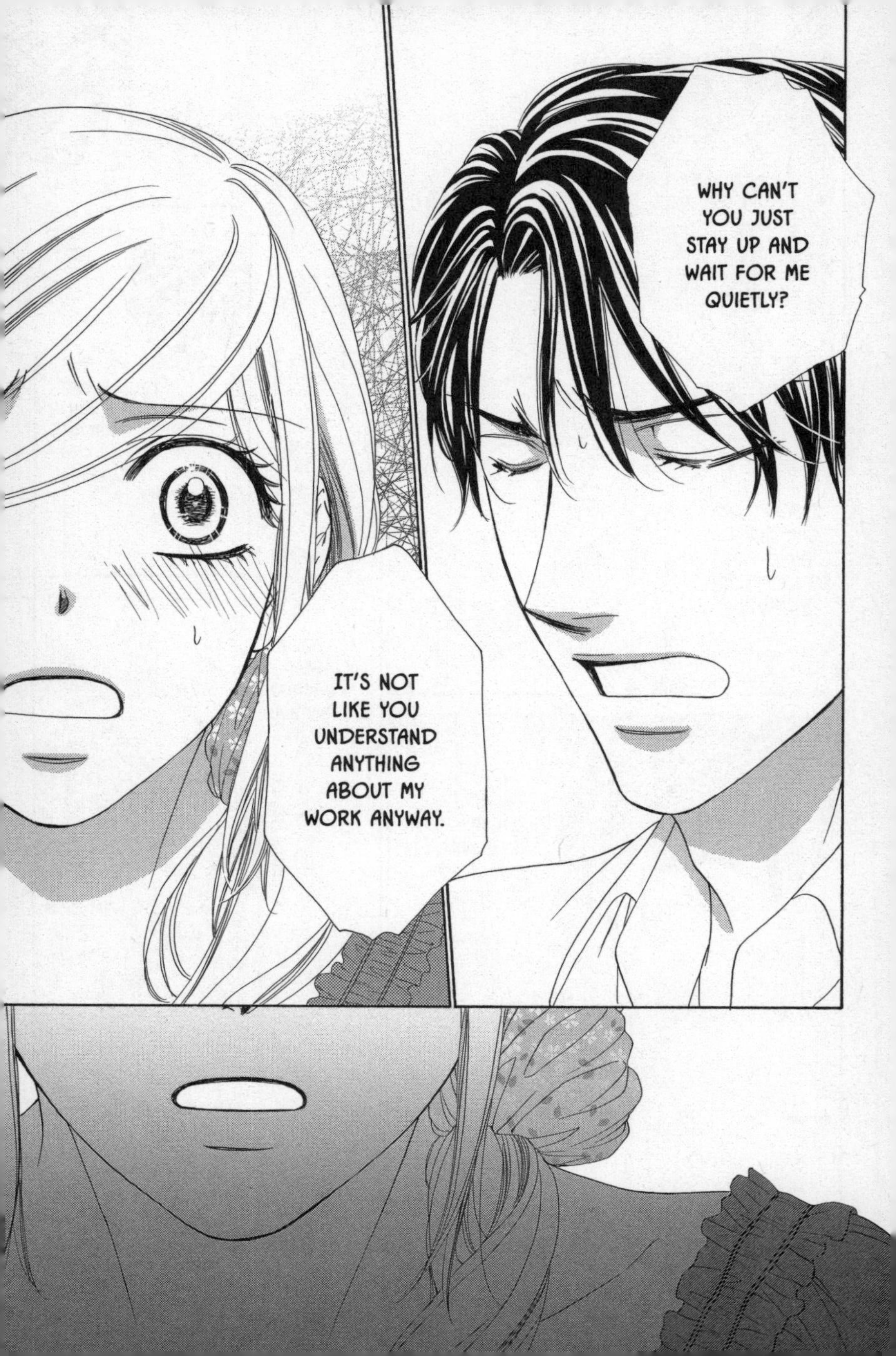
WHY CAN'T YOU JUST STAY UP AND WAIT FOR ME QUIETLY?
IT'S NOT LIKE YOU UNDERSTAND ANYTHING ABOUT MY WORK ANYWAY.

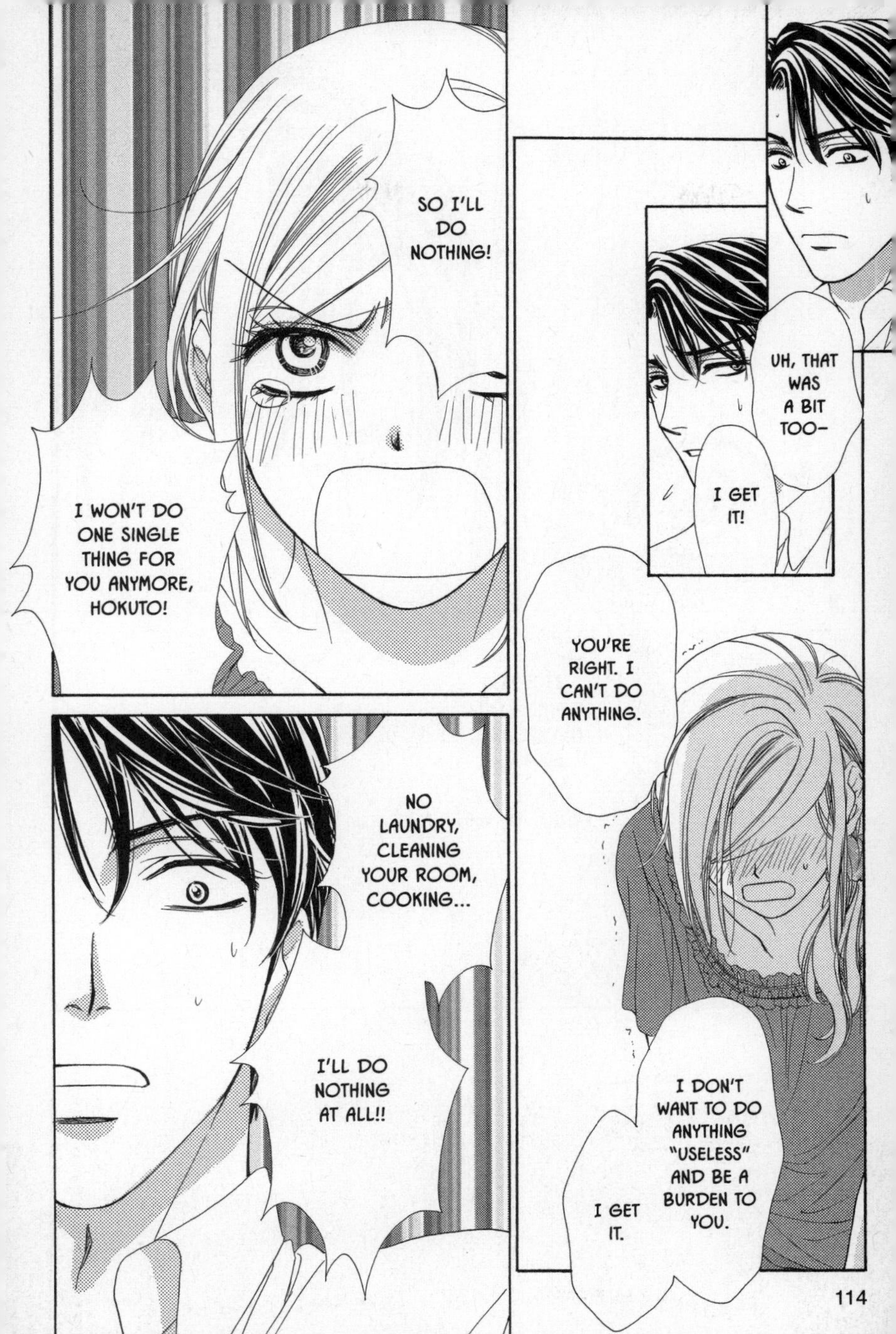
UH, THAT WAS A BIT TOO—
I GET IT!
YOU'RE RIGHT. I CAN'T DO ANYTHING.
I DON'T WANT TO DO ANYTHING "USELESS" AND BE A BURDEN TO YOU.
I GET IT.
SO I'LL DO NOTHING!
I WON'T DO ONE SINGLE THING FOR YOU ANYMORE, HOKUTO!
NO LAUNDRY, CLEANING YOUR ROOM, COOKING...
I'LL DO NOTHING AT ALL!!

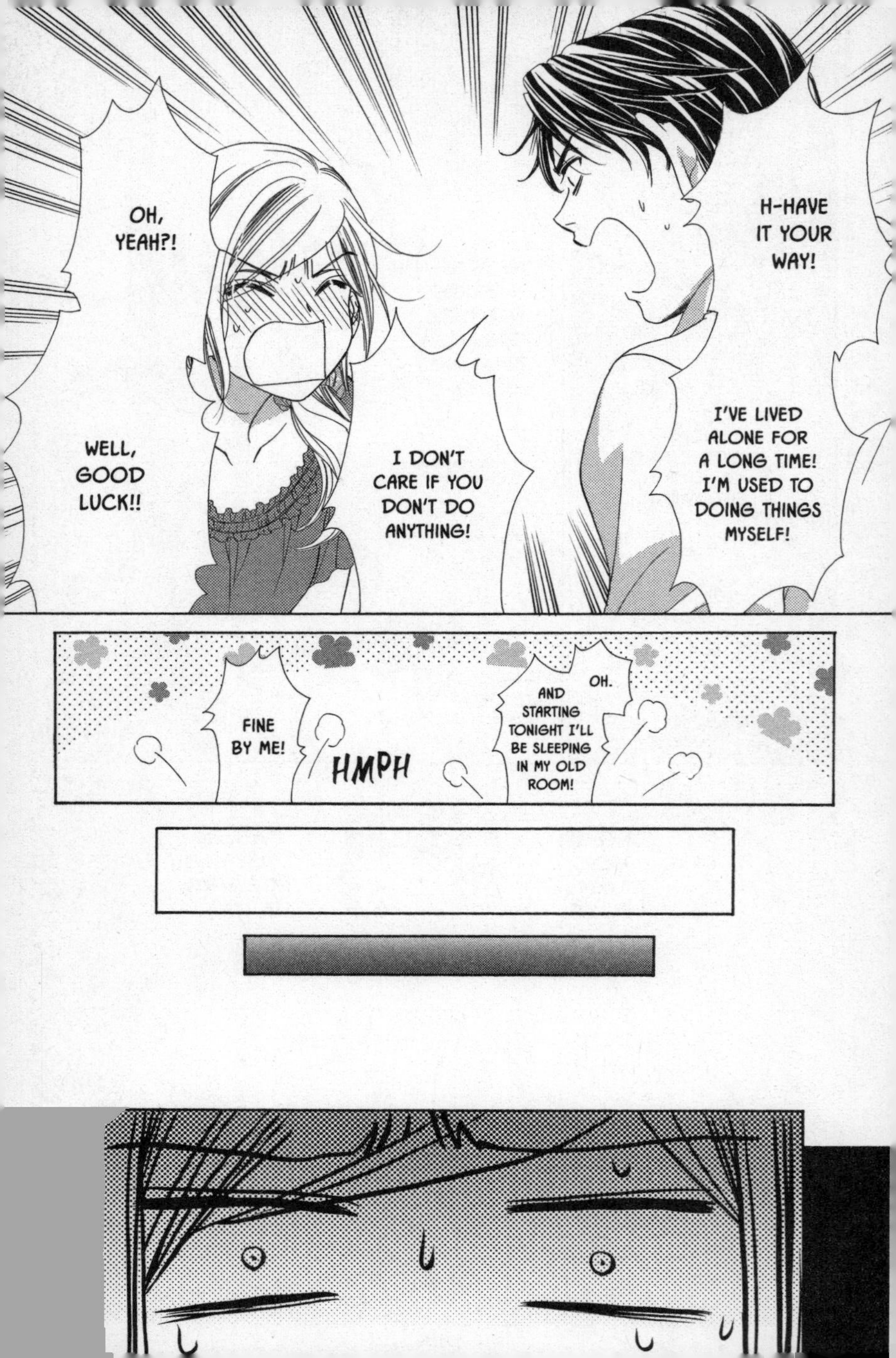
H-HAVE IT YOUR WAY!
I'VE LIVED ALONE FOR A LONG TIME! I'M USED TO DOING THINGS MYSELF!
I DON'T CARE IF YOU DON'T DO ANYTHING!
OH, YEAH?!
WELL, GOOD LUCK!!
OH.
AND STARTING TONIGHT I'LL BE SLEEPING IN MY OLD ROOM!
FINE BY ME!
HMPH

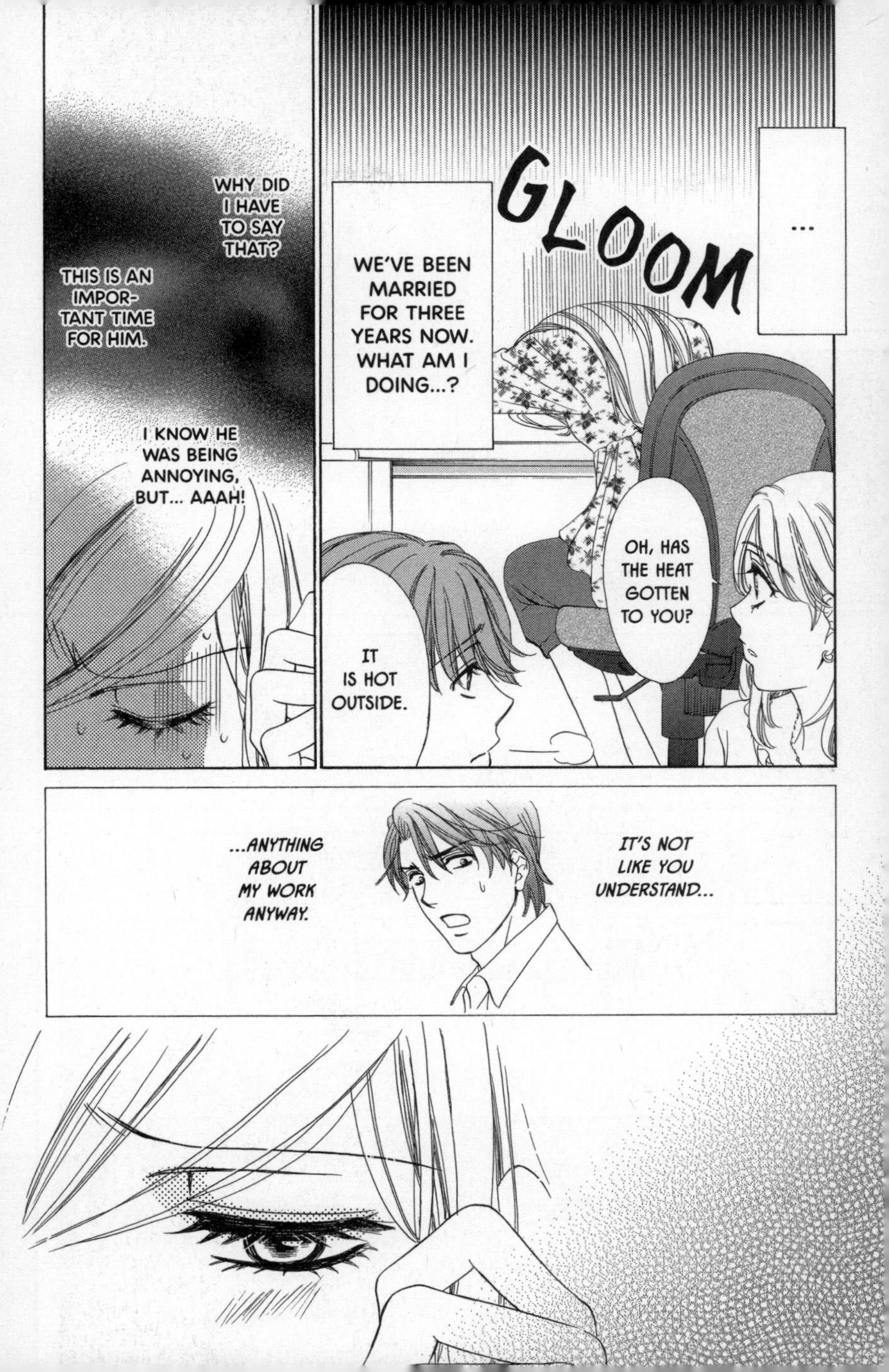
...
GLOOM
WE'VE BEEN MARRIED FOR THREE YEARS NOW. WHAT AM I DOING...?
OH, HAS THE HEAT GOTTEN TO YOU?
IT IS HOT OUTSIDE.
WHY DID I HAVE TO SAY THAT?
THIS IS AN IMPOR-TANT TIME FOR HIM.
I KNOW HE WAS BEING ANNOYING, BUT... AAAH!
IT'S NOT LIKE YOU UNDERSTAND...
...ANYTHING ABOUT MY WORK ANYWAY.

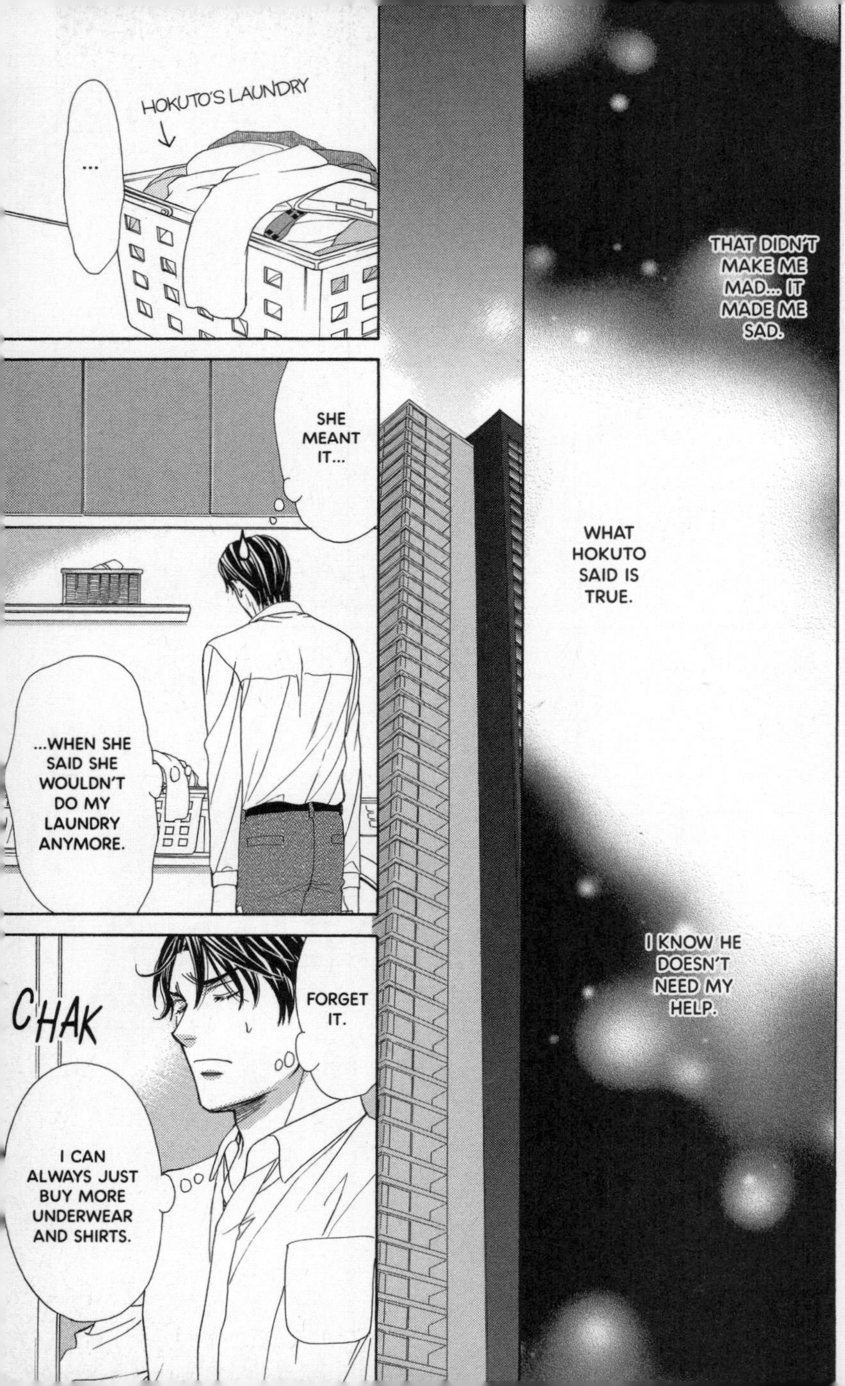
THAT DIDN'T MAKE ME MAD... IT MADE ME SAD.
WHAT HOKUTO SAID IS TRUE.
I KNOW HE DOESN'T NEED MY HELP.
...
HOKUTO'S LAUNDRY
SHE MEANT IT...
...WHEN SHE SAID SHE WOULDN'T DO MY LAUNDRY ANYMORE.
FORGET IT.
CHAK
I CAN ALWAYS JUST BUY MORE UNDERWEAR AND SHIRTS.

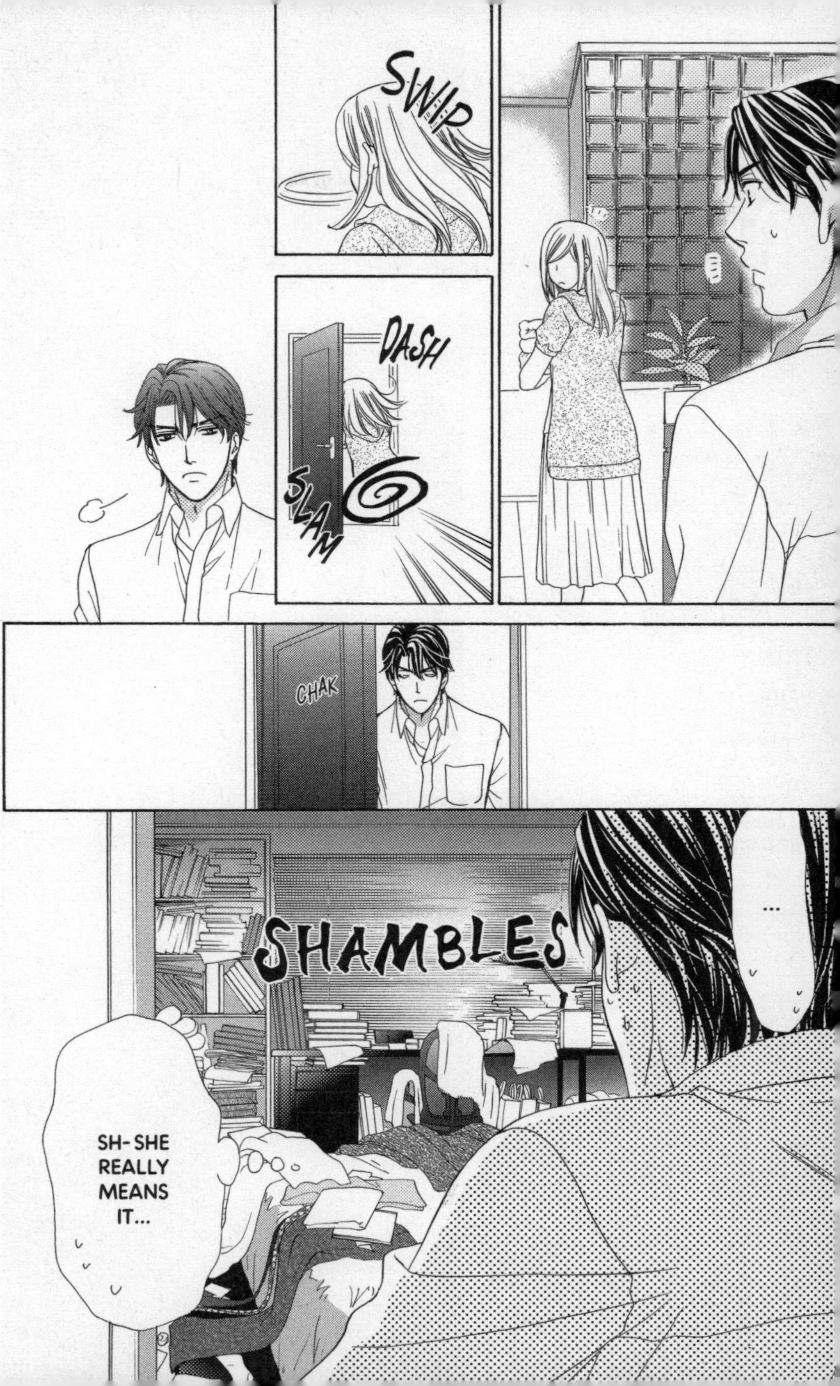
SWIR
DASH
SLAM
CHAK
...
SHAMBLES
SH-SHE REALLY MEANS IT...

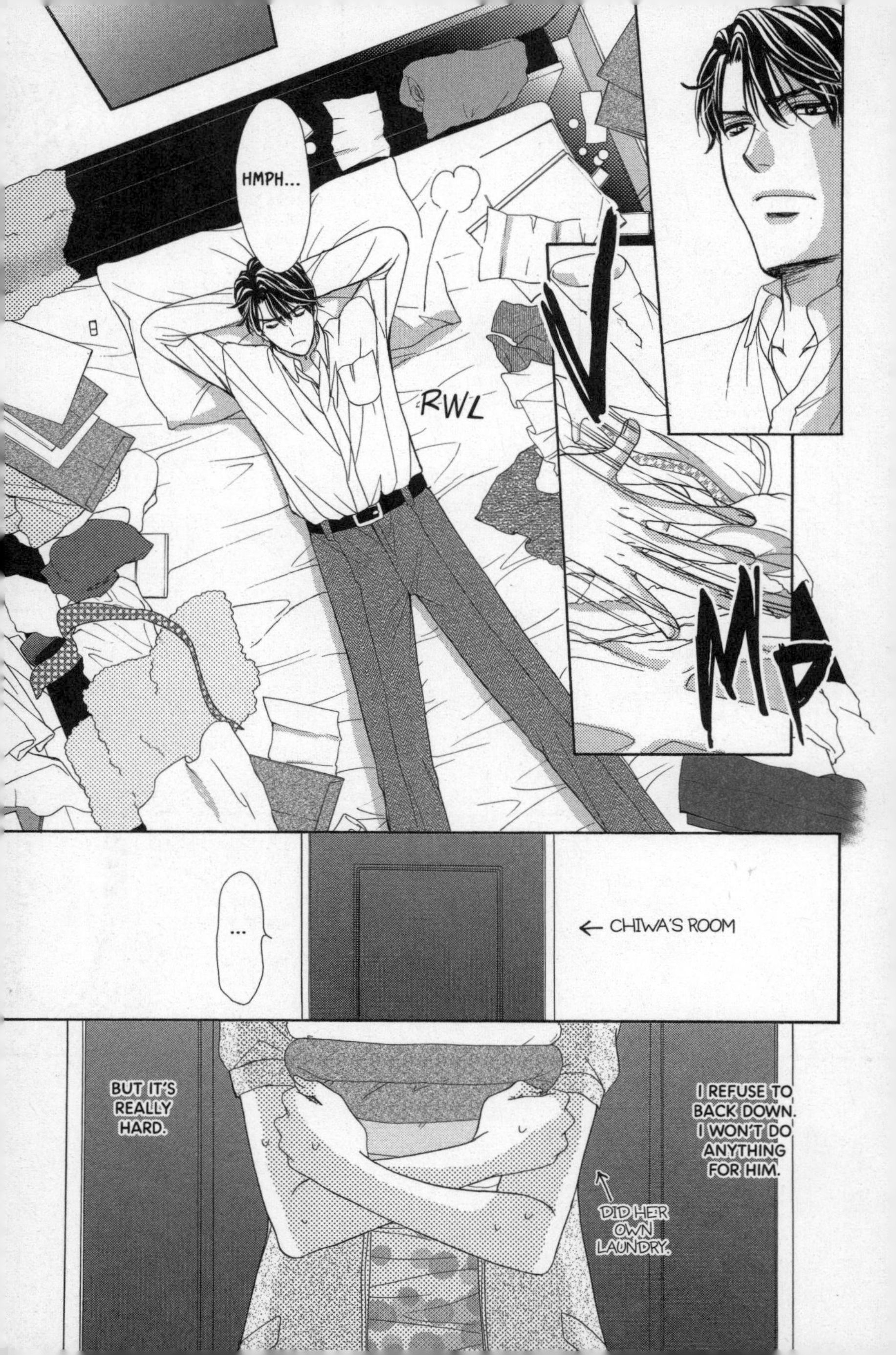
HMPH...
RWL
← CHIWA'S ROOM
...
I REFUSE TO BACK DOWN. I WON'T DO ANYTHING FOR HIM.
DID HER OWN LAUNDRY.
BUT IT'S REALLY HARD.

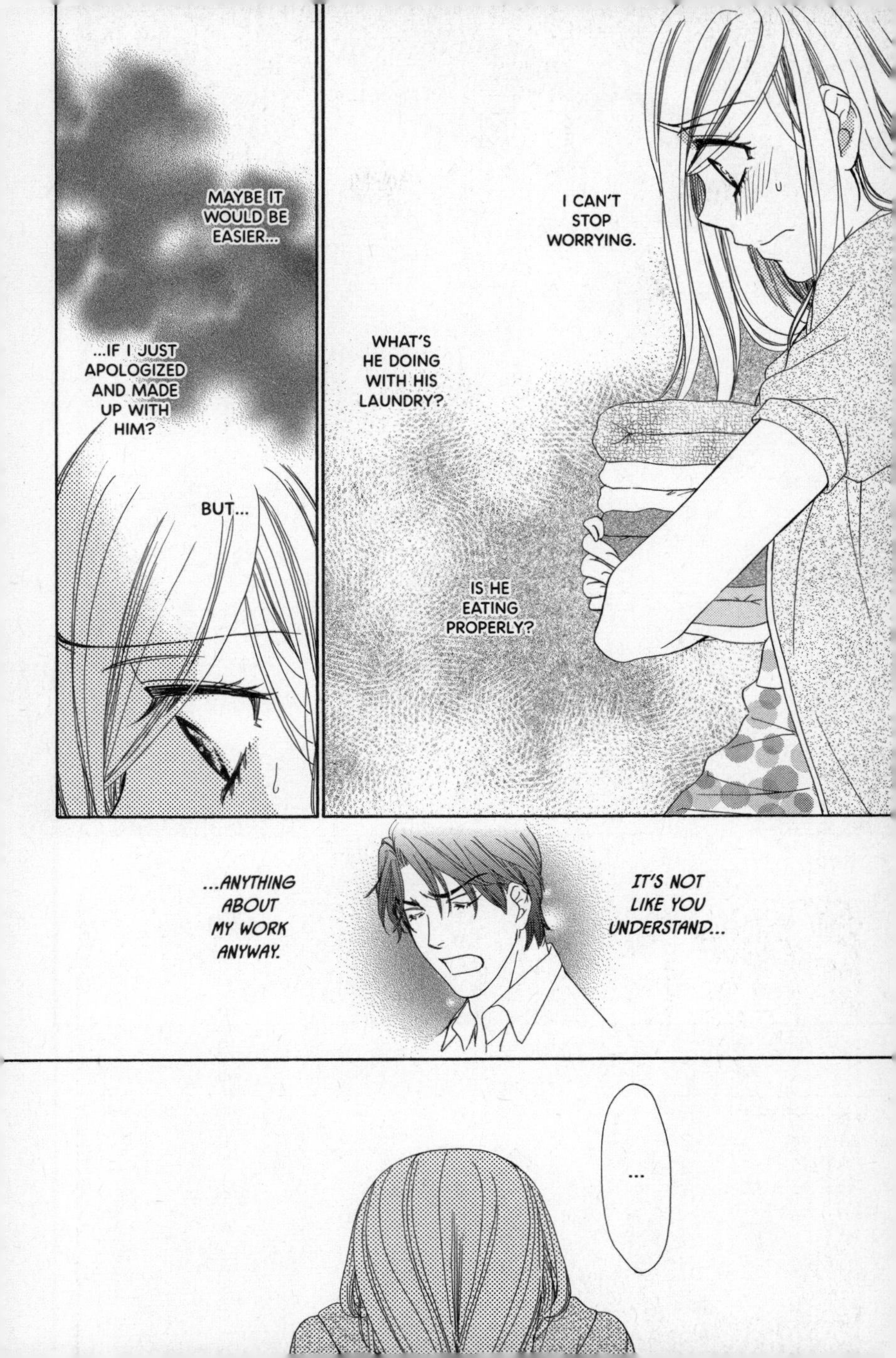
I CAN'T STOP WORRYING.
WHAT'S HE DOING WITH HIS LAUNDRY?
IS HE EATING PROPERLY?
MAYBE IT WOULD BE EASIER...
...IF I JUST APOLOGIZED AND MADE UP WITH HIM?
BUT...
IT'S NOT LIKE YOU UNDERSTAND...
...ANYTHING ABOUT MY WORK ANYWAY.
...

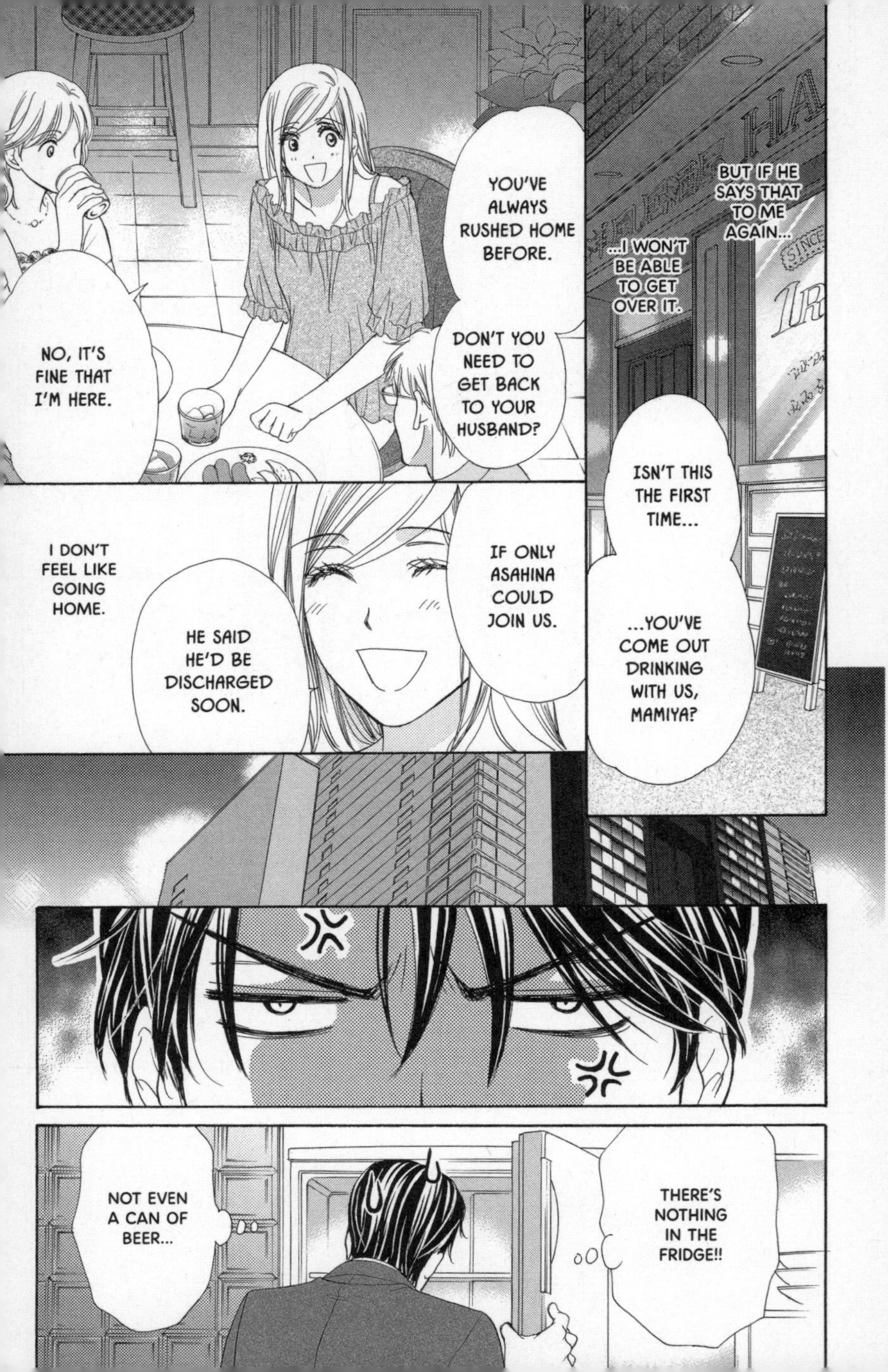
BUT IF HE SAYS THAT TO ME AGAIN...
...I WON'T BE ABLE TO GET OVER IT.
ISN'T THIS THE FIRST TIME...
...YOU'VE COME OUT DRINKING WITH US, MAMIYA?
YOU'VE ALWAYS RUSHED HOME BEFORE.
DON'T YOU NEED TO GET BACK TO YOUR HUSBAND?
NO, IT'S FINE THAT I'M HERE.
IF ONLY ASAHINA COULD JOIN US.
HE SAID HE'D BE DISCHARGED SOON.
I DON'T FEEL LIKE GOING HOME.
THERE'S NOTHING IN THE FRIDGE!!
NOT EVEN A CAN OF BEER...

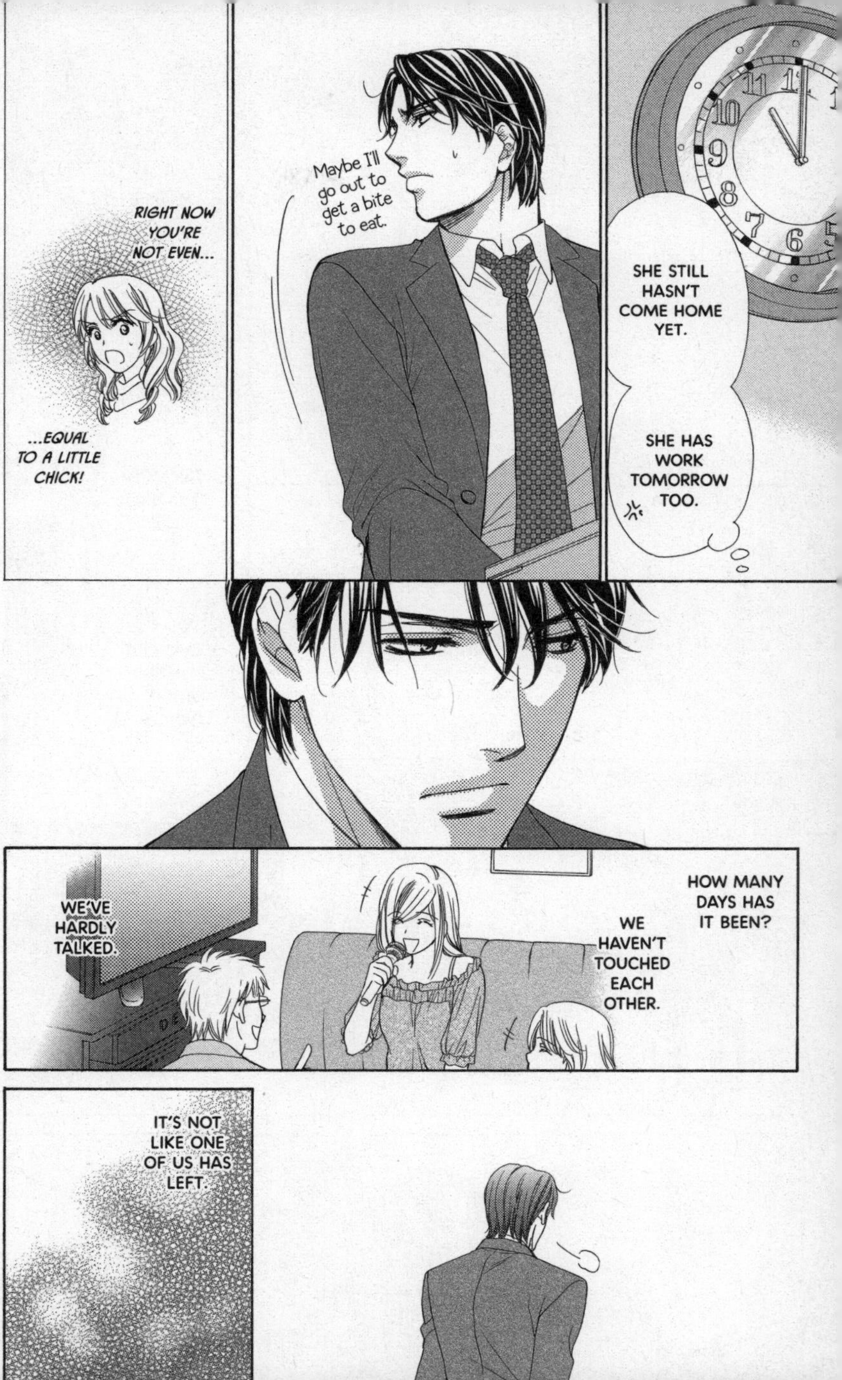
SHE STILL HASN'T COME HOME YET.
SHE HAS WORK TOMORROW TOO.
Maybe I'll go out to get a bite to eat.
RIGHT NOW YOU'RE NOT EVEN...
...EQUAL TO A LITTLE CHICK!
HOW MANY DAYS HAS IT BEEN?
WE HAVEN'T TOUCHED EACH OTHER.
WE'VE HARDLY TALKED.
IT'S NOT LIKE ONE OF US HAS LEFT.

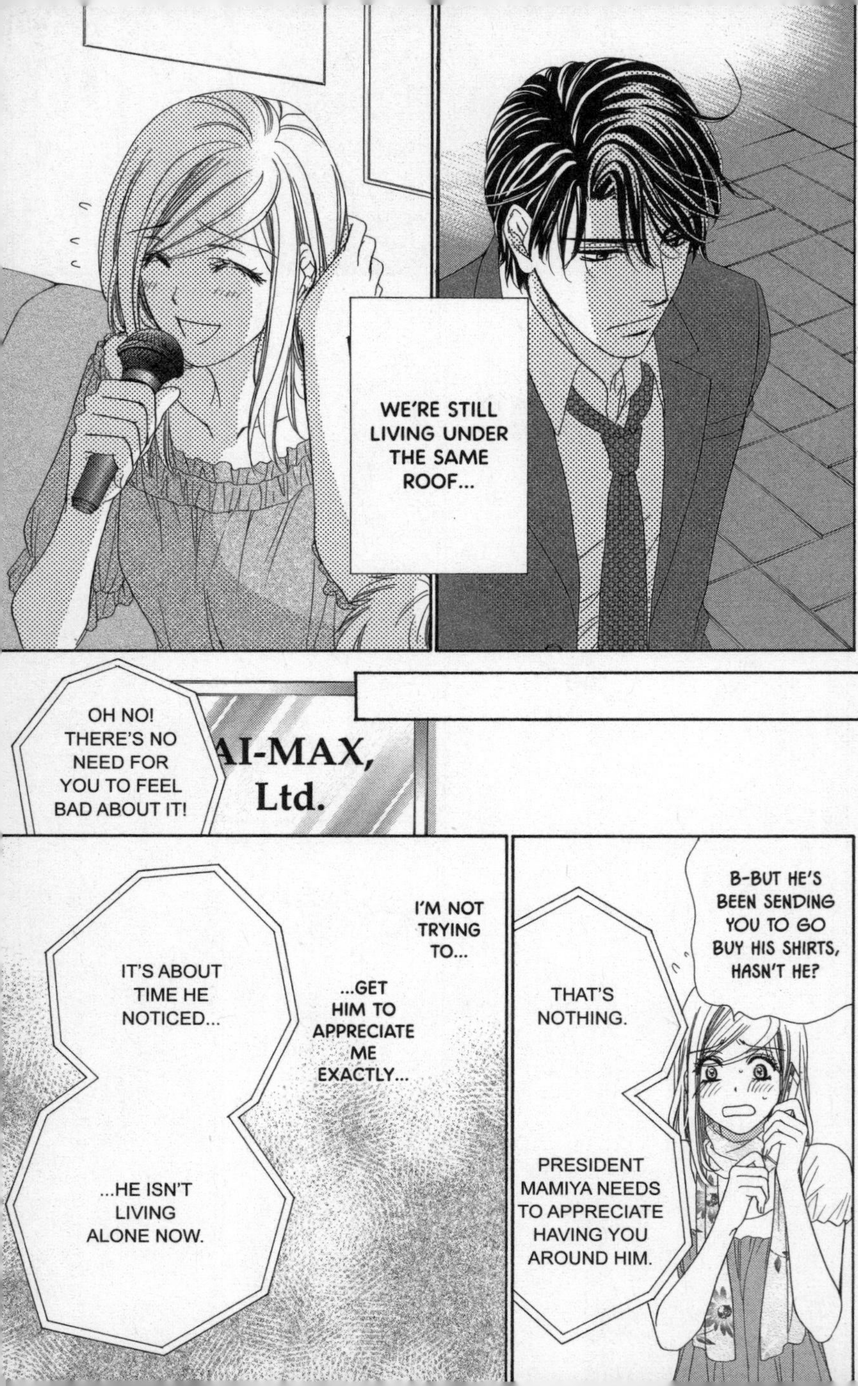
WE'RE STILL LIVING UNDER THE SAME ROOF...
AI-MAX, Ltd.
OH NO! THERE'S NO NEED FOR YOU TO FEEL BAD ABOUT IT!
B-BUT HE'S BEEN SENDING YOU TO GO BUY HIS SHIRTS, HASN'T HE?
THAT'S NOTHING.
PRESIDENT MAMIYA NEEDS TO APPRECIATE HAVING YOU AROUND HIM.
I'M NOT TRYING TO...
...GET HIM TO APPRECIATE ME EXACTLY...
IT'S ABOUT TIME HE NOTICED...
...HE ISN'T LIVING ALONE NOW.

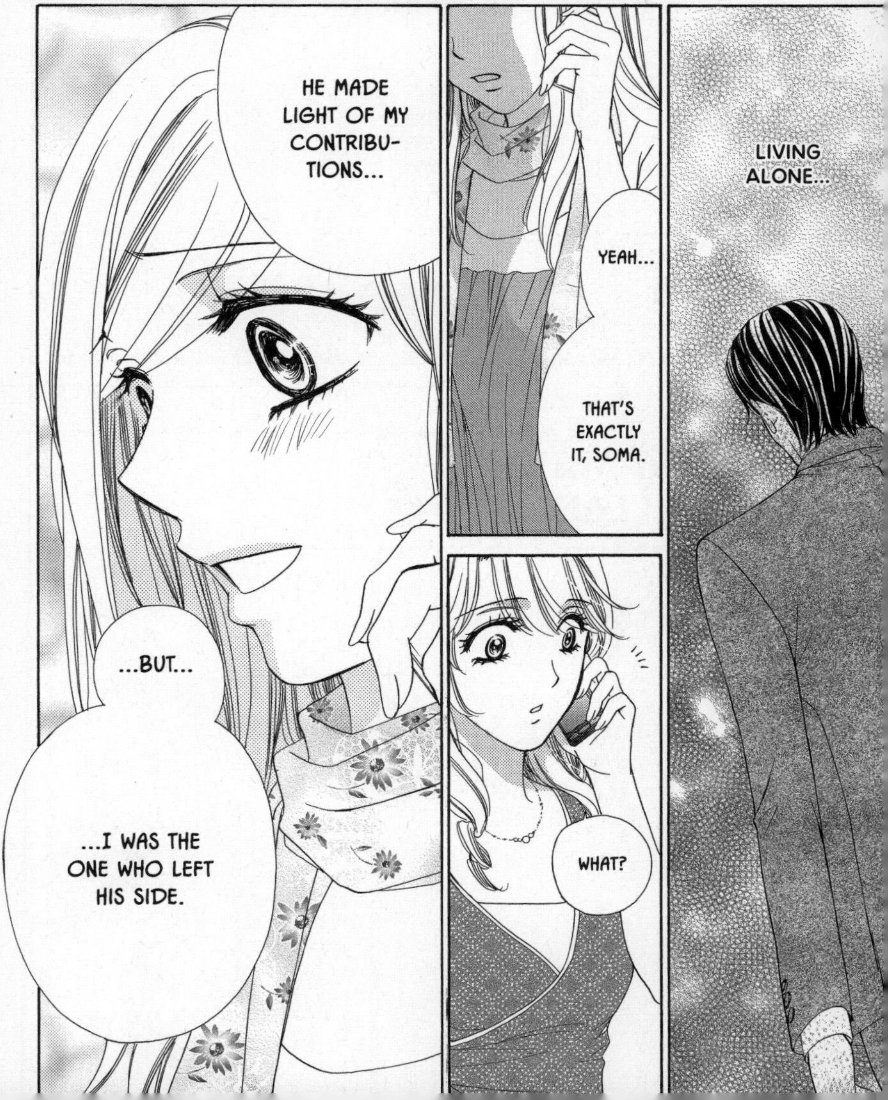
LIVING ALONE...
YEAH...
THAT'S EXACTLY IT, SOMA.
WHAT?
HE MADE LIGHT OF MY CONTRIBU-TIONS...
...BUT...
...I WAS THE ONE WHO LEFT HIS SIDE.

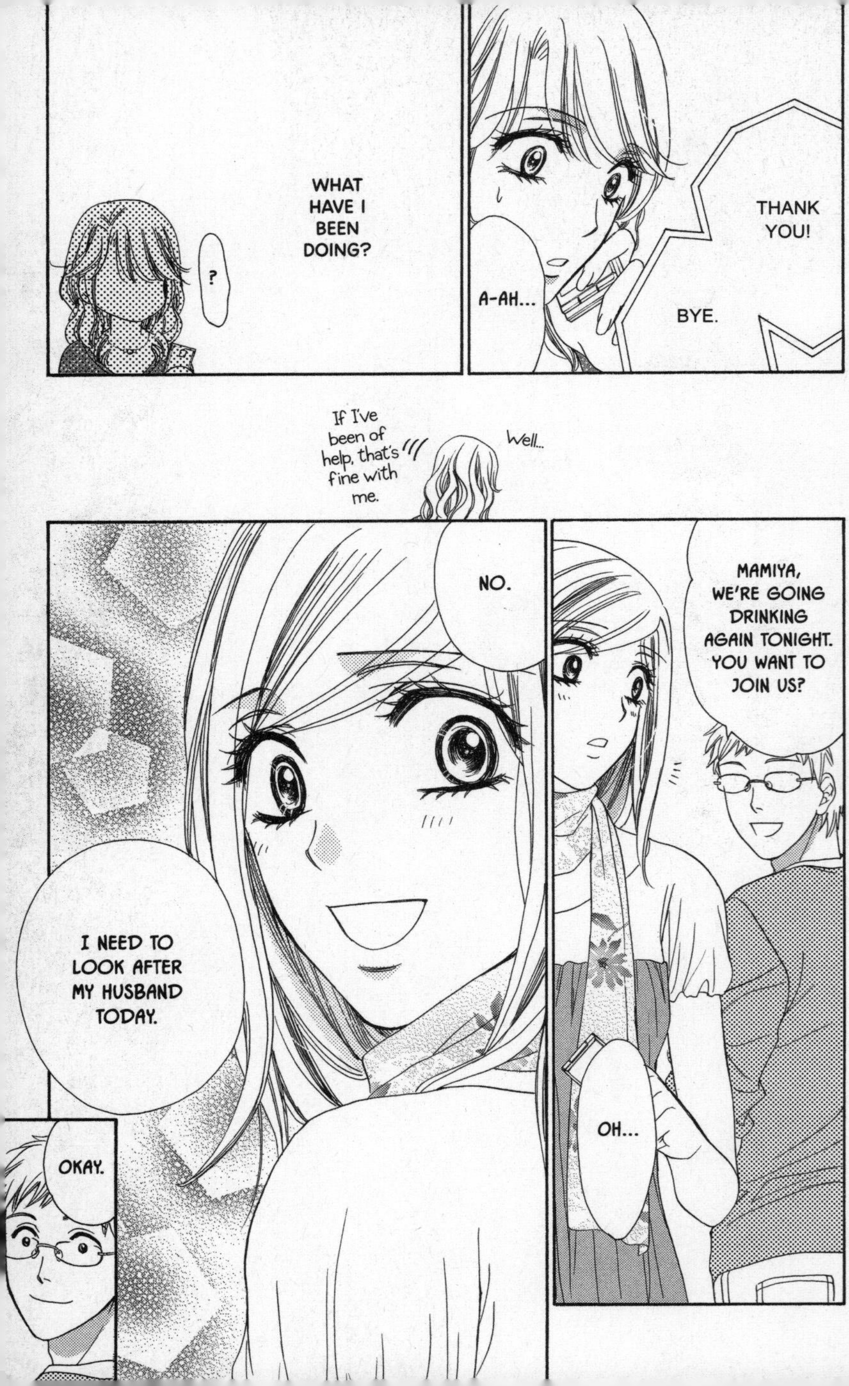
THANK YOU!
BYE.
A-AH...
WHAT HAVE I BEEN DOING?
?
Well...
If I've been of help, that's fine with me.
MAMIYA, WE'RE GOING DRINKING AGAIN TONIGHT. YOU WANT TO JOIN US?
OH...
NO.
I NEED TO LOOK AFTER MY HUSBAND TODAY.
OKAY.

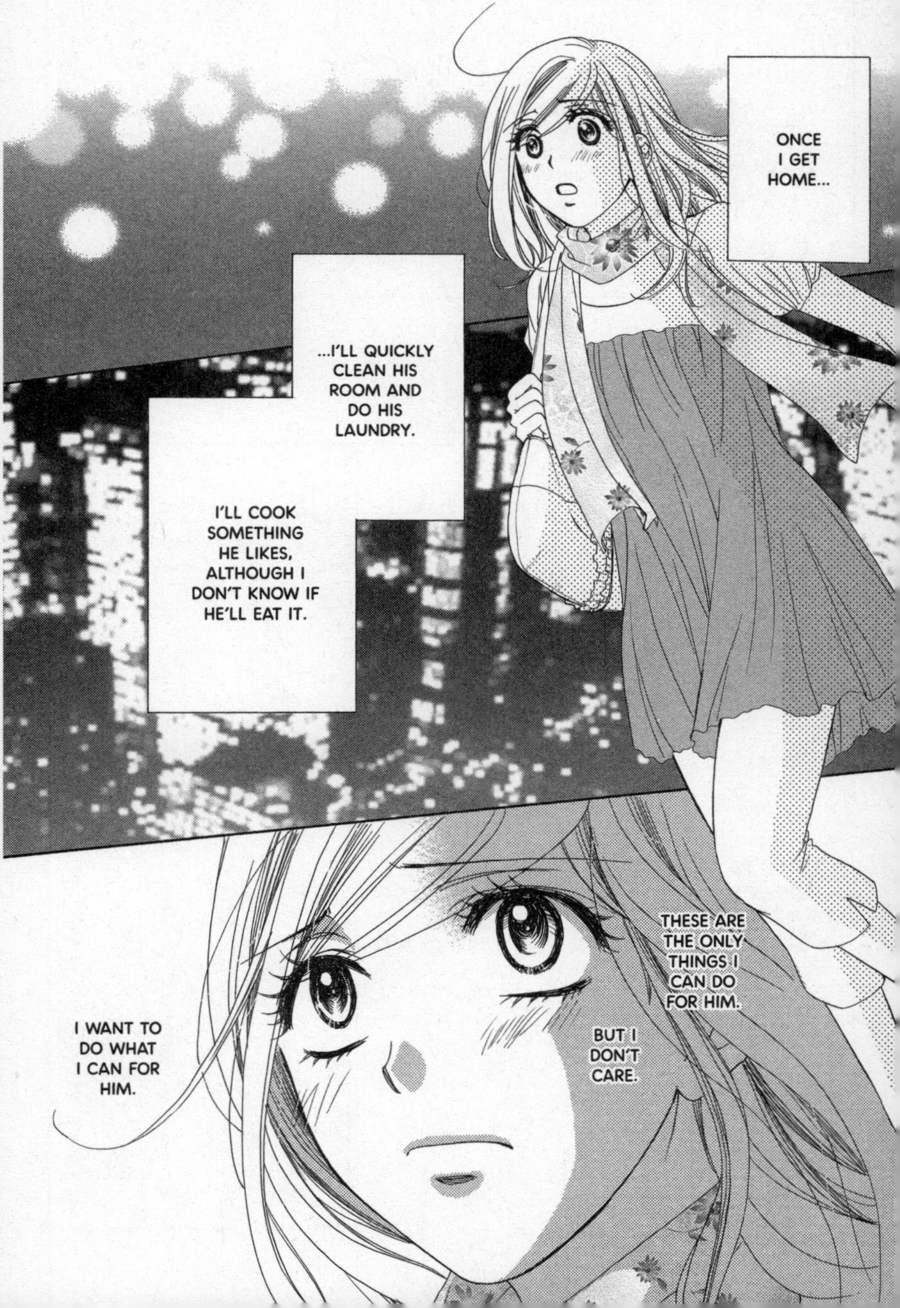
ONCE I GET HOME...
...I'LL QUICKLY CLEAN HIS ROOM AND DO HIS LAUNDRY.
I'LL COOK SOMETHING HE LIKES, ALTHOUGH I DON'T KNOW IF HE'LL EAT IT.
THESE ARE THE ONLY THINGS I CAN DO FOR HIM.
BUT I DON'T CARE.
I WANT TO DO WHAT I CAN FOR HIM.

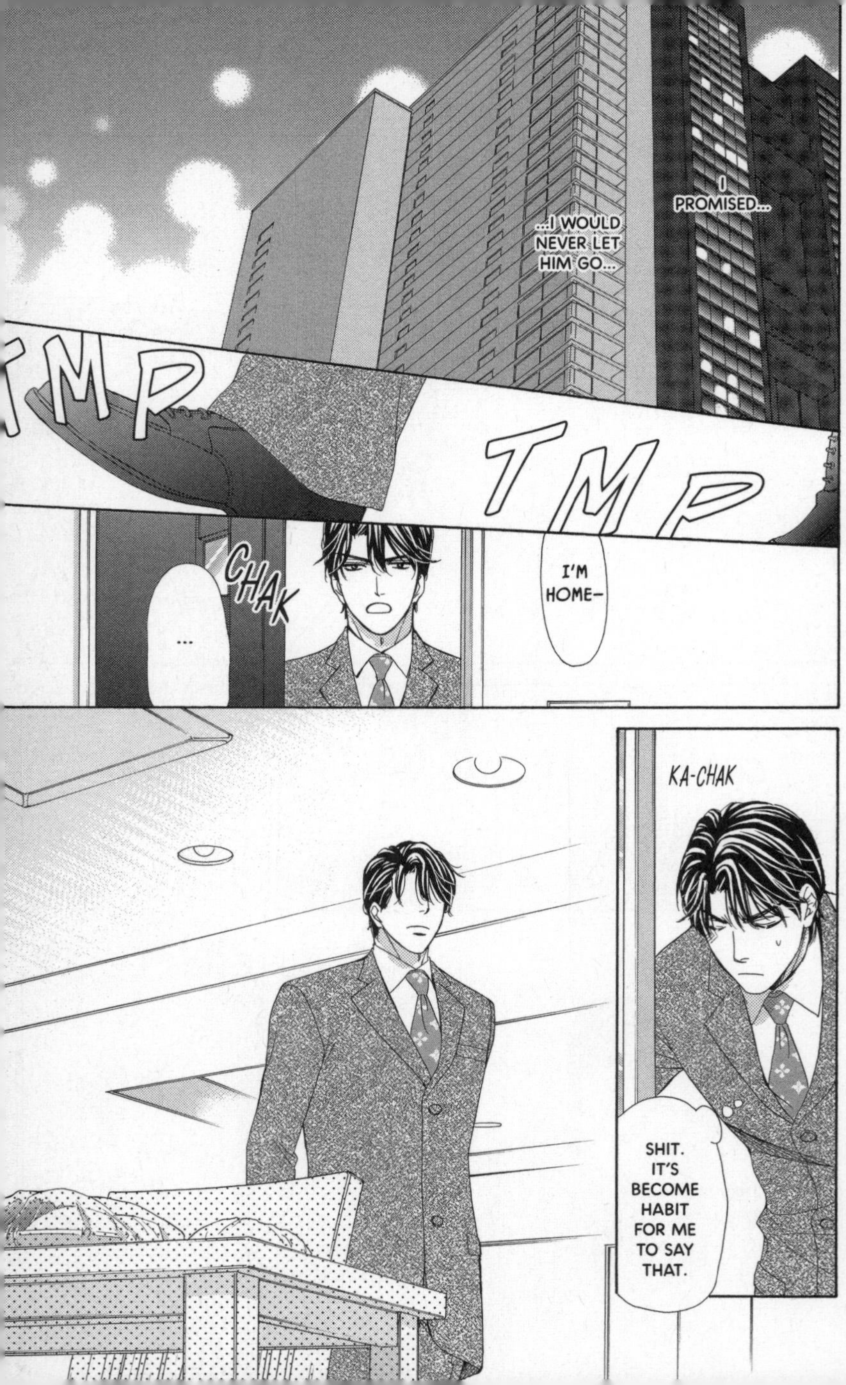
I PROMISED...
...I WOULD NEVER LET HIM GO...
TMP
TMP
I'M HOME—
CHAK
...
KA-CHAK
SHIT. IT'S BECOME HABIT FOR ME TO SAY THAT.

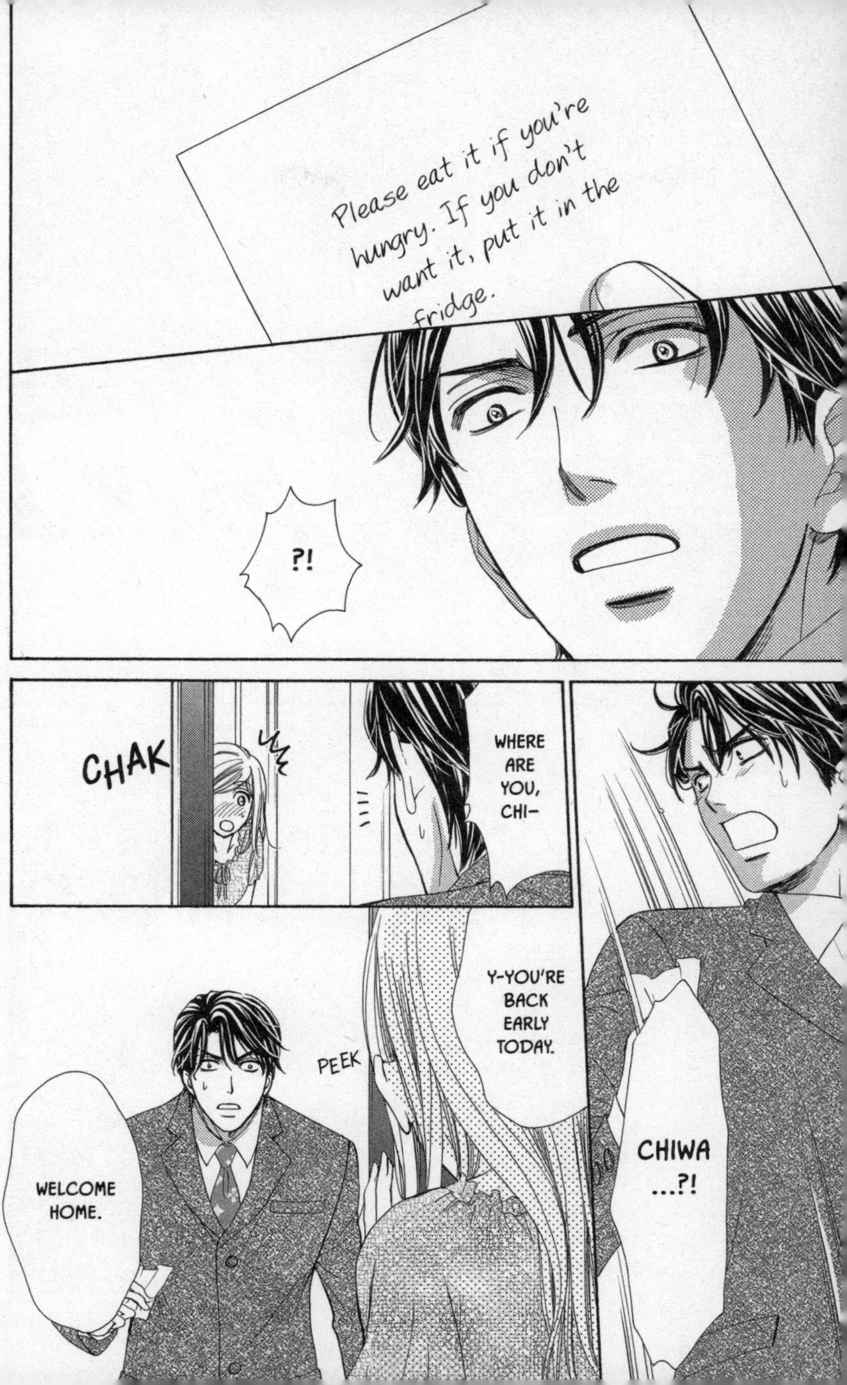
Please eat it if you're hungry. If you don't want it, put it in the fridge.
?!
WHERE ARE YOU, CHI–
CHAK
Y-YOU'RE BACK EARLY TODAY.
PEEK
CHIWA ...?!
WELCOME HOME.

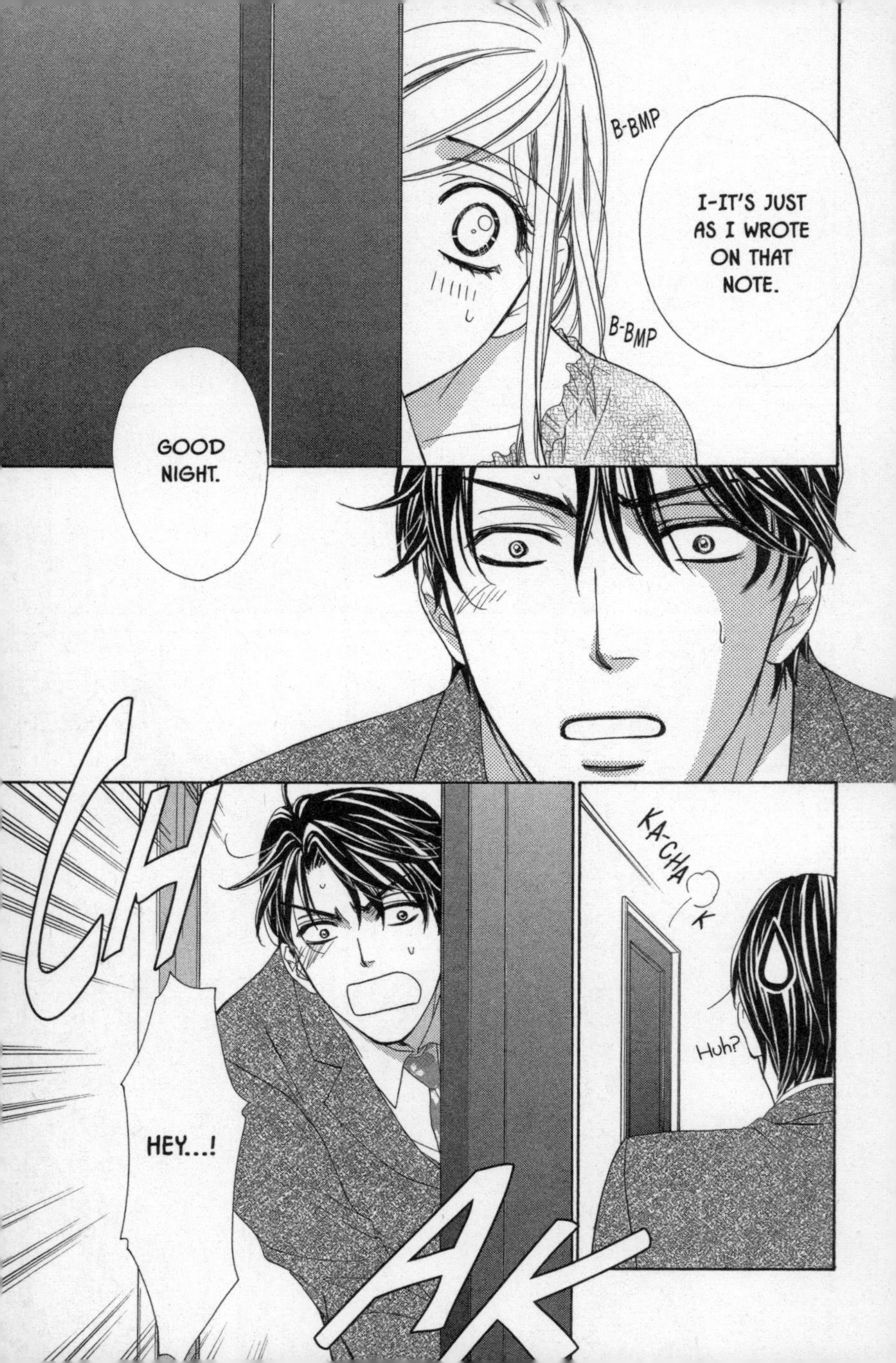
B-BMP
I-IT'S JUST AS I WROTE ON THAT NOTE.
B-BMP
GOOD NIGHT.
KA-CHAK
Huh?
CHAK
HEY...!

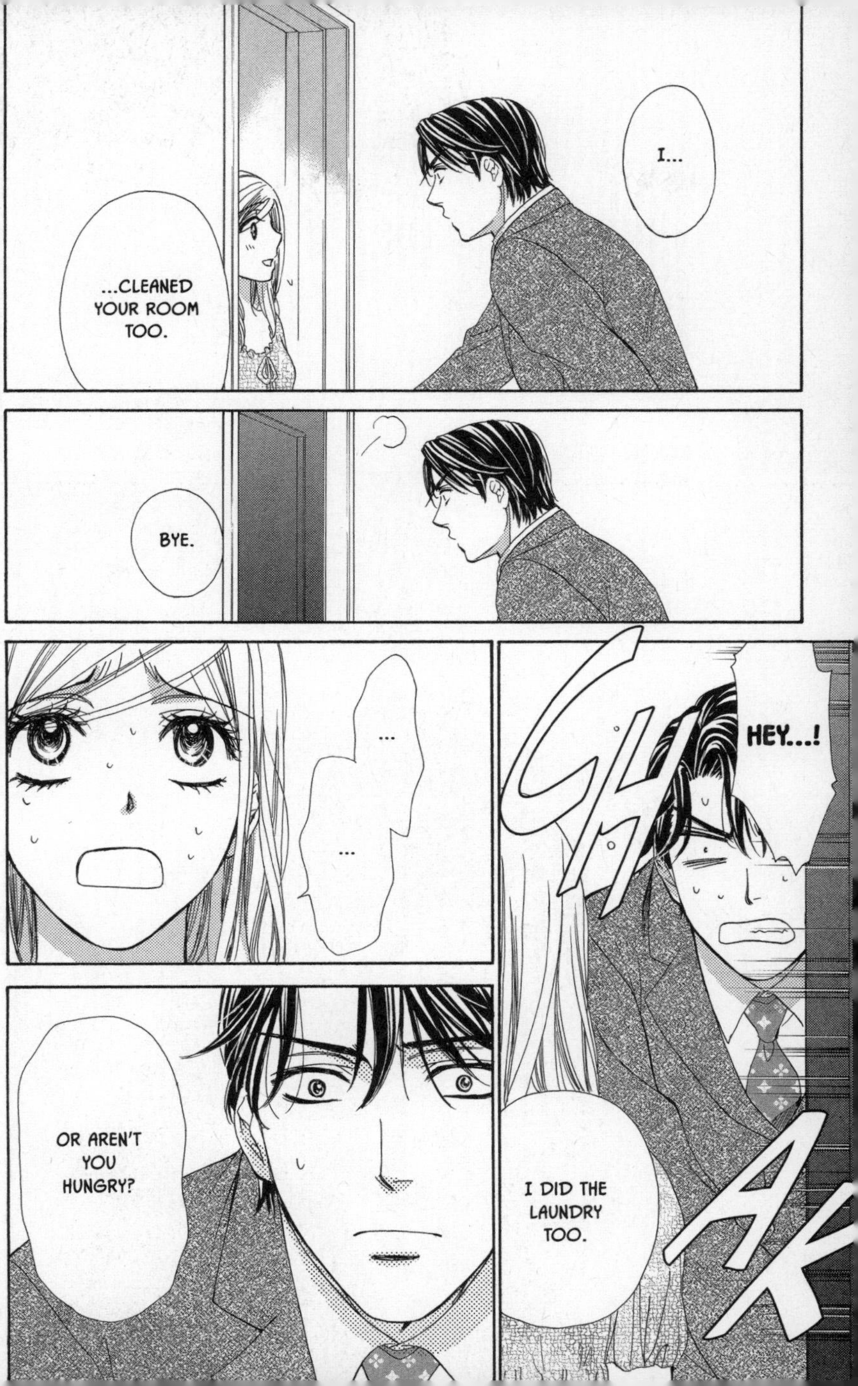
I...
...CLEANED YOUR ROOM TOO.
BYE.
CHAK
HEY...!
I DID THE LAUNDRY TOO.
...
...
OR AREN'T YOU HUNGRY?

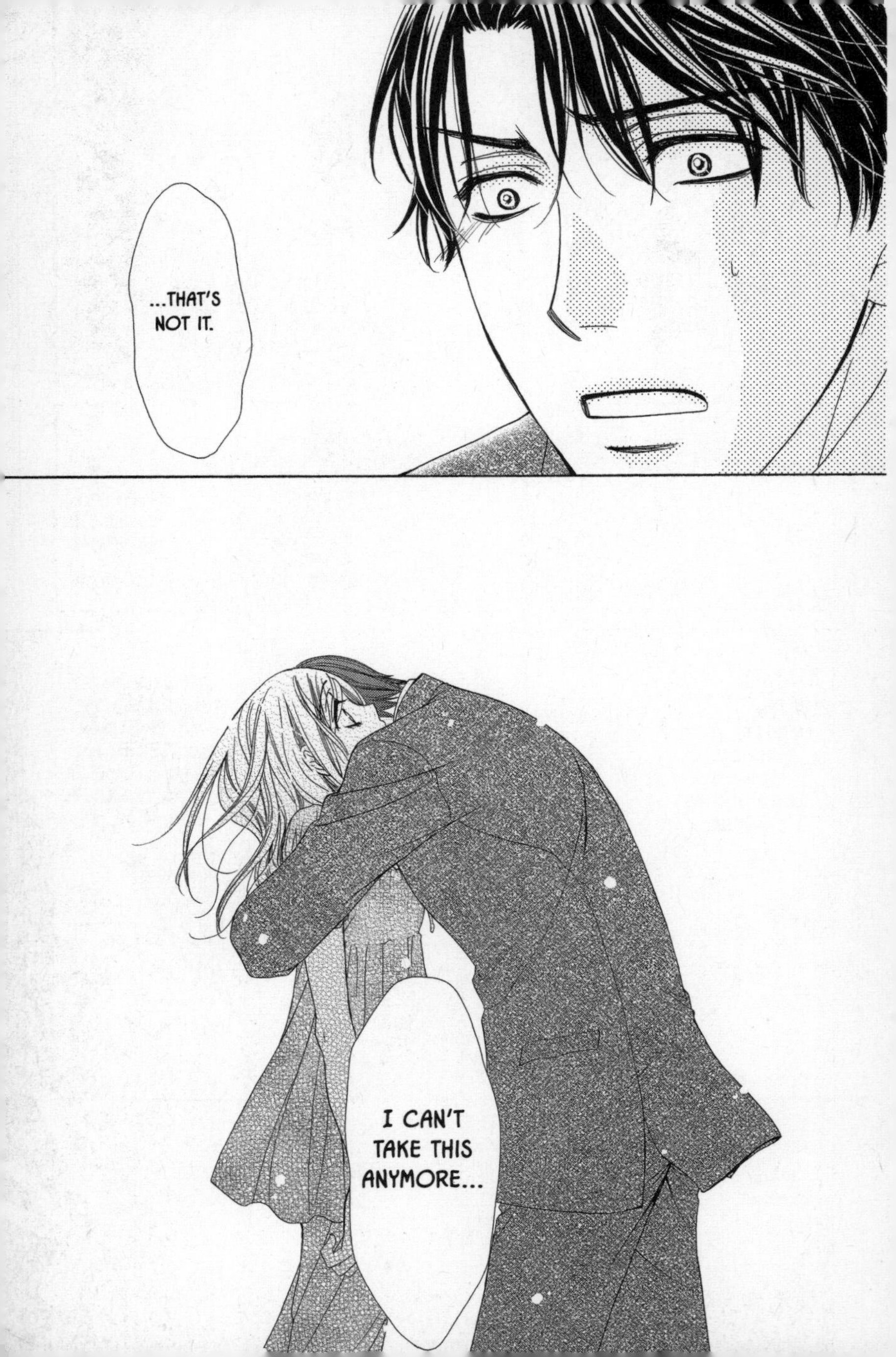
...THAT'S NOT IT.
I CAN'T TAKE THIS ANYMORE...

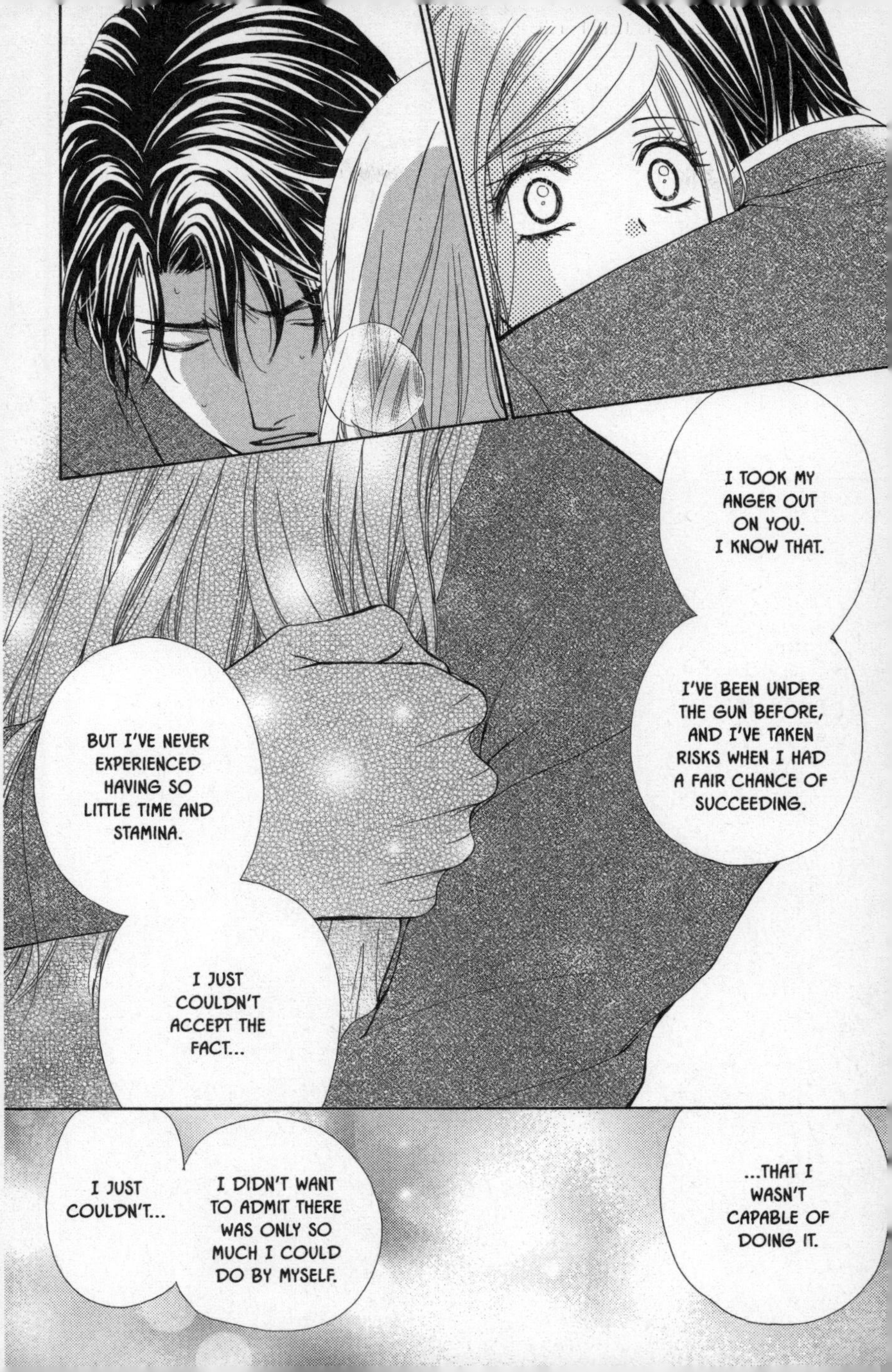
I TOOK MY ANGER OUT ON YOU. I KNOW THAT.
I'VE BEEN UNDER THE GUN BEFORE, AND I'VE TAKEN RISKS WHEN I HAD A FAIR CHANCE OF SUCCEEDING.
BUT I'VE NEVER EXPERIENCED HAVING SO LITTLE TIME AND STAMINA.
I JUST COULDN'T ACCEPT THE FACT...
...THAT I WASN'T CAPABLE OF DOING IT.
I DIDN'T WANT TO ADMIT THERE WAS ONLY SO MUCH I COULD DO BY MYSELF.
I JUST COULDN'T...

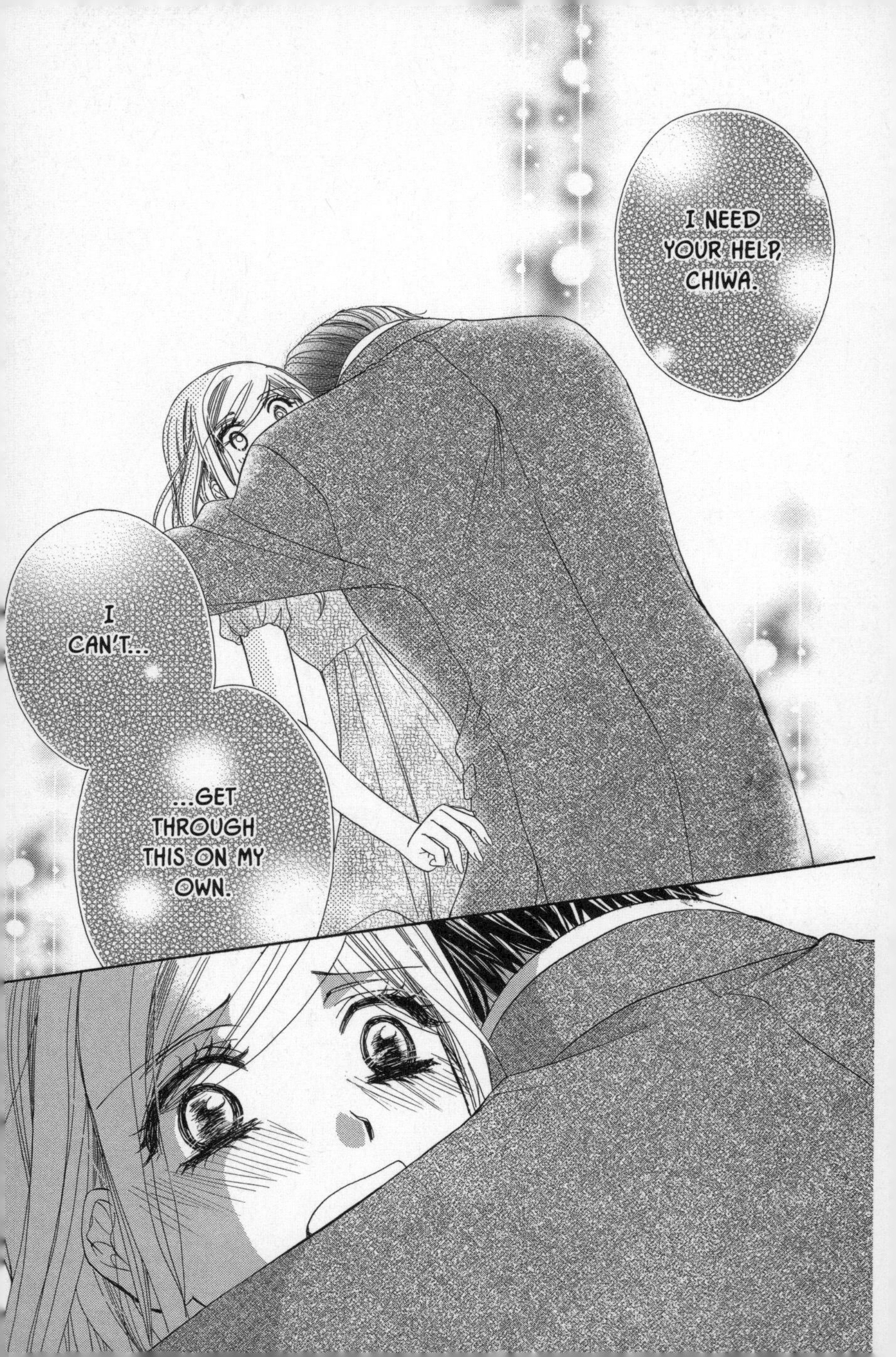
I NEED YOUR HELP, CHIWA.
I CAN'T...
...GET THROUGH THIS ON MY OWN.

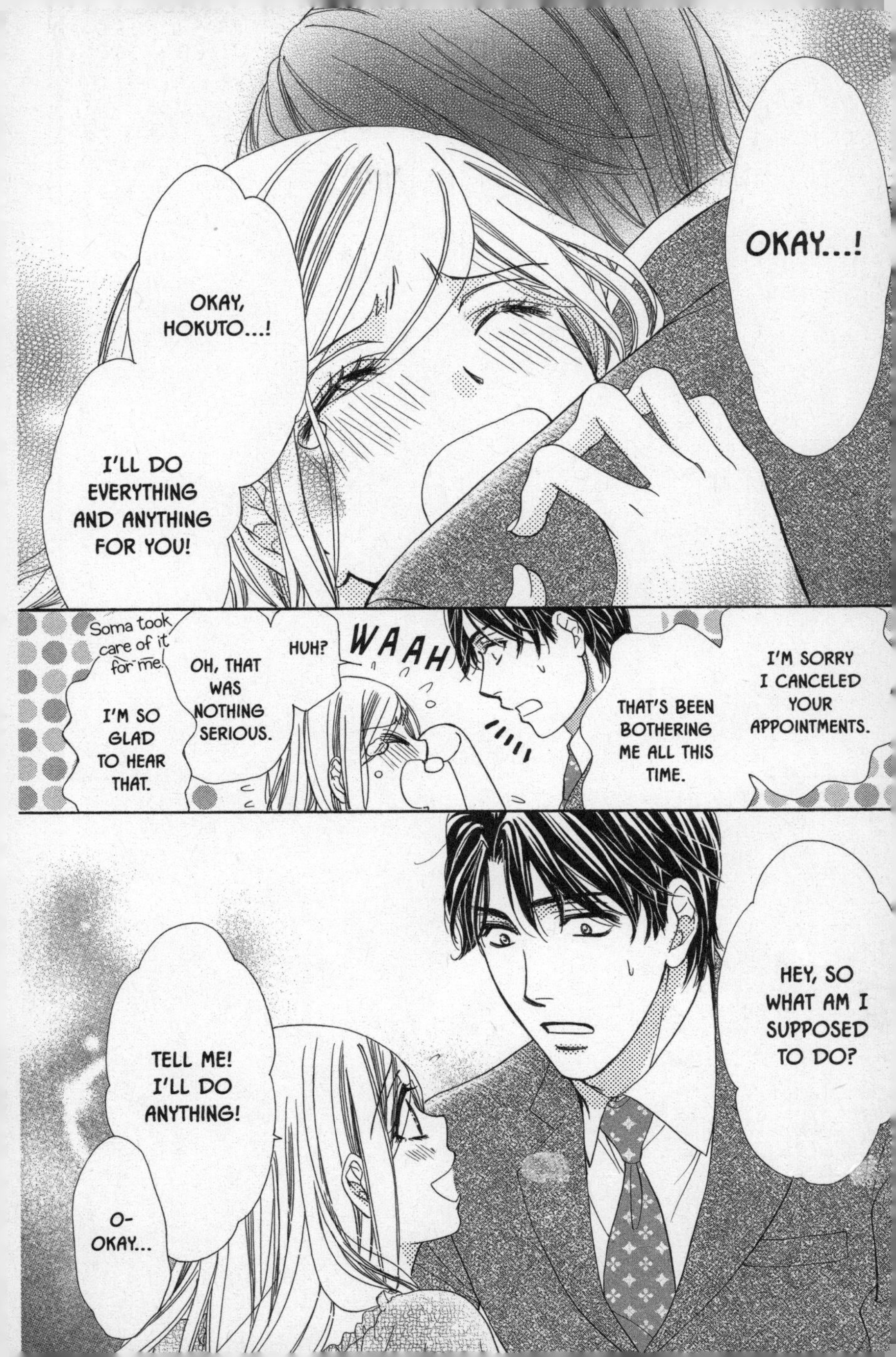
OKAY...!
OKAY, HOKUTO...!
I'LL DO EVERYTHING AND ANYTHING FOR YOU!
I'M SORRY I CANCELED YOUR APPOINTMENTS.
THAT'S BEEN BOTHERING ME ALL THIS TIME.
WAAH
HUH?
OH, THAT WAS NOTHING SERIOUS.
I'M SO GLAD TO HEAR THAT.
Soma took care of it for me.
HEY, SO WHAT AM I SUPPOSED TO DO?
TELL ME! I'LL DO ANYTHING!
O-OKAY...

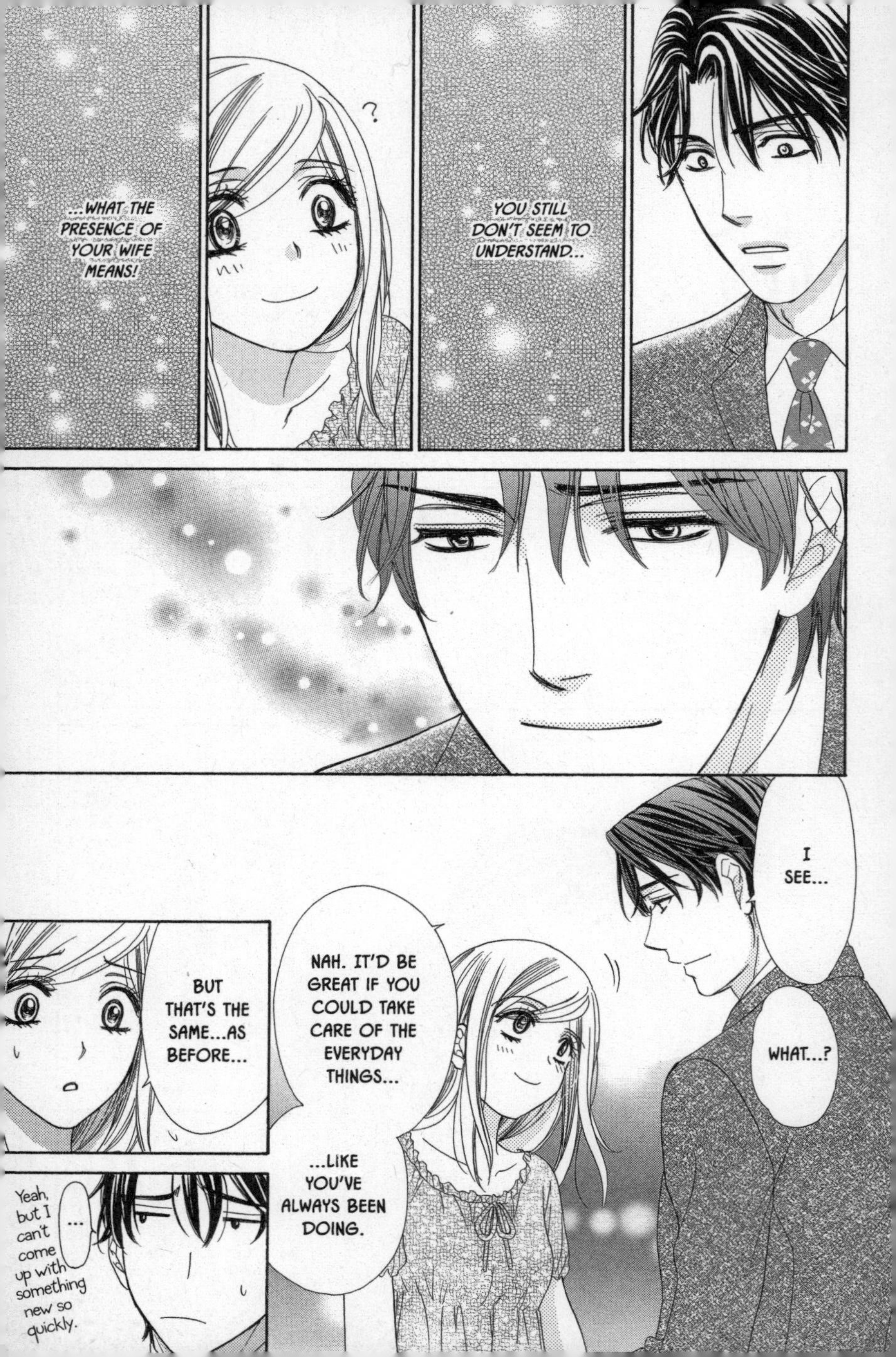
YOU STILL DON'T SEEM TO UNDERSTAND...
?
...WHAT THE PRESENCE OF YOUR WIFE MEANS!
I SEE...
WHAT...?
NAH. IT'D BE GREAT IF YOU COULD TAKE CARE OF THE EVERYDAY THINGS...
...LIKE YOU'VE ALWAYS BEEN DOING.
BUT THAT'S THE SAME...AS BEFORE...
...
Yeah, but I can't come up with something new so quickly.

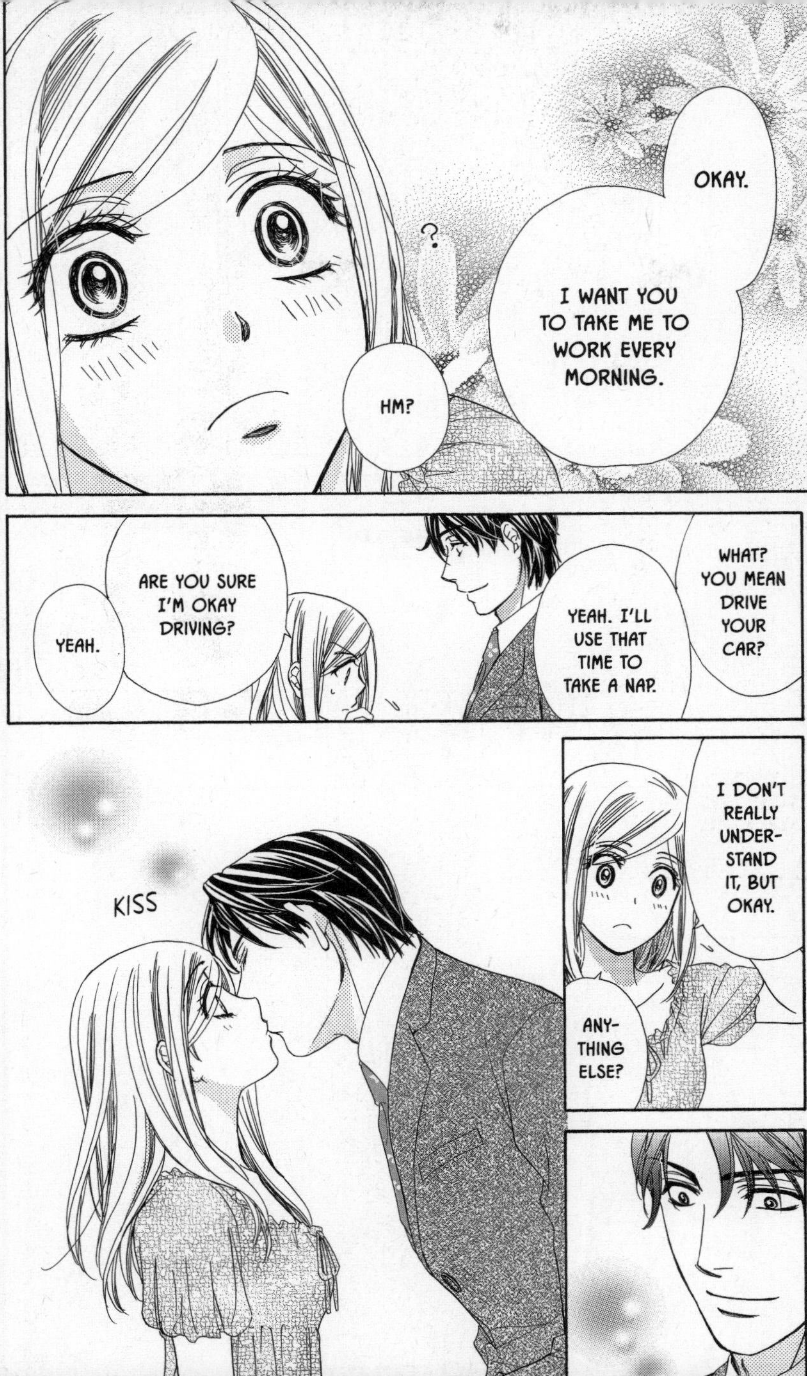
OKAY.
I WANT YOU TO TAKE ME TO WORK EVERY MORNING.
?
HM?
WHAT? YOU MEAN DRIVE YOUR CAR?
YEAH. I'LL USE THAT TIME TO TAKE A NAP.
ARE YOU SURE I'M OKAY DRIVING?
YEAH.
I DON'T REALLY UNDER-STAND IT, BUT OKAY.
ANY-THING ELSE?
KISS

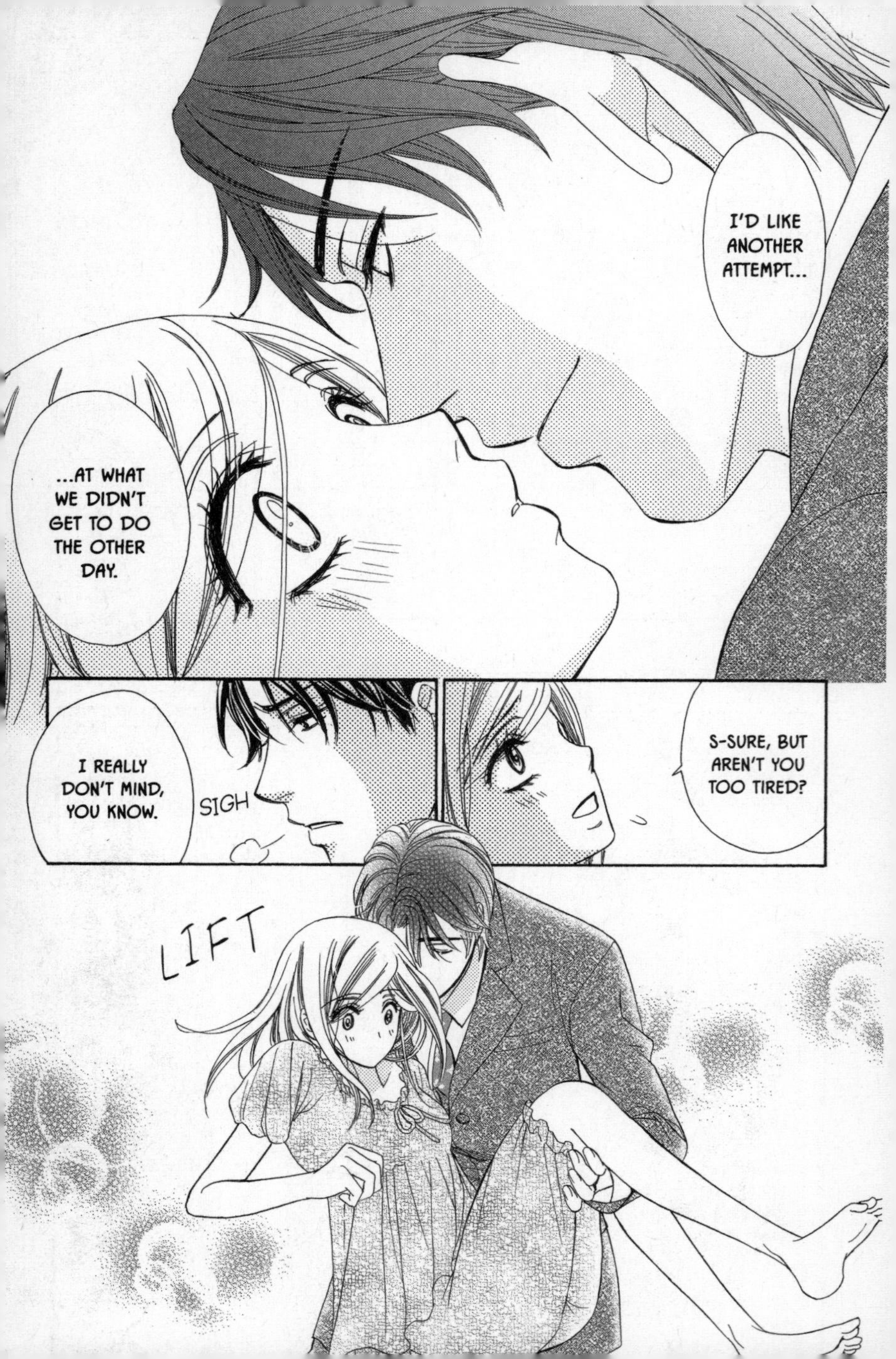
I'D LIKE ANOTHER ATTEMPT...
...AT WHAT WE DIDN'T GET TO DO THE OTHER DAY.
S-SURE, BUT AREN'T YOU TOO TIRED?
I REALLY DON'T MIND, YOU KNOW.
SIGH
LIFT

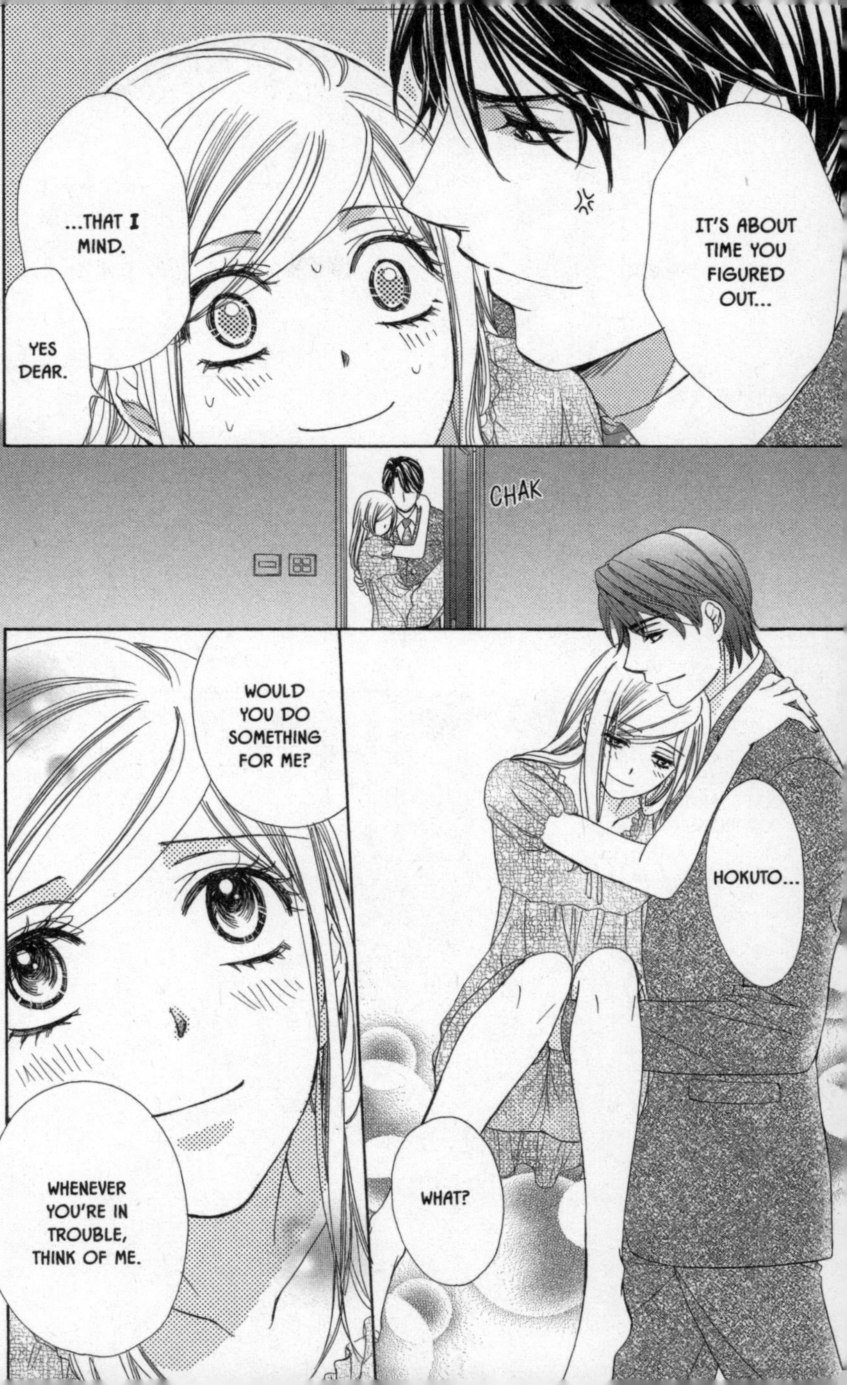
IT'S ABOUT TIME YOU FIGURED OUT...
...THAT I MIND.
YES DEAR.
CHAK
HOKUTO...
WHAT?
WOULD YOU DO SOMETHING FOR ME?
WHENEVER YOU'RE IN TROUBLE, THINK OF ME.

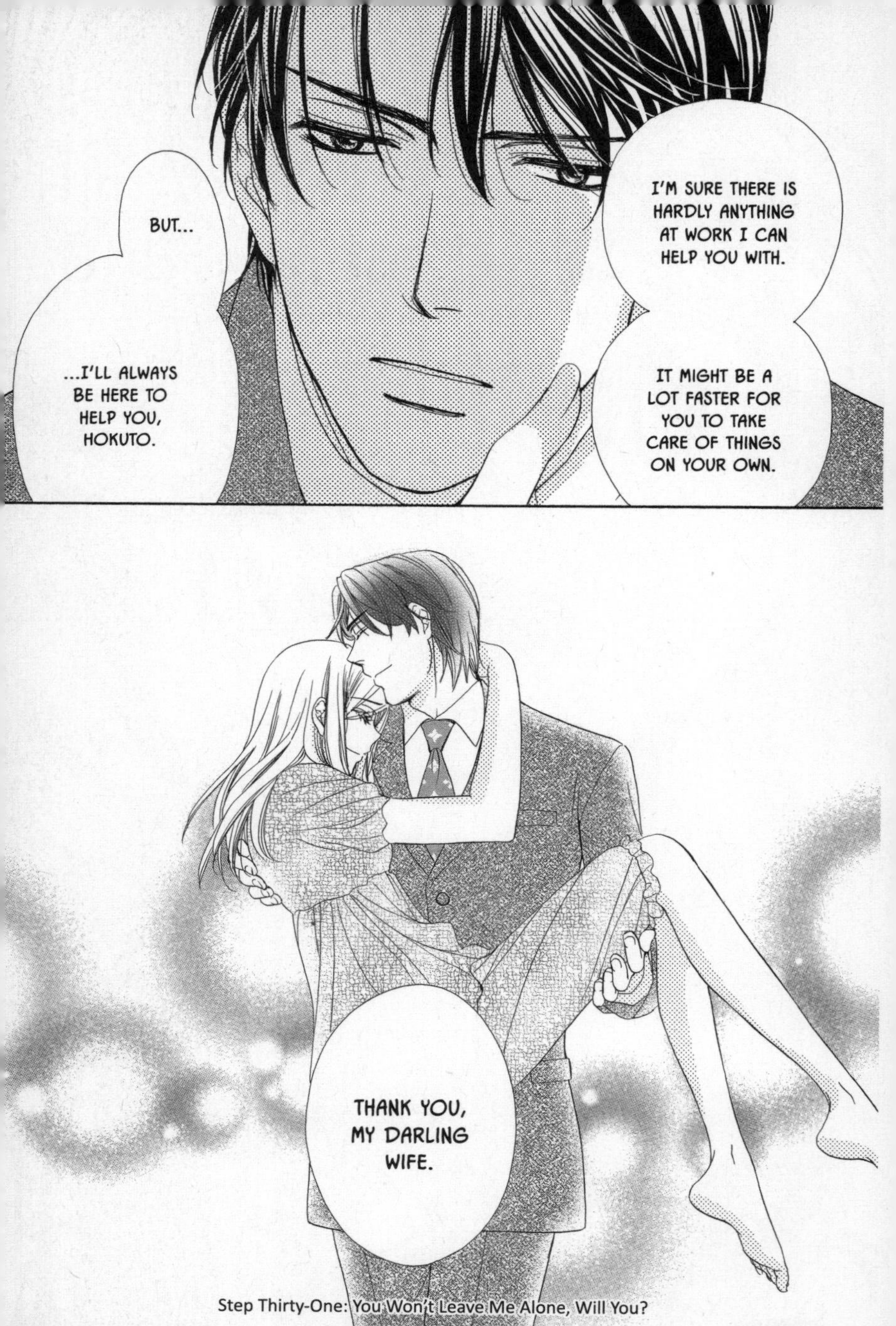
I'M SURE THERE IS HARDLY ANYTHING AT WORK I CAN HELP YOU WITH.
IT MIGHT BE A LOT FASTER FOR YOU TO TAKE CARE OF THINGS ON YOUR OWN.
BUT...
...I'LL ALWAYS BE HERE TO HELP YOU, HOKUTO.
THANK YOU, MY DARLING WIFE.

Step Thirty-One: You Won't Leave Me Alone, Will You?

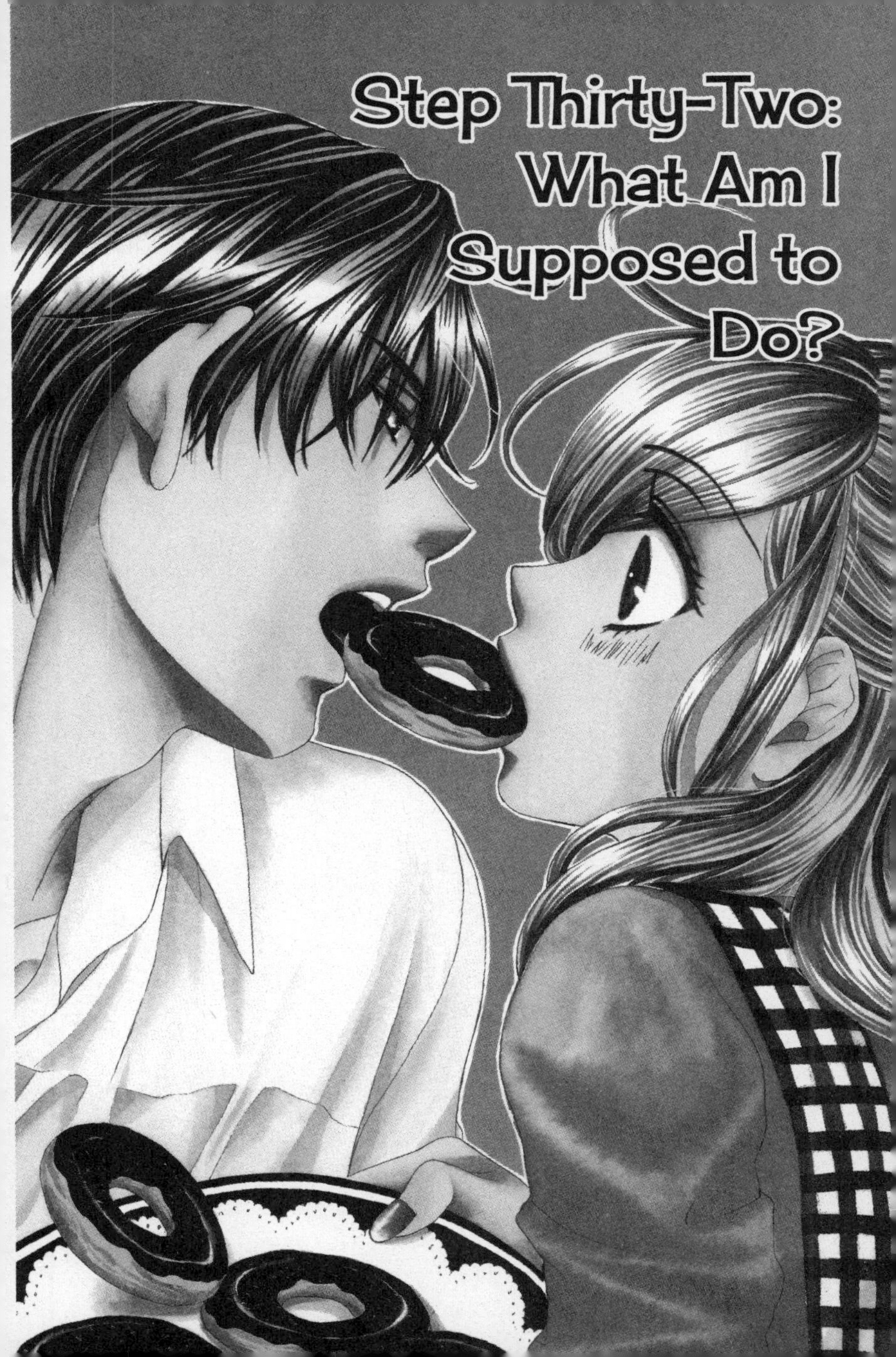
Step Thirty-Two:
What Am I
Supposed to
Do?

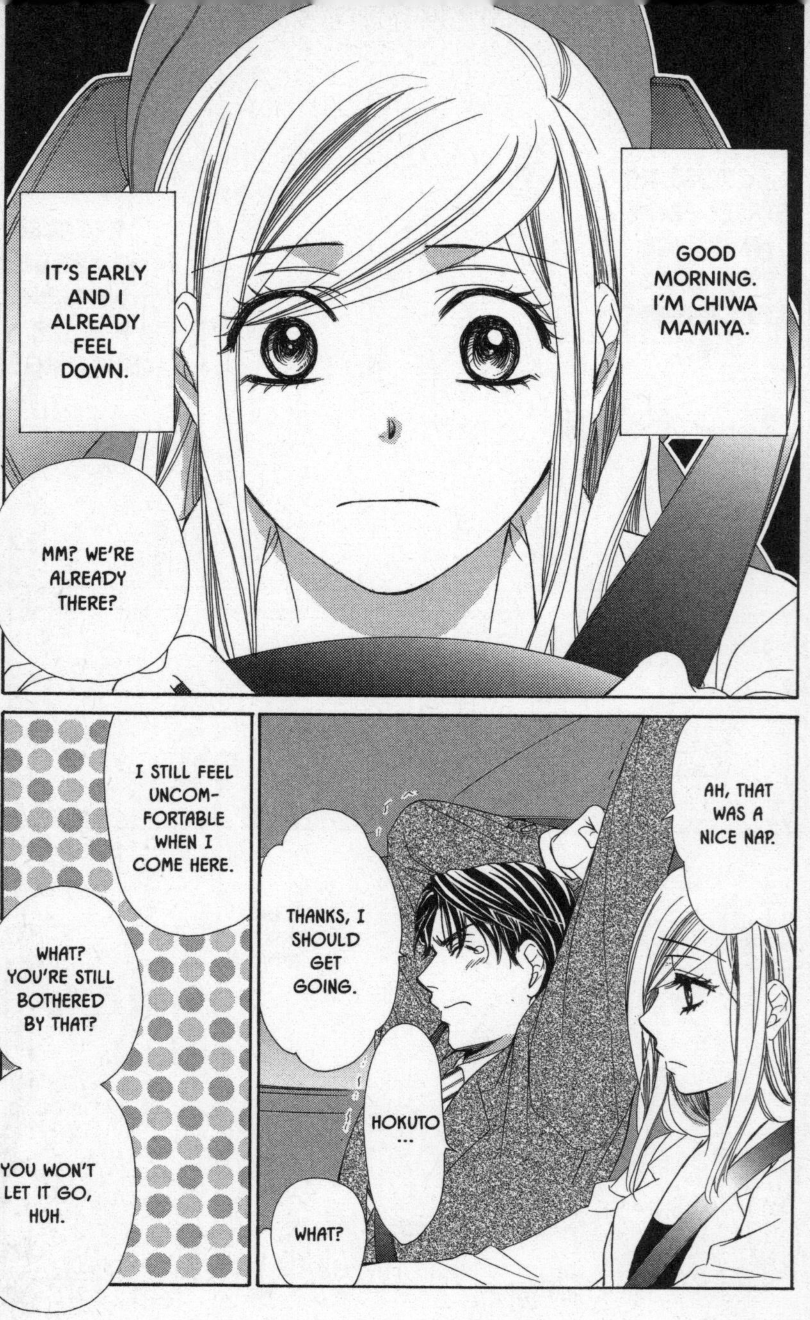
GOOD MORNING. I'M CHIWA MAMIYA.
IT'S EARLY AND I ALREADY FEEL DOWN.
MM? WE'RE ALREADY THERE?
AH, THAT WAS A NICE NAP.
THANKS, I SHOULD GET GOING.
HOKUTO...
WHAT?
I STILL FEEL UNCOM-FORTABLE WHEN I COME HERE.
WHAT? YOU'RE STILL BOTHERED BY THAT?
YOU WON'T LET IT GO, HUH.

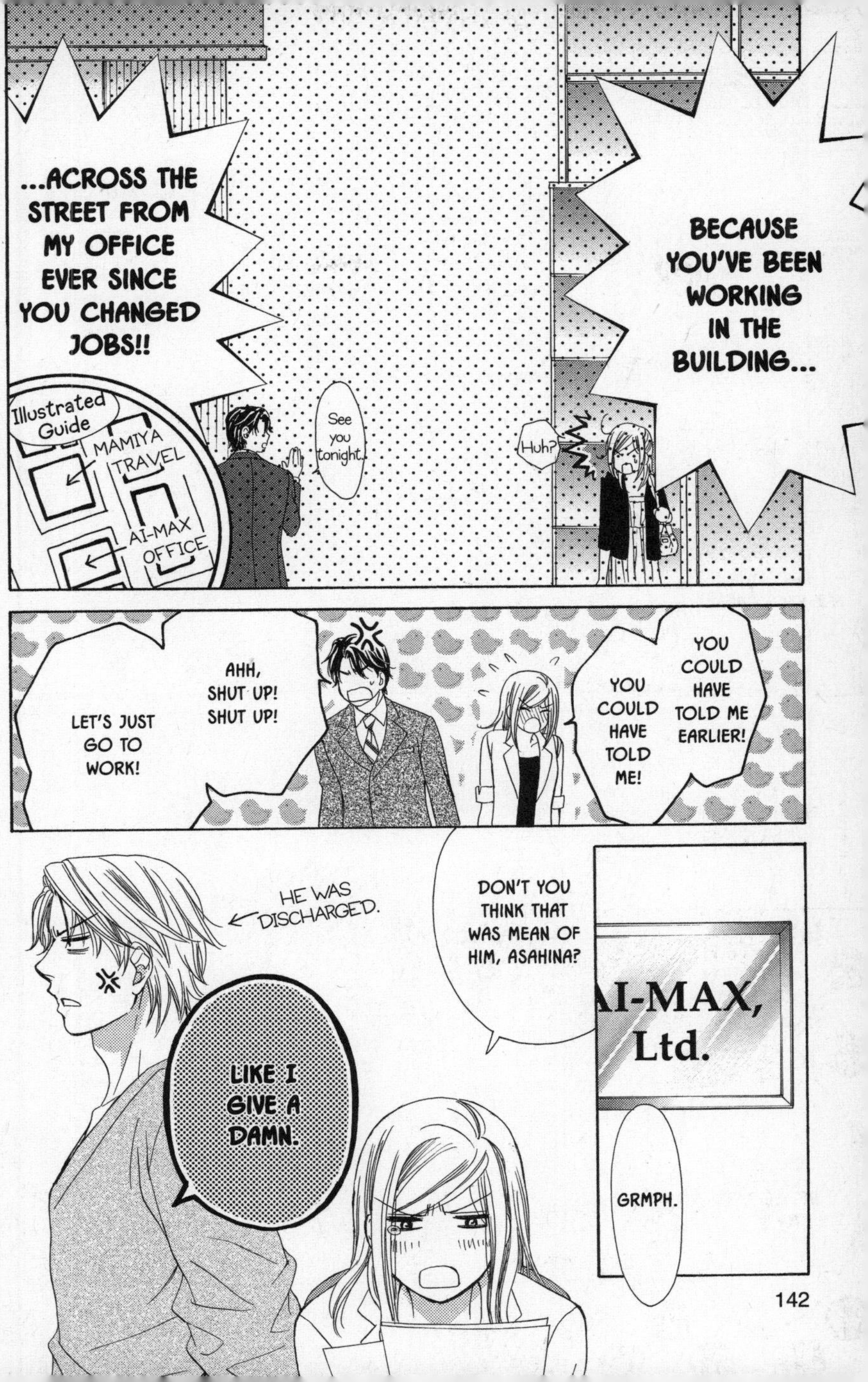
BECAUSE YOU'VE BEEN WORKING IN THE BUILDING...
...ACROSS THE STREET FROM MY OFFICE EVER SINCE YOU CHANGED JOBS!!
Huh?
See you tonight.
Illustrated Guide
MAMIYA TRAVEL
AI-MAX OFFICE
YOU COULD HAVE TOLD ME EARLIER!
YOU COULD HAVE TOLD ME!
AHH, SHUT UP! SHUT UP!
LET'S JUST GO TO WORK!
AI-MAX, Ltd.
DON'T YOU THINK THAT WAS MEAN OF HIM, ASAHINA?
GRMPH.
HE WAS DISCHARGED.
LIKE I GIVE A DAMN.

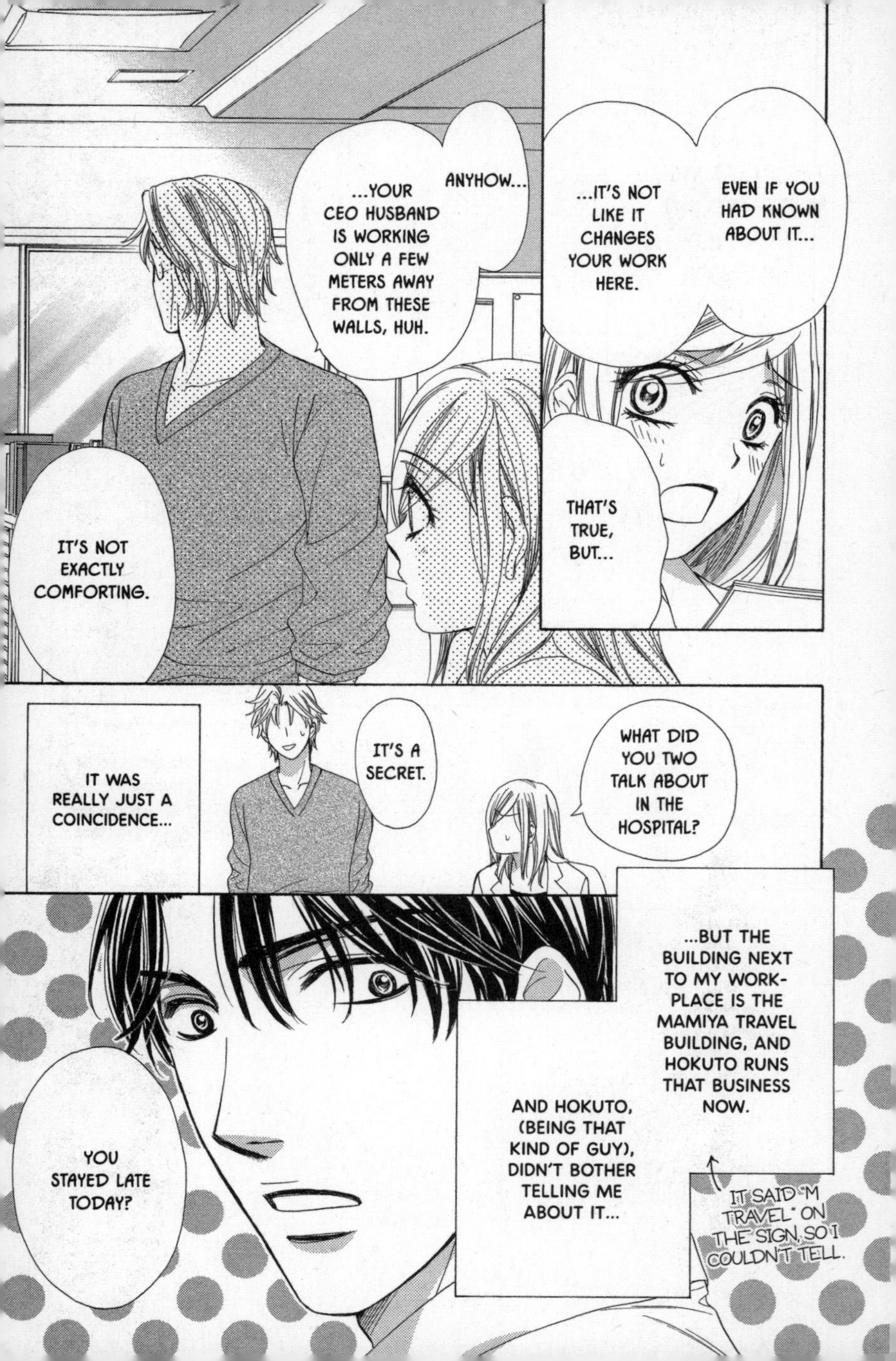
EVEN IF YOU HAD KNOWN ABOUT IT...
...IT'S NOT LIKE IT CHANGES YOUR WORK HERE.
THAT'S TRUE, BUT...
ANYHOW...
...YOUR CEO HUSBAND IS WORKING ONLY A FEW METERS AWAY FROM THESE WALLS, HUH.
IT'S NOT EXACTLY COMFORTING.
WHAT DID YOU TWO TALK ABOUT IN THE HOSPITAL?
IT'S A SECRET.
IT WAS REALLY JUST A COINCIDENCE...
...BUT THE BUILDING NEXT TO MY WORK-PLACE IS THE MAMIYA TRAVEL BUILDING, AND HOKUTO RUNS THAT BUSINESS NOW.
AND HOKUTO, (BEING THAT KIND OF GUY), DIDN'T BOTHER TELLING ME ABOUT IT...
IT SAID "M TRAVEL" ON THE SIGN, SO I COULDN'T TELL.
YOU STAYED LATE TODAY?

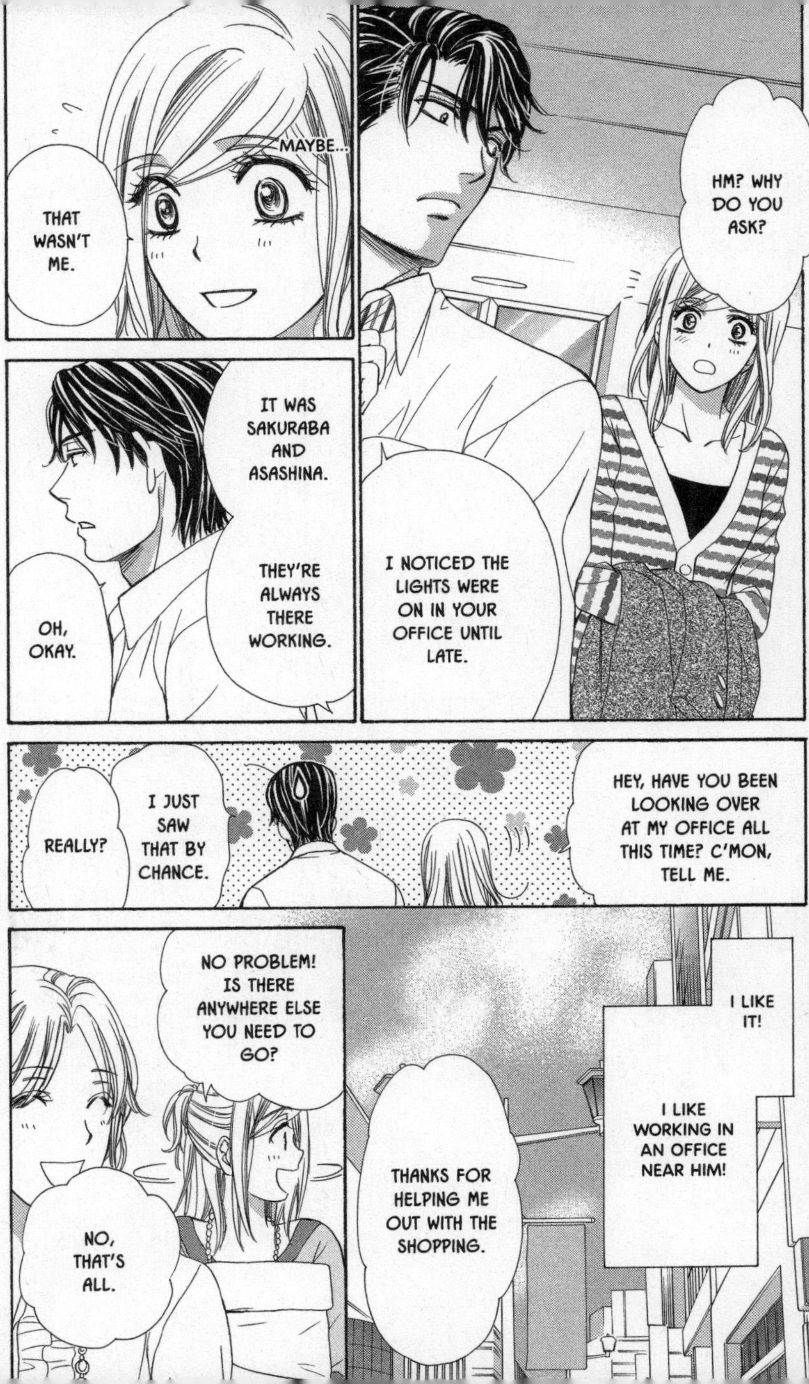
HM? WHY DO YOU ASK?
I NOTICED THE LIGHTS WERE ON IN YOUR OFFICE UNTIL LATE.
MAYBE...
THAT WASN'T ME.
IT WAS SAKURABA AND ASASHINA.
THEY'RE ALWAYS THERE WORKING.
OH, OKAY.
HEY, HAVE YOU BEEN LOOKING OVER AT MY OFFICE ALL THIS TIME? C'MON, TELL ME.
I JUST SAW THAT BY CHANCE.
REALLY?
I LIKE IT!
I LIKE WORKING IN AN OFFICE NEAR HIM!
THANKS FOR HELPING ME OUT WITH THE SHOPPING.
NO PROBLEM! IS THERE ANYWHERE ELSE YOU NEED TO GO?
NO, THAT'S ALL.

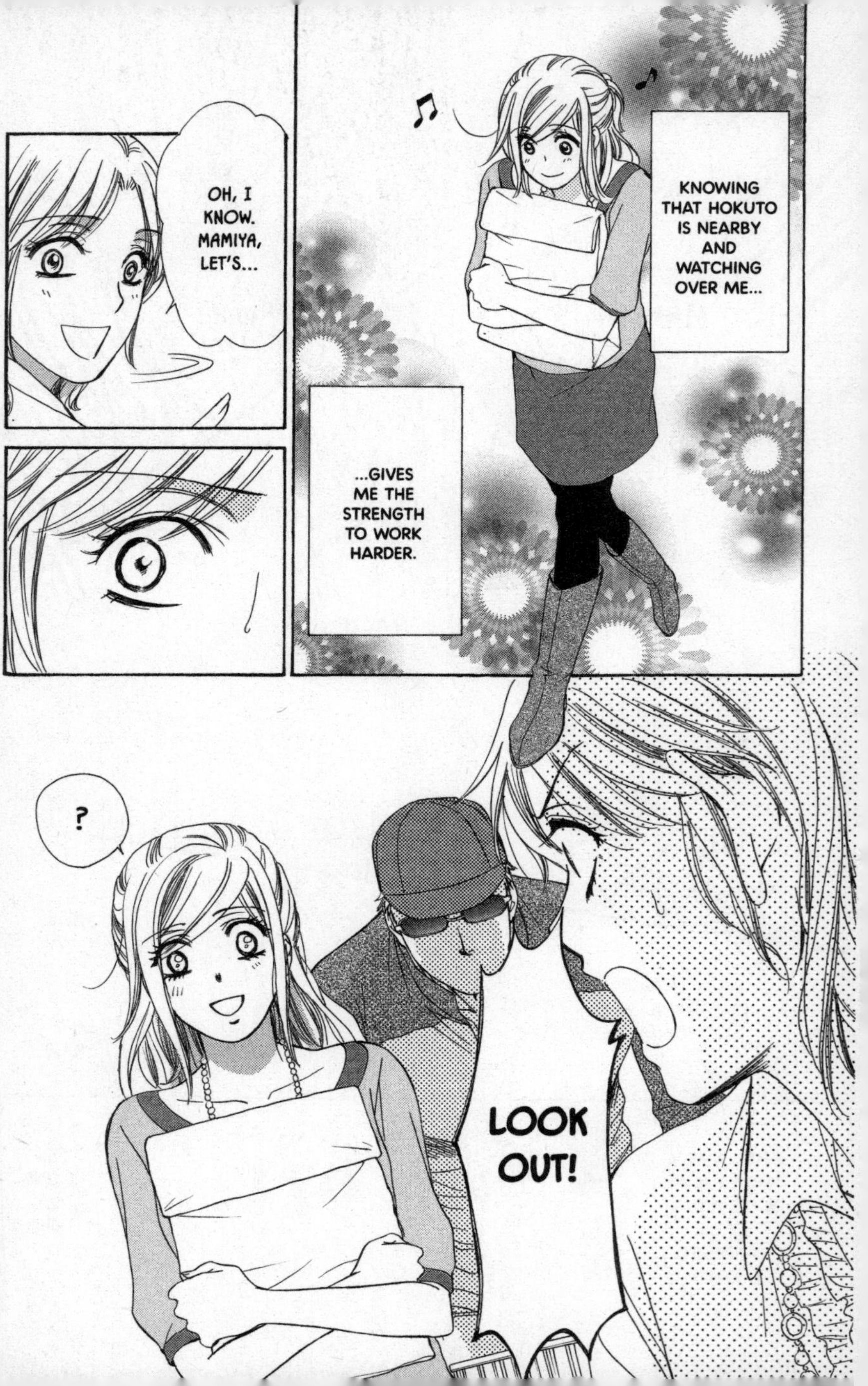
KNOWING THAT HOKUTO IS NEARBY AND WATCHING OVER ME...
...GIVES ME THE STRENGTH TO WORK HARDER.
OH, I KNOW. MAMIYA, LET'S...
?
LOOK OUT!

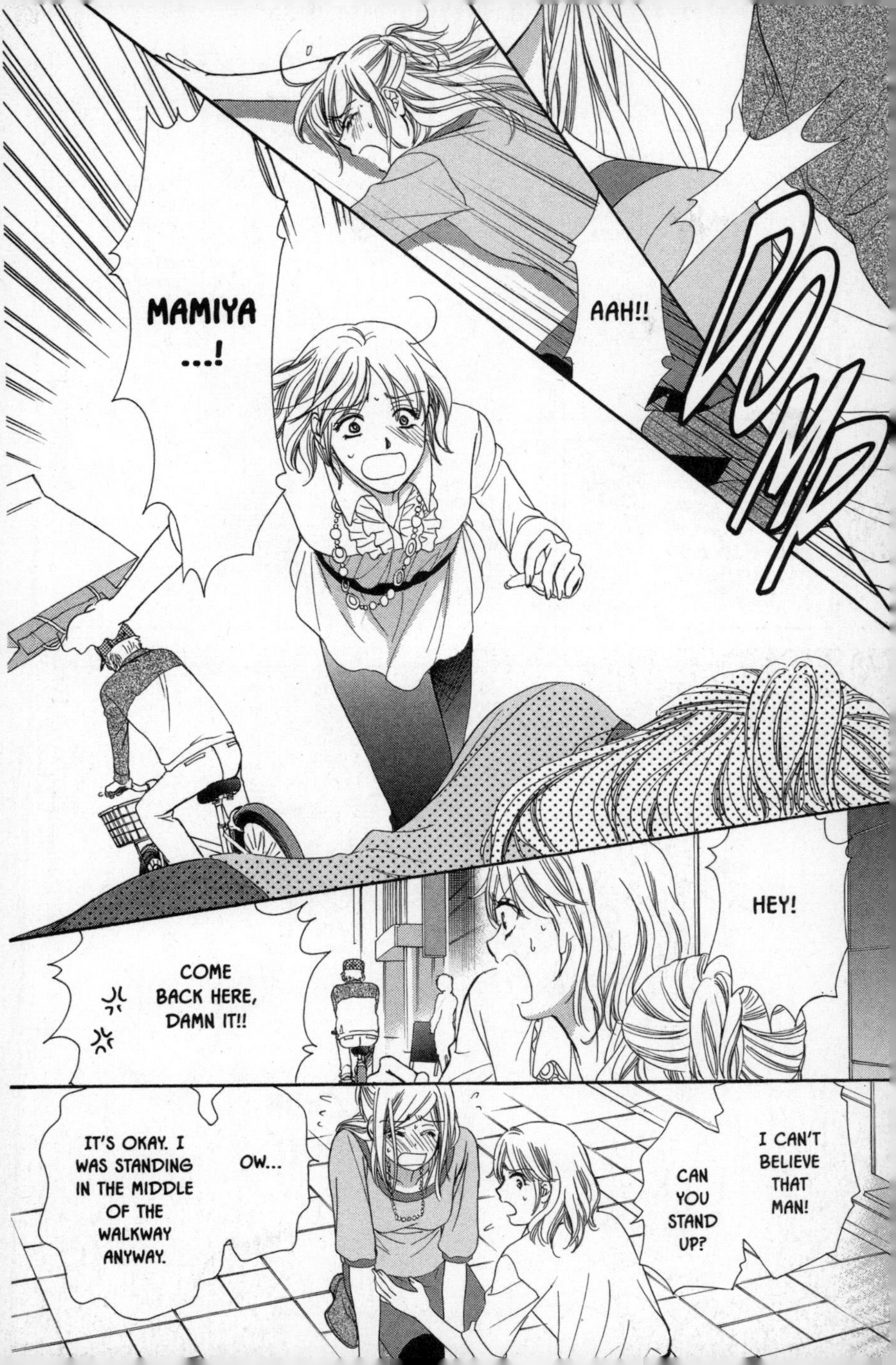
DOMP
AAH!!
MAMIYA ...!
HEY!
COME BACK HERE, DAMN IT!!
I CAN'T BELIEVE THAT MAN!
CAN YOU STAND UP?
OW...
IT'S OKAY. I WAS STANDING IN THE MIDDLE OF THE WALKWAY ANYWAY.

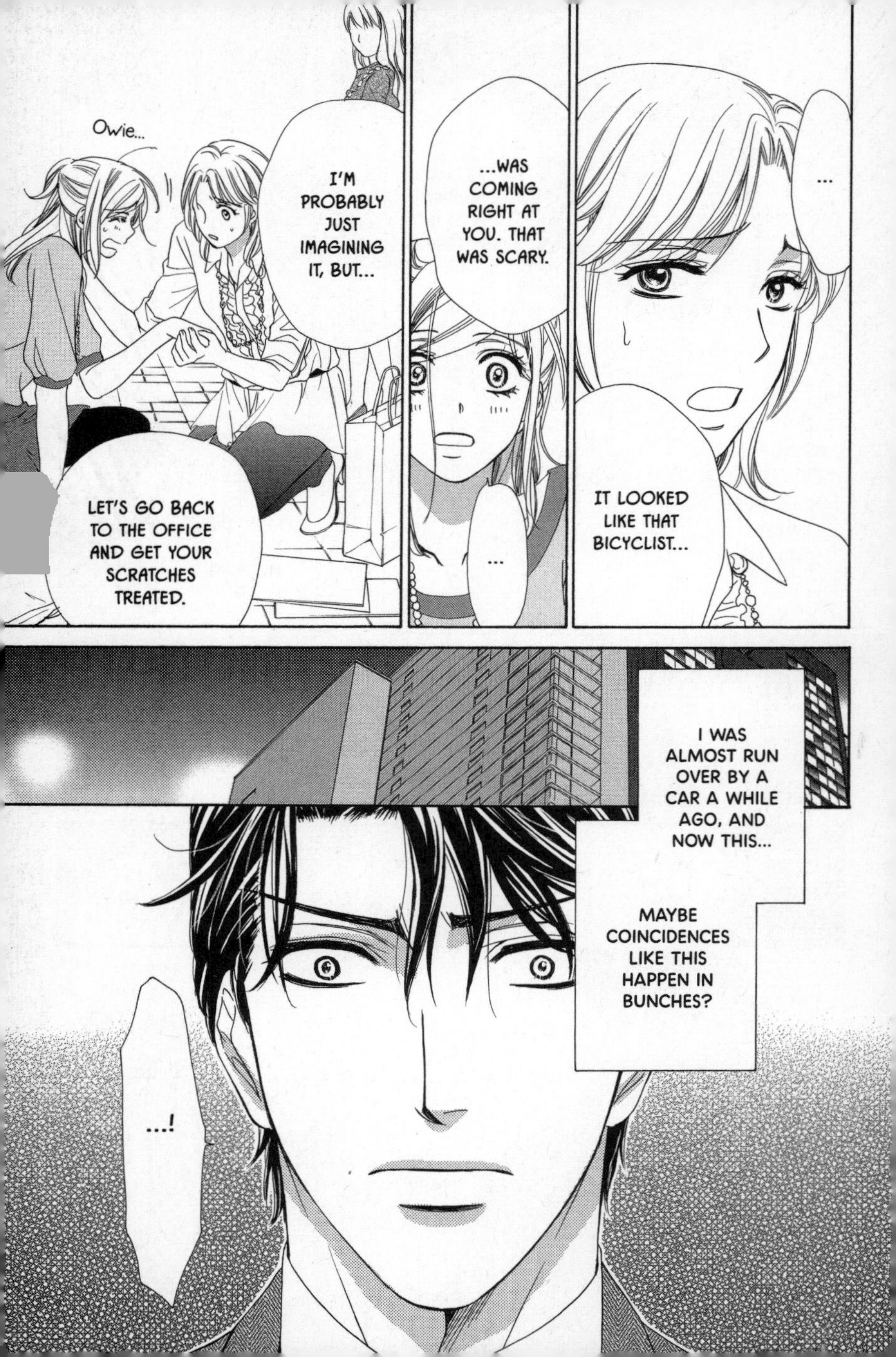
...
IT LOOKED LIKE THAT BICYCLIST...
...WAS COMING RIGHT AT YOU. THAT WAS SCARY.
...
I'M PROBABLY JUST IMAGINING IT, BUT...
Owie...
LET'S GO BACK TO THE OFFICE AND GET YOUR SCRATCHES TREATED.
I WAS ALMOST RUN OVER BY A CAR A WHILE AGO, AND NOW THIS...
MAYBE COINCIDENCES LIKE THIS HAPPEN IN BUNCHES?
...!

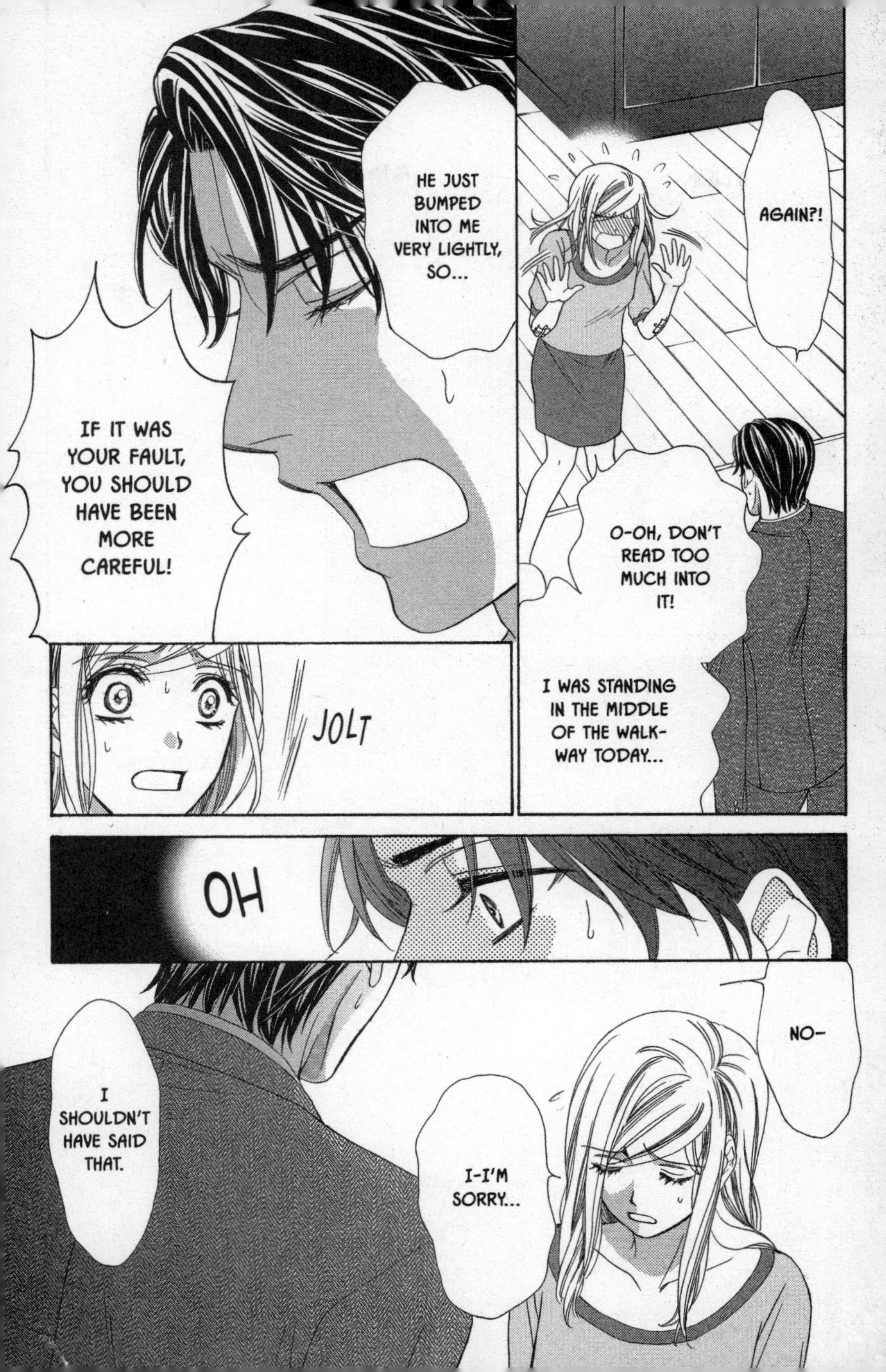
AGAIN?!
O-OH, DON'T READ TOO MUCH INTO IT!
I WAS STANDING IN THE MIDDLE OF THE WALK-WAY TODAY...
HE JUST BUMPED INTO ME VERY LIGHTLY, SO...
IF IT WAS YOUR FAULT, YOU SHOULD HAVE BEEN MORE CAREFUL!
JOLT
OH
NO-
I-I'M SORRY...
I SHOULDN'T HAVE SAID THAT.

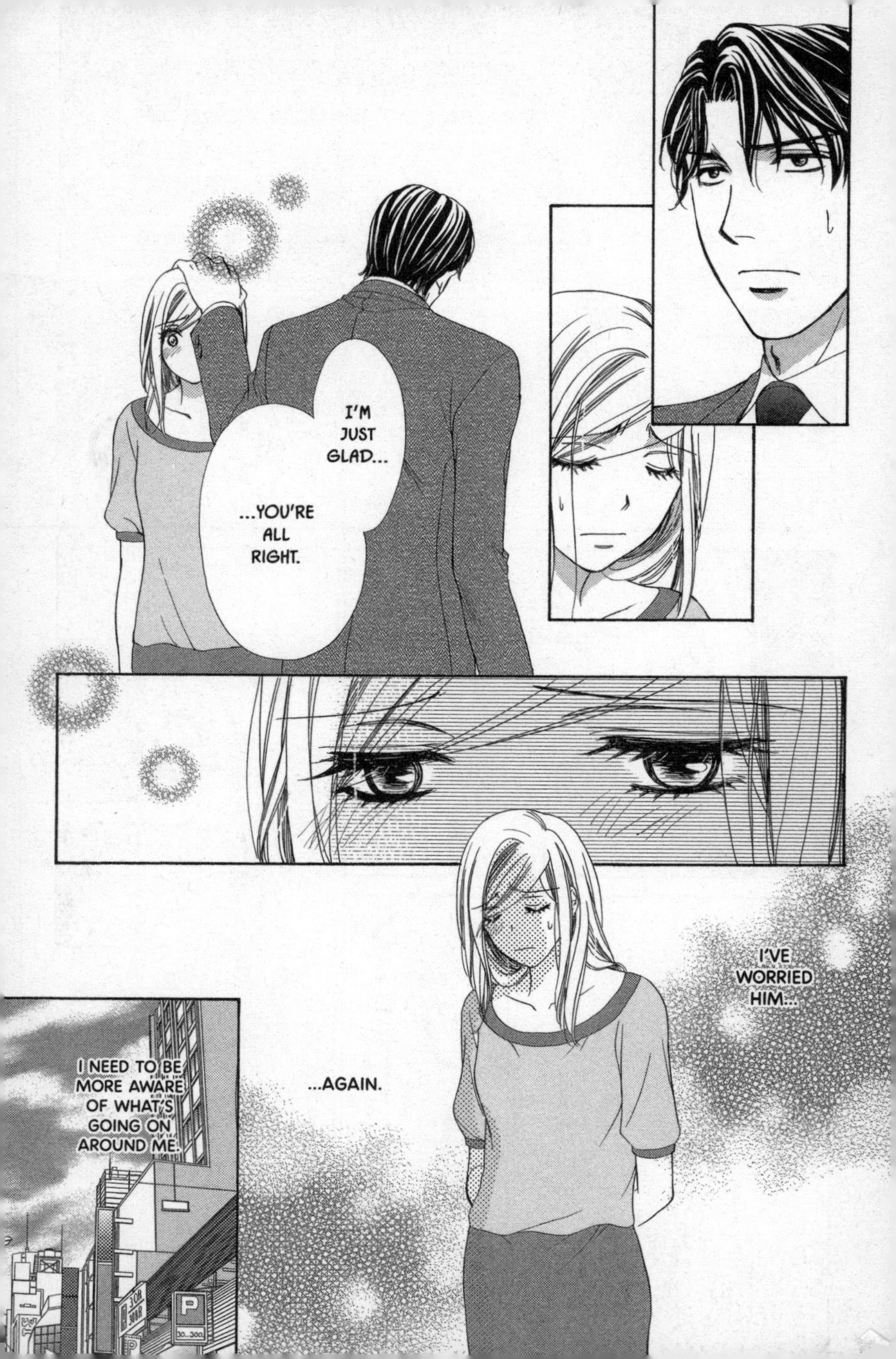
I'M JUST GLAD...
...YOU'RE ALL RIGHT.
I'VE WORRIED HIM...
...AGAIN.
I NEED TO BE MORE AWARE OF WHAT'S GOING ON AROUND ME.

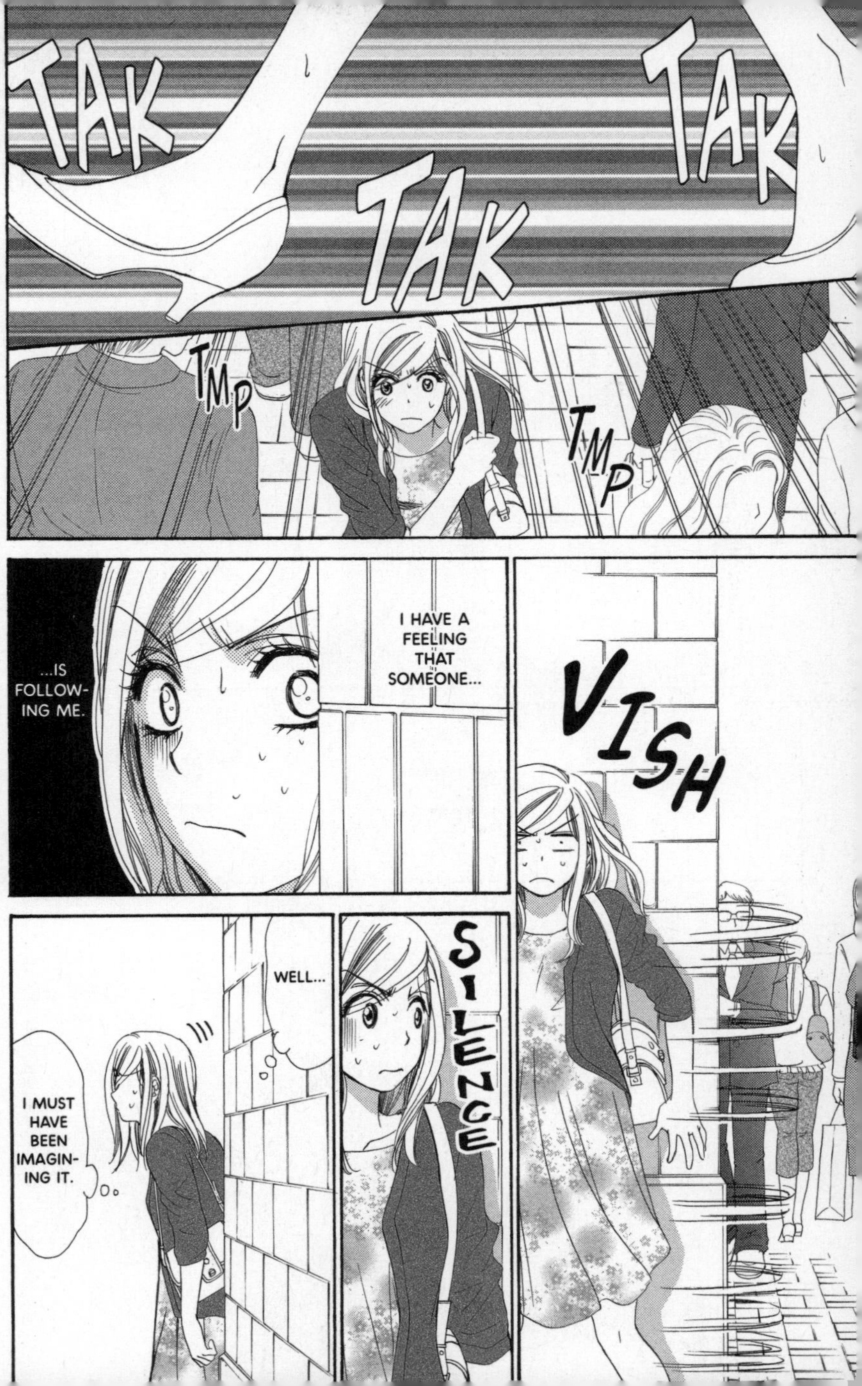
TAK
TAK
TAK
TMP
TMP
VISH
I HAVE A FEELING THAT SOMEONE...
...IS FOLLOWING ME.
SILENCE
WELL...
I MUST HAVE BEEN IMAGINING IT.

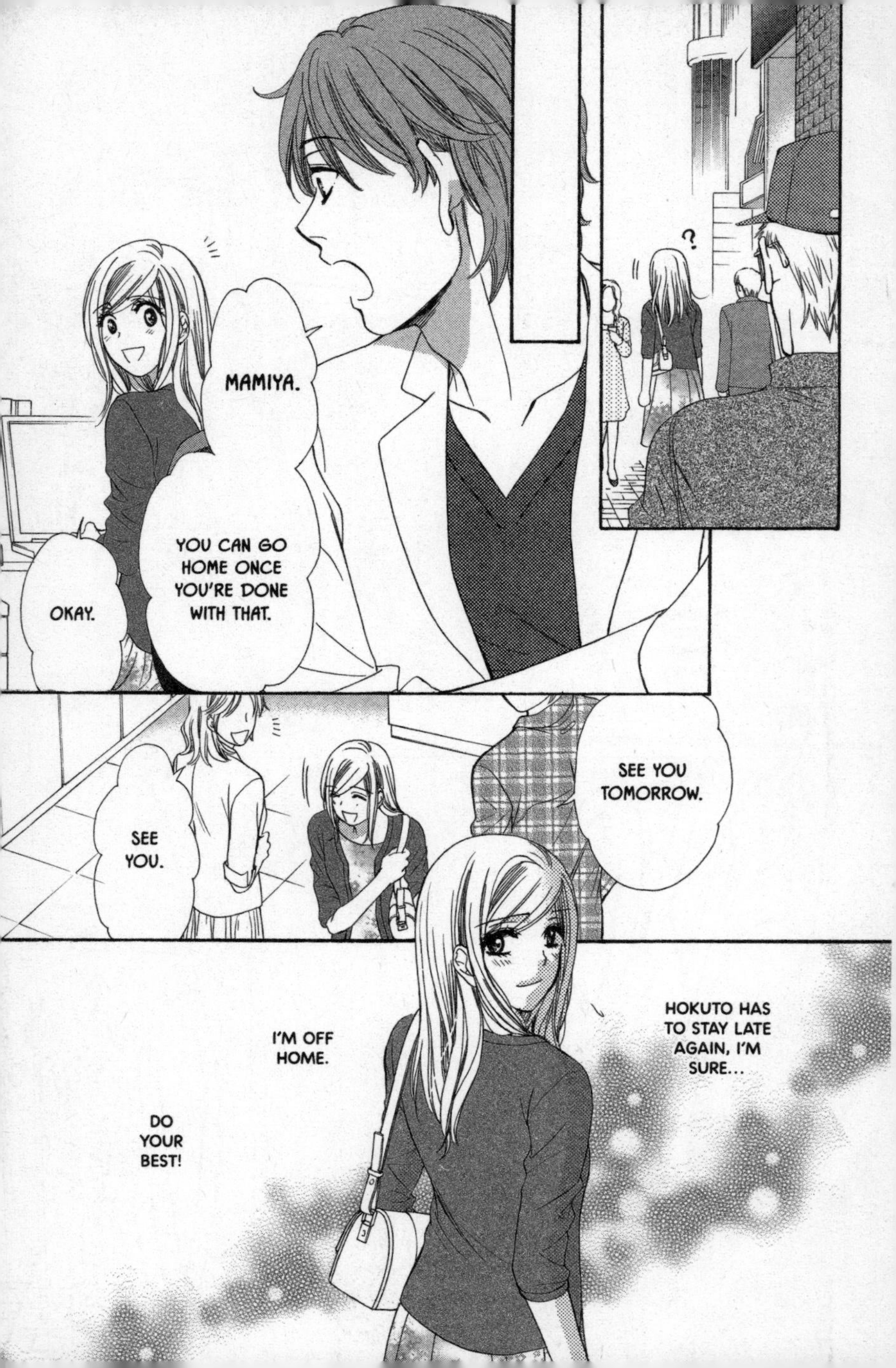
MAMIYA.
YOU CAN GO HOME ONCE YOU'RE DONE WITH THAT.
OKAY.
SEE YOU TOMORROW.
SEE YOU.
HOKUTO HAS TO STAY LATE AGAIN, I'M SURE...
I'M OFF HOME.
DO YOUR BEST!

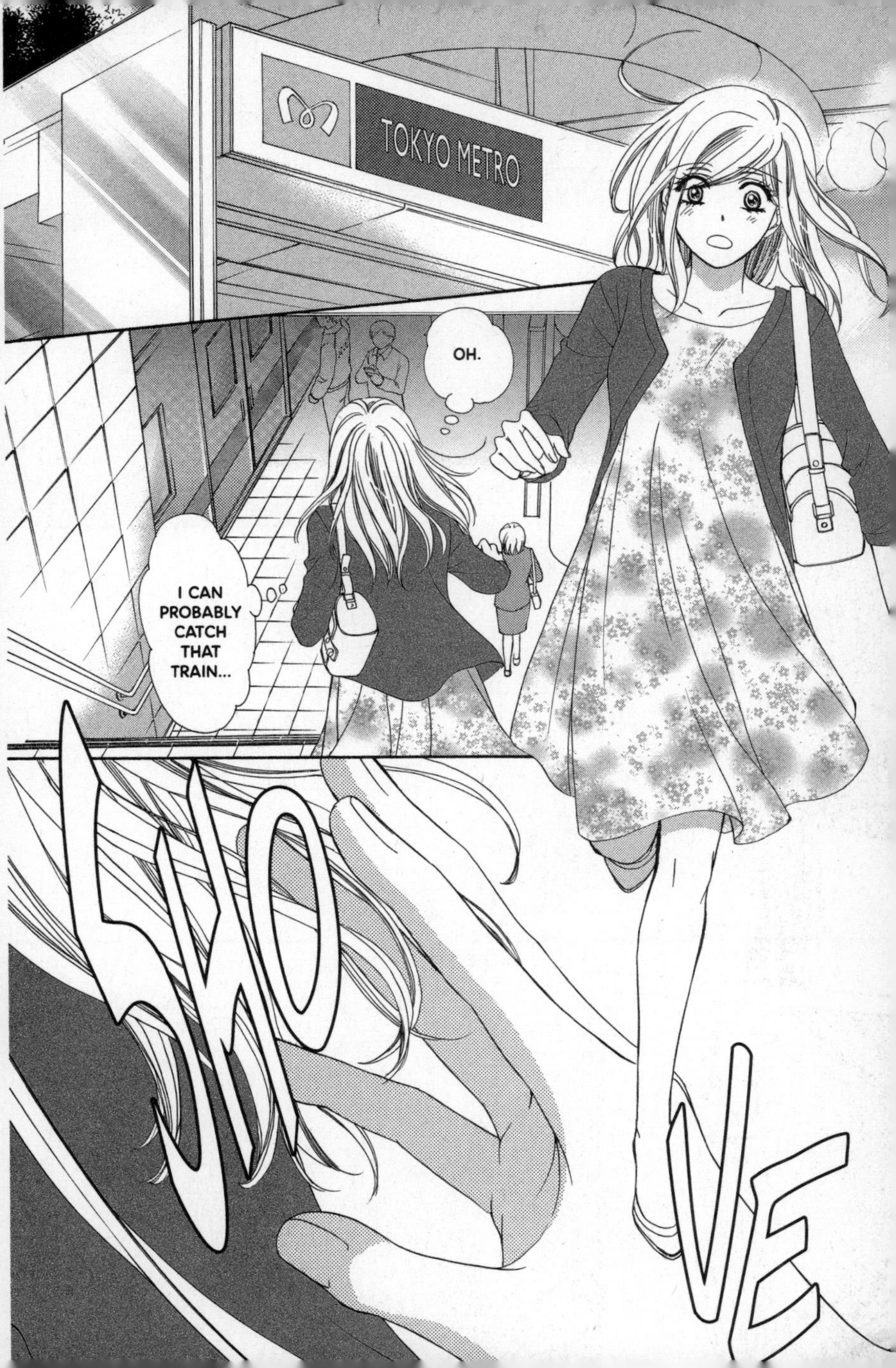
TOKYO METRO
OH.
I CAN PROBABLY CATCH THAT TRAIN...

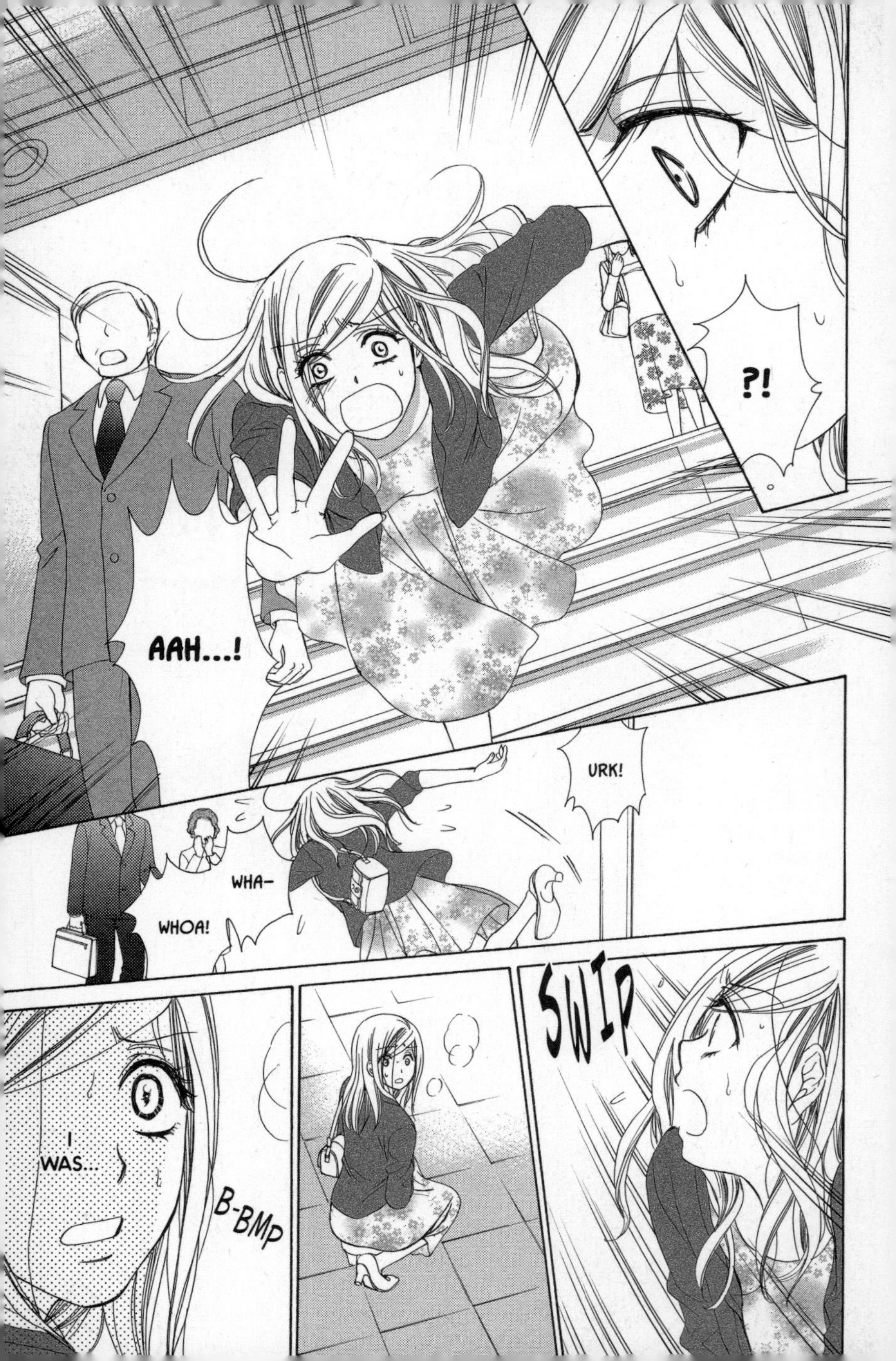
?!
AAH...!
URK!
WHA-
WHOA!
SWIP
I WAS...
B-BMP

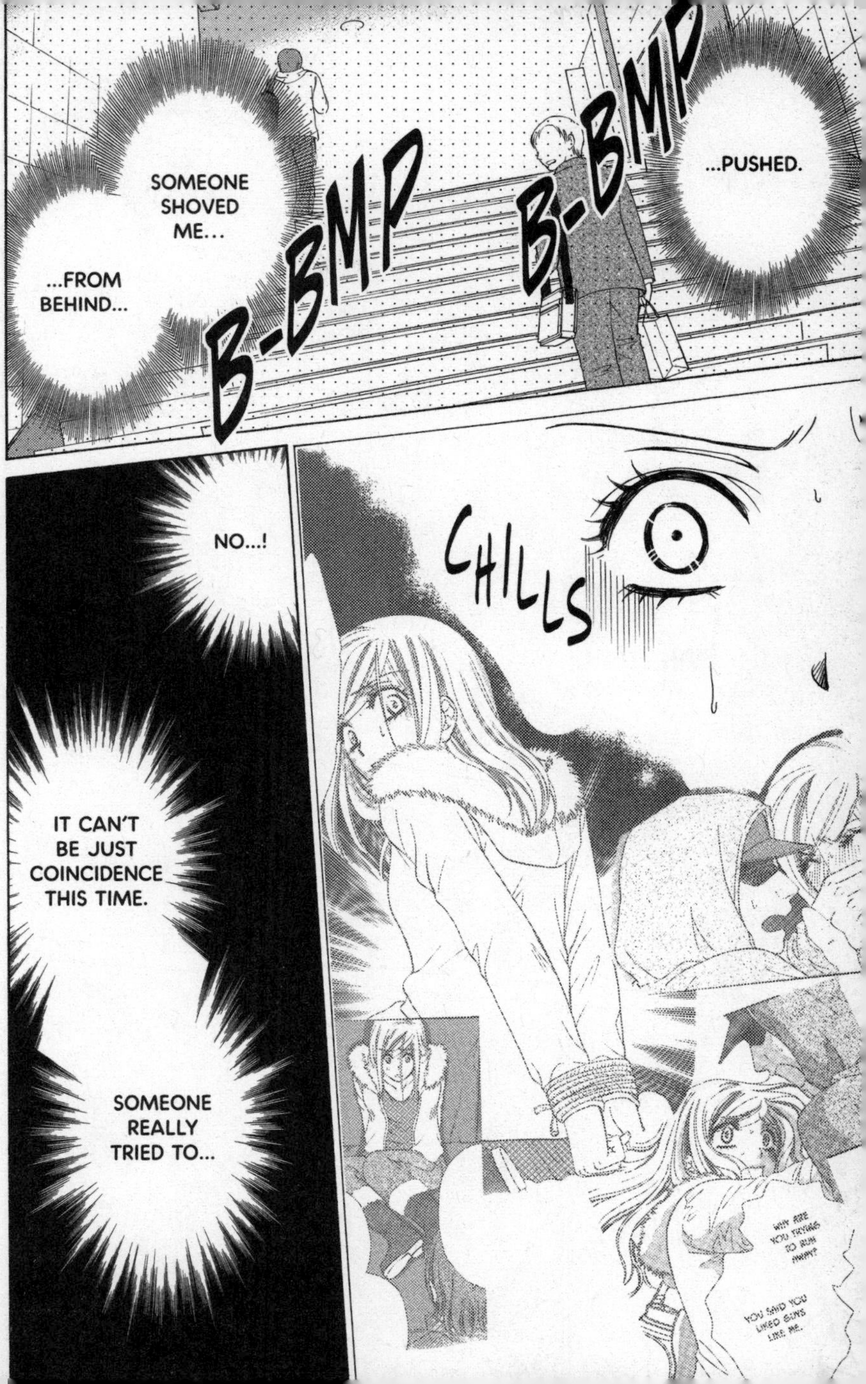
...PUSHED.
B-BMP
B-BMP
SOMEONE SHOVED ME...
...FROM BEHIND...
CHILLS
WHY ARE YOU TRYING TO RUN AWAY?
YOU SAID YOU LIKED GUYS LIKE ME.
NO...!
IT CAN'T BE JUST COINCIDENCE THIS TIME.
SOMEONE REALLY TRIED TO...

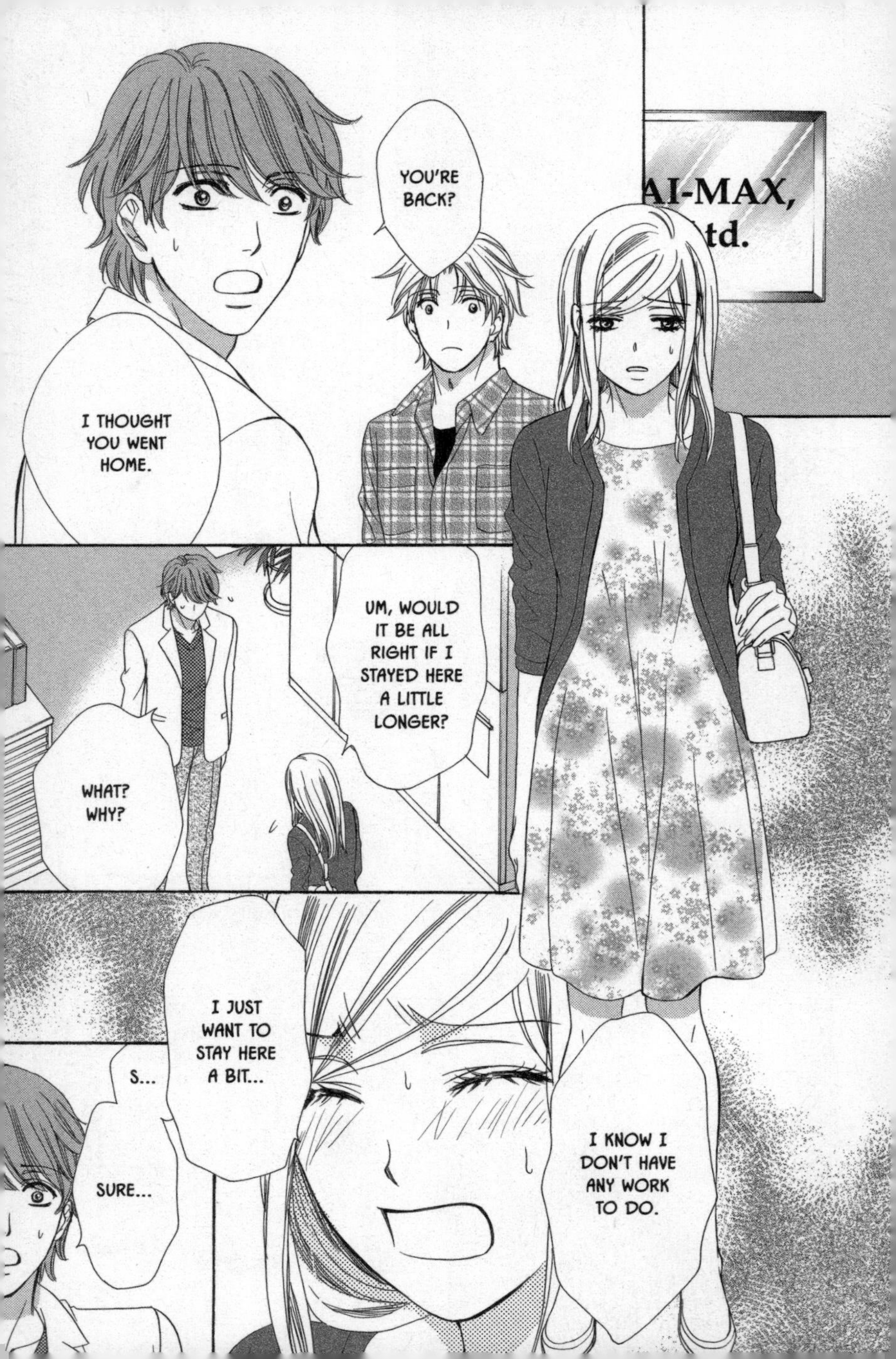

AI-MAX,
td.
YOU'RE BACK?
I THOUGHT YOU WENT HOME.
UM, WOULD IT BE ALL RIGHT IF I STAYED HERE A LITTLE LONGER?
WHAT? WHY?
I KNOW I DON'T HAVE ANY WORK TO DO.
I JUST WANT TO STAY HERE A BIT...
S...
SURE...

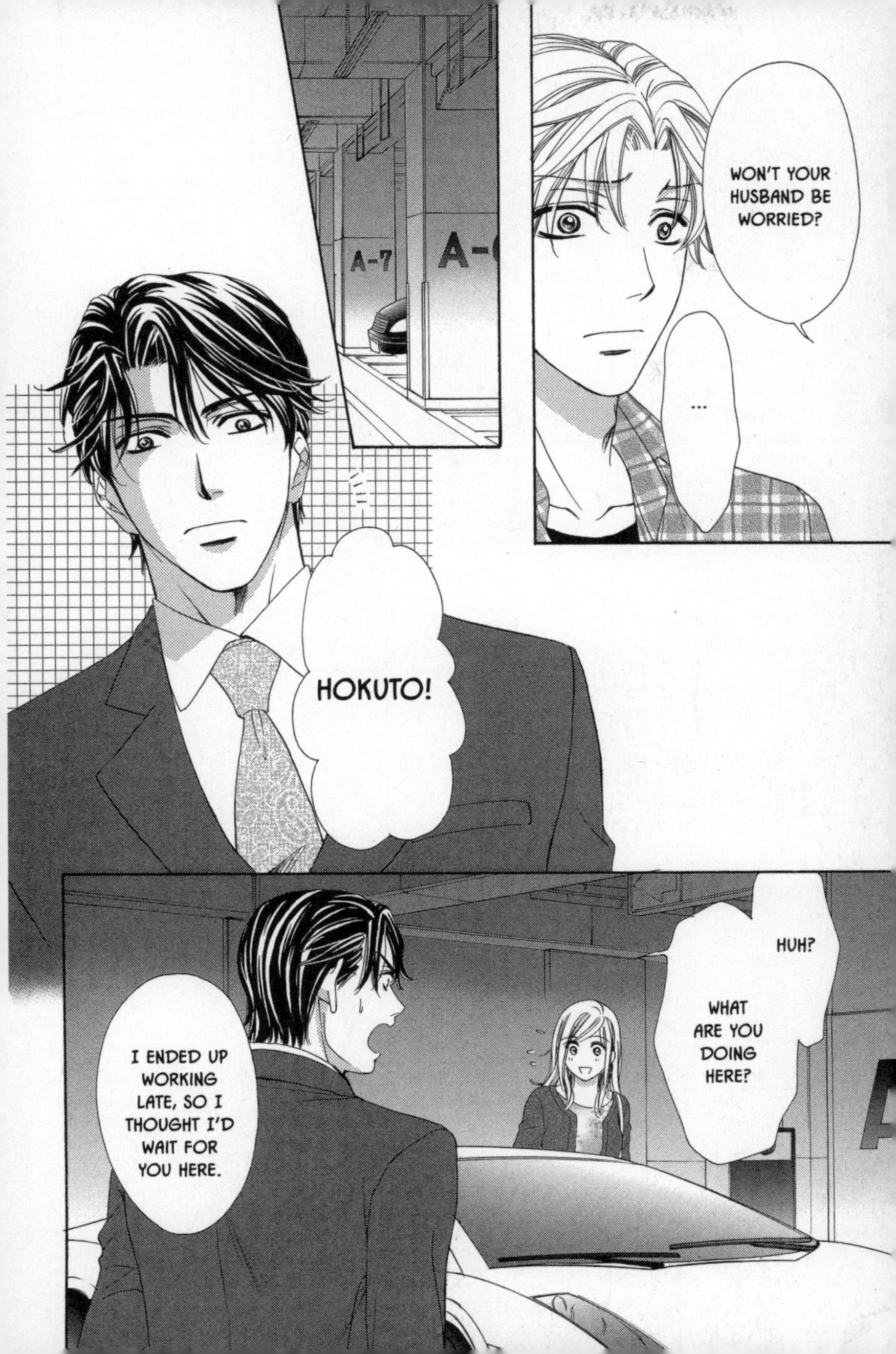
WON'T YOUR HUSBAND BE WORRIED?
...
HOKUTO!
HUH?
WHAT ARE YOU DOING HERE?
I ENDED UP WORKING LATE, SO I THOUGHT I'D WAIT FOR YOU HERE.

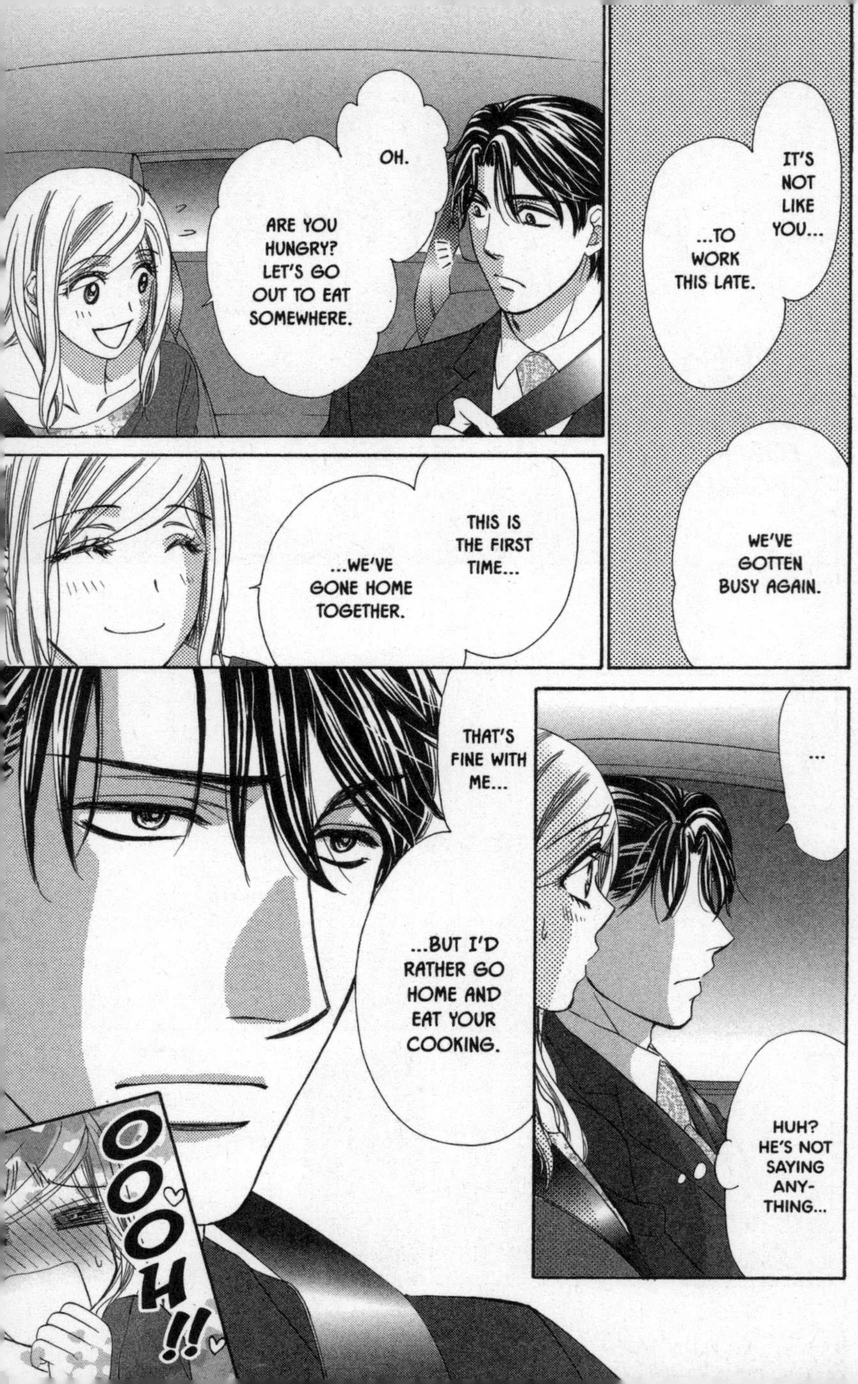
IT'S NOT LIKE YOU...
...TO WORK THIS LATE.
WE'VE GOTTEN BUSY AGAIN.
OH.
ARE YOU HUNGRY? LET'S GO OUT TO EAT SOMEWHERE.
THIS IS THE FIRST TIME...
...WE'VE GONE HOME TOGETHER.
...
HUH? HE'S NOT SAYING ANY-THING...
THAT'S FINE WITH ME...
...BUT I'D RATHER GO HOME AND EAT YOUR COOKING.
OOOOH!!

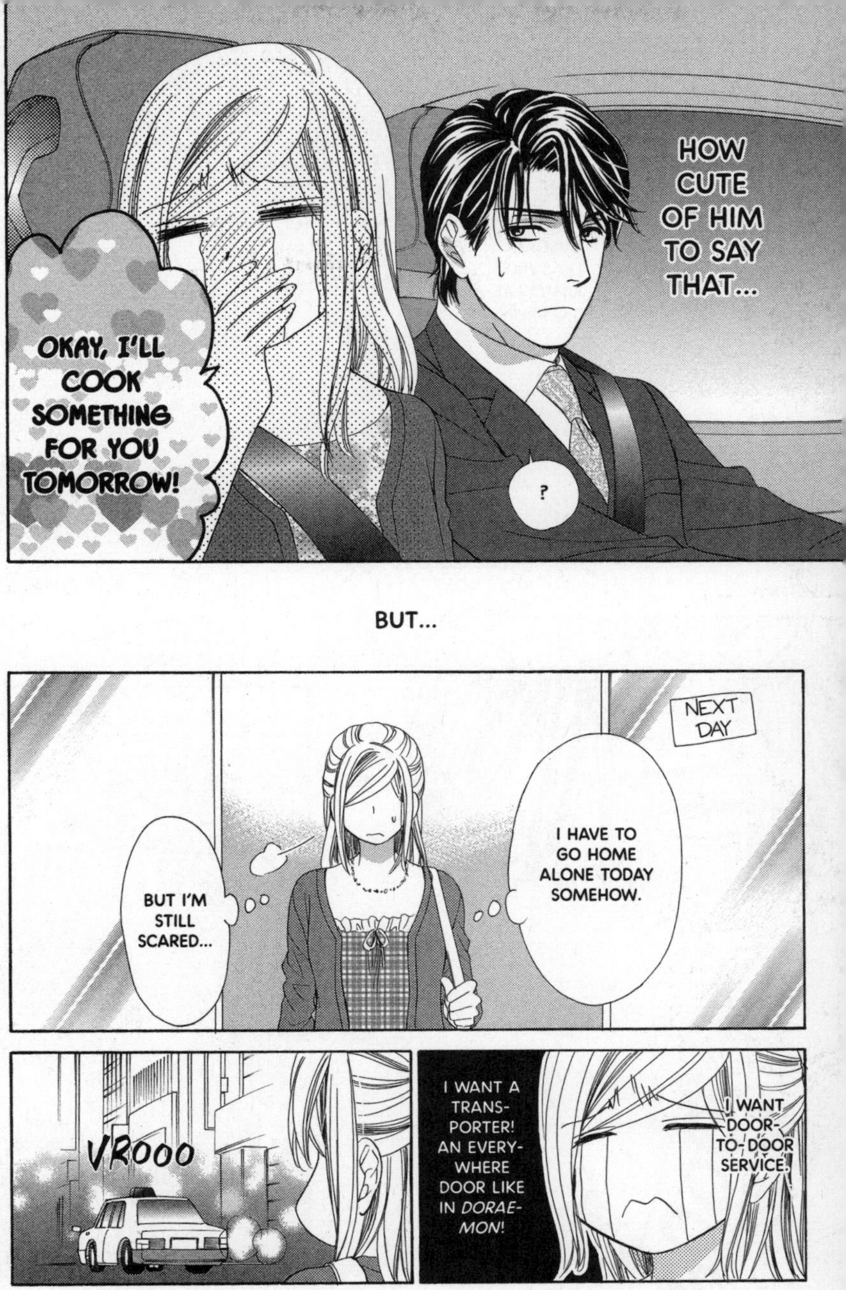

HOW CUTE OF HIM TO SAY THAT...
OKAY, I'LL COOK SOMETHING FOR YOU TOMORROW!
?
BUT...
NEXT DAY
I HAVE TO GO HOME ALONE TODAY SOMEHOW.
BUT I'M STILL SCARED...
I WANT DOOR-TO-DOOR SERVICE.
I WANT A TRANSPORTER! AN EVERYWHERE DOOR LIKE IN *DORAEMON*!
VROOO

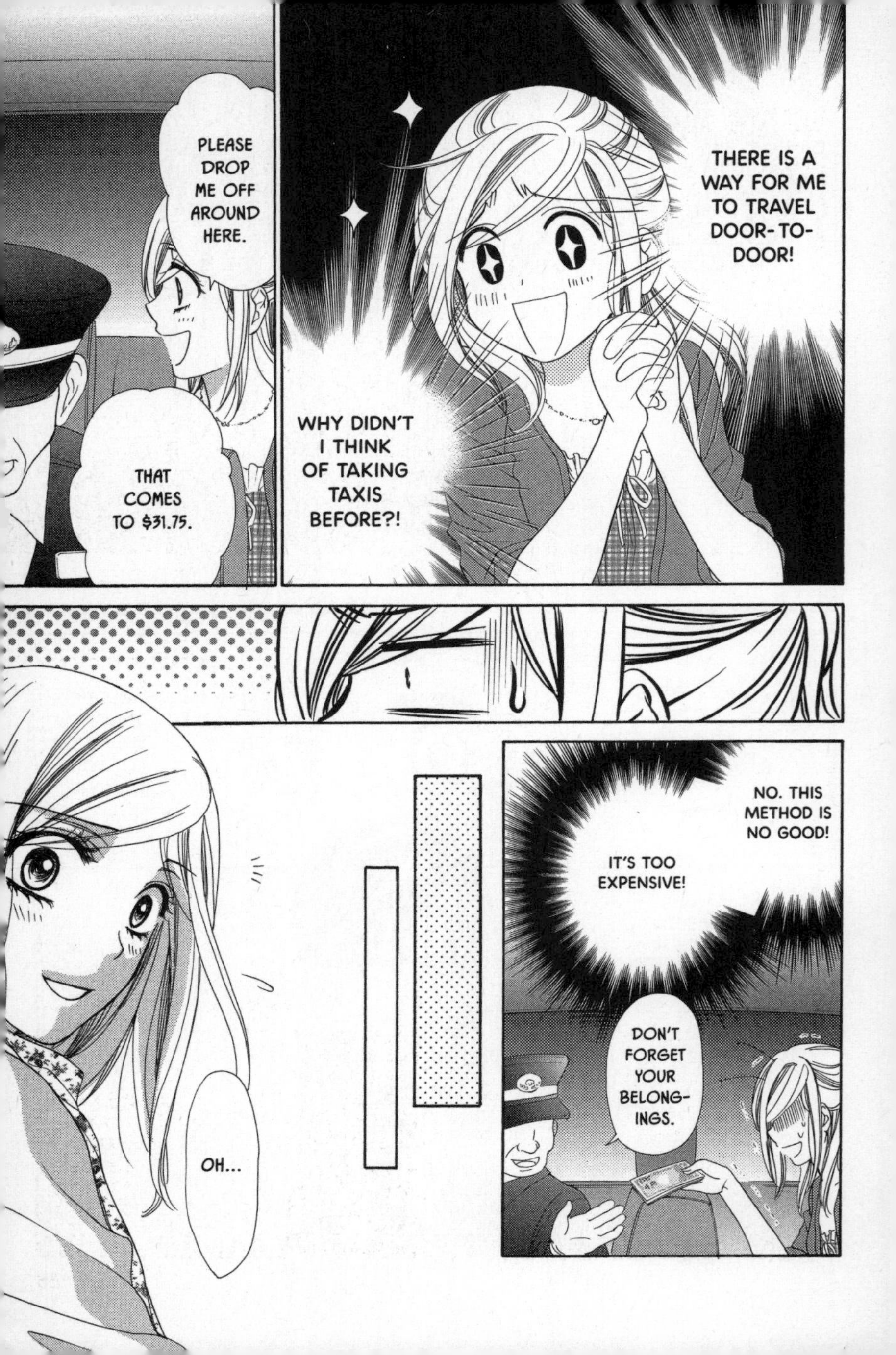
THERE IS A WAY FOR ME TO TRAVEL DOOR-TO-DOOR!
WHY DIDN'T I THINK OF TAKING TAXIS BEFORE?!
PLEASE DROP ME OFF AROUND HERE.
THAT COMES TO $31.75.
NO. THIS METHOD IS NO GOOD!
IT'S TOO EXPENSIVE!
DON'T FORGET YOUR BELONG-INGS.
OH...

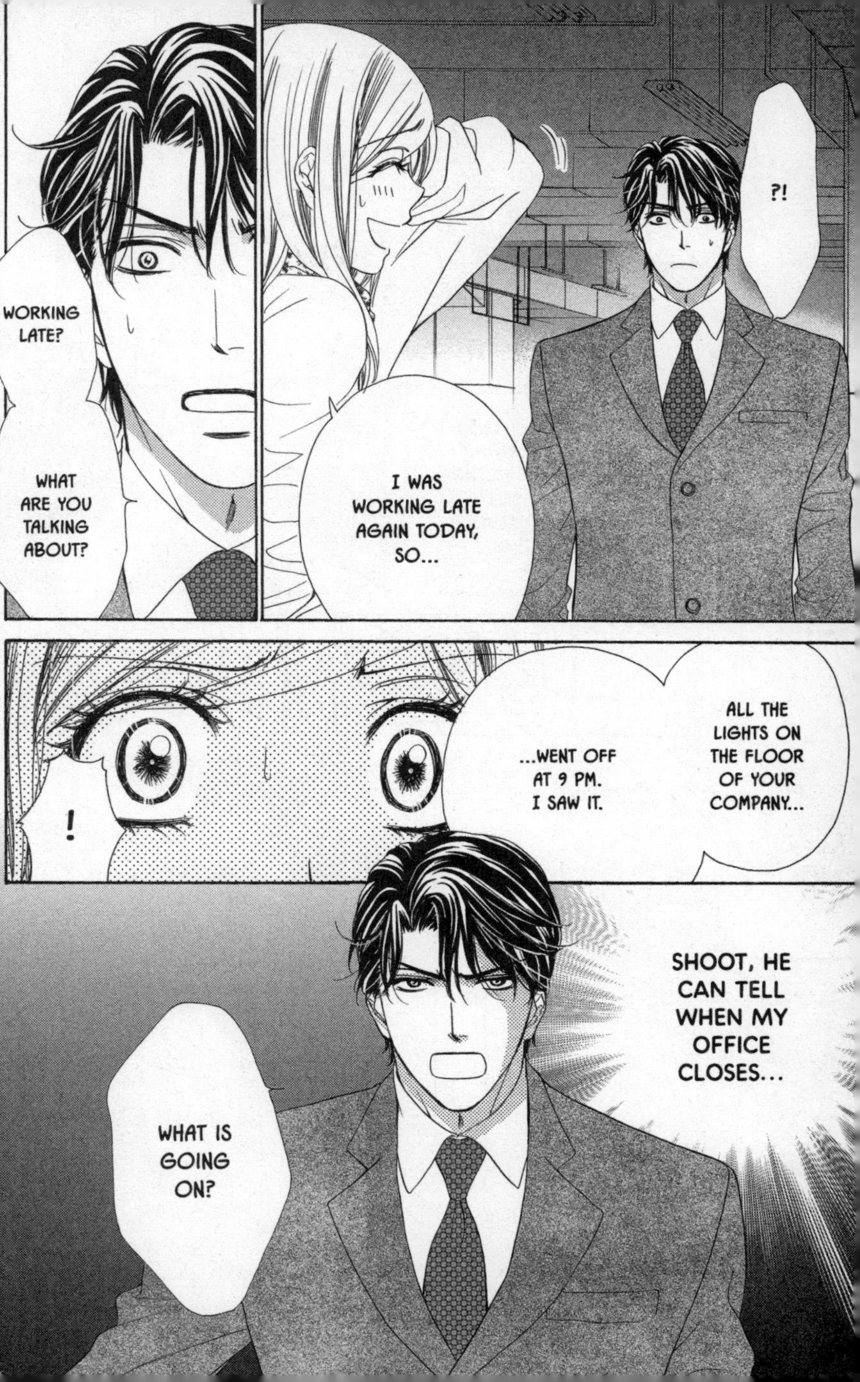
?!
I WAS WORKING LATE AGAIN TODAY, SO...
WORKING LATE?
WHAT ARE YOU TALKING ABOUT?
ALL THE LIGHTS ON THE FLOOR OF YOUR COMPANY...
...WENT OFF AT 9 PM. I SAW IT.
!
SHOOT, HE CAN TELL WHEN MY OFFICE CLOSES...
WHAT IS GOING ON?

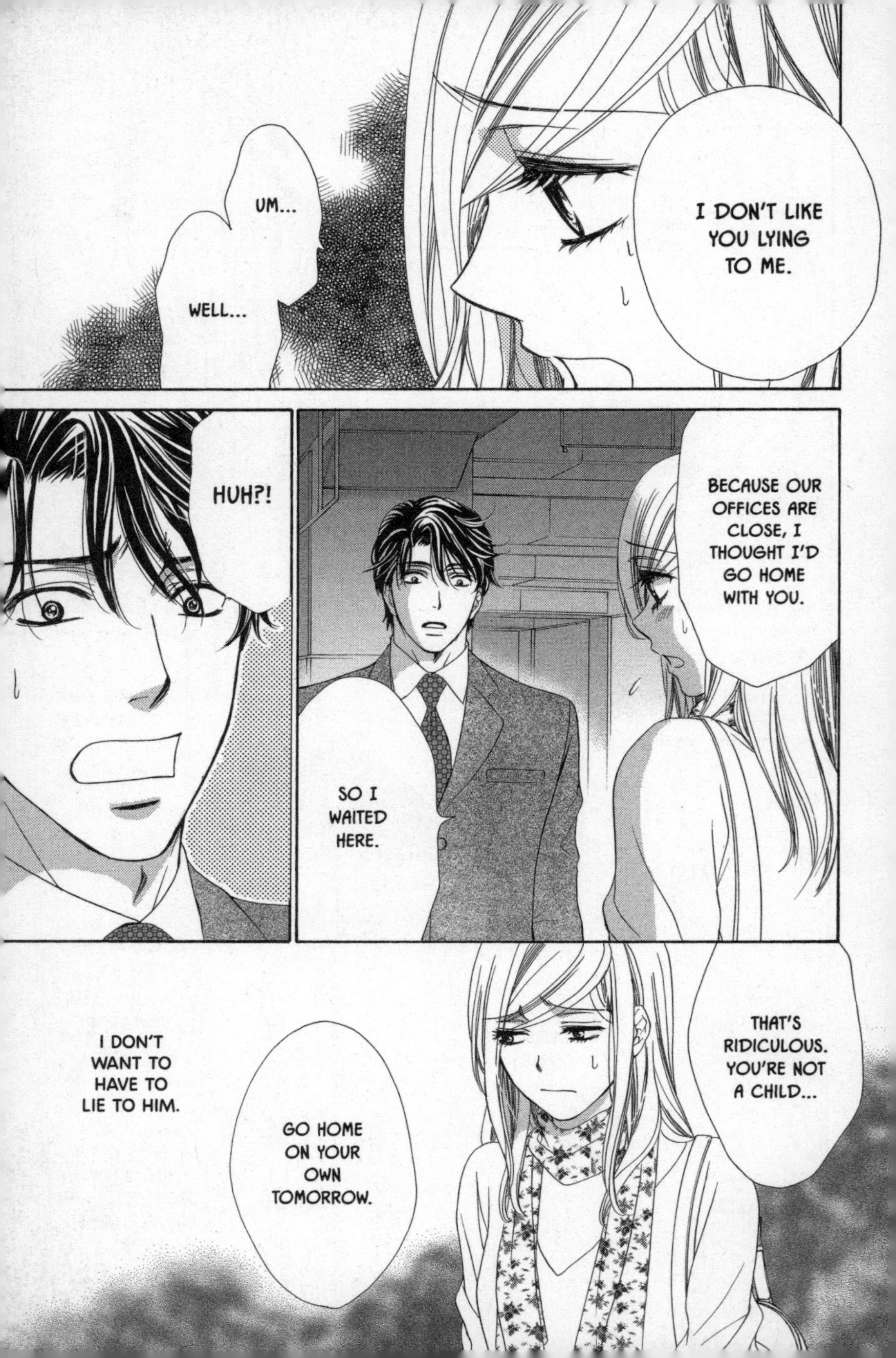
I DON'T LIKE YOU LYING TO ME.
UM...
WELL...
BECAUSE OUR OFFICES ARE CLOSE, I THOUGHT I'D GO HOME WITH YOU.
SO I WAITED HERE.
HUH?!
THAT'S RIDICULOUS. YOU'RE NOT A CHILD...
GO HOME ON YOUR OWN TOMORROW.
I DON'T WANT TO HAVE TO LIE TO HIM.

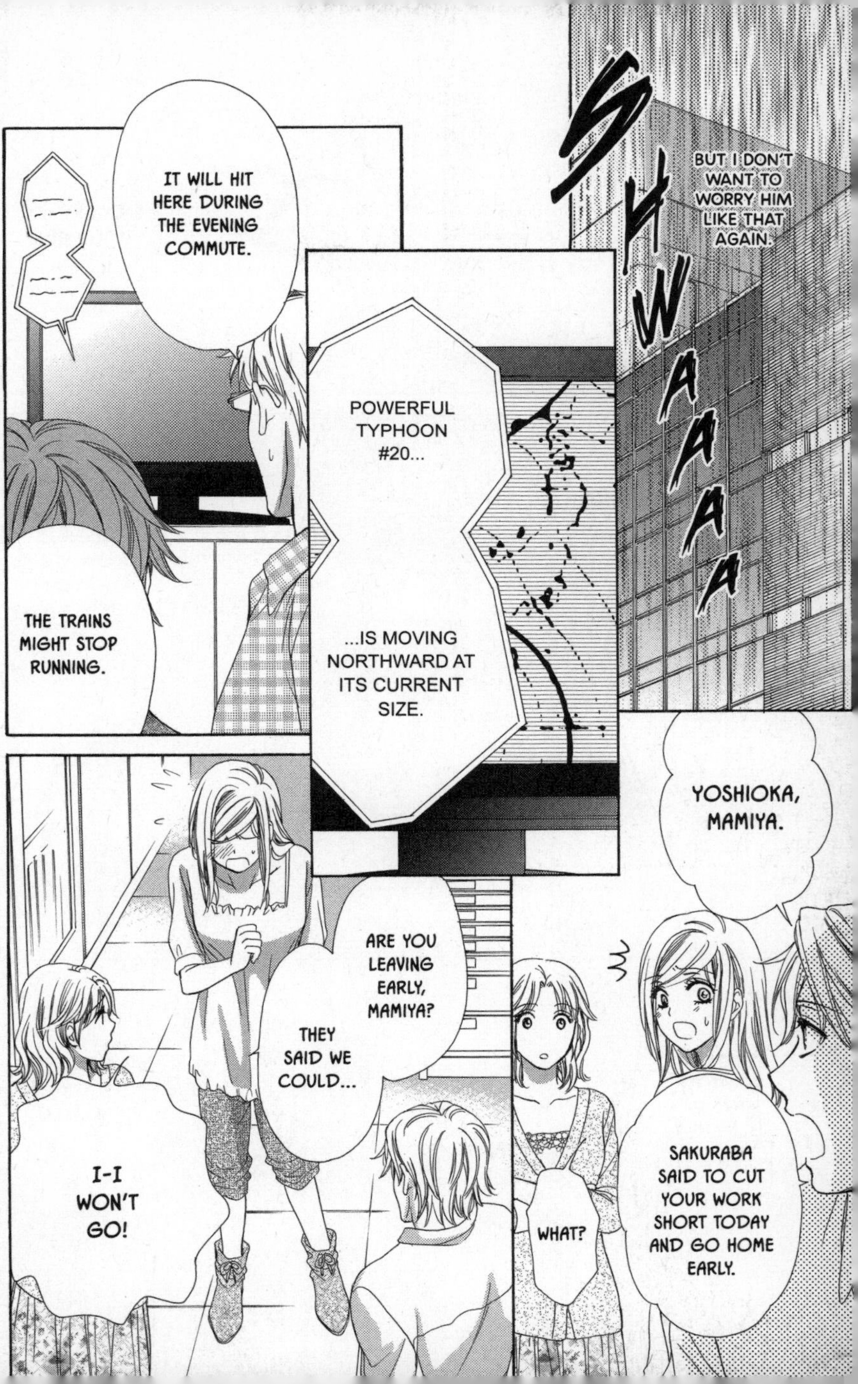
BUT I DON'T WANT TO WORRY HIM LIKE THAT AGAIN.
SHWAAAAAA
POWERFUL TYPHOON #20...
...IS MOVING NORTHWARD AT ITS CURRENT SIZE.
IT WILL HIT HERE DURING THE EVENING COMMUTE.
THE TRAINS MIGHT STOP RUNNING.
YOSHIOKA, MAMIYA.
SAKURABA SAID TO CUT YOUR WORK SHORT TODAY AND GO HOME EARLY.
WHAT?
ARE YOU LEAVING EARLY, MAMIYA?
THEY SAID WE COULD...
I-I WON'T GO!

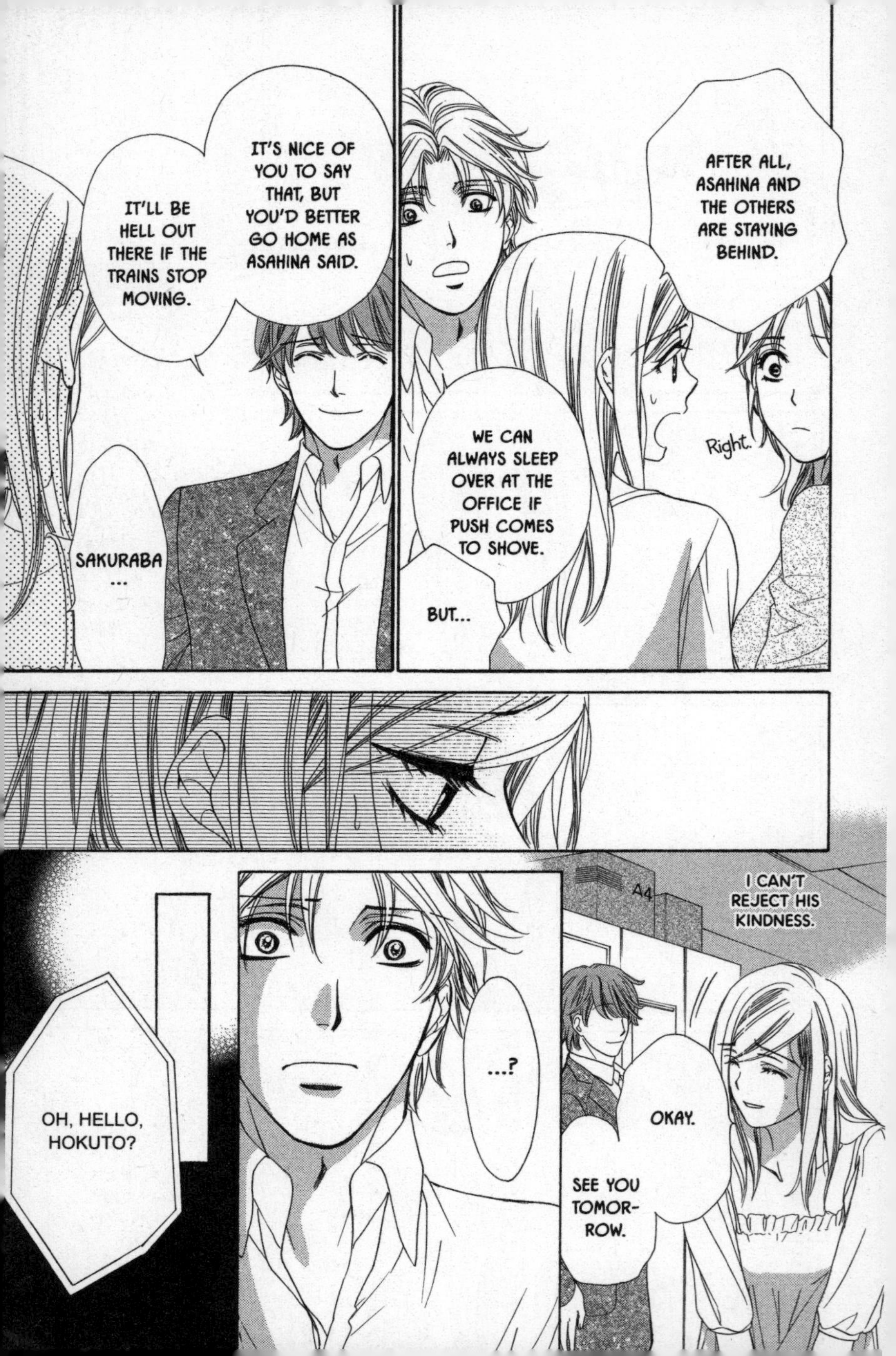

AFTER ALL, ASAHINA AND THE OTHERS ARE STAYING BEHIND.
Right.
WE CAN ALWAYS SLEEP OVER AT THE OFFICE IF PUSH COMES TO SHOVE.
BUT...
IT'S NICE OF YOU TO SAY THAT, BUT YOU'D BETTER GO HOME AS ASAHINA SAID.
IT'LL BE HELL OUT THERE IF THE TRAINS STOP MOVING.
SAKURABA ...
I CAN'T REJECT HIS KINDNESS.
A4
OKAY.
SEE YOU TOMOR-ROW.
...?
OH, HELLO, HOKUTO?

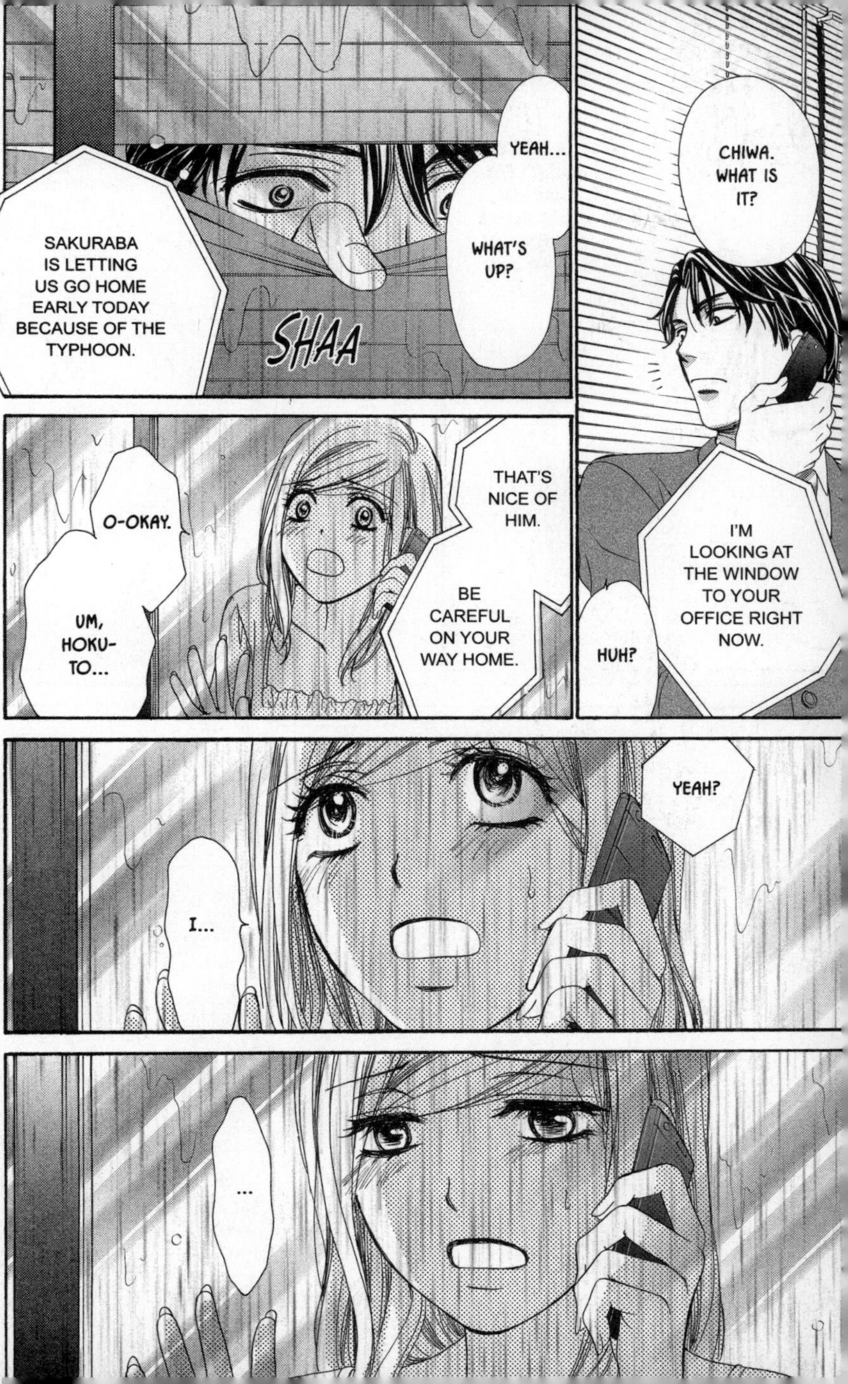
CHIWA. WHAT IS IT?
I'M LOOKING AT THE WINDOW TO YOUR OFFICE RIGHT NOW.
HUH?
YEAH...
WHAT'S UP?
SAKURABA IS LETTING US GO HOME EARLY TODAY BECAUSE OF THE TYPHOON.
SHAA
THAT'S NICE OF HIM.
BE CAREFUL ON YOUR WAY HOME.
O-OKAY.
UM, HOKU-TO...
YEAH?
I...
...

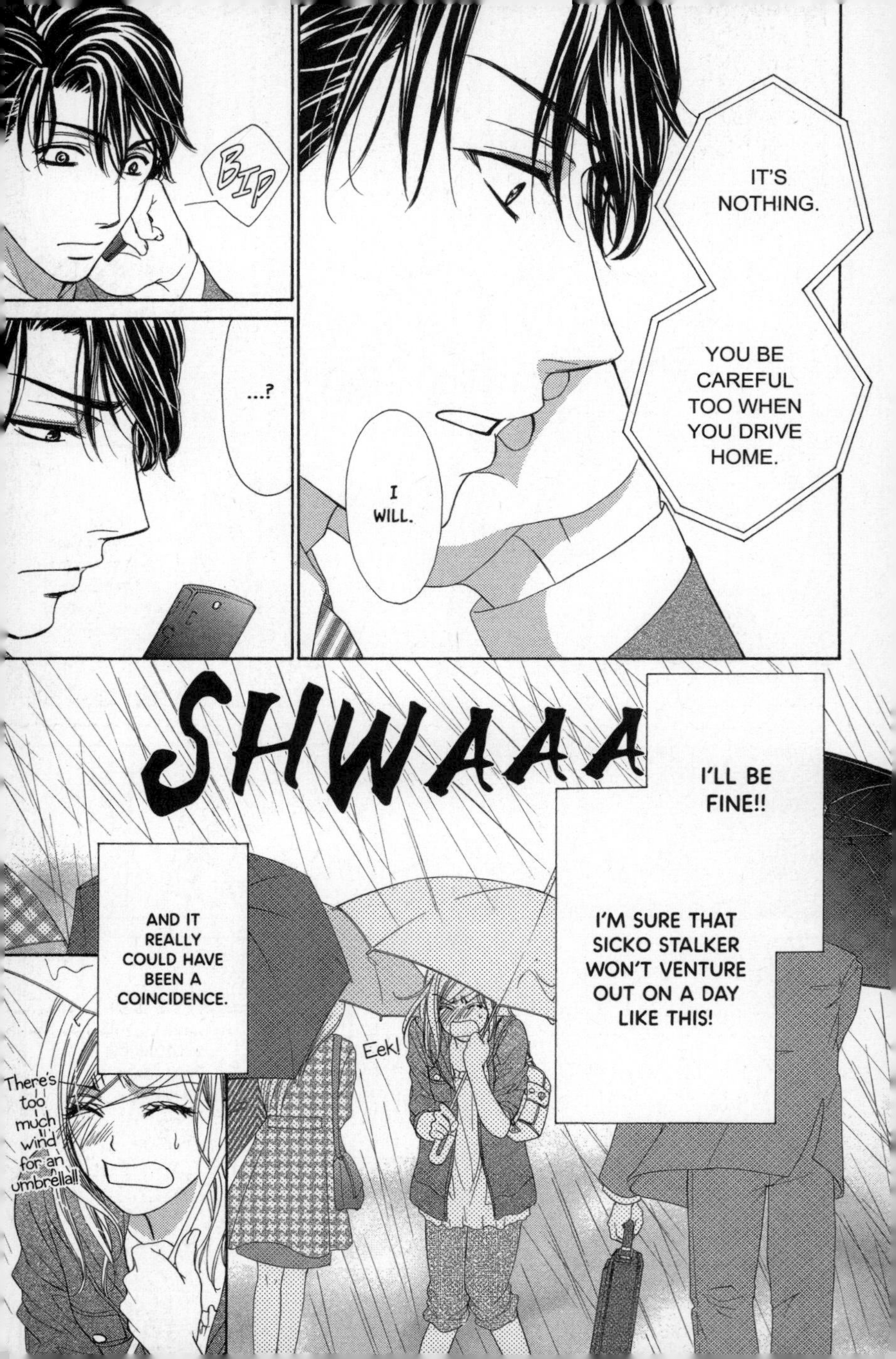
IT'S NOTHING.
YOU BE CAREFUL TOO WHEN YOU DRIVE HOME.
I WILL.
BIP
...?
SHWAAA
I'LL BE FINE!!
I'M SURE THAT SICKO STALKER WON'T VENTURE OUT ON A DAY LIKE THIS!
AND IT REALLY COULD HAVE BEEN A COINCIDENCE.
Eek!
There's too much wind for an umbrella!!

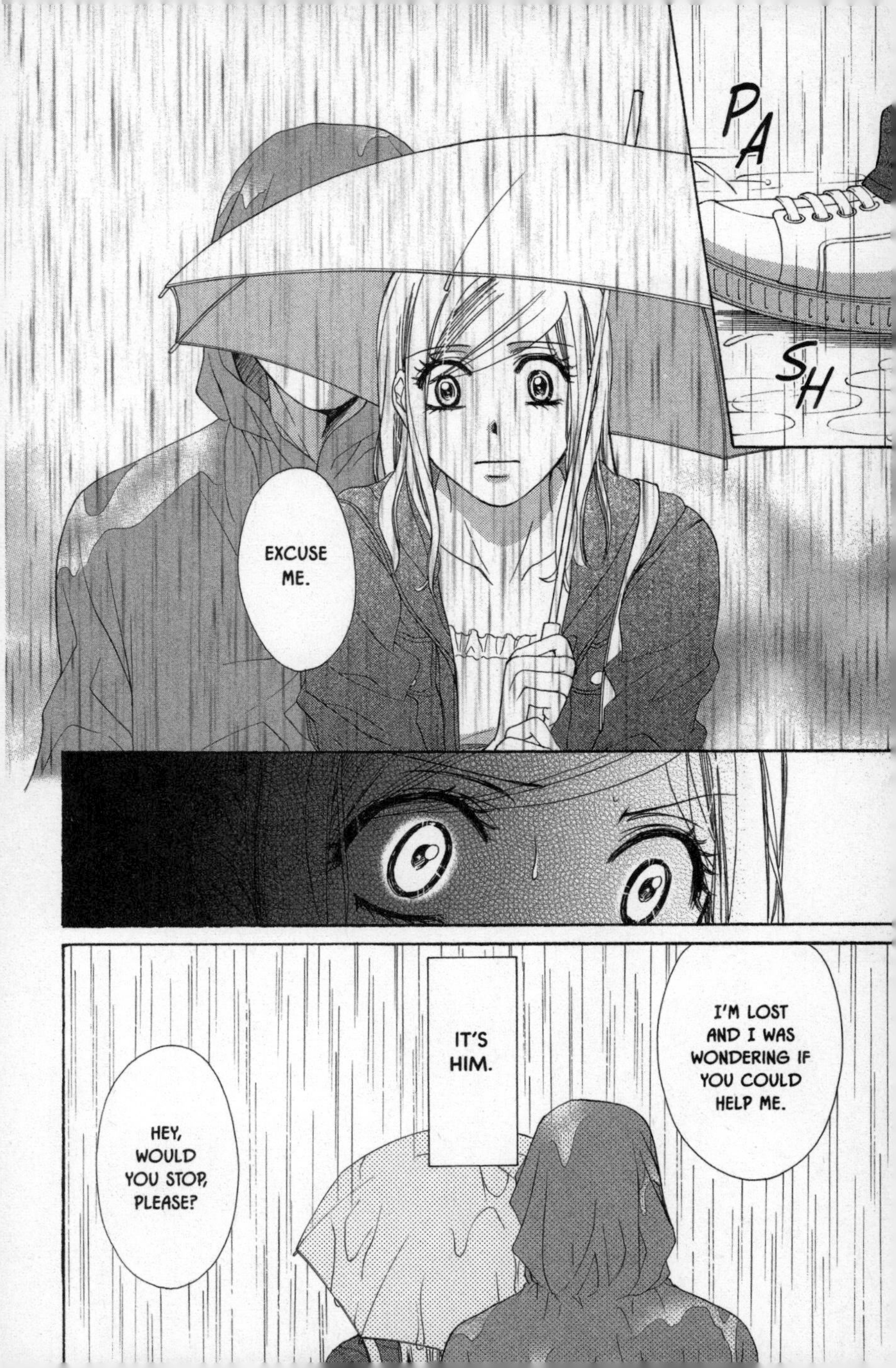
PA
SH
EXCUSE ME.
I'M LOST AND I WAS WONDERING IF YOU COULD HELP ME.
IT'S HIM.
HEY, WOULD YOU STOP, PLEASE?

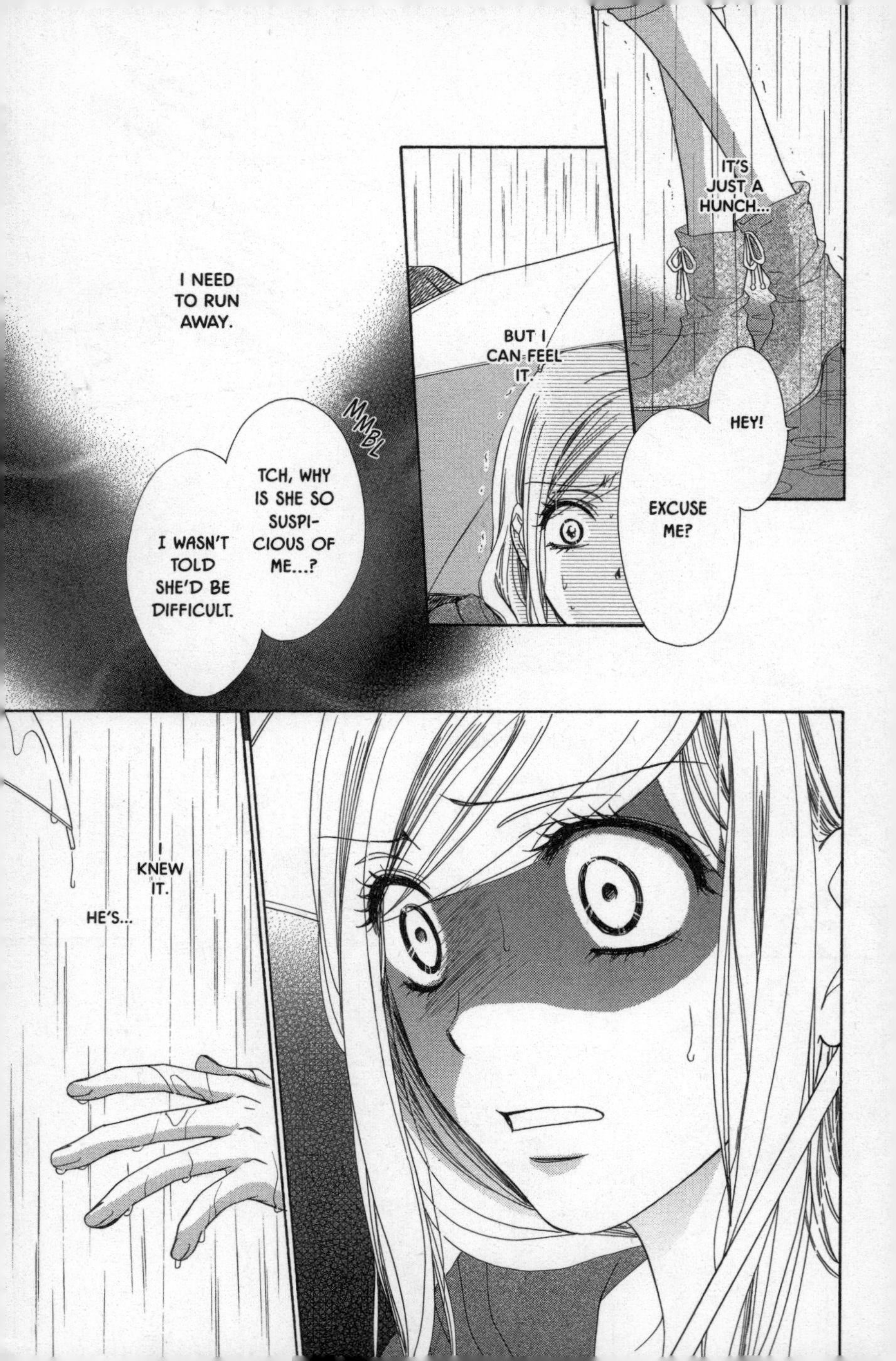
IT'S JUST A HUNCH...
HEY!
EXCUSE ME?
BUT I CAN FEEL IT.
I NEED TO RUN AWAY.
MMBL
TCH, WHY IS SHE SO SUSPICIOUS OF ME...?
I WASN'T TOLD SHE'D BE DIFFICULT.
I KNEW IT.
HE'S...

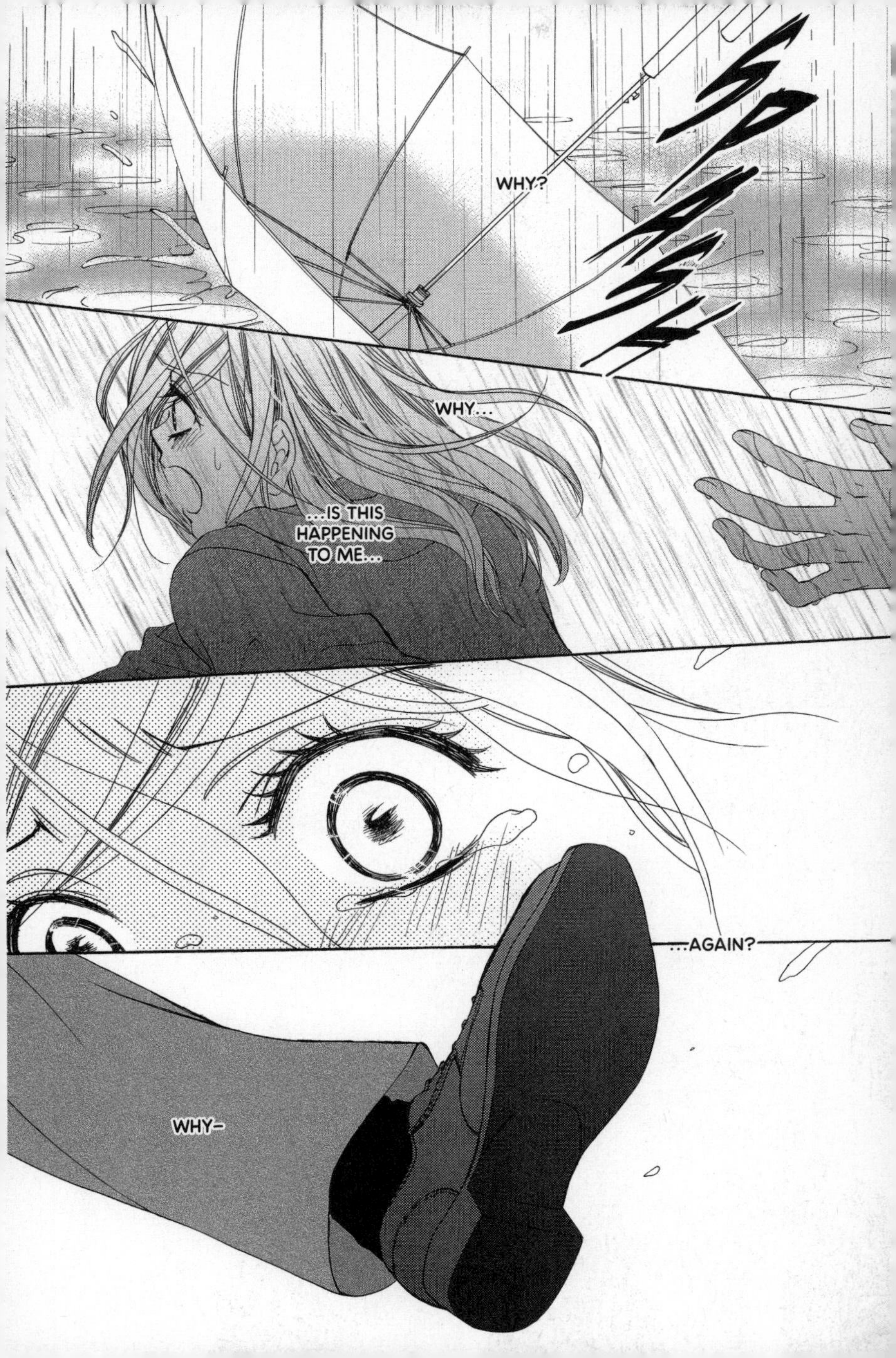
SPLASHH
WHY?
WHY...
...IS THIS HAPPENING TO ME...
...AGAIN?
WHY–

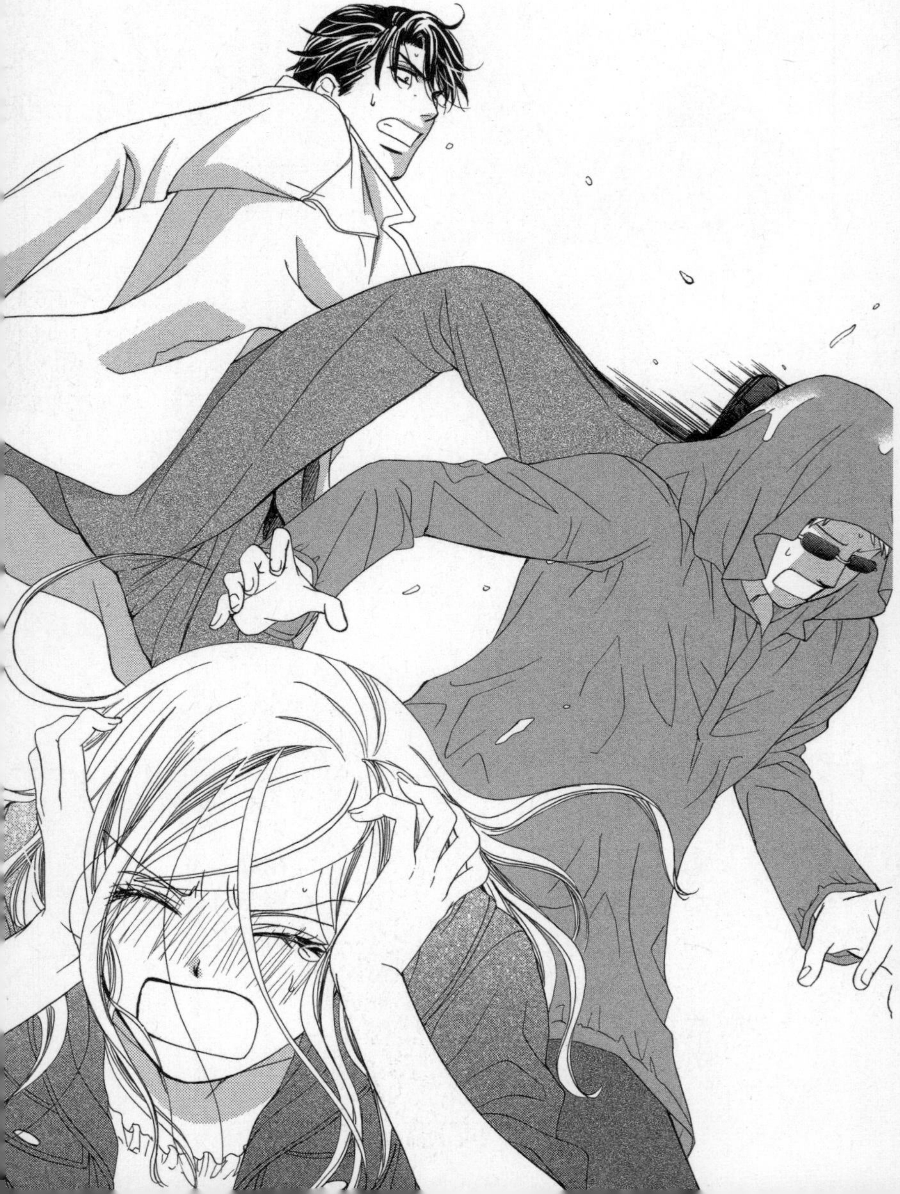

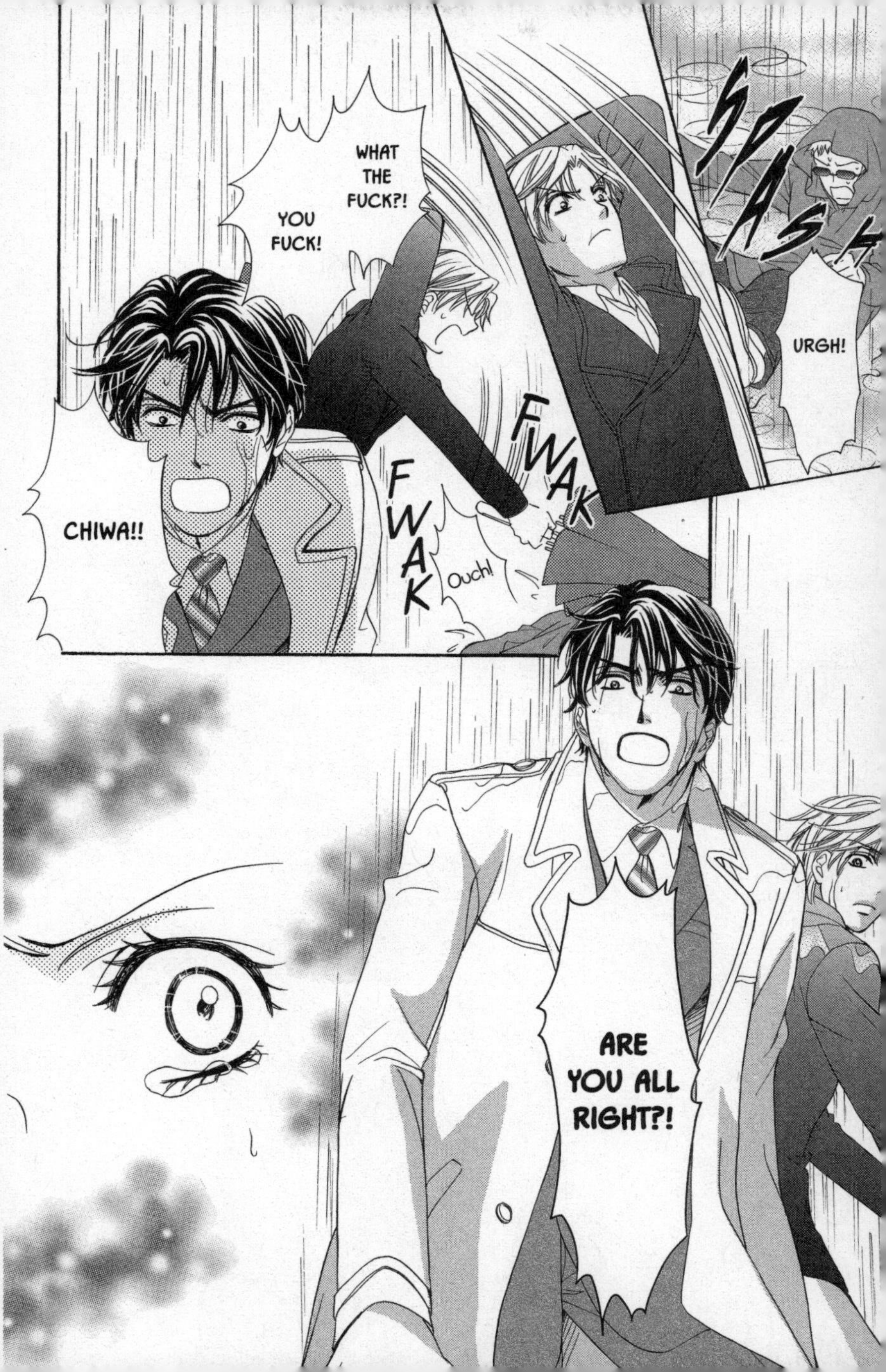
SPASH
URGH!
WHAT THE FUCK?!
YOU FUCK!
FWAK
FWAK
Ouch!
CHIWA!!
ARE YOU ALL RIGHT?!

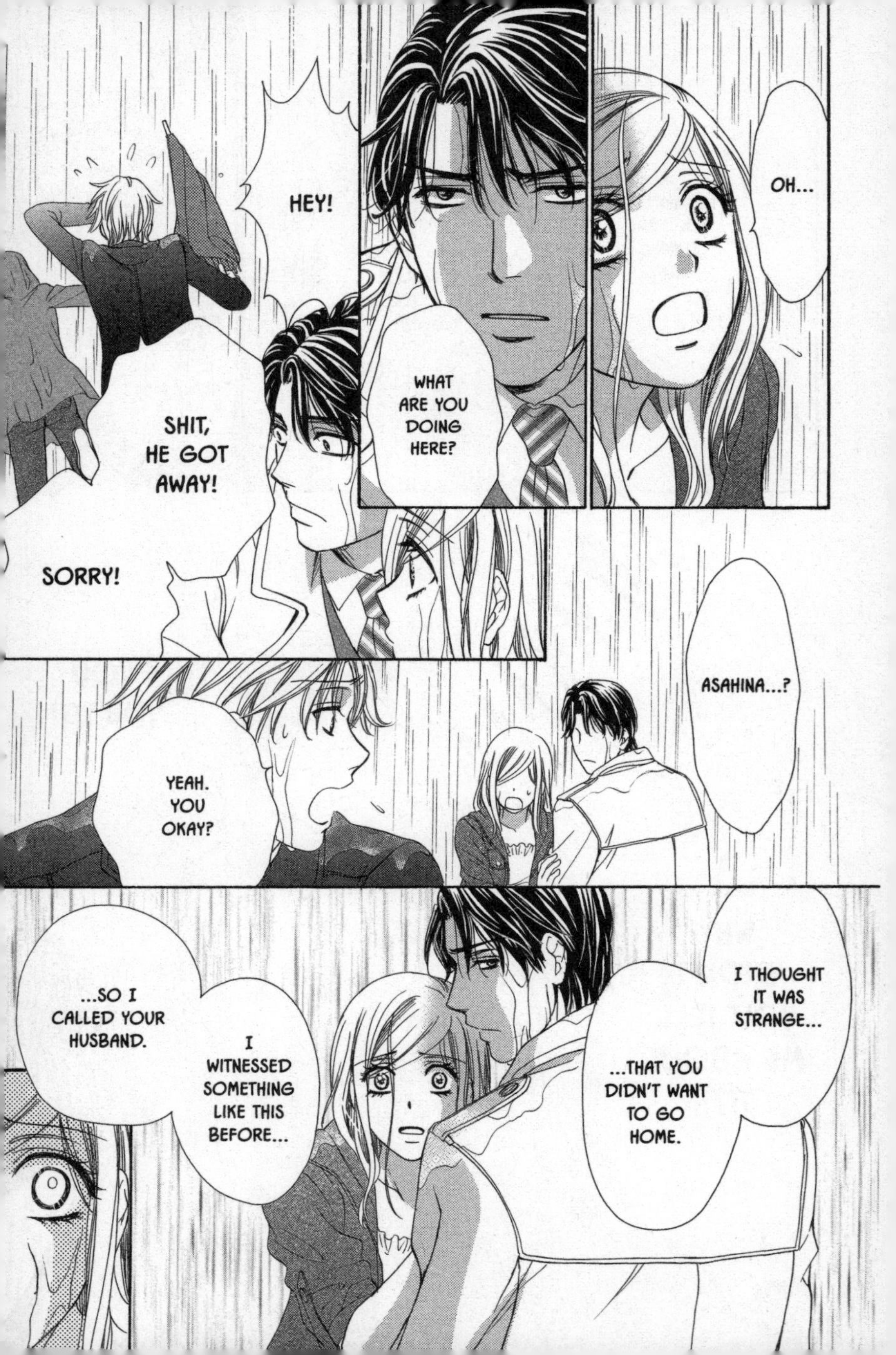
OH...
WHAT ARE YOU DOING HERE?
HEY!
SHIT, HE GOT AWAY!
SORRY!
ASAHINA...?
YEAH. YOU OKAY?
I THOUGHT IT WAS STRANGE...
...THAT YOU DIDN'T WANT TO GO HOME.
I WITNESSED SOMETHING LIKE THIS BEFORE...
...SO I CALLED YOUR HUSBAND.

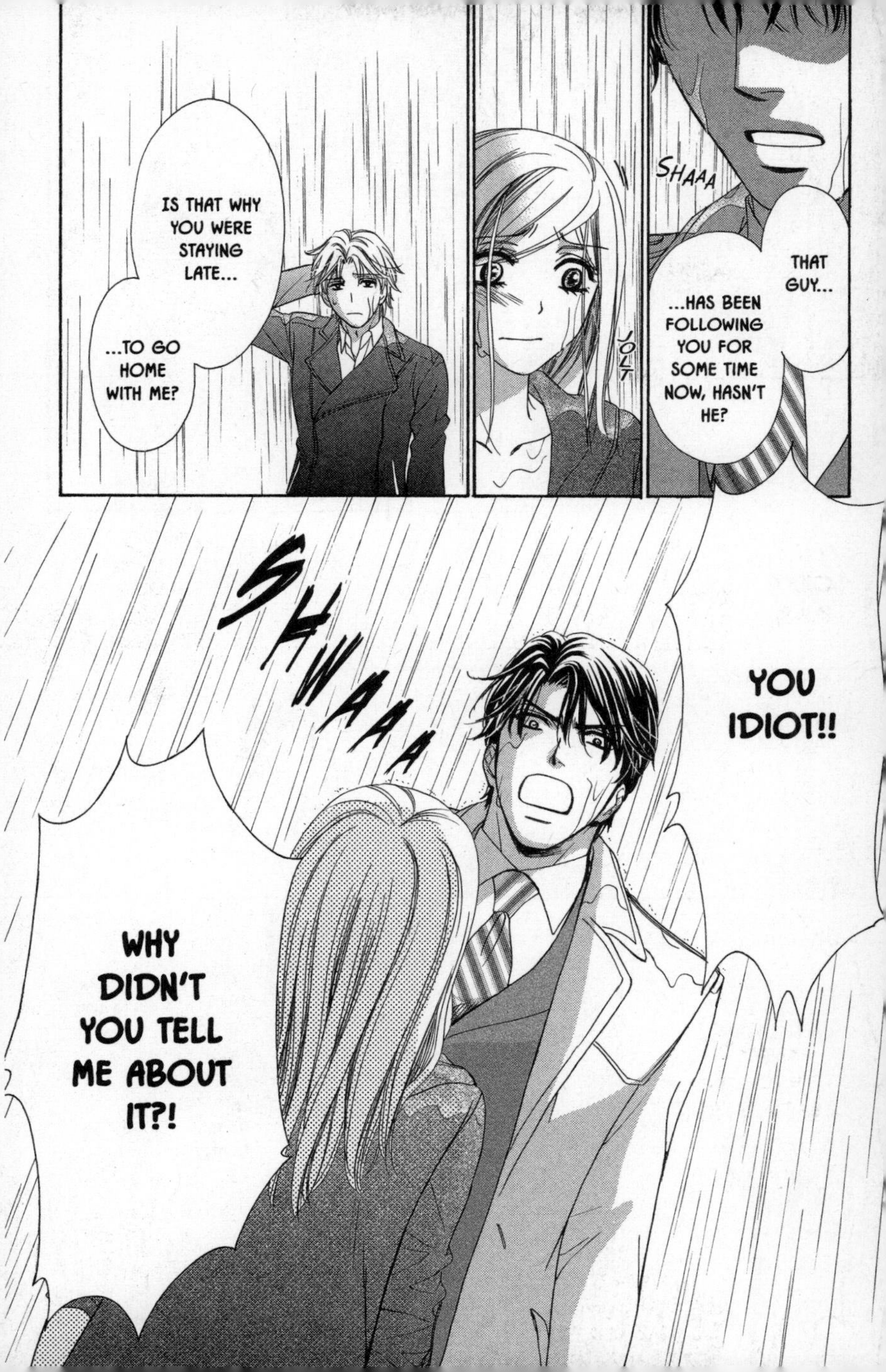
SHAAA
THAT GUY...
...HAS BEEN FOLLOWING YOU FOR SOME TIME NOW, HASN'T HE?
JOLT
IS THAT WHY YOU WERE STAYING LATE...
...TO GO HOME WITH ME?
SHWAAAA
YOU IDIOT!!
WHY DIDN'T YOU TELL ME ABOUT IT?!

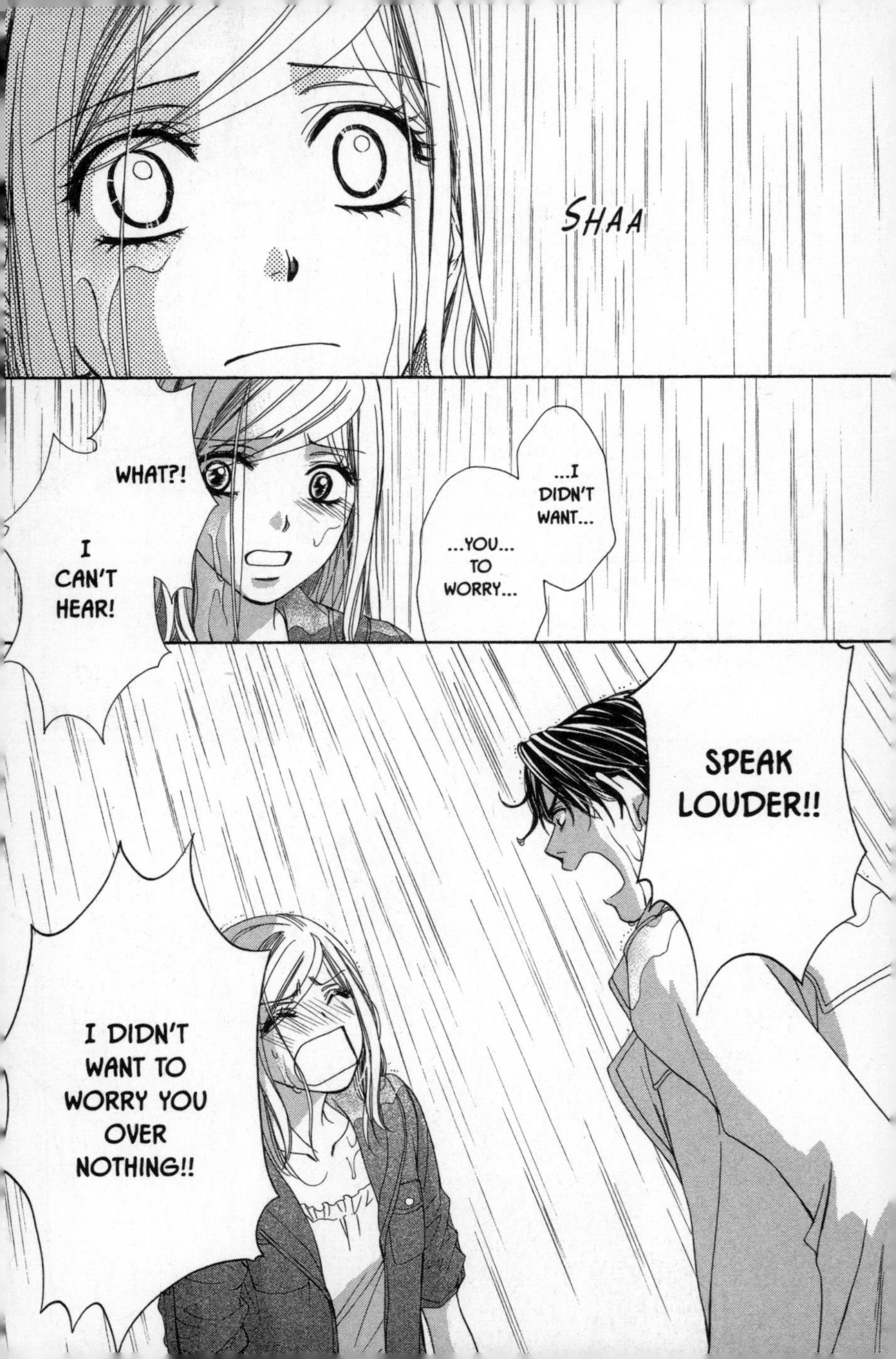
SHAA
...I DIDN'T WANT...
...YOU... TO WORRY...
WHAT?! I CAN'T HEAR!
SPEAK LOUDER!!
I DIDN'T WANT TO WORRY YOU OVER NOTHING!!

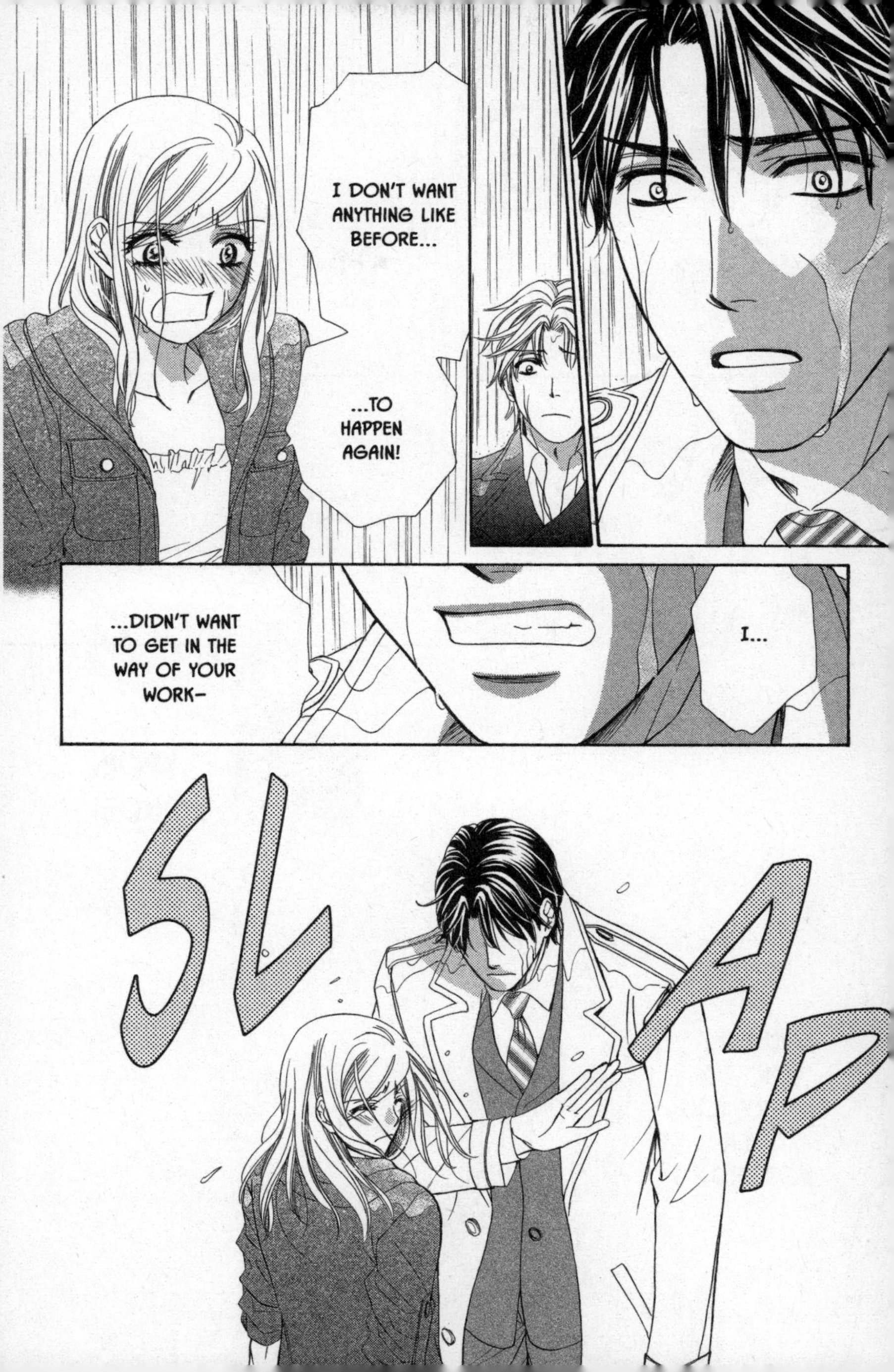
I DON'T WANT ANYTHING LIKE BEFORE...
...TO HAPPEN AGAIN!
I...
...DIDN'T WANT TO GET IN THE WAY OF YOUR WORK–
SLAP

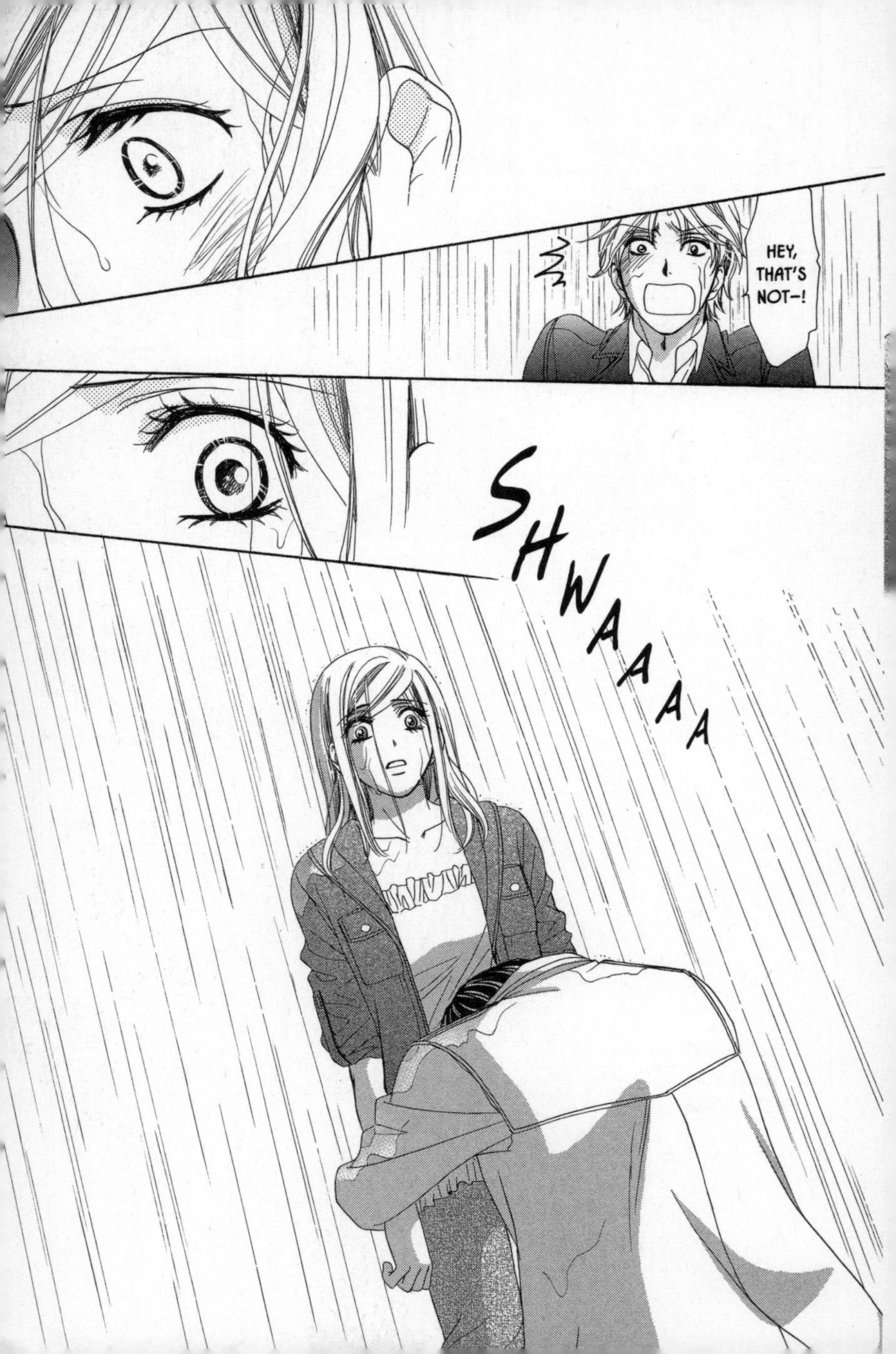
HEY, THAT'S NOT-!
SHWAAAAA

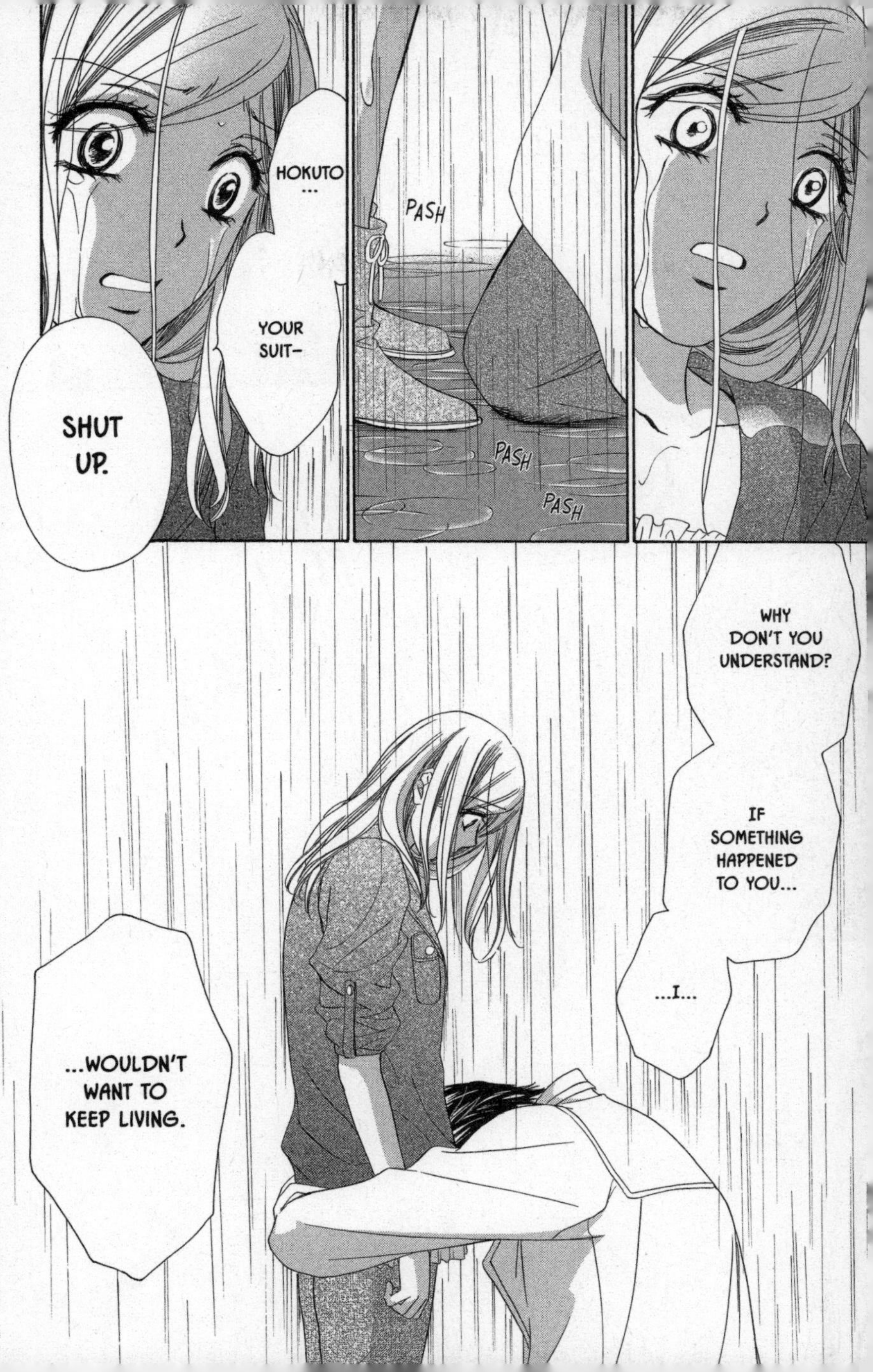
PASH
PASH
PASH
HOKUTO ...
YOUR SUIT-
SHUT UP.
WHY DON'T YOU UNDERSTAND?
IF SOMETHING HAPPENED TO YOU...
...I...
...WOULDN'T WANT TO KEEP LIVING.

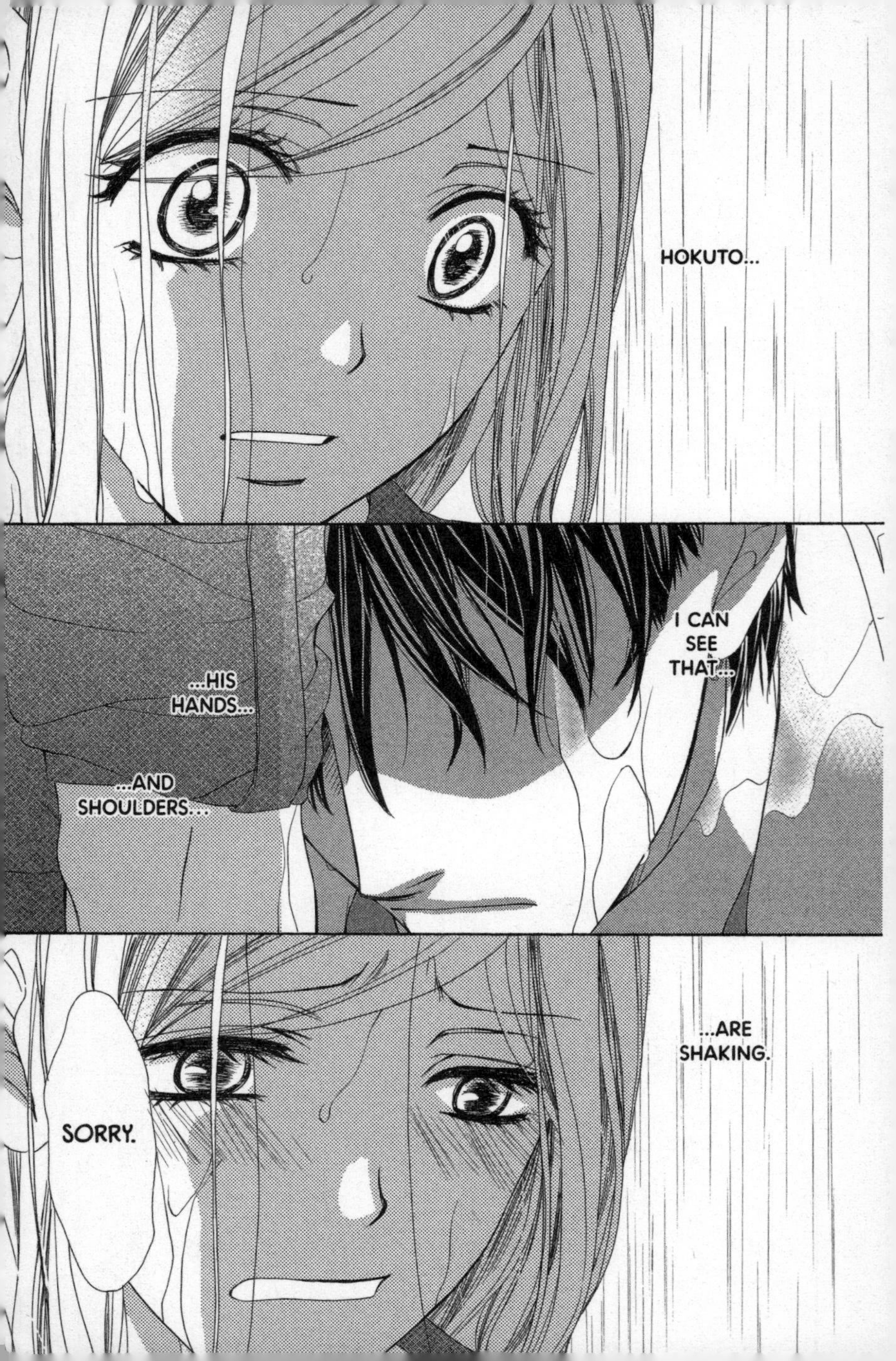
HOKUTO...
I CAN SEE THAT...
...HIS HANDS...
...AND SHOULDERS...
...ARE SHAKING.
SORRY.

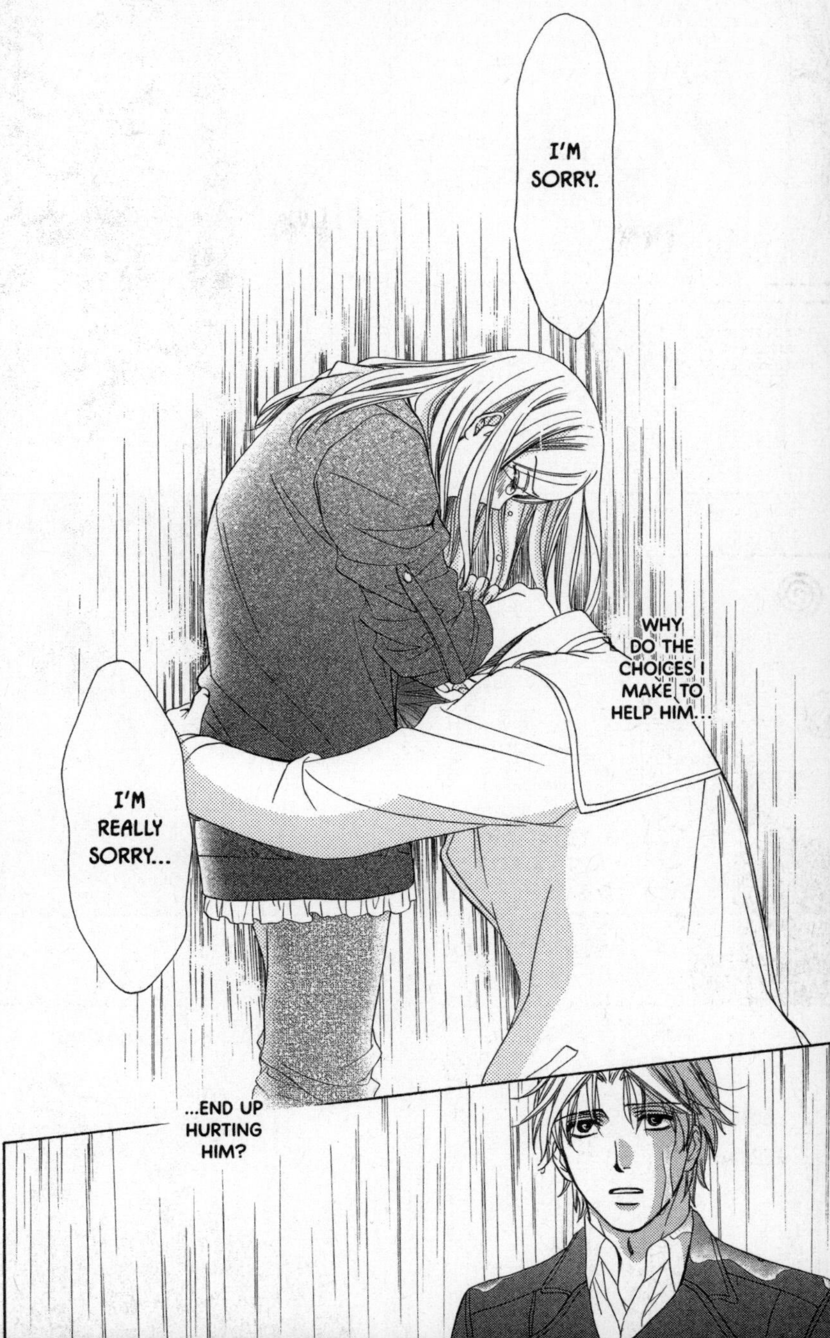
I'M SORRY.
WHY DO THE CHOICES I MAKE TO HELP HIM...
I'M REALLY SORRY...
...END UP HURTING HIM?

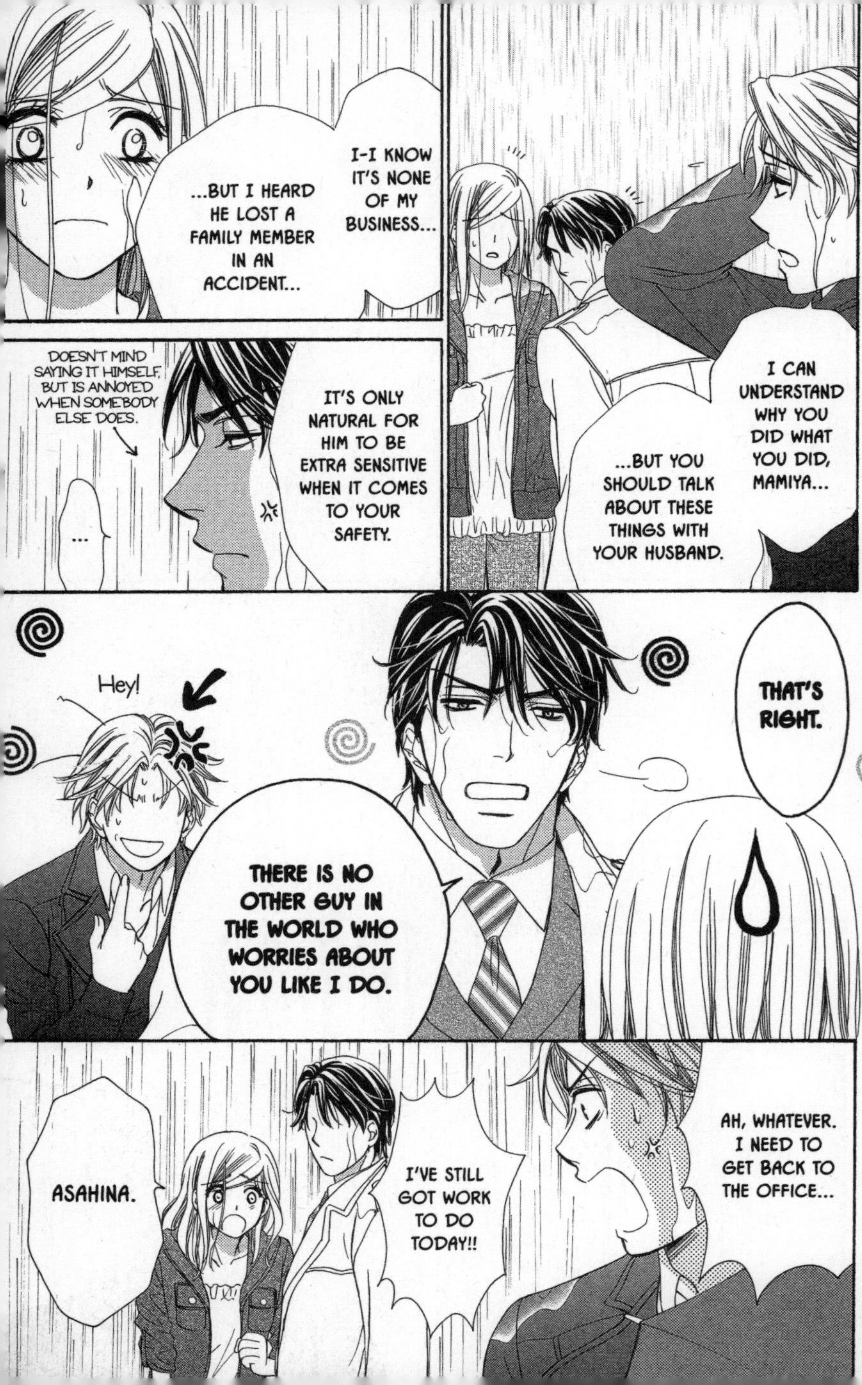
I CAN UNDERSTAND WHY YOU DID WHAT YOU DID, MAMIYA...
...BUT YOU SHOULD TALK ABOUT THESE THINGS WITH YOUR HUSBAND.
I-I KNOW IT'S NONE OF MY BUSINESS...
...BUT I HEARD HE LOST A FAMILY MEMBER IN AN ACCIDENT...
IT'S ONLY NATURAL FOR HIM TO BE EXTRA SENSITIVE WHEN IT COMES TO YOUR SAFETY.
DOESN'T MIND SAYING IT HIMSELF, BUT IS ANNOYED WHEN SOMEBODY ELSE DOES.
...
THAT'S RIGHT.
THERE IS NO OTHER GUY IN THE WORLD WHO WORRIES ABOUT YOU LIKE I DO.
Hey!
AH, WHATEVER. I NEED TO GET BACK TO THE OFFICE...
I'VE STILL GOT WORK TO DO TODAY!!
ASAHINA.

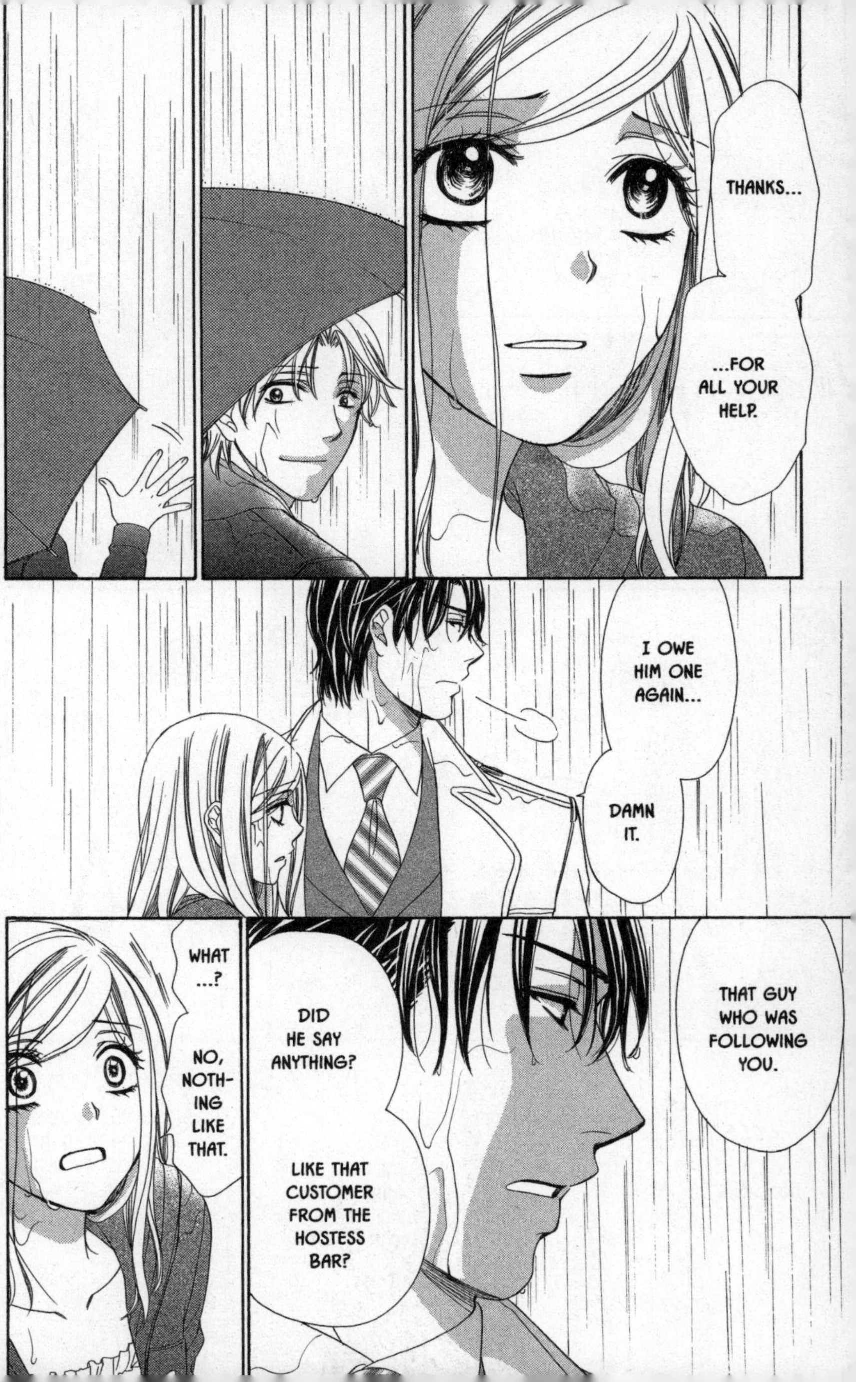
THANKS...
...FOR ALL YOUR HELP.
I OWE HIM ONE AGAIN...
DAMN IT.
THAT GUY WHO WAS FOLLOWING YOU.
DID HE SAY ANYTHING?
LIKE THAT CUSTOMER FROM THE HOSTESS BAR?
WHAT ...?
NO, NOTHING-ING LIKE THAT.

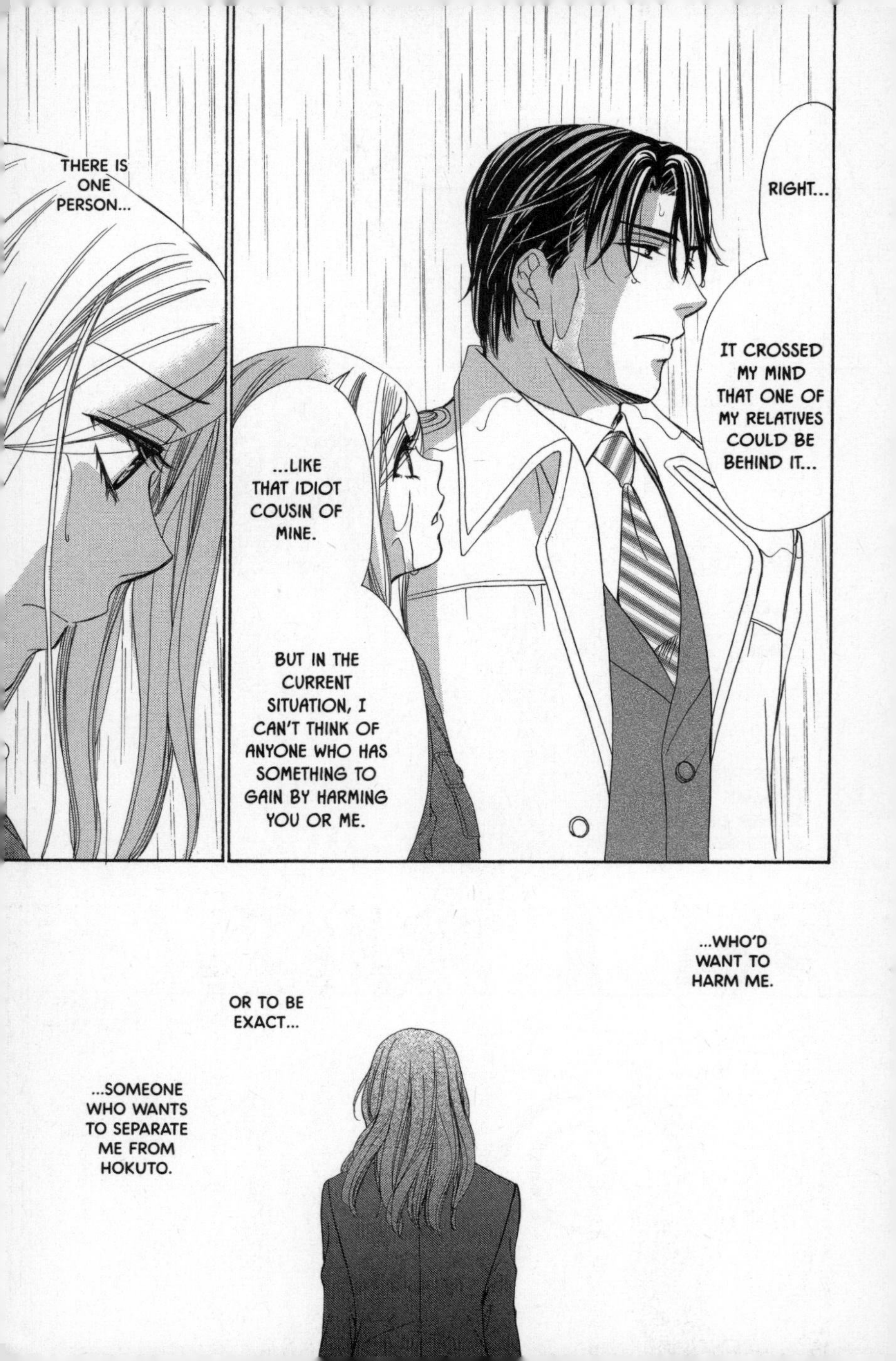
RIGHT...
IT CROSSED MY MIND THAT ONE OF MY RELATIVES COULD BE BEHIND IT...
...LIKE THAT IDIOT COUSIN OF MINE.
BUT IN THE CURRENT SITUATION, I CAN'T THINK OF ANYONE WHO HAS SOMETHING TO GAIN BY HARMING YOU OR ME.
THERE IS ONE PERSON...
...WHO'D WANT TO HARM ME.
OR TO BE EXACT...
...SOMEONE WHO WANTS TO SEPARATE ME FROM HOKUTO.

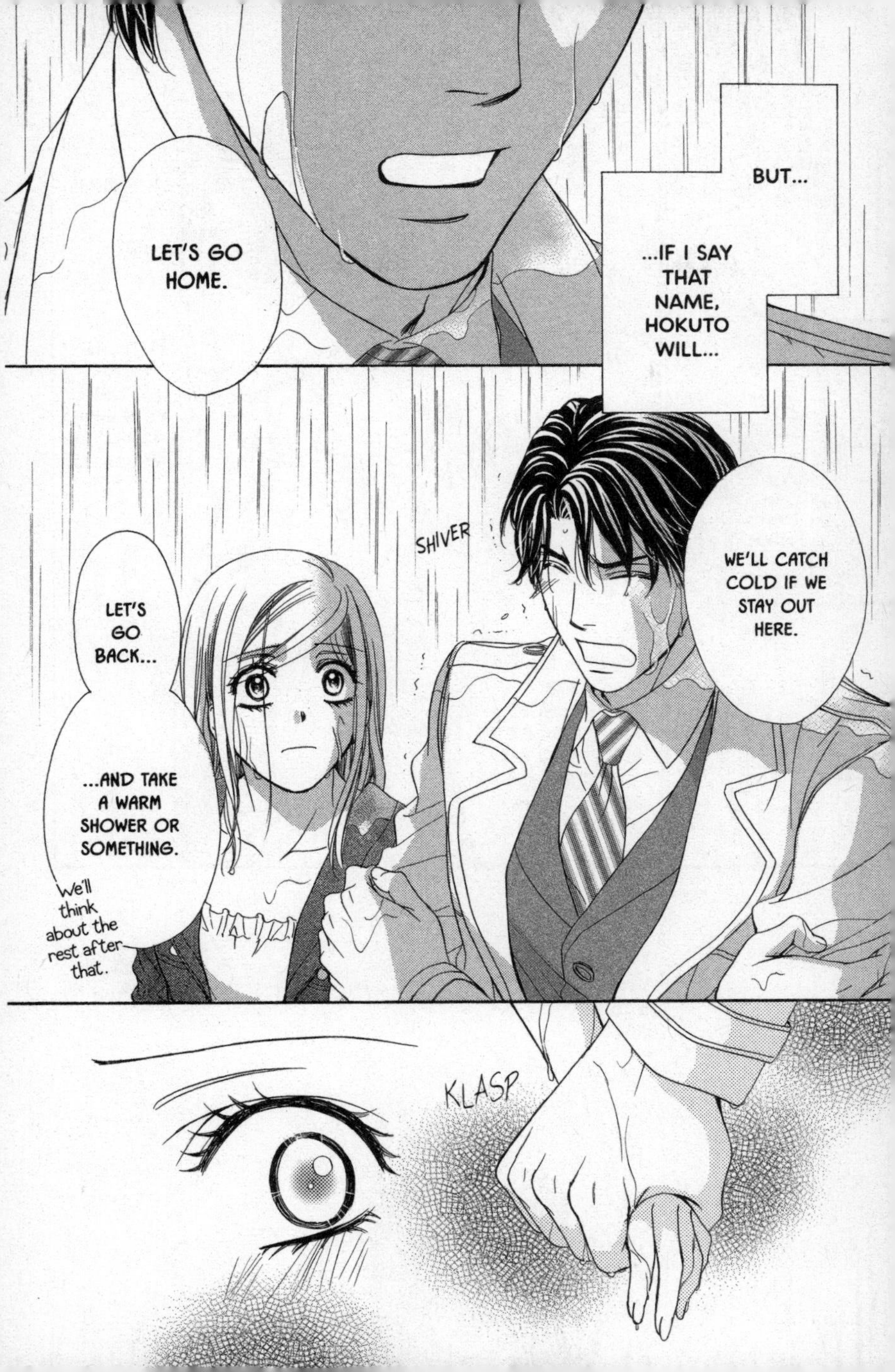
BUT...
...IF I SAY THAT NAME, HOKUTO WILL...
LET'S GO HOME.
WE'LL CATCH COLD IF WE STAY OUT HERE.
SHIVER
LET'S GO BACK...
...AND TAKE A WARM SHOWER OR SOMETHING.
We'll think about the rest after that.
KLASP

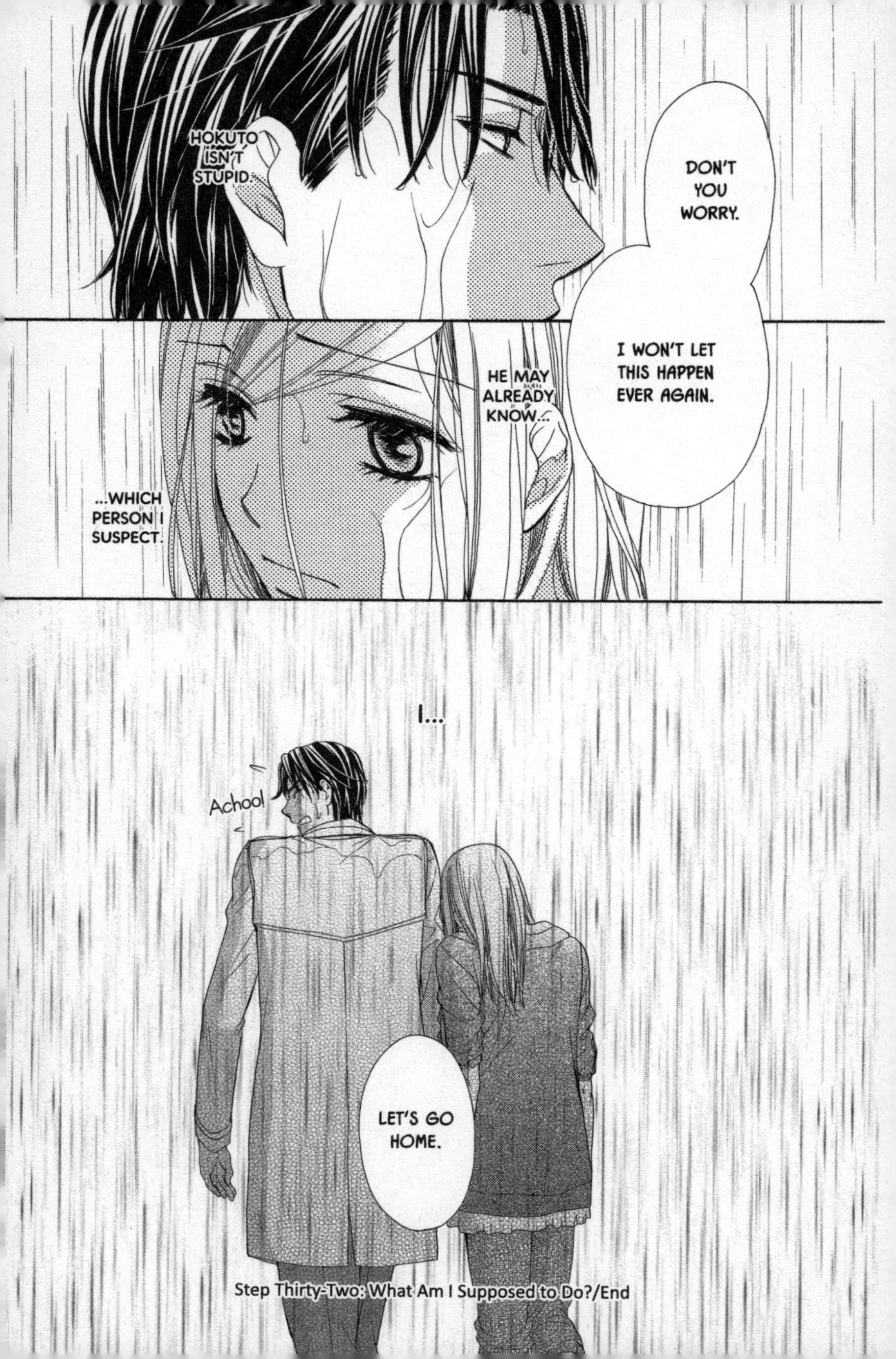
DON'T YOU WORRY.
HOKUTO ISN'T STUPID.
I WON'T LET THIS HAPPEN EVER AGAIN.
HE MAY ALREADY KNOW...
...WHICH PERSON I SUSPECT.
I...
Achoo!
LET'S GO HOME.
Step Thirty-Two: What Am I Supposed to Do?/End

Special Thanks

Assistants

K. Sano
E. Shimojo
Y. Nagashima
N. Hori

Editor

M. Okada

CHAPTER 31:
SHIRTS WEREN'T THE ONLY THINGS SOMA HAD TO BUY FOR PRESIDENT MAMIYA.

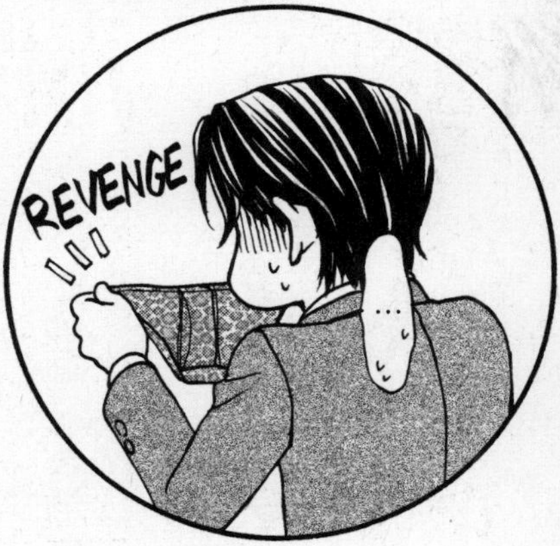
REVENGE
...

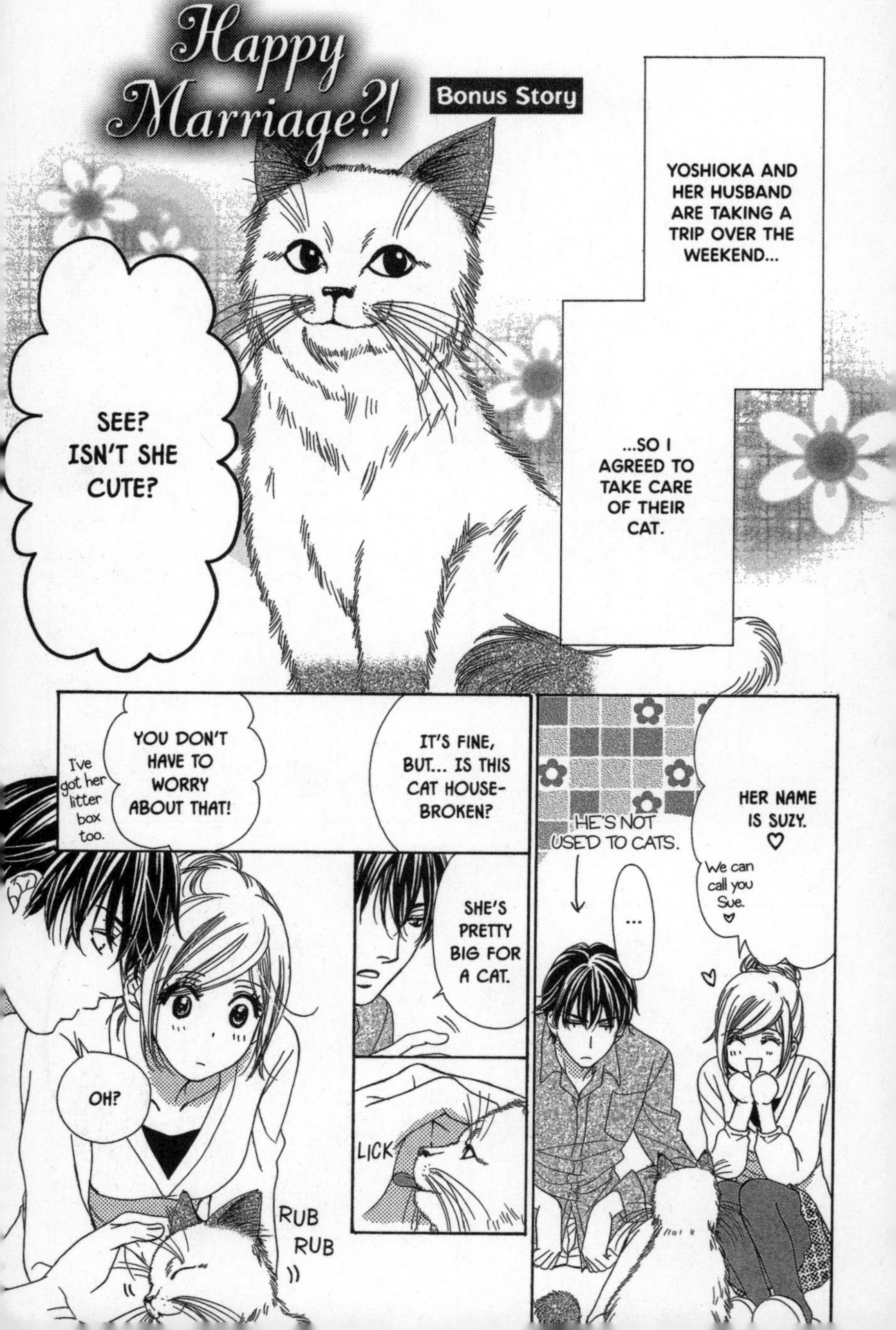
Happy Marriage?!
Bonus Story
YOSHIOKA AND HER HUSBAND ARE TAKING A TRIP OVER THE WEEKEND...
...SO I AGREED TO TAKE CARE OF THEIR CAT.
SEE? ISN'T SHE CUTE?
HER NAME IS SUZY. ♡
We can call you Sue. ♡
...
HE'S NOT USED TO CATS.
IT'S FINE, BUT... IS THIS CAT HOUSE-BROKEN?
SHE'S PRETTY BIG FOR A CAT.
LICK
YOU DON'T HAVE TO WORRY ABOUT THAT!
I've got her litter box too.
OH?
RUB RUB

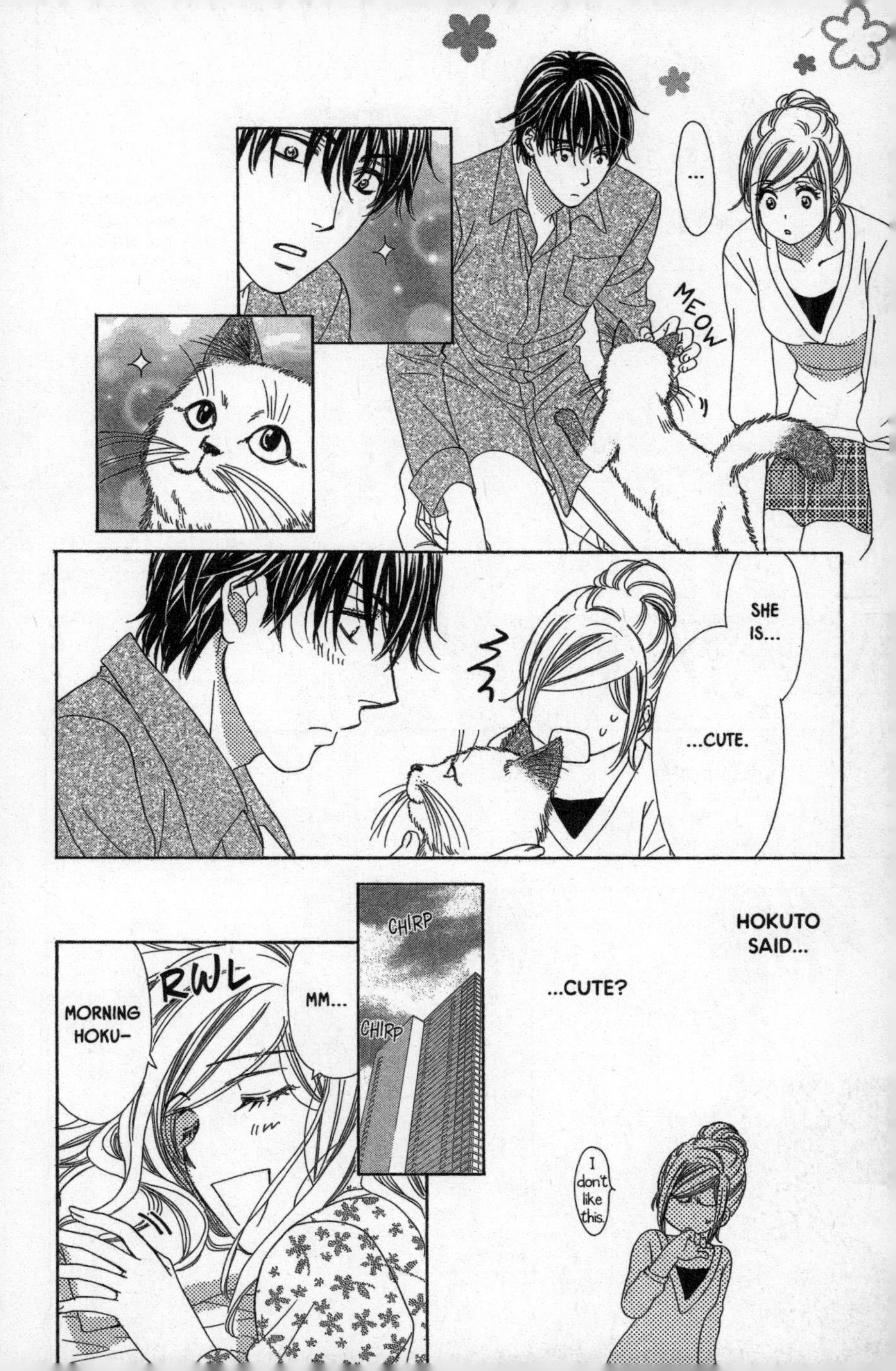
...
MEOW
SHE IS...
...CUTE.
HOKUTO SAID...
...CUTE?
I don't like this.
CHIRP
CHIRP
MM...
RWL
MORNING HOKU-

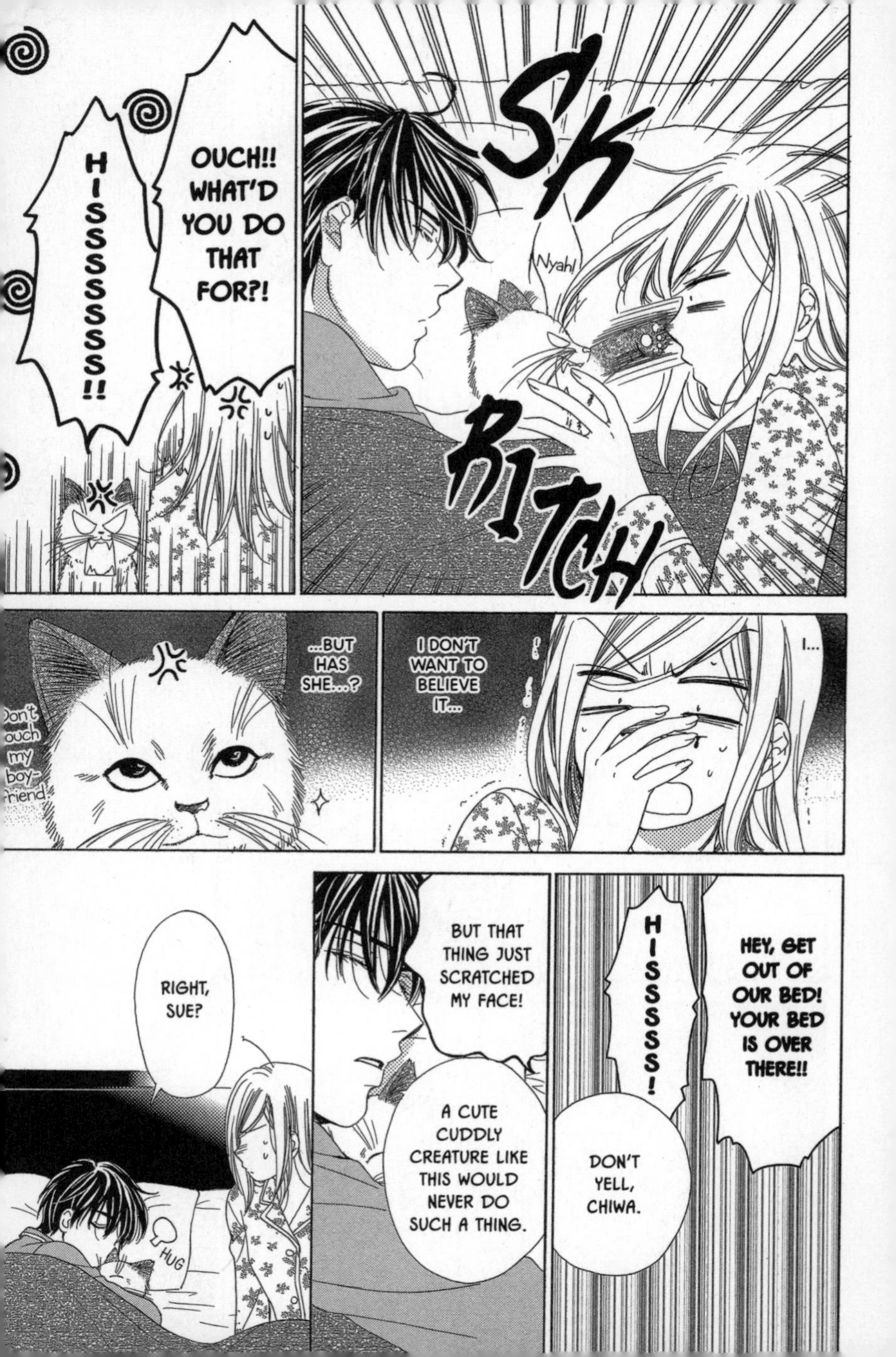
SK
Nyah!
RITCH
OUCH!! WHAT'D YOU DO THAT FOR?!
HISSSSSSSS!!
I...
I DON'T WANT TO BELIEVE IT...
...BUT HAS SHE...?
Don't ouch my boy-friend
HEY, GET OUT OF OUR BED! YOUR BED IS OVER THERE!!
HISSSS!
DON'T YELL, CHIWA.
BUT THAT THING JUST SCRATCHED MY FACE!
A CUTE CUDDLY CREATURE LIKE THIS WOULD NEVER DO SUCH A THING.
RIGHT, SUE?
HUG

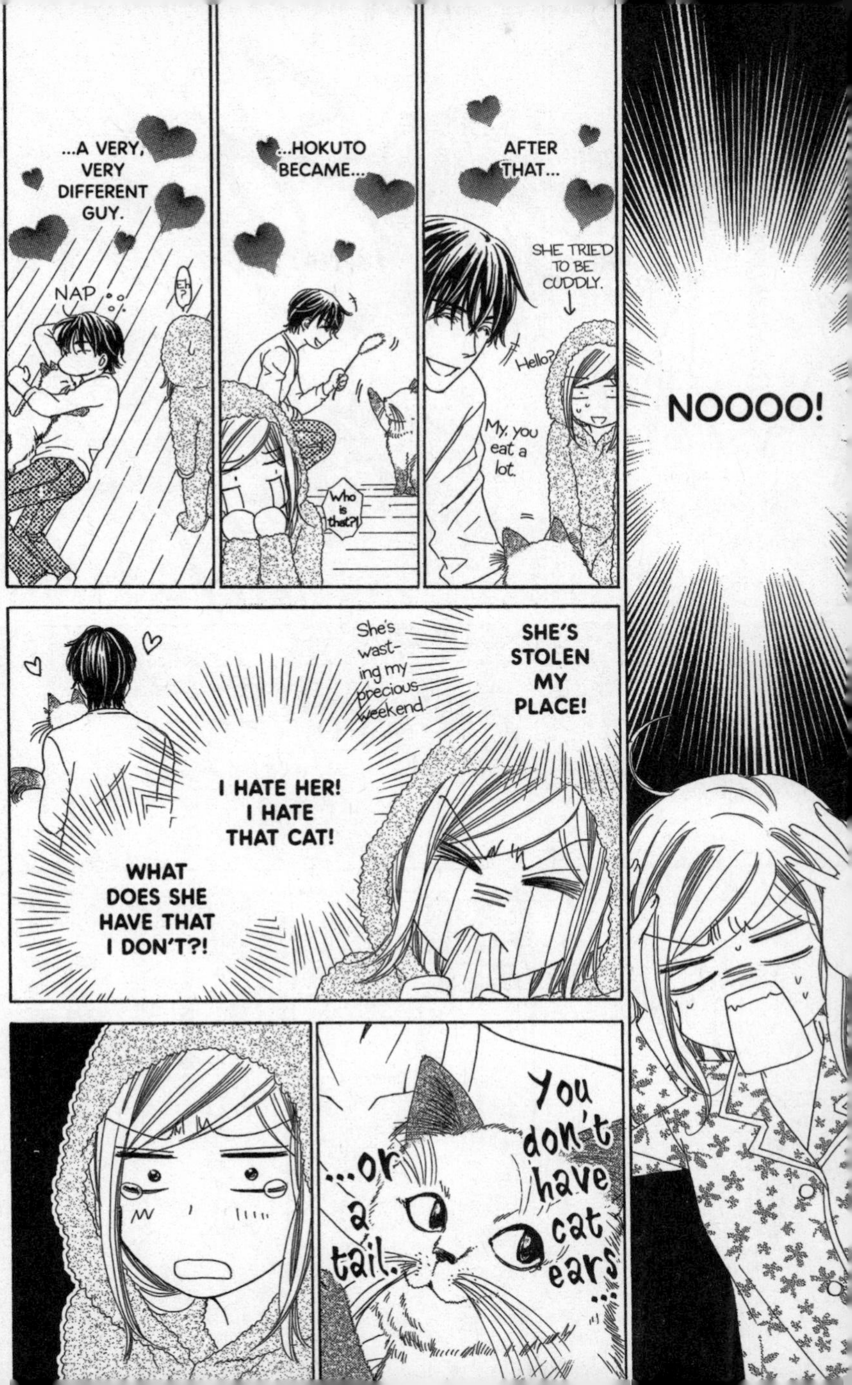
NOOOO!
AFTER THAT...
SHE TRIED TO BE CUDDLY.
Hello?
My, you eat a lot.
...HOKUTO BECAME...
Who is that?!
...A VERY, VERY DIFFERENT GUY.
NAP
SHE'S STOLEN MY PLACE!
She's wasting my precious weekend.
I HATE HER! I HATE THAT CAT!
WHAT DOES SHE HAVE THAT I DON'T?!
You don't have cat ears...
...or a tail.

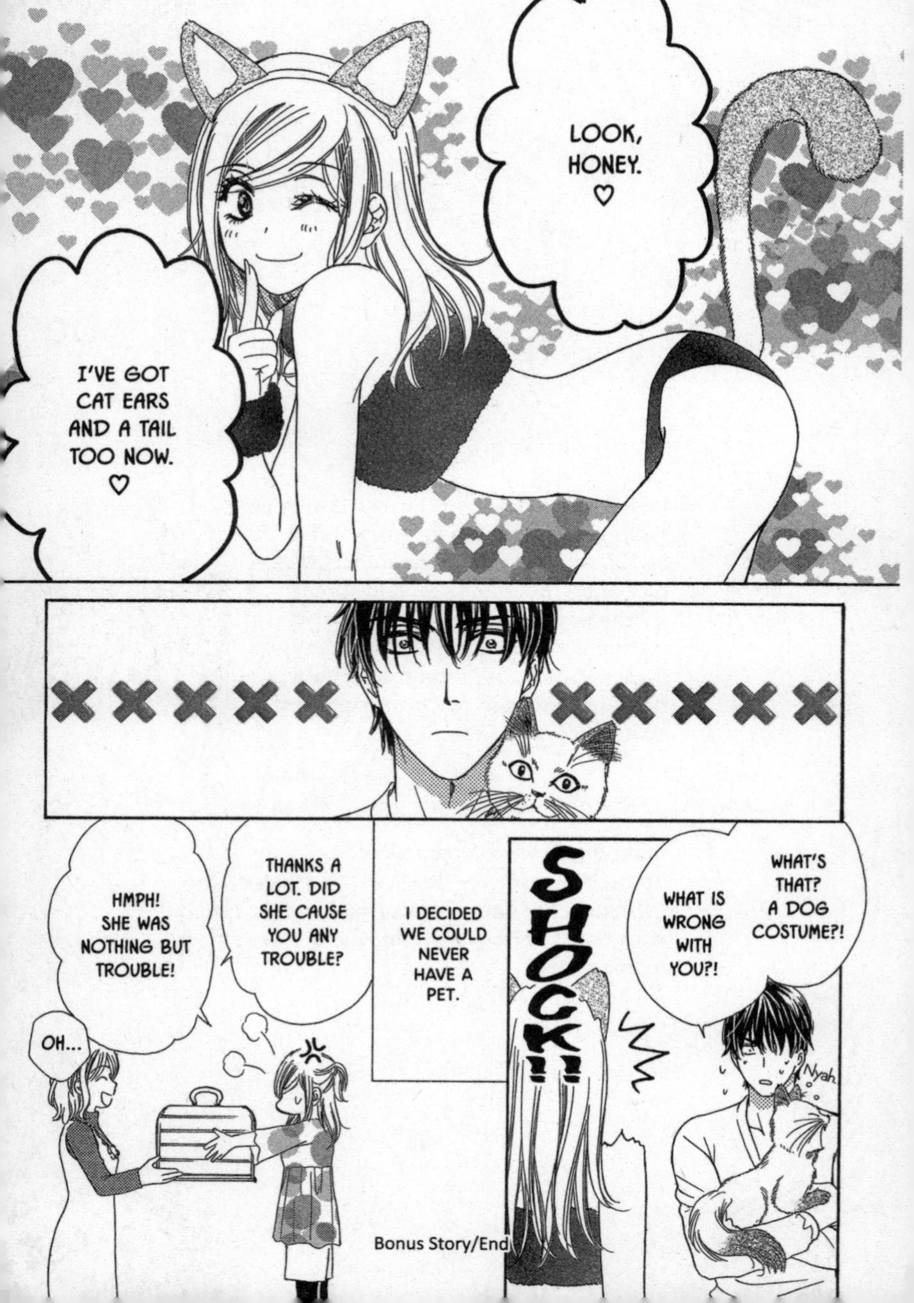
LOOK, HONEY. ♡
I'VE GOT CAT EARS AND A TAIL TOO NOW. ♡
WHAT'S THAT? A DOG COSTUME?!
WHAT IS WRONG WITH YOU?!
SHOCK!!
Nyah.
I DECIDED WE COULD NEVER HAVE A PET.
THANKS A LOT. DID SHE CAUSE YOU ANY TROUBLE?
HMPH! SHE WAS NOTHING BUT TROUBLE!
OH...

Bonus Story/End

A GIRL'S DREAM

Unlike the usual cover, I decided to draw
a seasonal illustration for this volume.
So I must apologize to the readers who
picked up this volume in midsummer...
By the way, the *Happy Marriage* novel
is coming out in Japan along with this
manga volume. It's very good! I drew
the illustrations in it. Please support the
novel too!

—Maki Enjoji

Maki Enjoji was born on December 8 in
Tokyo. She made her debut with *Fu•Junai*
(Wicked Pure Love). She currently works
with *Petit Comics*. *Happy Marriage?!* is her
fourth series.

Happy Marriage?!
Volume 8
Shojo Beat Edition

Story and Art by
Maki Enjoji

HAPIMARI - HAPPY MARRIAGE!? - Vol. 8
by Maki ENJOJI
© 2009 Maki ENJOJI
All rights reserved.
Original Japanese edition published by SHOGAKUKAN.
English translation rights in the United States of America, Canada, United
Kingdom, Ireland, Australia and New Zealand arranged with SHOGAKUKAN.

Translation/Tetsuichiro Miyaki
Adaptation/Nancy Thistlethwaite
Touch-up Art & Lettering/Inori Fukuda Trant
Design/Izumi Evers
Editor/Nancy Thistlethwaite

Printed in the U.S.A.

Published by VIZ Media, LLC
P.O. Box 77010
San Francisco, CA 94107

10 9 8 7 6 5 4 3 2 1
First printing, October 2014

www.viz.com   www.shojobeat.com

You may be reading the wrong way!

This book reads right to left to maintain the original presentation and art of the Japanese edition, so action, sound effects and word balloons are reversed. The diagram below shows how to follow the panels. Turn to the other side of the book to begin.

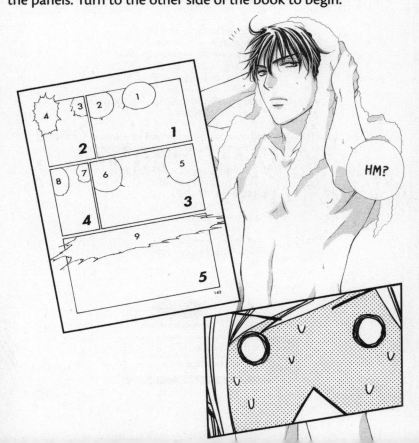